OZZY OSBOURNE

THE STORY OF THE OZZY OSBOURNE BAND
•
AN UNOFFICIAL PUBLICATION

OZZY OSBOURNE

THE STORY OF THE OZZY OSBOURNE BAND
•
AN UNOFFICIAL PUBLICATION

GARRY SHARPE-YOUNG

www.rockdetector.com

This edition published in Great Britain
in 2002 by Cherry Red Books Ltd.
Unit 17, 1st Floor, Elysium Gate West,
126–128 New King's Road,
London SW6 4LZ

Copyright © 2002, Garry Sharpe-Young.

All rights reserved. No part of this book
may be reproduced or transmitted in any
form or by any means, electronic or
mechanical, including photocopying,
recording or any information storage
and retrieval system, without
permission in writing from the publisher.

This book is sold subject to the
condition that it shall not, by way of
trade or otherwise, be lent, re-sold,
hired out or otherwise circulated
without the publisher's prior consent
in any form of binding or cover other
than that in which it is published
and without a similar condition
including this condition being
imposed on the subsequent purchaser.

All you need to know about the author:
Born: Münchengladbach 1964
Raised: On Judas Priest
Status: Decade of wedlock
Raising: Kerr, Krystan, Kjaric
Hair: By Vikernes

Typeset by Axis Europe Plc.
Printed and bound in Great Britain by
Biddles Ltd., Guildford and King's Lynn.
Cover Design by Jim Phelan at Wolf Graphics Tel: 020 8299 2342
Front cover photo by Matt Sampson.

ISBN 1–901447-08-1

Contents

Introduction	v
1. Chords of Disquiet	1
2. Killing Yourself To Live	17
3. The Reluctant Wizard	27
4. A Man For All Seasons	38
5. "It's A Band"	51
6. Mini Madmen	61
7. An Englishman's Castle	69
8. Luck Of The Irish	80
9. Hair By Sarzo Of Cuba	95
10. Way To Go	113
11. Enter Jake	118
12. Carmine Feel The Noise	128
13. Casting The Net	134
14. Tapping In	145
15. Next!	155
16. Eyes Closed To Success	163
17. Nailing It Down	172
18. Vai-able Options	181
19. Skol?	187
Postscript	198
The Ozzy Osbourne Solo Discography	199
Ozzy's Black Sabbath Discography	206
Other Ozzy Osbourne Recordings	214
The Ozzy Sidemen Discographies	220
Other Albums Which Include Sessions From Ozzy Osbourne Band Members	256
Ozzy Osbourne - Kith and Kin	257

Thanks

This book could not have been written without the generosity of the following Ozzy band members and associates: Don Airey, Tommy Aldridge, Carmine Appice, Jimi Bell, Lindsay Bridgwater, Randy Castillo, Paul Chapman, Fred Coury, Bob Daisley, Steve Fister, Lita Ford, Kelly Garni, Brad Gillis, Ray Gomez, Frank Hall, Bill Hunt, Lee Kerslake, Terry Nails, Dave Potts, Paul Shortino, Phil Soussan, Dana Strum, John Thomas, Bernie Tormé, Pete Way, Terry Horbury and Steve Vai. All the interviews with the above were conducted solely for this book. I would also like to add a nod of appreciation to Jon Hinchliffe, Jimmy Phillips, Michael Davis, Eric Parmeter and Ray Luzier.

Also, salutations to Rudy Sarzo and Brian Tichy who, although they did not feel able to contribute, declined in a gentlemanly manner and took valuable time out to respond.

I would also like to thank the members of Ozzy's band who, although wishing to remain anonymous, also contributed greatly.

Also worthy of note is Barry Scrannage. Sorry to say I felt I could not use any of our conversations but a few leads were prompted so you have my gratitude. I'm looking forward to your book.

For friends and sources of inspiration – my Mum, Grace-Anne, Kerr, Krystan, Kjaric, Peter, Sharon, Chris, Stevie, Phillip, Lucy, Gemma, Marisa, Sonia, Barry, Jane, Simon & Diana, Eddie & Helen, Bill & Zay, James & Belinda, Gregg Russell, Andy Southwell, Andy Pyke, Andy Dawson, Dave Reynolds and Michael Langbein.

The biggest thanks, though, go to Ozzy. Simply for providing

Ozzy Osbourne the inspiration and the music to fuel this journey. No, he did not contribute to this book in any way. I purposely did not use any material from my earlier interviews with Ozzy for this book. This book is about the music and the people that made it. And rock 'n' roll music doesn't come much greater than Ozzy's.

Dedication

This book is dedicated to three people all taken too early.

For Randy Rhoads who left a musical legacy so great that accomplished musicians struggle to adequately describe his uniqueness. A greatness that still envelops auditoriums and arenas to this day. I'm sure God's appreciation of the solo album is equal to what ours would have been.

For Randy Castillo. I was deeply saddened to learn of Randy's passing just as this book was being wrapped up. Everyone I spoke to had nothing but praise for Randy's musicianship, dedication and spirit of friendship. All his correspondence was upbeat and optimistic, even when discussing his illness. A great loss.

For my father Roy Sharpe who died in March 2001. Not only for letting his 13 year old son fixate on Judas Priest, grow his hair and clad himself in denim and leather but for saying nothing when at 33 that same son had shown little inclination of growing out of it. Watching my 9 year old raging to Linkin Park I hope I show the same tolerance.

Ozzy Osbourne

Introduction

This book is about the music of Ozzy Osbourne and the stories of those who made it. It is neither an exposé nor a catalogue of rock 'n' roll debauchery, drug blitzes and devil worship. That can be read about elsewhere and that, believe me, would have been a much easier book to write. Unfortunately the 'Madman' angle has been overplayed too many times over the years demeaning what I would call the real Ozzy – a gifted songwriter, an underrated singer who is blessed with an undeniable uniqueness when it comes to plain old-fashioned entertainment.

The story of the Blizzard Of Ozz has never really been told. Here I've attempted to portray the sequence of events from the viewpoint of the musicians who aided Ozzy in his cause. I do not claim that this is the definitive account – only Ozzy can provide that – but it does plug what were previously some very big holes in Ozzy's history. Over two decades Ozzy has chosen to work with some of the most talented rock musicians on this planet. He has consistently displayed a flair for keeping his band fresh, vital and up-to-the-minute. More than that, Ozzy has shown a knack, bordering on prescience, for hand-picking guitarists of exceptional and even unique ability.

This then is the story of the Ozzy Osbourne band.

Ozzy Osbourne

1
Chords Of Disquiet

Cited by many as *the* original Heavy Metal band, Black Sabbath have had a massive influence on the genre and have sold countless millions of albums. Black Sabbath, steered into their chosen doom / occult leanings by bassist and songwriter Geezer Butler, impose an enormous legacy upon the Heavy Metal scene. Guitarist Tony Iommi has laid down many of the classic all-time riffs and is a versatile Blues-inspired musician, revered as a guitar hero despite having lost some fingertips in a 1966 machine accident, which nearly put paid to his chosen career.

Until 1978 the band was fronted by the irrepressible Ozzy Osbourne. Now renowned as one of the true legends of Metal from his Black Sabbath years and his subsequent, massively successful solo career, Osbourne's trademark vocal style and outrageous on and off stage behaviour have gained the Brummie true rock idol status.

Created in 1967 in the heart of industrial Birmingham, a skinhead then known as Ozzy Zig, Tony Iommi, Terry 'Geezer' Butler and Bill Ward first united, albeit briefly, under the name Polka Tulk Blues Band. Osbourne's first attempts at singing came just after leaving school when, together with guitarist Jimmy Phillips, he founded the short-lived act The Prospectors. Previously Iommi and Ward had been part of The Rest, a band fronted by ex-Method Five vocalist Chris Smith. The group later changed its name to Mythology.

Osbourne and Butler, the latter a rhythm guitarist at this point, were members of Rare Breed, an act that lasted a mere two gigs. Prior to this Osbourne had stints with local bands The Black Panthers and Approach as well as having served a short term in the forbidding Winson Green prison for burglary. It was during his incarceration that the singer gave himself his now famous 'Ozzy' and smiley-face tattoos by rubbing floor cleaning paste into his skin.

The quartet joined forces when Mythology lost both singer and drummer. With the recruitment of Osbourne and Ward,

Ozzy Osbourne

Mythology changed its title to Music Machine adding saxophonist Alan Clark and Jimmy Phillips on slide guitar. Before long the Handsworth-based Music Machine became the Polka Tulk Blues Band and trimmed down to a quartet, with Butler adopting a new role as bass player by taking two strings off his lead guitar. Phillips meanwhile would go on to become a keyboard player performing with Purple Onion, Frog and Magic Roundabout. Within a short space of time the revised band had altered their moniker to the shortened Polka Tulk before another name change was enforced, the foursome becoming Earth.

Signing up to a management deal with Jim Simpson (who later was to manage fellow Birmingham boys Judas Priest) the band started the grind of playing the Rock and Blues clubs. Their first taste of Europe came when Simpson booked a tour of Germany. The shows included a date at Hamburg's infamous Star Club (the once famous haunt of The Beatles), before getting the band in a four-track studio to record their first demo. This recording, featuring the tracks 'Song For Jim' and 'The Rebel' in 1969, enabled the band to gain a deal with the then 'Progressive Rock' experimental label Vertigo Records, an arm of Fontana Records. Black Sabbath had already put in an appearance in the capital with a batch of gigs at the legendary Marquee Club in March 1969.

Upon signing they were to discover that another act called Earth had just released a single in Germany, thus necessitating a name change. According to legend it was a Dennis Wheatley novel that inspired Butler to come up with Black Sabbath. Despite the deal, Black Sabbath were financially in difficult times and it was at this point that Iommi actually left to join Jethro Tull for all of two weeks, to replace the departed Mick Abrahams.

Although Iommi's stay in Jethro Tull was brief he did appear with the band at the legendary Rolling Stones *Rock'n'Roll Circus* film session. However, he was soon back in the fold and Black Sabbath recorded their first Rodger Bain produced album for a miserly £600 on a four-track machine. (It is interesting to note as an aside that the engineer for the first two albums was

Chords Of Disquiet

none other than 'Colonel' Tom Allom, himself later to find fame as a producer for Judas Priest.)

The band's first product as Black Sabbath sank without trace. A single, 'Wicked Woman (Don't Play Your Evil Games With Me)', a cover of The Crows' track, had been released in January 1970. However, in February, the album *Black Sabbath* emerged upon an unsuspecting world, laden with many of what are now widely regarded as all-time classics such as 'Black Sabbath', 'The Wizard' and 'N.I.B.' The latter was allegedly at the time thought to be 'Nativity In Black' but was actually a strange reference to the shape of Butler's beard! The album's almost Neanderthal bludgeoning heaviness and thick industrial-strength riffs took rock fans by storm. The debut reached Number 8 in the British charts with virtually no assistance from radio airplay.

Live dates to promote the album saw the band opening up proceedings in Cardiff and would proceed through such salubrious venues as the East Ham Dukes Head, Salisbury's Alexis Disco and the Croydon Greyhound. Black Sabbath would venture into Germany, appearing at festivals alongside Rory Gallagher, Deep Purple, Free, Status Quo and Black Widow, and later supported Pink Floyd back in the UK before another German stint in August.

Shortly after wrapping up recording for their second album in June of 1970, provisionally entitled *War Pigs*, again with Rodger Bain, in August 1970 Black Sabbath played the 10th Plumpton Jazz and Blues festival alongside Humble Pie and Yes. Prior to the album release the record company, Vertigo, changed the album title to *Paranoid*; they were uneasy about the title *War Pigs* thanks to the ongoing war in Vietnam and also because there was a strong belief that the track 'Paranoid' itself could be a hit. Ironically, the title of 'War Pigs' had itself been changed, the original composition having been entitled 'Walpurgis'.

Indeed, the single 'Paranoid' reached Number 4 (which still remains Black Sabbath's biggest single hit to date), with the album reaching the dizzy heights of Number 1! The album, with the now more renowned classics such as 'Hand Of Doom', 'Fairies Wear Boots' and 'Iron Man', had Black Sabbath exploring a much more varied field of interests than its predecessor's predilection for the occult.

In America the second album reached Number 12 and settled in for a long chart stay, eventually clocking up a 65-week residency. The band's first American shows also occurred, with support slots to Mountain prior to their own headline tour (see below). There would be virtually no respite for the quartet as live promotion for the sophomore outing saw the band back on the road in the UK during September, starting off in Wales yet again – this time at Swansea's Brangwyn Hall. Three shows in Switzerland were undertaken before a short burst of live activity in the Low Countries, and by October Black Sabbath were playing their inaugural Scandinavian gigs. The close of the month witnessed another first as a Philadelphia appearance signalled the start of a long trail of roadwork in the United States. Black Sabbath's first headlining American trip would also see a run of three San Francisco Fillmore West gigs opening up for Arthur Lee's Love and The James Gang.

As 1971 commenced so did another stream of British dates. Black Sabbath would prove nowhere was safe with gigs in New Zealand and Australia followed by a return visit to America before returning to mainland Europe once again.

With the album's success came a valuable indicator to the band of the international potential of Black Sabbath. In a rather messy legal wrangle, Black Sabbath wriggled out of their management contract with Jim Simpson and signed up to Wilf Pine and Patrick Meehan, both of whom had previously been with the Arden Management company.

August 1971 saw the release of the last Rodger Bain-produced Black Sabbath album *Master Of Reality*. The record peaked at Number 5 in the British charts, but provided the band with a strong 'out of the box' seller in America, being certified gold before its release. The band backed up this success Stateside by a lengthy bout of touring, which by this time was beginning to take its toll both mentally and physically on the individual members. *Volume 4* (originally to be titled *Snowblind*) gave the band another top ten British album and featured the classic

Chords Of Disquiet

ballad 'Changes', featuring Yes keyboard player Rick Wakeman, alongside the more brutal 'Snowblind'. The band showed no sign of letting up, making another trip to New Zealand in early January 1973 gearing up for the by now familiar American dates. An Italian tour was completed and in March it was back for another round in Great Britain. Quite surreally, Black Sabbath would also make their presence felt at the Cascais Jazz Festival in Portugal.

The band returned to America to work on *Volume 4*'s follow-up but found for the first time their flow of ideas had ebbed. Relocating to rehearse in the suitably spooky setting of a Welsh castle dungeon, Iommi came up with the classic riff for the track 'Sabbath Bloody Sabbath' and the creative juices started to flow once more. In late 1973 Black Sabbath released the renowned *Sabbath Bloody Sabbath* album to worldwide critical acclaim. For live work, keyboard player Gerry Woodruffe was added and Black Sabbath put in one of their most important American appearances at the California Jam festival in 1974 alongside ELP and Deep Purple, playing to an audience of over quarter of a million people.

However, touring excesses and managerial nightmares had taken the band to breaking point, with Iommi and Osbourne becoming ever more confrontational. By now the band had shifted their business affairs to the notorious Don Arden. 1975's *Sabotage* kept the flame alive and the band put in another enormous American tour supported by Kiss.

The latest LP included a rarity for the band as initial copies included an unaccredited track 'Blow The Jug' – actually drummer Bill Ward singing the Nitty Gritty Dirt Band classic and captured unawares by a studio engineer.

The compilation *We Sold Our Souls For Rock 'n' Roll* charted well too, but many thought the 1976 experimental effort *Technical Ecstasy* to be somewhat below par. The album did include a first for the band though, as Ward took lead vocals for the first time ever on the track 'It's Alright'. American dates saw the band on the road supported by the unlikely duo of REO Speedwagon and The Ramones. Then, however, the unthinkable

Ozzy Osbourne

occurred. In the middle of rehearsals Ozzy left.

With the inevitable disintegration of Black Sabbath in the late '70s Ozzy had motivated himself to set about creating a fresh band. Ozzy's personal assistant at the time was Dave Tangye ('Tang') who also happened to manage Cumbrian heavy rock band Necromandus. Created under the original name of Hot Spring Water the quartet comprised vocalist Bill Branch, guitarist Barry Dunnery, bass player Dennis McCarten and drummer Frank Hall. A name change to Heavy Hand led eventually to Necromandus, a fusing of the words 'Nostradamus' and 'Necromancy'.

Frank Hall's first memories of Ozzy Osbourne date as far back as 1969. Black Sabbath would often play the gig circuit around the Lake District and it was at one of the band's very first gigs that Ozzy came to the fore.

"I first clapped eyes on Ozzy at the Towbar club in Nethertown in Cumbria," the drummer recalls. His memories of a pre-stardom Ozzy are in stark contrast to the onstage persona that would come to be known by millions. "I remember talking to Bill Ward who told me 'He's not long been out of prison' to which I replied; 'Better to break into music than houses I suppose!' Ozzy was a dramatic figure – he was really like a wild man. Onstage he used to whip his head up and down really, really fast and put his finger in his ear while he sang! I noticed he soon stopped doing that! The thing was though is that he was in fact a really friendly bloke, actually quite shy and nervous."

Ozzy's evolving dress sense, rarely captured in photographs during the formative years, would also give cause for concern. "In the early days he would always go onstage barefoot. God knows why. He certainly had a presence all of his own. I don't

---

Completists may wish to know that Iommi also recorded a session for FREEDOM / later SNAFU vocalist BOBBY HARRISON's solo album 'The Funkist'. FREEDOM were also part of Patrick Meehan's management stable and the band opened for Black Sabbath on numerous occasions. Titled 'The Funkist' the album saw a release in America on the Capitol label in 1973.

know why I remember this but he was wearing black corduroy trousers at that first gig. His hair was this long brown shaggy Rod Stewart kind of cut, spiky on top." This is not to say Frank too would not get caught up in the rock 'n' roll image stakes. "I had very long black hair and I would wear a black raven's feather in it," he admits. "People would say 'What tribe are you from?'"

Tony Iommi too would make an impression for reasons out of keeping with his media persona. "Tony is a great practical joker" Frank confides. "Both he and Ozzy are very, very funny but in different ways. Tony would often wind Ozzy up by putting eggs in his bed every night." (As we shall see this jape would be handed down through the rock generations in later years.)

Besides playing together on the live circuit, the band already had a strong Black Sabbath connection having cut a 1973 album *Orexis Of Death* for Vertigo Records during 1973 with Tony Iommi at the production desk. The Black Sabbath guitarist also had Necromandus signed up to his Tramp agency. Also involved with the agency were Judas Priest manager Dave Corke, one of the undisputed maverick legends of rock management, and Norman Hood. Necromandus would tour the Midlands area with Judas Priest as support band. "Priest had Al Atkins singing back then," Frank Hall affirms. "They did a lot of gigs with us and they had this great drummer, a black guy called Chris Campbell. Their manager Dave Corke would always buy my clothes from me for some odd reason. I would walk into the agency office with a pair of jeans and a denim jacket and Dave would say 'How much do you want for those?' So I'd sell them and walk out virtually naked.

"Dave was a hell of a character. Once he organised this freshman's ball gig with Necromandus, Vivian Stanshall and Keith Moon. As you can imagine it turned into a night of absolute lunacy."

The Necromandus album has been a constant source of fascination for Black Sabbath fanatics. Frank unveils the makings of a bona fide lost classic. "There were two attempts at making the album. The first was at the Marquee Studios at the back of the

Marquee Club and the second was in Blue Mink's Morgan Studios. The first time we came out with some pretty scrappy songs so Tony Iommi more or less said; 'Go away and come up with some better songs'.

The new material more than came up to scratch. Hall describes the bands music as 'Progressive Rock' not too far removed from today's acts such as Spock's Beard and Dream Theater. Finally getting down to recording, Necromandus found they were not the only ones ensconced in Morgan Studios. "Yes were there recording *Tales From Topographic Oceans*", Hall recalls. "I saw Jon Anderson walking in the middle of the street one day and told him, 'You're from The Warriors!' I used to go and see him with that band before he joined Yes. As you can imagine he was quite surprised. But we got talking and he introduced me to Rick Wakeman."

The world-renowned keyboard maestro was doubling up on duties at the time, recording for Yes and mixing his own solo work *The Six Wives Of Henry VIII*. Necromandus were on the night shift starting work at 9 in the evening and emerging as dawn broke. Frank was forthright in his approach to Rick. "We had this one track which I really thought could benefit from an outro using cellos, violins and keyboards so, being cheeky, I asked Rick if he would do it. I really got into his ribs about it, really pestered him but in the end it turned out he wanted to do it anyway. 'Yes' he said 'I'll do it for a crate of Guinness!' Rick actually thought it was a good idea."

This union never transpired though, as Frank relates. "When I told Tony that Rick wanted to put piano on this song he simply didn't believe me. Tony's first question was 'What does he want?'. He thought Rick would charge us megabucks. I told him he only wanted a crate of Guinness but it just didn't happen because Tony thought I was only joking and naturally thought too much money would be involved. I'm sure Rick would have done it for the beer."

The focal point of Necromandus was always guitarist Barry 'Baz' Dunnery. Although never to break into the public arena, Dunnery's talents left many open-mouthed in astonishment.

"He was incredibly fast," reckons Hall. "I remember Steve Howe being very impressed as Baz was going through his legato runs and speed picking. I'll never forget that look on Steve's face, like, 'fucking hell! What's he doing?'"

Ozzy's reputation for targeting guitarists with exceptional abilities was evident even then. With Black Sabbath on a global commercial high, the singer had nevertheless earmarked Dunnery as Frank Hall explains. "Everyone knows Baz's brother Francis from It Bites but, believe me, Baz leaves his brother standing. Baz was, and is, a fantastic guitarist. Both Ozzy and Glenn Hughes really rated him. Ozzy, I'll never forget, really tried to push Baz. He told Baz that he had the world at his feet."

Iommi himself would guest on one track, putting guitar down on 'One Fine Lad', a song about army life. However, Frank has some problems with remembering which song was which because, for a reason the drummer never discovered, all of the song titles would be changed. "The first Necromandus single was to be 'Don't Look Down Frank', a song about me. For some reason that title got changed to 'Nightjar'. All the titles were changed."

With Black Sabbath riding high internationally, an Iommi production credit, a guitar hero in the making and signed to a major label, it seemed as though the future looked bright indeed for Necromandus. It was not to be. *Orexis Of Death* was shelved. The reasoning behind the decision remaining a mystery for nearly three decades.

"The album was axed because Baz left the band," Frank sighs resignedly. "He said that he didn't want to go but he felt he had a conflict with the musical direction of the band. This was our big chance. We just couldn't understand it at all. We were devastated." With Dunnery out of the picture Iommi thought Necromandus was dead in the water. "We offered to try and get another guitarist as good as Baz but Tony thought this would be unlikely. He was right. We tried to get someone to keep the band going and get the album out but it was just impossible. Then of course Black Sabbath got back out onto the road so Tony was busy with that and the whole thing was just forgotten."

Ozzy Osbourne

Frank though was picked out by Glenn Hughes, vocalist for noted funk-rockers Trapeze. "Glenn was always asking for Necromandus to open for Trapeze. He asked me to consider joining the band because he could see things were shaky with Necromandus. I was just so low and disappointed by the whole thing at that point I went back home."

The *Orexis Of Death* album would remain consigned to the vaults until the late '90s when curiosity regarding all things doom-laden prompted its semi-official release on a series of small labels.

With Necromandus consigned to the history books Hall travelled back up to his native Cumbria, soon reforging links with Dunnery in a band called Nerves. At first a covers act, Nerves, with Steven Hatfield on keyboards and Don McKay on vocals, would evolve into the hard-edged R&B outfit Tantrum. Hall's musical career gradually fizzled out and the drummer would find himself working on a building site to make ends meet. Returning home from work one day in 1976 he would be given a jolt to see a familiar car outside his house.

"I recognized it straight away," he declares. "It was Ozzy's Range Rover. I got inside the house and there in my living room was Dave Tangye – Ozzy's P.A., Baz and one other guy." Frank and Dave Tangye went back a long way; "I actually got Dave the job with Ozzy," Frank maintains. "Ozzy asked me one day if I knew of someone to mind him and I suggested Dave straight away. I told Ozzy he was totally trustworthy and you could rely on him. Dave became Ozzy's P.A. and minder for many years."

Tangye did the talking. Frank remembers the exact words. "Right, Ozzy wants a guitarist, bassist and drummer and you lot in Necromandus are the likely candidates." Piling into Ozzy's car, the new recruits journeyed down to Staffordshire and Ozzy's home at Bullrush Cottage. Enter Blizzard of Ozz…

The original incarnation of Blizzard of Ozz was in an enviable position. Ozzy was a globally known figure and with Baz Dunnery the quartet was blessed with a world-class guitarist. Frank Hall had many reasons to be optimistic. "Ozzy had a lot of offers on the table from a few record companies. The potential was just huge at that point because the press would jump on any new Ozzy album. Ozzy was really keen to show the world how good Baz was too."

The musical persuasion of the inaugural Blizzard Of Ozz was not what the average Black Sabbath fan would have ever anticipated, however, as Frank elaborates. "Necromandus was always a kind of progressive, jazzy type rock band. I suppose you could put us in the same camp as Greenslade or Gentle Giant – that type of thing. We didn't actually change much when we worked up the songs with Ozzy. Some of the material was extremely complex, lots of time changes, and it sounded great. Ozzy of course wanted heavyweight detuned guitars all the time but the combination really was striking."

The band spent over a month working up new songs and gathering together some 15 or so, enough to be whittled down for a full album's complement. The chaotic circumstances prevailing in Ozzy's personal and business life would take their toll, though. "Ozzy was having a really hard time dealing with a lot of Black Sabbath stuff, his personal life and management troubles too. He had an awful lot to contend with." Frank confirms.

Naturally these early sessions would be peppered with famous Ozzy tomfoolery. "It was a fun summer!" the drummer laughs. "I don't know how we managed to get so much work done. Ozzy would often seek what he called 'Inspiration' at his local pub The Hand & Cleaver. By the time he got back around 11 at night he would want to rehearse!

"I remember one night Ozzy got really bothered by rats. He had this old dog kennel at the back of his house and he was obsessed with the idea it was full of rats. Well, he had been talking about rats all day and then suddenly I saw him marching off to this kennel with a can in his hand. 'Where are you going with that petrol can?' I said. Before I could stop him he had covered this thing with petrol and set light to it. Now, Ozzy was growing a beard at the time and he was standing far too close to this building when he lit it. Boof! It went up in flames and blew back on Ozzy, singeing off his beard and eyebrows!"

Frank would witness another Ozzy trick that had the band

members fearing for their singer's life. "There was a field at the back of Ozzy's place that he rented out to the local football team. In the corner of this field was a large pond. Well, one day Ozzy got into his Range Rover and, God knows why, drove straight into the middle of this pond! Ozzy thought it was hilarious until he realized the car was stuck in the mud. Not only that but it was sinking with Ozzy in it! I mean – it was going down fast! We thankfully got him out but he had to wait for his car until the farmer pulled it out in the morning with his tractor."

The band did manage to prevent one of Ozzy's potentially near-fatal exploits though. "We were having this big barbecue one day" Frank reminisces. "Ozzy is a great cook and would come up with these fantastic curries. God knows what he would put in them because we would feel stoned for days afterwards! Anyway, we were eating and this helicopter was flying low over Ozzy's house which really bothered him. I seem to remember he thought it was the press trying to get some pictures. Ozzy loved shotguns, and so he marched into his house and got out this Remington pump-action shotgun and started to fire at the bloody helicopter! We just managed to stop him but he did get a few shots at the thing."

All these exploits (and many more besides) were naturally having a serious effect on the work schedule. "Baz got very disillusioned with it all. We spoke one night and agreed to move out. It was a shame because the music was great – I could still sit down and play it today.

"Ozzy was obviously having to deal with too many things at once. Baz was being approached by other bands at the time – he was asked to replace Peter Banks in Flash. Some friends of mine from Barrow-in-Furness knew Phil Collins well and had recommended me for the position in Genesis. They liked my jazz-rock style but of course I was with Ozzy at the time and had to decline the offer."

And so Blizzard of Ozz Mark I split up. McCarten joined Birmingham band Grit while Dunnery and Hall reformed Nerves back in Cumbria. There were no hard feelings and Hall, along with his parents, would be invited to Ozzy's house for a mam-

Chords Of Disquiet

moth celebratory bash in honour of the Queen's Silver Jubilee in 1977. This is when the drummer would discover Ozzy had other strings to his bow besides singing.

"For that party the house was totally crammed – hundreds of people" he recounts. "My Mum and Dad were in awe. My Mum always tells people that she slept in Ozzy's bed. She did actually; Ozzy let her have his big four-poster covered in carved gargoyles for the night.

"Now Ozzy had this very impressive and extremely expensive Steinway piano in his sitting room. He showed me that there were more ways than one to play it. I couldn't believe my eyes when he climbed up on top of it. He stood on it and urinated inside it. He was playing the strings by directing this endless stream of urine, trying to get a tune! We were in absolute hysterics and I was pushing against the door as hard as I could praying my mother wouldn't try to come in!" Beat that, Keith Emerson.

In later years Dunnery would become a member of the ELO offshoot Violinski whilst Hall's career has most recently seen him playing with jazz band The Children. He can also be found touting his own band project, The Binmen, also featuring former Sweet singer Malcolm McNulty.

Meanwhile, with the Necromandus musicians no longer on the scene, Ozzy had another stab at forging the Blizzards. His manager, the ubiquitous Don Arden, had discovered that an acquaintance of his handled business affairs for a band who at the time were in limbo. That band was Dirty Tricks, signed to Polydor Records, and who had just completed a run of three albums, the first of which happened to be produced by Rodger Bain – the man responsible for the early Black Sabbath albums. The band comprised vocalist Kenny Stewart, guitarist John Fraser Binnie, bass player Terry Horbury and drummer Andy Bierne. Arden played Ozzy the band's new tapes, for the Tony Visconti-produced *Hit And Run* album, to a favourable response and a meeting was duly arranged.

Bassist Terry Horbury takes up the tale. "We'd split up really. But the three of us, myself, John and Andy stuck together planning on starting another band. Our manager had decided he wanted out of the business but unfortunately would not let us out of our contract so we were in an impossible situation. It wasn't just that. Punk and New Wave had come in and really set us back too. For Dirty Tricks to do a gig we'd need our full crew, etc. which was costly, but these new bands would just turn up and plug in. Basically we were in a jam.

"What happened though was that we got the call to meet up with Ozzy. We first met him in Don Arden's office in London, we all had a banter then arranged to travel up to Ozzy's house near Stafford to get some songs together. So, we all went up to Ozzy's place. I think all in all we stayed there three weeks. I remember that almost as soon as we arrived Ozzy seemed distracted by something outside the window. Next thing we knew he's grabbed this shotgun and then we see he's crawling along the hedgerow like a commando. Well, after a time he came back with this dead partridge he'd just shot. He just stood there with a big grin on his face, dripping blood all over our guitarist's wah wah pedal. That was our 'Ozzy greeting' if you like.

"It was quite a house. In the yard Ozzy had this big bus he had bought. He was in the middle of turning it into a tour bus. He's ripped out all the seats and was painting it black inside and out. Ozzy had Marshall amps and cabs everywhere, which for poor musicians like us were the holy grail, but he was using them for tables! Oddly though, despite the Marshalls everywhere else, he had no P.A. set-up in the actual rehearsal room. What he did have in there was a Revox tape recorder, a microphone and a large stuffed bear which looked like it had been attacked a few times!"

There would be no hint of the former material in use as this new proto-Blizzard of Ozz Mark II started out from scratch, and writing new material. Terry Horbury: "It was a bit like an old Blues session really because the only way Ozzy could record was through this Revox. We'd be blaring away and we could see him singing, reading ideas from his lyric books he had, but not hear him. It was only when we played the tapes back we got the full picture."

Terry remembers distinctly the name 'Blizzard Of Ozz' being mentioned as the moniker for the band. Pointedly, no Black

Chords Of Disquiet

Sabbath material was attempted.

"I don't ever recall doing any Sabbath songs. Ozzy said that we would probably do 'Paranoid' as an encore or something but he wanted all new stuff. I think all in all we got about half a dozen songs together. It was good stuff, just good solid hard rock. I've still got tapes of the rehearsals.

"The problem was that, to be truthful, Ozzy really wasn't in the best shape to get a band together at that time. We would be ready to work at 10.30 but Ozzy wouldn't wake until midday and then he'd go down to the local pub until 4. Glenn Hughes came round once while we were there. I'll never forget it, Glenn was so out of shape that after he had sat down in a chair he found he couldn't get up again! We all had to lift him out of the thing – he had literally become part of the furniture!

"With Ozzy though it's just so easy to forget because he was full-on *all the time*. Every five minutes he would tell us a hilarious story about his past. One of the few I remember was that apparently one day Ozzy and Geezer were standing next to each other at the urinals having a piss. Ozzy, for some reason, had a can of silver spray paint in his pocket so he whips this out and sprays Geezer's manhood with it! Of course Geezer couldn't do anything because he was in mid-stream so he just had to stand there while he was sprayed silver! We'd get about a hundred stories like that every day. So much so that we actually had some serious discussions between the three of us just what we were letting ourselves in for!

"Ozzy was having a real hard time of it really. Money was a big problem. Ozzy even told us it would be a good idea if we all signed on the dole in Birmingham!"

The three musicians suggested to Ozzy that rather than travelling to Staffordshire it would be more practical to pursue matters in London. "Ozzy thought this was a good idea too so I went ahead and booked a month's rehearsal at The Tunnel studios for us" relates Terry. "The day before we were scheduled to go in I phoned Ozzy to make arrangements and he simply said 'Oh, I've just rejoined Black Sabbath'. So that was that."

After their Ozzy adventure the Dirty Tricks musicians would

all follow differing paths. Binnie wound up with the much vaunted Rogue Male. Horbury and Bierne would work with Alvin Lee for a while before the bassist hooked up with German ex-UFO guitarist Michael Schenker and then Vardis. He would also become acquainted with another figure in the Ozzy saga – Bob Daisley.

"There was a time when Bob was in Uriah Heep but had got the call to go back to Ozzy. We were trying to work out a plan for me to temporarily fill Bob's role in Heep while he sorted out the Ozzy thing. Although I would have loved to have done I was committed to another band at the time so it never happened."

Author's note: Another source close to Ozzy at this time has stated that the band Ozzy attempted to assemble at this time only had one rehearsal at Bill Ward's house and nothing was achieved outside of a drunken jam. This is obviously at enormous variance with Frank and Terry's accounts of events. Interestingly, the conflicting source (who would not be interviewed) claimed there was nothing worth finding out about Ozzy's time away from Black Sabbath.

2
Killing Yourself To Live

Like light on the brink of an insatiable and irresistible black hole, Ozzy was sucked back into the *Götterdämmerung* of Black Sabbath's dying star, ousting his temporary replacement, former Savoy Brown and Fleetwood Mac man, Dave Walker, to re-record the vocals for the *Never Say Die* album.

Black Sabbath had actually got on with the business of recording with Walker while Ozzy had taken his leave. Although a vocalist of some repute, Walker was the first to face the insurmountable obstacle placed in the way of all pretenders to the Sabbath throne. Simply put, Black Sabbath don't need a lead vocalist – they need Ozzy Osbourne. Caught on the hoof, studio time intended for cutting tracks with Walker in Toronto was hastily rescheduled to accommodate the returning Ozzy. Here the band started from scratch, the material demoed with Walker being completely unsuitable for Ozzy.

With such constraints, and still dealing with the tumult of the previous months, it is quite remarkable that *Never Say Die* turned out as respectable an album as it is. The lyrics to the eminently catchy 'Hard Road' were probably a bit more poignant – given the band's situation – than many outsiders would have dared guess. The record fared well in the UK and Europe but would wallow in the lower reaches of the American Billboard Top 100. With Ozzy back in the fold the band staggered through a subsequent world tour. On home turf the band had been supported by the electrifying spectacle of the then-novel Van Halen and Ozzy was not shy in his praise for the Americans. Sabbath, anaesthetized by their own excesses, had looked slow and awkward in comparison to the exuberance of David Lee Roth and the sheer wizardry of Eddie Van Halen.

Black Sabbath retired to California, ostensibly to work on a fresh album, but came up against an unassailable brick wall of apathy. Wisely, Ozzy got the sense of a new dawn and, breaking free, went to ground in Los Angeles. Minus Ozzy Black Sabbath, or rather the remaining duo of Tony Iommi and Bill Ward, tenaciously clawed their way into some much needed breathing space enrolling Geoff Nichols on bass and Ronnie James Dio on vocals. Nichols had a long history with Iommi as guitarist with fellow Brummies, Quartz, a band Iommi had long been assisting, firstly as producer for their 1977 Jet Records eponymous debut. Quartz would duly act in the support role for Black Sabbath's subsequent UK tour dates. What is not so well known to fans of the band is that an outtake from that first record, 'Circles', boasted not only Iommi on guitar but Queen's Brian May and even Ozzy himself on harmonica. Inexplicably, the track never made the album. It would be relegated to the B-side of the 1980 single 'Stoking The Fires Of Hell', Osbourne's involvement being, almost incredibly, overlooked by a music media at the time obsessed by heavy metal.

Nichols would eventually switch to keyboards when erstwhile Rainbow man Craig Gruber took the role and has stoically figured in the Black Sabbath saga ever since. Ronnie James Dio though, another Rainbow refugee, was a figure of quite awesome vocal talent and would steer the band into renewed vistas of success. Dio, in possession of a voice of extreme pedigree, both rich in texture and blessed with a mighty power, had onlookers and listeners startled when judged against – it has to be said – Ronnie's less than towering physique.

Born Ronald Padova, he had brought his talents to bear on school outfits, including Ronnie and The Red Caps who actually went so far as to release a single, 'Lover'/ 'Conquest' in 1958. The '60s had Dio fronting Ronnie Dio and The Prophets, a band in which he not only sang but played piano, bass and trumpet. In 1967 a fresh project, The Electric Elves (latterly Elf), was forged with Dio's guitarist cousin and latter-day Rods mentor David 'Rock' Feinstein.

With the whimsical Elf, Dio began to break into the big league supporting Deep Purple and issuing progressively better albums. He would, along with Elf in their entirety (minus their guitarist, naturally), be plucked from obscurity and groomed for stardom by Ritchie Blackmore. The Dio-era Rainbow, which

Killing Yourself To Live

found the singer's sense of majesty and grandeur coming to the fore, would provide a reliable barometer of what was to come for Black Sabbath. Dio had always imbued his projects with Gothic kitsch and medieval romanticism with such familiar imagery as dragons and rainbows. Dio branded Black Sabbath as his own simply by steering the band towards more malevolent and brooding lyrical themes. Quite deliberately, Osbourne's replacement was his complete and unequivocal antithesis and as such would, over the next few years, provide the fuel to a publicly played-out feud unparalleled in rock 'n' roll.

As 1979 dawned Los Angeles was a seething hotbed of hard rock bands. It was a unique primeval soup fired by the inspiration of the '70s rock leviathans, the over-the-top exploits of Kiss and the latter-day heroics of Van Halen, whilst still smarting from the bruises left by Punk. Within this maelstrom of talent and determination, band members switched allegiances in order to place themselves in the right camp while bands scrabbled to find ever new and daring stageshows and images to set them apart from the crowd.

This new generation would include names such as Snow, London, The Boyz and Mickey Ratt. Later developments would throw up Ratt, Dokken, Great White, Mötley Crüe, Quiet Riot, Poison, Warrant, LA Guns, Faster Pussycat, Guns N'Roses and W.A.S.P., not to mention a labyrinthine succession of descendants.

Outside this den of madness, and oblivious to all but a chosen handful, sat Ozzy Osbourne in a purgatory delivered by his own hand. He had finally severed his ties with Black Sabbath and was determined to erase the memory of the last decade. Into this void would walk Dana Strum.

Strum was racing on the treadmill of the Los Angeles rat run with his act Badaxe. The band differed from the melting pot of other desperate souls in that the group was firmly rooted in a more rustic traditional earthiness akin to the pioneering British acts and, in particular, Black Sabbath. The act shunned the prevalent Glam trend and went for a back-to-basics long hair and jeans look.

Along with the pivotal figure of Strum, Badaxe was formed of drummer Steve Ward, guitarist David Carruth and a succession of singers. The mike was initially in the hands of Toronto-born Stacey Morland, who then relinquished his role to Bob Geadreau out of Phoenix, Arizona. Badaxe's last line up was fronted by Louie Merlino. Recordings were undertaken for an album but this never surfaced. A 7" single for a Canadian label Earth Breeze in 1978, 'Cry For Me' / 'All You Can Stand', did emerge, however, and would come to the attention of Billboard magazine who singled out Badaxe for their 'Pick Hit'. The group gigged hard pulling off many notable supports and guest slots to such diverse artists as Judas Priest, Black Oak Arkansas, Starz, The Dogs, Eddie Money and Michael Des Barres' Silverhead. They would also make it onto celluloid, featuring in the Emilio Estevez movie *17 And Going Nowhere* and one of their amateur video clips would earn the director Mark Goldberg a UCLA Jim Morrison award.

All in all though, Badaxe missed the bus commercially. Not unnaturally they wanted to break it big time like every other hungry-eyed band but they could not compromise on the music. Strum himself, is nowadays philosophical. "Mainly it was a very Sabbathy trip but a kinda American version. We were not set out to be a hit type of act at the time although maybe now 20 years later it might have been."

It was probably their marked rawness that brought Badaxe and in particular Strum to the attention of Jet Records' Pat Sicillano. Scouting for talent to build a band back around Ozzy the enterprising Sicillano had marked Strum out, giving him the address of Frank Zappa's Hollywood studio where the label was setting up sessions in order to entice Ozzy out of his self-imposed exile.

A week later Strum received the call to attend. "I got a phone call telling me at what time to arrive but not what we would be playing or doing. I always thought that was odd but I knew most of the Black Sabbath stuff anyway and I figured who gave a fuck…"

The first meeting with Ozzy was to provoke a wave of

Killing Yourself To Live

conflicting emotions which would become a part of Strum's life for the next few months. The sense of disbelief at the opportunity afforded to him was triggering instincts in Dana that had him mentally shouting "Wow! It's him…Ozzy!!!" but pragmatism soon took over. "This was not the glitz and dollars and fun that anyone would think." There was work to be done.

Strum's sensibilities were assailed further when he walked into Zappa's studio startled to see the renowned figure of former Thin Lizzy guitarist Gary Moore performing. The scenario was somewhat surreal. Being invited to try out for Ozzy was hard enough to take in but being confronted by one of the greats of rock guitar set the bass player's mind reeling.

Moore's status within rock echelons was undoubtedly of the highest ranking but the Irishman came with baggage and a reputation. Like Ozzy the effects of the demon alcohol had generated Moore as much media print as his guitar abilities. On top of this, his clashes with Thin Lizzy mentor and driving force Phil Lynott had boiled over into expensive mid-tour walk outs. In spite of all this Gary Moore was an awesome lead guitarist and at this stage in his life was slowly rebuilding his life and career. On paper the union of Moore and Ozzy, both Jet Records artists, had huge potential. Strum notes that Moore's playing ability was "unreal" but he could detect a severe clash in styles, finding it hard to imagine Moore as part of any post-Sabbath outfit.

Nevertheless the trio, together with more than one drummer whose names have evaporated into the ether, jammed on whatever came into the sphere of operations. Pointedly there was never any attempt at or discussion of any Sabbath run-throughs. Although the mood overall was relaxed, Moore and Ozzy simply didn't gel.

From the outset Ozzy's state of health had made an obvious impression on Strum and signalled a quick mental game of questions and answers to assess the situation. "He is a bit fucked up – what to do? Fuck it – I love the music. I know it will be a good thing," he surmised. Strum was committed and hoped the relaxed rapport struck up with Ozzy was an indicator that he had got the gig. Shortly after this jam Moore would go his own way and

Ozzy Osbourne

forge an alliance with ex-Deep Purple vocalist Glenn Hughes and drummer Mark Nauseef for what was to become G-Force.

Although the first sessions had ruled Moore out of the picture, Ozzy was keenly impressed by Strum and invited him over to his residence at the Le Parc Hotel in West Hollywood to discuss further plans. The singer's room was a stark visual clue to the overall chaos surrounding Ozzy that Strum would in time have to weave together into some kind of grand plan. "It was a wreck; beer cans, smell of dope, piles of dirty clothing, old food and pizza boxes. Nothing too incriminating out in the open – he was smart. It looked like Oz had been having some good rock 'n' roll fun in a high dollar hotel!" Fortunately the hotel, used to the eccentricities of bored rock stars, let it all pass as long as the bill was paid.

It was here that the bass player learned that although Jet Records had given Ozzy a list of potential guitar recruits there was no band as yet. The pair talked of future plans and the evening rounded off with Ozzy stating "Kid, you got the job". Strum responded boldly enough, to Ozzy's surprise, that he was sure he knew the right guitar player for his band.

"That night was odd, not just because I had just got the Ozzy gig." Strum was totally convinced of his choice and although Ozzy questioned his judgement, Strum would not be deterred. It was a big risk. Here he was, a relative unknown, telling Ozzy Osbourne, a cast iron true-as-they-come rock 'n' roll legend, in no uncertain terms that someone equally obscure was the man to resurrect his whole career.

So convinced was Strum that he describes this conversation in almost fatalistic terms. "A strange feeling came over me in that I knew the guy that I had told him should be the guitar player. It was Randy Rhoads – I was certain of that. I really saw it happen very clearly in my head. Like it was just a fact in time that was meant to be. I had no doubts."

Strum may have felt the firm hand of destiny placed on his shoulder at that point, but Ozzy and Randy Rhoads were oblivious at this point. It would transpire that not only were both parties ambivalent about the union but, as it turned out, Strum had to fight tooth and nail to make it happen.

This was driven by conviction and also that Strum personally had nothing to gain in the short term from hooking Ozzy up with Randy. The club circuit at that time was a vicious back-biting charnel house of aspiring – usually broke – musicians who would trample on anyone and anything to make it to the top. Landing the gig with Ozzy Osbourne was a one-way ticket to superstardom and Strum was putting forward an arch rival for the position.

"All of the hard rock bands were kinda fighting each other for that magic record deal. Badaxe and Quiet Riot were not the best of friends." This is putting it mildly; Quiet Riot were led by one Kevin DuBrow, a man who by his own admission badmouthed colleagues, compatriots and rivals to such an extent that his own band became completely ostracised. In a matter of years, though, Quiet Riot would soar meteorically, scoring an American Number 1 album and, for a brief moment, eclipse all but the very biggest of established bands.

For now, though, this ascendancy was in the future and Strum faced an uphill task in contacting Randy. "I had a trip to break through which was to get hold of Randy without anyone really catching on."

Dana Strum set about his mission with zeal, drawing up a candidature of possibles for Ozzy. It was a short list headed by Randy but also including George Lynch of The Boyz and Carlos Cavazo of Snow. From an acquaintance at the Starwood Club Strum got a contact number for Randy at his mother's music school in Burbank. Once the deal had been put to Rhoads though, Strum was taken aback by the guitarist's response. "Randy was not really into the idea and he didn't like Sabbath that much. He was kinda into Glam rock and fancied himself more of a Mick Ronson, T Rex or Brian May of Queen type of vibe."

Strum's sense of purpose took hold once again. "At this time I felt myself almost telling him that he had to try, because it would be great." Rhoads then awkwardly confessed that he had never auditioned for anyone before and simply would not know

Ozzy Osbourne

what to do. Strum considered, and then began discussing one of Randy's solos that had impressed him at the Starwood. "I told him that would be a great start and we could just go from there". Further conversations throughout the day finalized the details of the audition. Strum still had his "strange feeling" but little would he know that his campaign to unify Ozzy and Randy had only just begun. "I knew that this was to be a very meaningful day in rock history, I will never forget." Not knowing the tribulations he still had to face Strum set up the meet.

Although this was without question a pivotal juncture in Ozzy's life, he was far from fighting fit and not exactly in the best shape. He was physically heavy and the blitz of drink and drugs that had numbed the immediate wrench of leaving Sabbath had now become his own personal ball and chain. Strum still had in his memory the images of Sabbath in their prime and resolved himself to better times to come, convinced that if a good band could be assembled Ozzy's renaissance would be inevitable.

"Despite Ozzy's condition I always thought it would work out," he confides. "It just needed time. He might have had times where he did not really know what to think. He was a bit unclear a lot of the time and much later I would understand just how meaningful Sharon's role in his life would be."

For the time being though, Strum simply had to deal with Ozzy's troubles, often acting as a sounding board. "I didn't do drugs and drink much at all at that early point in my life. Our meetings at the Le Parc Hotel would often turn into talks about life and booze. More than once in the apartments across the street we heard someone playing 'Iron Man' kinda out of nowhere. It was really funny shit from day one. He really was like a three ring circus all of the time."

In the midst of this somehow the true spirit of Ozzy managed to break through. "One night in the hotel he kinda came up with a few melody lines," says Strum. "I knew then and there that the magic Sabbath sound was something other than the killer guitar and bass riffs. The vibes and melodies were all Ozzy. I was really happy as I had learned what I thought to be true was a fact. Ozzy was the centre of that great sound I loved."

Killing Yourself To Live

Often the singer would share tales of his past with Dana who was enthralled by stories of Ozzy's pre-Black Sabbath bands, his job at an abattoir and his exploits stealing televisions. The two even discussed a wild scheme to start an agency with Strum slated as 'Super Agent'. Weighed down though he was by emotional, alcoholic and chemical shackles, the atmosphere around Ozzy was nevertheless electric. "One night he went out and yelled at the sky in Hollywood and seemed to make it rain" Strum recalls. The magic was tangible and the excited American was honoured to be chosen as the sorcerer's apprentice.

This was the Ozzy that Strum drove around to check out the guitarists on the agenda. By now Strum had realized that not only was he Ozzy's bass player but his driver and all-round organizer as well. Even the normally patient hotel staff were getting irate at the sheer volume of calls Strum was patching through and receiving in his efforts to assemble a band.

Typically the auditions were an enlightening experience. "We saw a few real freaks" Dana admits. "One guy kept singing Hendrix songs while he played the guitar and Ozzy kept saying "No, just play – I'm the front guy!" It was crazy."

Interestingly number two on Dana's list of three was blissfully unaware of the proceedings. Ensconced in his pre-Dokken band The Boyz, the band's manager had neglected to inform George Lynch that there was an interest in him from the Ozzy camp. "He was never told that I ever thought that he should be my second shot," Strum relates. "Oh boy, was he upset!"

Another applicant was the towering, tattooed figure of Chris Holmes, later of W.A.S.P. infamy, about whom Strum is diplomatic "That just was not right…"

In between viewing each candidate Strum drove Ozzy in his Triumph TR7 sports car to the next audition, all the while attempting to convince his employer that Randy Rhoads was the man. "It was kinda nuts. I think that he thought that I was selling him a friend." Little did Ozzy know that Strum's intentions were totally altruistic and that he and Randy were to all intents and purposes, adversaries on the circuit. Having his nerves assaulted by American hopefuls Ozzy simply wanted to go home.

Ozzy Osbourne

"Let's just go to England," he told Strum. "We can find a real bloke." His colleague maintained his stance "I kept on with the fact that he needed to see Randy."

Ozzy's daily ritual was still revolving around liquid sustenance and the evenings would invariably be spent at the notorious Rainbow Bar & Grill on Sunset Boulevard. "Ozzy kinda liked the circus of that place, I guess that it made him feel at home. There were very many wild cool nights – after all he was Ozzy so anywhere we went… I was new as hell to all of that. Don't forget, I was young, dumb and full of cum," Strum fondly and vividly remembers. "Really each day at that time in his life was kinda get up, get high, get drunk and…who knows…"

Ozzy could hold his own, though, as a public figure and celebrity. Strum has recollections of being extremely nervous when Jet Records laid on some media interviews. "I took him to the interviews and we both kinda sat there. I wondered what he was going to say, being that there was no band and no songs. He did just great."

Author's note: I have my own experiences of Chris Holmes. The first is of trying to maintain an air of decorum interviewing an earnest Blackie Lawless on the 'Electric Circus' dates whilst behind him a showering, soaped-up Holmes was pressing his features – facial and otherwise – up against the unfortunately unfrosted glass panel to distract my attention from his boss. I had to bite the insides of my cheeks to get through that experience with a straight face. Latterly he invaded the British metal band Marshall Law's trailer backstage at a German festival and stayed there – for four hours! During his residency he quite candidly admitted most of his gig that night would be on tape. Watching his 'guitar solo' that night alongside two extremely accomplished but open mouthed and agog guitarists, I could only admire the man's nerve! What a hero.

3
The Reluctant Wizard

Randall William Rhoads, the youngest sibling to brother Doug and sister Kathy, was born on December 6, 1956 at St. John's Hospital in Santa Monica, California. His mother Delores was left a single parent when his father, a music teacher, baled out of the relationship. This severing of ties would provide Randy with an extended family of two half brothers, Dan and Paul, in later years. Both Randy and Kathy would take up folk guitar from a very early age, the youngsters getting to grips with an acoustic Gibson belonging to their grandfather. Their musical environs would be fashioned by the fact that Delores was the owner of the North Hollywood music school Musonia.

Prompted by his mother in an effort to instil a practical knowledge of sight reading, Randy also took up piano lessons. Randy, though, had set his sights firmly on the guitar, despite the fact that his semi-acoustic Harmony Rocket's sheer size, when compared to the waif-like Randy, presented physical challenges all of its own. Randy's close friend Kelly Garni would also get sucked into this pursuit of rock music. The two had met when just 11 at Junior High school and were both fired by a love of rock music. It was a glue that would create a friendship for life. Garni has vivid memories of the Randy he was first drawn to.

"There was just something about him that stood out, he really had a presence about him. At school Randy actually had a big problem with it. He actually looked feminine so other kids would give him a hard time over that. The thing was though, that he had this Mozart-like talent. We both wanted to be rock stars, even at 11, it's all we ever spoke about." The two budding stars resolved to learn the craft of playing music and form a band as soon as they were able.

"When we first met, Randy only knew rhythm, no lead. I would spend every day hanging around his house just learning. It was quite a house - his mother played, his sister played and his brother played too. Of course I wanted to join in so Randy said "How about bass?" I would play the root notes to his rhythms, runs and patterns."

Randy was eager to add lead playing to his skills and this is where tutor Scott Shelly comes into the picture. "Randy worshipped Scott," Kelly recounts. "He learnt how to play lead from Scott and add it to his rhythm playing, so pretty soon he was playing both rhythm and lead over my bass runs. Music just took over our world. We both cared about little else and as fast as he was learning guitar I was learning bass. I don't think his mother knows this but we would both cut school and jam at my house all day. When Randy's mother left for work at the music school about 3 o'clock we would grab our amps and haul them two or three blocks to Randy's house to carry on playing there. Nothing would stop us except the *Beverly Hillbillies*. When that came on TV we dropped everything!"

In their early teens the duo graduated from theory to application, bowing in with a debut act, Violet Fox. With Randy's brother Doug on drums, Violet Fox's ambitions flickered for a matter of months but it was enough to set Randy and Kelly onto the path of rock 'n' roll. Sojourns ensued on the Burbank party scene with further acts including Mildred Pierce and The Katzenjammer Kids. "We were performing as a band by the time we were 13," admits Garni. "Often it would just be grabbing whoever was available to act as a drummer and we'd just play these surfers' backyard beer bashes, mostly without a singer. I think we got through about four or five guys on drums."

These embryonic outfits would pad out their live sets with covers of songs by the likes of The Rolling Stones, Mountain and Alice Cooper. Garni: "Randy was a major, major Leslie West fan. Not enough is said about that. Mountain was a major influence on Randy. We also did a lot of Stones – stuff like 'Street Fighting Man' and 'Sympathy For The Devil'. Also at that time Alice Cooper was very big for us both. We both loved Alice and Randy was especially taken with Glen Buxton's style of guitar playing. It's interesting to note that not many people have picked up on that, even the guitar magazines, which I think is because of the Ozzy/Sabbath association. Randy's inspiration really came from Leslie West, Glen Buxton and Mick Ronson."

The Reluctant Wizard

Next in the trail of fledgling bands would come Smokie – Still just 13, Rhoads and Garni had elevated their status to the Hollywood club scene and would be patronized by KROQ radio anchor Rodney Bingenheimer, performing on a regular basis at the DJ's club. "That was a great club, great for us too because Rodney was very influential on the scene," Garni maintains. "Everyone in the club was only 15 or 16 but everyone got served liquor. We had this huge transsexual guy, Smokie, as a singer. He couldn't sing a note but he looked incredible. On drums there was a guy named John Barber."

Smokie would be perfectly poised to capitalise on the latest influential wave to hit America – Glam. "We really got into it – Slade, Mott the Hoople, David Bowie. We'd start to play all their songs. Randy really got off on Mick Ronson. If you've ever seen the *Ziggy Stardust* video you can see it all – Randy looks exactly like Mick Ronson from that video, the hair, the clothes, the Les Paul – even Randy's facial features."

Ultimately Smokie bit the dust, unfortunately in less than salutary circumstances. "Basically Smokie himself didn't have all his faculties," Garni says bluntly. "In fact, he was crazy and violent with it. We had to get rid of him because he got violent with us – he was a big guy and, remember, we were still just kids. From then on we had a few singers – Cagey, Glenn, all of these when the band had no real name as such."

In 1976 the band Little Women would provide a useful step up to a semi-professional outfit in search of more than just a good time. Rhoads and Garni were now 15 and more enthused about the prospect of rock superstardom than ever. There was, however, a problem – the lack of a frontman. The story of just how Kevin DuBrow enters the scenario has been elaborated on time and time again, albeit with less and less reliability. DuBrow is a pivotal figure in the saga as it was his drive and ambition that would, as Kelly Garni recognises, push Randy Rhoads into the public arena by way of his first recording contract.

Garni: "Randy and I were at our good friend Hillary's house," relates Kelly taking up the tale. "We had been partying pretty hard, hadn't slept at all and it got to early morning. I heard

Hillary in the next room talking to someone on the phone about a singer, a guy who sounded like Rod Stewart. Of course I caught this because any mention of a singer was useful so I asked Hillary "Who was that guy? Tell me all about him." I got a name and number and called him. I said "We've got a band...of sorts. I think we should meet."

Bearing in mind that Garni and Rhoads were too young to drive, a friend gave them a lift to Kevin DuBrow's house. There they were treated to a 8mm film reel of Kevin performing live with guitarist Stan Sobel of The Dickies, but unfortunately without sound. "He was dressed up just like Rod Stewart – he even had the scarf!" Garni laughs at the memory of it. "Both Randy and I thought this was really silly and, in truth, we weren't very impressed. We both kept looking at the door wondering how we were going to get out."

The budding musicians crossed DuBrow off their list but the singer had other ideas. "He would not leave us alone," Garni recalls. "Kevin would just keep phoning us day after day after day. In the end it just became too much so we gave in and invited him around to audition in the garage at our house. Well, he was just horrible. He was like the worst singer you ever heard in your life. We told him not to call us any more but still he persisted." Figuring DuBrow's persistence must surely account for something, and still lacking an all-important frontman, Rhoads and Garni relented – again.

"We thought if the guy is that keen to promote himself it can't be all bad. Kevin is certainly not what you would ever call shy. Randy and I spoke about it and thought, well, perhaps we could try and teach him to sing. Kevin was a big Steve Marriott fan so we agreed we would try to teach him to sing in that style. To his credit, Kevin got it down pretty good – he really worked at it. Then of course, as soon as he had his foot in the door, he took over everything. Kevin wanted to be a rock star more than any of us."

DuBrow's gung-ho attitude soon snared management – of a sorts – for Quiet Riot. "Actually this guy was a coke dealer who put some money into us" laughs Kelly. "He was actually pretty

The Reluctant Wizard

helpful, got us our first gigs and arranged our first recordings, got us from the embryo into the carriage so to speak. Unfortunately he had a tendency to violence so our parting with him was very bitter." The singer would then strike a deal with a more soundly-based management set-up – the Toby Organisation run by David Joseph and Warren Etner, business advisors to whiter-than-white pomp-metallers Angel.

"The new managers really got things moving for Quiet Riot," admits Garni. "They refined us from the raw product that we were." However, the Toby Organisation had a game plan set out for Quiet Riot that was not in keeping with the band's ideal path of career enhancement. "We were a hard rock band but they had different ideas. Some of it was just plain goofy. They wanted to portray us as innocent little schoolboys but with a mischievous side to our nature. They even got me to dress up in a sailor suit. This period is actually pretty interesting because it's where Randy's trademark bow tie comes from. They kept telling us to think like The Knack! They had plans for a TV show and everything. Randy and I just wanted to play spookier more, menacing stuff like Alice Cooper but every time we tried they would say no."

What the Toby Organisation did achieve was a record deal. Unfortunately it was in the wrong country. Quiet Riot were rejected by every major American label without exception, despite a seemingly interminable round of showcases at the Starwood Club. Refusing to acknowledge defeat, Joseph and Etner spread their net further and, following a few trips to the land of the rising yen, snared a deal with CBS in Japan.

Quiet Riot would then enter into a four-year period of life inside a bubble. The band had a debut album out but no-one could buy it in the stores. Their reputation as a live act was also being bolstered by a rapid climb up the ladder at the Starwood Club. Starting out booked by Michelle Meyer as an opening act Quiet Riot rapidly elevated themselves from amateur night on a Sunday up through the mid-week rankings to score a regular residency. And that's where they got stuck. "We spent four years languishing at the Starwood Club," says Garni wearily. "At the time it was great because we packed the house every night we played but we couldn't break out of it. It's great to be playing in front of a thousand people who come back to see you week after week but we were going nowhere. We were also broke."

There were other gigs, such as at the Santa Monica Civic guesting for Angel, but in reality Quiet Riot were anchored at the Starwood by a very short chain. There were internal problems too. Garni and DuBrow were growing farther and farther apart. The frustration of their treadmill career predicament and an ever-growing resentment building between bassist and singer triggered Garni's next move.

"I'd had enough. I'd only ever known music. I was 19 and had no money. The lifestyle was getting to me too" he readily admits. "I had an ever-growing problem between Kevin and me. It wasn't just his fault; I was drinking a lot, I said stupid things, got thrown in jail. Kevin had his hands full with me. I was constantly provoking him." Eventually the atmosphere had worsened to such a degree that the two could not even bear each other's presence in the same room. Garni had been seriously considering a career in the emergency services and, after the conclusion of a band meeting, it was time to jump. "I became a paramedic which I stuck at for ten years and loved every minute of it. I kept my friendship with Randy. Nothing could change that."

Randy and Quiet Riot persevered, enlisting a young Cuban by the name of Rudy Sarzo to fill the void left by Garni's departure. A second album for the Japanese market came and went. Quiet Riot was treading water, still waving, not yet drowning…

******

Came the day of the first Ozzy / Randy / Dana tryout at Dirk Dalton's studios all was not going to plan. Strum has a vivid recollection of the day. "Ozzy had had a few drinks and kinda did not want to go. I kept telling him he had to go. Trust me. This is the guy!" However, despite the pair getting to the audition, Ozzy's mood could not be lifted. "You could see he was as frustrated as hell. He hated life, he hated LA and he missed England

and his home."

About 10pm the studio rear buzzer rang and Randy made his way in with Strum helping set up his gear – a small old Gibson amp, a dist box and an echoplex. "Randy was nervous because he still did not know what to play. I assured him it would be fine." Unbeknown to Randy Rhoads he was not the only one whose nerves were on edge. Dana Strum was deeply concerned. "Ozzy was in the lobby drinking and getting pretty fucked-up. I was concerned that he might pass out and not get all of this. I was freaking!" Strum set about getting Randy into action before his boss flaked out. Wisely, he had set the studio up prior to the guitarist's arrival. "I got a sound on Randy, just so that we could hear him, he still kept telling me that he did not know what to play. I played a bit of bass with him to relax the vibe and told him the Starwood solo would be the shit. This was the first time I had played with him and he was…great!"

The bass player rushed out into the lobby and found Ozzy sound asleep. He was not prepared to come this far though to simply let the opportunity slip through his fingers. "I woke him. He was fucked-up and asked me to take him home, just take him home," he relates. "This was a crazy night. I had a guy who wanted to go home and a guitar player that did not really want to try!" Strum was by now afraid of losing everything he had worked for, but felt there was no turning back. "I got Ozzy up and told him firmly that he had to at least see this guy." A degree of self-preservation also crept in as Strum admits. "I also told him that I live in Los Angeles and he can't do this to me." Somehow Ozzy, with Strum's physical assistance, made it out of his torpor and into the studio room. Desperation was in the air now. "I sat him down. I told Randy, who had no idea how fucked-up Ozzy was, to play."

Randy replied "Like what?"

"The Starwood solo trip – just play!!"

Strum continues; "I fucking cranked the big speakers in that place. Ozzy's eyes opened and he listened, looked at me and laughed," the bass player recalls.

"Have him come to the hotel tomorrow" beamed Ozzy. "Tell

him he's got the job".

Later that night Strum got on the phone to Randy still trying to convince him to join the band.

Dana Strum, according to Kelly Garni, is correct in the assumption that Randy was far from keen on the proposed alliance. "I can't think of any other way to say this but Randy and I both had the same opinion of Black Sabbath – we thought they were fools. In truth Randy thought it was just silly and had very little musical interest there," explains Garni in terms which may come as a shock to Ozzy fans. "Randy came from a fairly religious background and had a big problem with all the black magic stuff. It was against everything he believed or had been taught. Musically we thought Black Sabbath was music for old farts, the kind of people who sat around all day and smoked pot – old hippies. I can't express it in any other terms, we thought it was downright silly. This might sound odd because we were both heavily into Alice Cooper...

"But, Quiet Riot was going nowhere and Randy was sick of having no money..."

Fortunately, and in spite of Randy's misgivings, the relationship between the three personnel did solidify. More significantly, and in spite of the guitarist's wariness of the whole 'dark' side of Black Sabbath, Ozzy and Randy would quickly develop a unique friendship. Rhoads did turn up at the Le Parc as instructed but his appearance was not all Strum or Ozzy expected. The bassist met Randy, clad in a polka dot shirt and rings, in the rain outside the hotel and took him up to Ozzy's room. Randy was offered a beer but declined in favour of a diet coke. "Oh no, not another one," grunted Ozzy resignedly. Randy's unusual choice of attire provoked another question that needed settling and a less than tactful Ozzy was as forthright as ever. "You're not gay, are you?"

Randy stared at Strum in disbelief. "No doubt he wondered why he was there again," Strum laughs. "No doubt!" The guitarist, probably wondering what on earth his hairdresser girlfriend Jodi would make of this madness, was simply dumbstruck.

The Reluctant Wizard

Subsequent interviews given by Ozzy suggest that Randy replied that while he wasn't gay he was nonetheless a Catholic. It broke the ice and soon plans were made for another jam session. This time Randy suggested he knew of a great drummer – Frankie Banali. Making his departure, he discussed details such as pay, the name of the band and other details. He also reminded Strum that he still had commitments teaching at his Mom's music school.

The second workout took place at Mars Studios. Strum had organized everything, as was becoming the norm. Badaxe roadie Bill Birch was conscripted to help move Randy and Dana's gear as both only had small cars. Banali brought his own drums along. It was the first time Strum and Banali had met and while the trio were setting up their gear they listened to an R&B band rehearsing next door. They were surprised to find out the soulful tones were those of Glenn Hughes.

Ozzy was late and so a relaxing jam ensued. "We jammed and played riffs, some of my stuff, some of Randys'. 'Crazy Train' vibe. The magic was unfolding big-time."

When Ozzy arrived so did Jet Record's owner Don Arden. This notorious and powerful figure in the music industry was also Osbourne's official manager. The comfortable atmosphere evaporated but soon the four were so deeply involved in the music that Arden's presence was soon forgotten. Strum is effusive; "Ozzy sang kinda any lyric he thought of just to get a feel. He really is a gut feeling type of guy. It was fun for all of us and Randy played fucking great. He was on fire. You had to know that this was it. History!"

Sitting in the same room, Strum's friend and roadie Bill Birch must have been one of the happiest men on the planet.

Further run-throughs would take place after this event but without Banali who, coincidentally, hooked up with Quiet Riot. Many of the riffs and formative ideas which would eventually surface on the first Ozzy album were worked out during these sessions in the studio and in Ozzy's hotel room.

Outside of the studio Strum's role as general organizer was being stretched to the limit. "There were lots of phone calls to keep it going. Randy was still not certain, my band was pissed and Kevin DuBrow was pissed. The truth was, though, that Randy was having mixed feelings about Quiet Riot and did not like the band's last album. He hated the guitar sound. Professionally he felt really bad about it." To this day DuBrow has not forgiven Strum for poaching his star guitarist.

The next move was a relocation to England but concerns over the financing of the whole endeavour were raised by the precocious Randy who, out of the blue, demanded to to know who was going to pay for everything. Strum, after all, was just in it for the experience.

"At this point none of us had a dime. All my phone bills, my time and Randy's time were on us," he states matter-of-factly. "My vibe was to just let it roll but I later felt that Don Arden did not feel the same way. I was to learn more about that later but at that moment I just wanted to be in the game. I loved Black Sabbath and the music that Ozzy did and that was it. The dollars did not matter because I loved the shit. It was a treat."

Dana Strum believes that his energetic stage performances and his general up-and-at-'em manner in getting things done did not endear him to Arden. There is even a suggestion that Strum, by necessity, had taken too much control of the situation and Arden felt he needed to regain the initiative. The bass player began to get a sense of foreboding that, in his words, he "was in the wrong place at the wrong time."

"I'm a strange guy to be a bass player really. In fact I make a better manager or producer" he confesses. Although these qualities and skills would come to the fore with Strum's very public success in his later acts, right then and there the people pulling the strings were sensing potential trouble. Not only was Ozzy's new bassist playing the four-string role but getting intricately wrapped up in the day-to-day affairs of running the star's life. Dana was making the phone calls, Dana was driving the car, arranging the meetings, placating the nervous, enthusing the faithful and smoothing the rough edges.

Within this whirlwind of activity Strum first met Don's daughter Sharon who was then in the employ of her father and

The Reluctant Wizard

working at Jet Records. He also cultivated a career outside the Osbourne orbit, just in case; he was earning by editing and cutting radio spots. Sensing all was not well within the Ozzy camp, he was also getting plans in mind for a new band. "There were many phone calls and lots of work still for Ozzy and Randy but the more the cards played out, I felt I was about to be the low draw." Ozzy journeyed to England on his own whilst Randy and Dana waited anxiously. Randy was grounded because he lacked a passport. High and dry in Los Angeles and with no word from England or Jet Records, Strum tried to convince the guitarist that Ozzy would get in touch.

The call eventually came – but only for Randy. Undaunted, Strum simply got on with matters in hand and became a major mover and shaker in American metal circles.

Strum's formative years with Badaxe and his endeavours with Ozzy Osbourne have given the bassist a practical nous which enabled him to succeed throughout the '80s and '90s. Known in the business as a sharp operator, he owns his own digital studio and touring production company.

"The world of hard rock and those that stake a valid claim in it is – and always was – small. It's like the porn industry. The same people over and over. So, I learned, over and over," he maintains. "I never really fitted into many of the circles. I wouldn't kiss ass to get a deal or play at fake friends just because I wanted to make it. I've been a slave to my trade. I would not trade a day of the way I have had to work my way up through the music business. I've loved it all and it's made me a stronger person – no silver spoon shit with me."

The rewards for Strum have been rich indeed. Now a native of Las Vegas, Strum resides in a palatial, self-designed retreat reminiscent of a castle in Moorish Spain. Over the main fireplace hangs a swordfish coated in dollar bills, a win in a bet Strum had with an attorney. All in all a home of a bona fide rock star.

"I love it all, the music, the vibe, the women and the rock 'n' roll life. I don't regret a day."

4
A Man For All Seasons

The next character to enter the saga would prove, over the unrolling years, to be an ever-reliable foil for Ozzy Osbourne. Although bassist Bob Daisley and Ozzy have had many spats and altercations over more than a decade, the Australian four-stringer's talents both musically and as a songwriter would see him playing a sometimes pivotal role off and on over the next decade.

Daisley's dues were paid with Stan Webb's illustrious blues rockers Chicken Shack although he was for a while, by his own admission, tempted away for a spell by the bright lights and quick success of pop music.

"I joined Mungo Jerry in 1973," Bob admits. "Remember them? It was actually the management who thought I would be right for the job. We had a couple of hit records, three I think, and I did *Top Of The Pops* and all that. Although it was fun it wasn't credible so I went back to Chicken Shack to play some serious music. Those were great times. We had Robbie Blunt on guitar then from Silverhead, Well, that all ended for me in '75. There was Luther Grosvenor Ariel Bender. He had a good track record with Mott The Hoople and Spooky Tooth. On drums was Paul Nichols of Lindisfarne, which is how Widowmaker came together. That was a great band although Steve Ellis had a severe drinking problem which messed things up quite a bit. We got in John Butler for the second album."

The band would land the honours of opening for The Who on a series of mammoth dates across the UK when Roger Daltrey had caught the band's appearance on the TV show *The Old Grey Whistle Test*. Bob explains how these prestigious showcases came about. "Steve Ellis knew Roger Daltrey and of course Roger knew of Steve's drinking problem. So, when Roger saw Widowmaker on the TV he phoned Steve congratulating him for getting his act together and for putting together such a good band."

Widowmaker also famously supported Uriah Heep on their

A Man For All Seasons

UK 'High And Mighty' tour of 1976 which is where Bob came across drummer Lee Kerslake. With Hawkwind man Huw Lloyd-Llangton on guitar, an American tour would lead to the final disintegration of Widowmaker but offered a fresh opportunity for the bassist. At the close of the tour in Los Angeles Daisley's colleague from Mungo Jerry, guitarist Dick Middleton, hooked up a meeting with a friend of his.

"Dick introduced me to Ritchie Blackmore who told me he was looking for a bassist," Daisley reveals. "The auditions were held at this huge film studio, I seem to remember. Well, anyway, I was told I had got the gig but I wasn't sure I wanted it. I was really wary of being a side-man but I spoke to friends who convinced me it was a good step up and would do my career some good. After all, Rainbow were an arena band."

Bob Daisley became a member of Rainbow at a time when many would judge the band to be at their creative peak. "I did the *Long Live Rock 'n' Roll* album and the following world tour which went everywhere." Daisley put in his live debut with Rainbow at the Swedish capital, Stockholm, before trekking around America, Japan and Europe. The band were riding on a high but Rainbow's famous tradition of instability would present itself. Rainbow vocalist Ronnie James Dio offered Bob Daisley his opinion on the circumstances unfolding and a lot more besides.

"There came a time when Ronnie took me aside to tell me that in his opinion Ritchie was considering changing players and that he in turn was looking to set up his own band. Would I be interested? Well, of course I was. Ronnie has a world class voice and Rainbow was looking a little shaky for all of us except Ritchie. So I went back to my home in London and waited on Ronnie who told me he was lining up a deal and it was all looking good. Ritchie did of course get his new people in as Ronnie predicted. I hung on and spoke to Ronnie numerous times who was saying, "hang in there, we've got a guitarist, we'll fly you over when we're ready". I was still hanging around until I finally read in a magazine that Ronnie had joined Black Sabbath! Well, all I could think of was 'thanks a lot Ronnie!'"

Ozzy Osbourne

Then fate intervened. "It was ironic," Bob relates. "Soon after that episode I met Ozzy at a gig in London. I had gone to see Girl at the Camden Electric Ballroom and Arthur Sharp, from Ozzy and Girl's record label Jet Records, introduced me to Ozzy. We got chatting and that's when he told me he was getting a band together and it was arranged that I should visit Ozzy at his house." The initial conversation led to a trip to Ozzy's house in Staffordshire. "Ozzy's house was set up for auditions as he had a kind of rehearsal studio built onto the side of it," Daisley recollects. He would be surprised to discover he was not the first to arrive. "There were two different guys there already – a red haired guitarist and a drummer. To this day I don't remember who they were, we were never properly introduced. I think Ozzy just said 'Meet Jim,' or something like that. Well, we started to play a bit and afterwards Ozzy took me into another room and asked me what I thought. Frankly my honest opinion was that these guys were not really good enough and I said so. Ozzy thought about it a bit and then marched into the studio and said 'It's not working out, guys. Pack up your gear and go home'. I was stunned but they just did as Ozzy ordered. They just left without saying a word. Never did find out who they were."

At this stage Ozzy resolved to get a serious band together and Randy was flown over from Los Angeles. Further sessions were held at Ozzy's house where songs were starting to get knocked into shape. By now Ozzy and Randy were beginning to develop a close friendship that was becoming apparent to all. Randy and Bob too enjoyed a moment of synchronicity when, just as they were finishing a song, the pair said simultaneously to each other, 'I like the way you play'.

An old friend of Ozzy's called Barry Scrannage (more popularly known as 'Spencer') was helping out on drums and a lot more besides. "Spencer was a useful bloke to have around," opines Bob. "He was our general helper, our roadie, our drummer and our driver. In fact we used him a bit like a drum machine. He was never at any stage discussed as being the drummer for the band though." There have been tales filtering through the years that this unit of Ozzy, Randy and Bob with Spencer on

A Man For All Seasons

drums actually gigged. The truth, according to Daisley, is that one jam session was put on for the locals in order to test out the new songs.

Bob brings to mind the event that sparked the rumours. "We were working up these songs at a place in Ilkeshaw owned by Transam Trucking. It was a really nice live-in situation and we had use of this proper rehearsal studio in a big barn-like building. Because we had got to know quite a few people down at the local pub we invited maybe eight or ten of them back. Spencer sat in and played drums. We needed to see what it felt like to play these songs in front of people so that's what we did. It certainly wasn't a 'gig' in any sense."

This 'public jam' did not pass off without incident though as the bassist reveals. "I remember one local kid was pissed and got really mouthy. In fact he soon got to be a pain in the arse. He got really pushy and actually tried to get into a fight with Ozzy. It was quite funny because Ozzy broke a cup over the kid's back and told him to fuck off. There was a bit of a scuffle and this troublemaker was thrown out. Well, later, I went and found Ozzy and he was sitting in front of this open fire drawing himself a fake black eye with an eyebrow pencil!"

Spencer and Ozzy, although long-time compatriots, would during this time have their fallings-out. Daisley summons up an altercation between the two which set Randy Rhoads into a state of panic. "Ozzy and Spencer had gone off to a neighbour's house while Randy and I stayed back at Ozzy's house. Well, they came back arguing, obviously having had a few. I don't know what the reason was but Ozzy was really annoyed at Spencer for insulting his neighbour somehow. Ozzy got so angry he picked up this piece of wood and started to chase Spencer around and round his yard! It was really funny but Randy took this deadly seriously and ran up to his room. All we could was the noises of him barricading himself in his room by pushing all his furniture in front of the door! Randy didn't live that down for a long time."

In the midst of all this male bonding, and with auditions taking shape, it seemed as though Spencer's role in the whole situation became a point of contention. "Spencer was never the drummer for the band at any stage," states Bob categorically. "We never told him he was the drummer either. He was very useful to have around, driving to London for us, running errands and so forth and we did use him to lay down a beat so that Randy, Ozzy and I could work up the songs.

"Jet Records were paying us a living wage at the time from our advance, just £100 a week I think. I remember that Spencer got his envelope and it had written on it 'Roadie's Wages' with about £50 or something in it. He was pretty pissed off with this and threw his money into the fire. He may have thought that he was in line to be the drummer but I don't understand that because we were actually auditioning drummers for a long time so he knew the score. Spencer still stayed with us for quite some time afterwards as our helper."

With Randy, Bob and Ozzy now really beginning to work off each other the proto-band now began an earnest search for a drummer. It proved to be a more arduous task than any of them could have possibly imagined. The efforts in structuring a new band were put sharply into focus when the rejuvenated Ronnie-led Black Sabbath released *Heaven And Hell* in April of that year. The record not only achieved a No. 9 placing in the UK, the highest for any Sabbath album for the past five years, it was already being heralded as a classic. Iommi had also persuaded Geezer Butler back on board. Ozzy was truly out on his own.

Bob's memory of the pressure of those auditions is of a seemingly endless run through of musicians who simply were not up to scratch. "We tried out a German guy who was very good but just not quite right. There was a guy from Birmingham called Yatta and a bloke who played for Wings, Geoff Britton. We tried out Dixie Lee from Lone Star for about a week I think. Dixie was the guy who we used to record the demos at a studio in Birmingham for the American label. He was so upset that he apparently cried when Ozzy told him he had not got the job." Frankie Banali, who had bashed the tubs the one time in Los Angeles when Randy Rhoads first tried out with Ozzy and Dana Strum, was also approached by Randy but had prior recording commitments in Germany.

A Man For All Seasons

The band's frustration was evident toward the tail-end of these tryouts. By now the trio were ensconced in the legendary surroundings of Rockfield Studios in Monmouthshire. They had been endeavouring to finalize the band for three months. Next on the list was Dave Potts, previously with Skip Bifferty and Ten Years After.

"All of us were really frustrated by it" sighs Bob. "We had been through at least 40 drummers and nothing was close. We nearly picked Dave Potts but I think Ozzy told him he had got the job to close the issue rather than because he was right for the job. Don't get me wrong, he was a very good drummer, but again just not right."

Nonetheless the Osbourne/Rhoads/Daisley/Potts quartet stuck at it for the allotted time. "I stayed there for the whole week but I think my drumming wasn't as good as that first session" Dave concludes. "We used to go running into the nearby town, which I guess was Monmouth. We would run into the town as if we were going to keep fit and then we would have a drink and run back. As a little team, with Ozzy and Bob Daisley, we hit it off. We would all have a drink, even Bob who was always looking after his health, and then run back to the studio afterwards. That last night I was with them they got me absolutely blitzed. It was a good laugh. So, it was a good relationship, but to be honest, sitting down at the kit I worked out after about three days that I wasn't going to get the gig but we were definitely going to have a bit of fun. If I had gone in there at the level I was at with Praying Mantis I think I would have been the drummer, but because I had been inactive for a while I could see something was lacking."

Dave Potts walked off to a career with NWoBHM pomp rockers Praying Mantis, later laying down his sticks to manage the band and also look after the business affairs of Clive Burr's Escape. But his path would later cross Ozzy's once again.

"Around 1980 I bumped into Ozzy in John Henry's Studios. Ozzy came over to me. He remembered me which is not unreasonable after a week together but he also asked "Have you still got that blue Ludwig drum kit?" I was rather stunned because I couldn't have told you what drum kit I had when I auditioned. Ozzy has got a very good memory for a lot of things. You know Ozzy is a crazy guy but underneath it all he is a very sensible guy. When I first met him and saw all those tattoos all over his knuckles I thought 'fucking hell'. You know I was going with the first impression but it was completely wrong."

Bob Daisley too kept up with Dave. "I developed a good friendship with Bob Daisley" Dave affirms. "Back in the days of Praying Mantis I had bumped into him and he had taken me to some Buddhist classes and introduced me to that way of thinking. He absolutely amazed me. You look at him and think he is just another rock 'n' roll guy but there is so much more to him."

What made the whole auditioning process irksome in particular for Ozzy was that his personal choice was unavailable. "Ozzy really wanted Tommy Aldridge," Bob affirms. "They had met when Black Sabbath had done a lot of touring in America with Black Oak Arkansas during the mid '70s. Ozzy really rated him but he was tied up." Indeed, approaches had been made surreptitiously to Tommy Aldridge who, while filling in at the time with Gary Moore, had been in the employ of Canadian master guitarist Pat Travers since 1977.

Whilst the fledgling unit was focused on tracking down a drummer, there was another musician who entered the frame during the Rockfield sessions. Stourbridge-based keyboard player Bill Hunt was a teacher by profession but had solid rock credentials under his belt. Hunt had been a member of the post-Bakerloo progressive rock act Hannibal. The band, whose business affairs were handled by Black Sabbath manager Jim Simpson, had released one now extremely rare Rodger Bain-produced album and toured as support to Black Sabbath on early German dates.

Switching to, of all things, the cor anglais, the versatile musician had been involved with the debut ELO line-up and later, as a pianist, wangled his way into Wizzard prior to entering the teaching profession. The call from Ozzy Osbourne would come not only out of the blue but at a typically ungodly rock 'n' roll hour. "I got a phone call from Ozzy at 3 o'clock in the morning!"

A Man For All Seasons

Bill Hunt recalls vividly. "He said, 'my mate Spencer has been bending my ear about you'."

The keyboard player actually took a Monday off work to journey down to Monmouth. "Well, I had heard about Ozzy's reputation of course so I had already had a couple of pints to give me Dutch courage by the time I arrived. When I got there only Spencer was there. He said, 'they're all on this health kick and they are out running.' Seeing as they were out jogging, Spencer and I went down the pub."

With the return of Ozzy, Rhoads and Daisley, the group settled down in front of the TV. Hunt remembers some disparaging remarks from Ozzy regarding the late Ayotallah Khomeni were curtailed by Randy and Bob's eagerness to get back to work. "I really wasn't there long enough to judge anyone's true abilities" Bill maintains. "What I do remember was how keen Randy was, He was a really nice lad – very eager and enthusiastic."

A jam ensued with Hunt taking on the keyboard role. "Randy and I tried a few things I had been working on, just chord patterns really. Then Bob came in and we were all just jamming. Well, Ozzy heard this and thought it sounded like something they had been working on called 'Mr. Crowley'. It was a similar feel and similar key. That's as far as it went really."

Bill's jam session did leave a little but important legacy with the Ozzy crew as Bob Daisley relates. "Bill actually instigated the intro to 'Mr. Crowley'. He was playing around with this keyboard chord progression, piddling about with some rough ideas. It was just a small part but that would become the opening sequence to 'Mr. Crowley'."

Bill did not return the next day. "I had a young family and different pressures to the other guys. It would have been a bit of a luxury to hang around waiting for something to happen. If I would have known of course… Anyway, we just jammed and left it at that but looking back it was a huge privilege."

Bob backs this up. "Bill was a decent enough bloke but we weren't seriously looking for a keyboard player at this stage. I think he was a bit older than us too. Randy must have been 22 or thereabouts, I think Ozzy had just turned 30. Bill had short grey hair so Ozzy called him 'Grecian 2000'! We were actually much more concerned with getting a drummer to put the actual core band together."

Bill would return to teaching but later would become involved with another West Midlands legend, Slade. Hunt co-wrote songs for both Slade and Dave Hill's later offshoot Slade II. In later years Bill, courtesy of Dave Hill, would have the opportunity to meet Ozzy again at the Castle Donington 'Monsters Of Rock' festival. Watching the show from side stage Bill was taken aback to recognize his 'Mr. Crowley' contribution still in place. "I was really surprised when they did 'Mr. Crowley' because that little chord progression was still there which was nice to hear. I was quite chuffed actually!"

With keyboards temporarily put aside and Aldridge firmly out of the equation, Daisley describes the arrival of Lee Kerslake as a godsend. "Lee was the last drummer we auditioned," Bob remembers. "He ca me in at a very difficult time as the record company was straining at the leash. If Lee had not worked out they would have to get someone like Cozy Powell in or another session drummer. Time was running out."

Time was not all that was weighing on the musician's minds. That summer Black Sabbath were enjoying a renaissance bout of sell-out shows and their single 'Neon Knights' was also floating in the top thirty. *Heaven And Hell* was also making a strong showing giving Tony Iommi his best American chart placing since 1975's *Sabotage* and, to rub salt into the wound, passing the million sales mark with consummate ease. Fate would, however, intervene to redress the balance in Ozzy's favour. In what must have been galling to Iommi's new ratings, though, was that in July a less than welcome collection of poorly assembled live tapes of Ozzy-era Sabbath had usurped even *Heaven And Hell*. The downright shoddy *Live At Last*, using material from as far back as a Manchester Free Trade Hall gig in 1973 and roundly panned by critics as well as band members past and present, nevertheless struck gold at Number 5. Even the Ozzy anthem 'Paranoid' was dusted off for another stab at the singles charts and catapulted its way to Number 14 in August. If Ozzy needed

A Man For All Seasons

any motivation, it was arriving in spades.

1979 found Lee Kerslake divorced from Uriah Heep after a mammoth eight-year run. During that time Kerslake had seen Heep achieve dizzying heights of success internationally with the seminal and undeniably grandiose *Demons And Wizards* and *Magician's Birthday* albums. The band had made huge inroads into traditional territories, as America and mainland Europe, but were also of bona fide superstar status in such remote climes as Australia and Asia. However, during the mid-seventies the Uriah Heep institution had hit troubled times with fracturing line-ups and the tragic death of their New Zealander bassist Gary Thain.

Kerslake, along with mentor and guitarist Mick Box, had remained a stabilizing influence – weathering the many storms that assailed the band – but by the time of 1978's *Fallen Angel* Kerslake's position had become untenable. Friction between band members and record company boss and manager Gerry Bron about the musical direction of the band had been slowly but surely pulling the band apart for many years. Eventually, giving it all up as a thankless task, the drummer walked, intent on proving his ability as a songwriter and arranger with an ambitious solo venture.

Not one to remain idle, Kerslake was quick to set up a band with Manfred Mann bassist Colin Pattendon and the then unknown vocalist Pete Cox. "This was of course years before Go West, you understand," smiles Kerslake. "He had a phenomenal voice even then. I had about 20 or so of my songs, all good strong melodic rock stuff, and we were shaping up for a solo album. I really needed to prove a point after having been hassled so much in the past. I'm not just 'the drummer' and in Uriah Heep there was this big battle going on between Ken Hensley and Gerry Bron as to the arrangements and the songs. It had been going on for too long and it was beginning to affect the band's success. One day I had a big argument with Bron and just left." The new band never even reached the naming stage. Kerslake had received a call from an old friend.

"A very old friend of Uriah Heep's named Ossie Hoppie called me up one day. Ossie is a big promoter in Germany and has been for donkey's years; all the bands know him as someone to be trusted. Well, he'd read an article in a German magazine about me leaving Uriah Heep and was surprised to say the least. When he gave me the message I nearly fell off my chair."

By now a seasoned veteran of behind the scenes skulduggery and the inner machinations of major rock bands, Lee was understandably cautious if not more than a little curious. "When Ossie asked me if I'd be interested in working with Ozzy I have to admit my first reaction was 'no bloody way!!' I'd been ripped off to buggery already and wanted nothing to do with that side of things any more. Once bitten twice shy.

"Of course I wanted to work with Ozzy and when I heard Bob Daisley was involved too it began to look very attractive. The business side of it was a major worry, though. Ossie explained that this was a brand new thing and that all the band members would be in it together – that it was a proper band and not just a bunch of backing musicians for Ozzy. That I liked. Well, I left it with Ossie and told him that I'd play it like this – they can audition me at the same time I audition them. Ossie relayed the message, got back to me and we went from there."

Kerslake was sent a rough demo tape, which included an early work-out of 'Crazy Train', and arranged to meet the Ozzy trio at a rehearsal studio in London where Lee's kit was already set up. Ozzy, Randy and Bob were apparently in defeatist mood having spent many fruitless months searching for a drummer. The prospect of a session with Lee had lifted their gander somewhat. Bob and Lee had known each since Daisley's old act Widowmaker had opened for Uriah Heep whilst Randy was a keen Uriah Heep fan. Lee remembers his introduction to Ozzy. "He was very frustrated at not being able to find a drummer. He actually said 'fuckin' 'ell, 50 million drummers we've been through! Not one of 'em had a chance!' It was quite a challenge but I knew I could click in with Bob straight away."

"When I listened to the demo tape I knew that this was just my style," relates Lee. "I knew Dave Potts had had a try out before me but there was another guy on the tape, I don't know who that was. Anyway, this demo had 'Crazy Train' but with a

A Man For All Seasons

strange kind of disco drum beat that didn't fit at all. To me it was obvious what I should do."

The atmosphere in the studio changed as soon as the former Uriah Heep man began to play. "I remember Randy and I looking at each other instantly as soon as Lee started," says an excited Daisley. "Randy was very excited and so was Ozzy. We all thought the same thing. 'Fuckin' hell – This is the guy!' I'm sure we told him so too."

Lee describes what happened from his vantage point. "We had this little cassette player to play back the demo so we gave it a quick listen then got on with it. Randy went into the 'Crazy Train' riff and I just put down what I thought would work". [Note: Lee actually verbalized his version of the guitar riff and then his drum pattern here. Apologies to the reader. There are times when words simply fail!]

"Bob looked at Ozzy and they gave each other a big smile but Randy leapt about four foot in the air! 'We got one!' he shouted. It was really funny, he was so excited he simply couldn't contain himself. 'Oh, man! At long last, we got one!' he kept shouting. Ozzy and Bob looked relieved and happy that this was obviously going to work but Randy was just over the top. I remember Ozzy had this big fox-fur coat on and he said to Bob and Randy 'Are we happy now?' We were all grinning like little kids."

This moment became imprinted on Lee's memory for more reasons than one. "Well, we all knew there and then. Ozzy shook my hand and said to me 'Here's my hand, here's my heart, 'till we're dead, 'till we part'. That was good enough for me. I was in."

"Lee was absolutely perfect" recalls Bob Daisley. "It was all sorted out there and then. Myself, Ozzy and Lee went out to a Chinese restaurant afterwards to celebrate."

It must be remembered that Lee Kerslake was walking into an already entrenched trio. Of course Bob Daisley was a known quantity to Lee while Ozzy's reputation was legendary. But how did Lee take to Randy? "The only thing you can say about Randy is that he was very, very special. A lovely, lovely guy," Lee states emphatically. "He was truly gifted, quite simply a fantastic

Ozzy Osbourne

natural player. The things he could come up with were mind-blowing. His capabilities seemed to know no bounds."

As the quartet got into serious rehearsal they naturally began to gel musically. "Randy was just amazing. I'd come up with something on the piano and Randy would just put down something that was near perfect. Bob would get himself out of bed and start scribbling down lyrics. We created some real magic. It's a very rare thing. He could play the blues phenomenally. Some of the stuff just blew me away."

By the stage that Lee became involved, Ozzy, Bob and Randy had already put together nearly a complete album's worth of material. "I just put my oar in a little bit on the arrangements, little directional ideas and of course put my drums down. We did some more writing, though, to include one of my ideas in a new song called 'No Bone Movies'. Mainly, though, the album was about there but ideas were already flowing for the next record. Creatively it was an amazing time."

Bob apostrophises this feeling of comradeship. "In fact we were so keen on it being an equal unit that when Lee joined we wrote another song, all four of us as a joint effort, to make it fair. 'No Bone Movies' was written as an intended B-side but in the end it made it onto the album." The title passed most British fans by but the American audience got the reference straight away. "We all went to see this porn film in London," Bob admits. "Me, Randy, his girlfriend Jodi, Ozzy and Sharon. I kind of got, er…inspired! It was Randy who was partly responsible for the title because, being American, he called porn 'bone movies'. You have to remember that when we were writing and recording the album we had no idea of how big the album would become so I thought 'No Bone Movies' was obscure enough to be kind of hidden for an English audience."

5
"It's A Band"

With the set-up of the band now cast, the quartet began looking at other areas requiring attention. The first matter that needed resolving was that of a name. "It was very much a four-way band," observes Bob. "That was the deal and it was clear to everyone. The problem was that the record company, as they do, insisted on just calling it 'Ozzy'. We told them in no uncertain terms that this was a band and not a solo artist. Ozzy wanted this too. Ozzy fronted the band and came up with vocal melodies, Randy was the guitarist and riff-writer, I wrote both music and lyrics and Lee was a drummer with proven writing abilities too."

Rehearsals began apace at Clearwell Castle and Rockwell to work up the album songs. The band was kicking around proposed names for the band but were none memorable enough that Lee can recall. "It was around this time that Blizzard Of Ozz was decided on though," he remembers.

Jet Records, however, were insistent on promoting the act as a solo venture. "They kept up with this campaign but we said no. The band is called Blizzard Of Ozz. You can put 'featuring Ozzy Osbourne' on the first couple of albums to start with but it's a band."

Bob is also very clear about how the band name came about. "Ozzy's dad thought of Blizzard Of Ozz. Ozzy told him he was starting a new band before he left Black Sabbath the very first time, in 1977, and his dad suggested it then. Ozzy even got T-shirts made up with it on."

Ozzy himself was, by all accounts, feeling trapped in a self-made dilemma. Lee maintains that Ozzy was raring to get working again but, also in some trepidation at the prospect. This is an aspect of Ozzy's character often voiced by the man himself over the years. "He was a little lost, if you want the honest truth," Lee reckons. "A lovely warm-hearted bloke was Ozzy, I'm sure everyone will tell you the same, but he was really struggling with himself. He was in a rush to get on the road but scared shitless of it at the same time. He also had a lot of problems at home. He'd often be forced off onto a tangent by outside distractions."

The band's rhythm section would often play on Ozzy's fears and found his trusting nature an Achilles heel that was too tempting to ignore. "We used to go for a good long walk around the country fields before we went into the studio," Lee laughs. "We would start work about midday and work through until two or three in the morning then. Anyway, Ozzy would be so easy to wind up. Both Bob and I were in on it. We once started talking about the news and saying 'What are we going to do about the country?' Ozzy would be listening to this wondering what on earth was going on. 'What do you mean?' he would say. 'The news, didn't you hear about the invasion? The outbreak of war. We're at war again, they're coming over right now.' Ozzy believed it totally. 'What are we going to do?!!' he said. You should have seen the look on his face. He was so terrified he literally ran back to the studio! When he found out it was only a joke he said that when we had told him he nearly had a heart attack. He's a very funny guy.

"That was an example of how little things really bothered him. The big things he could handle easily with no problem. Ozzy was a very funny, warm guy to be around. All four of us actually got on really well. It was a great team."

When the foursome got into the studio the feeling that something special was on the cards really began to materialize. "We'd be rehearsing songs and I'd notice riffs and for the first time in a long time I was thinking this is really, really good" Lee recalls. "We would chop and change things all the time to get things right. Randy had ideas just pouring out of him and Bob and I totally understood how the other was thinking. There really was a unique magic. When Ozzy started to put down the vocals I said to Bob, 'Bloody hell, this is going to be a fuckin' fantastic album!' We all knew it."

The first album was required quickly although proceedings at Ridge Farm Studios did not start according to plan. "We were working with Chris Tsangarides as producer but after a week we dispensed with his services," Bob states. "We had a talk and said, 'fuck it – we'll do it' and decided that we were working so well

"It's A Band"

together anyway that we didn't need a producer so we just kept the engineer who was Max Norman."

What really began to strike home at this point was the burgeoning talent of Randy Rhoads. An obviously-impressed Daisley is quick to praise: "Randy, you could tell, was going to be a major talent. He would play an absolute blinder of a solo and then double it note for note exactly. Everything was completely worked out to the finest degree in his head. That's a rare talent."

Outsiders were equally enthralled. "People came down from the record company on a pretty regular basis," says Bob. "You could tell they could sense the band chemistry. It's either there or it's not. When they heard Randy you could see they were thinking *what planet is this kid from?* We were all very proud of the magic that we had. We had certainly stumbled onto something unique."

The band was complemented in the studio by the highly regarded figure of Don Airey lending his keyboard talents. Airey's CV reads like a *Who's Who* of rock starting with Cozy Powell's Hammer, then Babe Ruth, and includes performances with Rainbow, Whitesnake, Colosseum II, Gary Moore, Uli Jon Roth and Jethro Tull.

Although a session player for the recording, Airey's invaluable contributions should not be underestimated. The haunting monolithic cathedral of sound, that makeup the intro to 'Mr. Crowley' were in the main arranged by Airey. Although he cannot recall the inspiration for the tune, the practicalities of composition are still clear. "I sent the band out of the studio for half an hour while I dreamt it up and recorded it," Don reveals. "When they came back it was all done."

Airey would also add his deft touch to the overall atmospherics of the album by donating the instrumental passage in 'Revelation Mother Earth' and the outro to 'Suicide Solution'.

The lyrics of 'Suicide Solution' would become the subject of heated debate in later years when they were accused of leading directly to the deaths of three American teenagers. The first of these occurred in October 1984 when a 19 year old, named in

Ozzy Osbourne

court as 'John M.' shot himself in the head whilst apparently listening to the song. The teenager's body was found with the headphones still on.

"Ozzy set the ball rolling for that song by coming up with the first line 'Wine is fine but whiskey's quicker' which inspired me to come up with the rest of the words" records Bob. "I've seen mentions in magazines previously which say that the song is about Bon Scott. That's bullshit. I wrote the words about Ozzy and the state he was getting in after leaving Black Sabbath. Basically Ozzy was drinking himself to death when he got booted out of Sabbath and the lyrics were my way of telling him to stop before it was too late. I came up with the title as a bit of a play on words – 'Solution' being the solution to a problem but also with the double meaning of a liquid solution. It was me saying to Ozzy, look – stop: you're killing yourself." As for hidden vocal lines or subliminal messages, "there's nothing there, that's absolute rubbish," Bob defends. "Totally untrue. Who on earth would be so stupid as to write a song telling people to kill themselves?"

The slurred narrative entangled in the outro to 'Crazy Train' has lent itself over the years to over many eager theories as to the exact 'meaning' of what Ozzy is saying. In actual fact it isn't Ozzy at all as Bob Daisley explains.

"We had this young kid helping out in the studio as a bit of a roadie. Well, he was talking about how much he could drink so of course we took him down the pub. After a pretty heavy drinking session we ended up literally carrying this lad out. Well, we got back to the studio and after he came to he started telling all these silly stories in this funny voice. I remember he had a really odd laugh." The sozzled youngster's guffaws made such an impression on the assembled musicians they decided to capture it for posterity on tape – but not before subjecting the hapless individual to a practical joke of the highest order.

"We put raw eggs in his bed!" Daisley laughs. "Of course when he got in they all broke. In the morning he was telling us this story and he was talking in such a strange manner, a bit like a madman actually, we got it all on tape. So, what you hear at the

"It's A Band"

end of 'Crazy Train' is not Ozzy but this young kid answering our question *what was in your bed?* 'An eegggg!!!!'"

With Airey committed to American touring with Rainbow, the search was on for a replacement in order to replicate the intricacies and fills laid down in the studio for the live environment. Jet Records placed an advert in the Melody Maker classifieds requesting, surprisingly, the services of a keyboard player-cum-rhythm guitarist.

"I was 22 at the time and I really fancied joining a rock 'n' roll band and touring America. I had my classical training and had gone through Cambridge to get my music degree. Up until then I had been playing in a folk-rock band – seven people in the back of a Transit van. I think I was just eager to go to the States really" admits an aspiring Lindsay Bridgwater. "As soon as I saw the advert I thought, that's for me! Jet Records sent me the tape and I was immediately impressed." Expecting a bludgeoning Heavy Metal album, Bridgwater would be taken aback to hear a guitarist free-forming in ecclesiastical Hypo-Dorian and Mixolydian modes. "I loved the guitar playing and the fact that songs such as 'Mr. Crowley' had a lot of classical influence, almost Vivaldian in structure, really appealed. I sat at home and scored everything then went to the audition and played it all note for note. They were surprised to say the least."

Lindsay recollects the competition on the day. "I was quite surprised. There were some people there who were simply there to say they had played with Ozzy. A lot of the stuff was quite complex, 'Revelation Mother Earth', 'Mr. Crowley', etc. No-one I heard that day quite managed it." After impressing the band on the ivories Lindsay was keen to show he could fulfil the full criteria required. "I picked up Randy's guitar and hacked away on a few chords but it became quickly apparent that Randy could pull off all the guitar parts live so any rhythm guitar from me simply wasn't needed," Lindsay explains.

"The way Randy could switch from lead to rhythm and vice versa really showed his virtuosity – in fact his ability knocked you flat. On the albums there was an awful lot of guitar, sometimes seven or eight tracks with electric overlaid with acoustic and then lead too. When I first heard it I remember thinking 'How the hell are we going to do that live?' but as soon as I heard Randy play it became obvious. Randy could do it all. He was such a dynamo live. You wouldn't believe some of the things he could do."

Rehearsals ahead of live shows took place at the converted church that held Nomis Studios. UFO were sharing the same facility and Paul 'Tonka' Chapman, a guitarist of no mean standing himself, had heard that Ozzy had got himself a new wonder kid. "It was the talk of the building when we arrived. Everyone was talking about Ozzy's new guitarist," Chapman maintains. "UFO were in there writing I think and Ozzy was rehearsing. They were right at the end of the complex next to this coffee shop thing so of course, being nosy, I went down there for a look. Well, when I got there I found this tiny little guy with blond hair playing this big classical acoustic guitar. He had his music stand set up and he was playing the Stanley Myers cavatina from *The Deer Hunter*.

"'You must be Randy,' I said and of course we got talking. Everyone else, typically, was down the pub." UFO bassist Pete Way has memories of the same period. "Randy was a massive Schenker fan, he knew all the UFO songs. He was an absolute sweetheart of a guy. Ozzy kept talking to me about his 'secret weapon', this is before I'd heard Randy and I didn't work out what he meant. I thought, 'what is he talking about?' Paul had burnt his fingers I remember. He'd fallen asleep with a lit cigarette and was so out of it he was still snoozing when the cigarette burnt into his fingers! Ozzy was a bit alarmed at this when Paul showed him and to take his mind off the pain he invited us to see his 'secret weapon'. We walked in and there they were – Randy, Bob, Lee and Ozzy – although you couldn't hear Ozzy at all."

Paul elaborates, "Now I'm used to loud music but they were unbelievable! They had a full P.A. set up so it was bloody loud when Randy, Bob and Lee were playing but every time Ozzy sang, the red warning light came on to indicate an overload so Ozzy looked like he was just mouthing the words. It was totally deafening!"

"It's A Band"

Pete was dumbstruck. "I knew what Ozzy meant by 'secret weapon'. Randy was just unreal."

"The Nomis rehearsals were great fun. It really was an inspiration being able to appreciate just how good individually everybody was" affirms Bridgwater. "For the most part Randy, Bob, Lee and myself would just run through the set. Randy was such great fun to work with because he was not your run-of-the-mill guitarist, quite unlike anyone I have ever played with before or since. Bob and Lee of course were extremely professional. Absolute top-class musicians. Both had had success in their own right and I suppose they took me under their wing a bit. I think after the first album had been done, keyboards came as a bit of an afterthought. Initially I was kind of an extra really and it took a while to find my feet and become a valid member."

Bridgwater also backs up the feeling of camaraderie present at the time. "It was never Ozzy and a group of session musicians. Not only did everyone believe it was a band but, more importantly, it felt like a band. They had all written the tracks, Bob more so than most. Lee was highly skilled with arrangements, Bob contributed the words and lots of chord progressions and Randy had the riffs. Ozzy was kind of seen as the guiding light - he would show everyone the direction in which to go.
There was no drunken debauchery, none of that. Quite unlike the image portrayed to the outside world we just got on with the job night after night getting the set absolutely right."

Ozzy debuted the Blizzard Of Ozz with two low-key anonymous club gigs in front a favoured few. The exact venues would pose a memory test for the rhythm section. Lee thinks they were in the far-flung climes of Cromer in Norfolk and Skegness. Daisley is unsure of their whereabouts but ventures "Blackpool was one, I'm sure." Completists might wish to note that the band's most recent member Lindsay Bridgwater confirms that the first gig was Blackpool, the second West Runton near Cromer.

The band went out under a pseudonym to keep the media at bay. "David Arden at Jet came up with the cover name Law." relates Daisley. "Of course local people soon found out who it was. I remember Roy Wood came to the first gig. We signed a lot of autographs too. What was funny was that Ozzy, Lee and I were known to the kids from Black Sabbath, Uriah Heep and Rainbow but Randy was pretty much left alone as no one knew him."

The band road-tested much of the debut album packed out with Sabbath staples such as 'Children Of The Grave' and 'Iron Man'. With such high profile players, this brace of supposed low key gigs turned out to be anything but. The grapevine had resulted in hundreds of fans crammed into the tiny venues, as Bridgwater recalls. "I was staggered. The gigs were packed out. I don't know how they got to know it was Ozzy. Strangely for us, the band, we only then really appreciated how big this whole thing could be. It was awe-inspiring seeing this devotion to Ozzy at first hand."

Bob has reason to remember a small incident afterward which in some small way, would signal the misapprehensions that all the band members would be forced to come to terms with as the band's profile grew. "After the gig we did these signing sessions and this kid brought along a Black Sabbath album for Ozzy to sign. Just as he was leaving this kid said to Ozzy, 'are you still into black magic?'.

Lindsay Bridgwater confirms this. "This chap – who looked a little strange – sidled up to Ozzy and took him to one side. He said he was into black magic and didn't know what to do about it. Ozzy's advice was to change to Milk Tray! It was absolutely wonderful how Ozzy dealt with that one. He didn't belittle the kid in any way – just put him in his place."

Standing next to Ozzy, Daisley took all this in too. "You should have seen this poor kid's face! He soon got the joke though and all the kids standing in line had a good laugh too."

The following full-scale British tour, kicked off in Glasgow on September 12th 1980, saw Ozzy welcomed back as an all-conquering hero. *Blizzard Of Ozz* crashed into the UK charts peaking at Number 7 on September 20th and lending a huge boost. Even a reissued 'Paranoid' made it back into the charts, but not everything was complying with the grand plan. "At Hammersmith there was a plan for Ozzy to rise out from under the stage during 'Crazy Train'," recounts Lee Kerslake. "Well,

"It's A Band"

we had to do this on a fork lift truck to make it work. When Ozzy came out of the smoke from the floor in his white tassels, flashing his peace signs, the crowd just went into uproar. What people don't know is that there was a plan for me too. They were going to put a pyrotechnic device under my seat and blow me up! The idea was for the explosion to go off and I would be launched into the air by the aid of wires and four roadies. We had half of the ELO crew on the road with us then, great guys. The problem was that we tried it at rehearsal and not only could the block and tackle not lift me up but it took eight roadies to get me off my seat!" Uriah Heep fans will know that Lee's stature could never be described as slight.

Support band for the tour were Welsh veterans Budgie, enjoying a second wind of popularity with their *Power Supply* album. Strange to imagine now, but Budgie's addition to the billing actually brought so many of their fans to shows, it was only after their confirmation, a lot of the shows sold out.

Lindsay Bridgwater would double up each night performing with both bands. "I did both bands' sets. I would come off after Budgie, grab a half-hour break then go straight back on with Ozzy. It never seemed like hard work.'

"John Thomas, Budgie's guitar player, was absolutely smitten by Randy. The whole band was just in awe of him. The two guitarists got on great and I remember John trying to glean as much as he could from Randy 'What's that progression?' or just simply 'How do you do that?' They got on famously."

As Bridgwater recalled, Budgie's guitarist John, or J.T. as he is more commonly known, would click instantly with Randy, both as a musician and as a friend.

"That tour was the best I have ever done" J.T. records. "I've known Ozzy for years and he was keen for me to meet Randy so he introduced us both backstage at the first night, the Glasgow Apollo. We hit it off straight away, Randy knew all about us. Well, we both picked up guitars and didn't put them down from that point on!... he totally knocked me back. I can remember telling everyone – this guy is just brilliant. He looked an absolute star. He was an absolute magician on the guitar. His approach was

Ozzy Osbourne

just superb, he didn't play 'dark' like a lot of players then. Randy was very melodic. Absolutely perfect for Ozzy. I know Randy pretty much impressed the world – that's how good he was."

Randy would be enthralled by J.T.'s huge Gibson collection and his intimate knowledge of guitars. This would lead to a small disappointment for the young American though. "Randy had this white Les Paul he was very keen on" J.T. recalls. "He asked me how old it was so I told him – 1972. He was gutted. 'I thought it was a 1963!' he said. That little incident really, really upset him. You have to remember, he was very young. He loved going through my guitars – I had hundreds of them. He would open up each case and either say 'Wow – great,' or 'That's crap!' He wanted to play them all."

In the midst of this run of UK dates it was decided that a live version of 'Mr. Crowley', already making a radio impact in America, should be issued as a single. A mobile recording studio was dispatched to capture the song on the British tour. However, the record company were keen to make this single release doubly collectable by including an unreleased track. With no excess material left in the can from the 'Blizzard' sessions the band was faced with a challenge, coming up trumps with 'You Said It All' in record time.

"We wrote that track in one afternoon during a soundcheck, at Oxford I think" observes Bob. "It was quite funny how it came together. Lee had the vocal melody and Randy put down the music. All very quick. After I had recorded this on tape from the desk I came up with the lyrics back at the hotel."

But where was Ozzy? "While we were writing the song Ozzy was fast asleep underneath the drum riser!" Bob laughs heartily. "We recorded the song that night with Lindsay on keyboards. I suppose what we should have done was to record Ozzy's snoring for the intro!" The track would remain a highly sought-after rarity. With the exception of the single B-side it would only resurface on the Japanese compilation album *The Other Side Of Ozzy Osbourne*, noted not only for the inclusion of 'You Said It All' but also the even scarcer 'You, Looking At Me Looking At You' studio outtake.

6
Mini Madmen

The UK dates led straight into pre-production for a second album. "Arden wanted another album quickly. The first record was selling much faster than anyone had anticipated and he wanted a follow up straight away," Lee emphasizes.

The *Diary Of A Madman* album was cut swiftly after the debut as the label needed it ready for an American tour. The first album sales were going through the roof but it was initially released only in Europe. Indeed, *Blizzard Of Ozz* would have to wait until March of the following year to see an American release. New songs were coming faster than the band could record them. Lee was now able to lend his arranging talents fully and ended up contributing melodies to about six songs. At the close of 1980 the Blizzard Of Ozz were back in the studio, once again with Max Norman acting as engineer.

Lee recalls this hectic period. "With *Diary Of A Madman* we just clicked. We matched and progressed from what we had done before and took it to a whole new level. Those songs just flowed."

Bob remembers the sessions for another reason. "During the *Diary* sessions Ozzy had his car, a classic green Mercedes, just repainted and restored. He had parked it on this dark country lane just outside a pub named The Plough near Ridge Farm Studios." Ozzy's choice of parking would not prove opportune. A red Mini smashed into the back of it causing major damage.

"You can imagine, he was really pissed off," records Bob. "Well, I didn't know this yet and I had just brought a new car – a red Mini! So I see Ozzy in the pub looking really pissed off and was telling him about my new car. When I told him it was a red Mini I'm absolutely certain he thought that I had smashed his car up!" Car crash coincidences were not the only mysteries to be dealt with. One of the album's songs had been put to bed minus a suitable title and this simple practical point would engender a little fable all of its own. Lindsay Bridgwater for the first time unveils what he believes to be the true meaning of the track

Ozzy Osbourne

'S.A.T.O.'

The exact nature of the title has been expounded and hypothesized upon over the years. It has been credited to anything from Ozzy (then still married to his first wife) extolling his clandestine love for Sharon by cryptically putting his love's initials into a song title (wrong), or some devilish combination of mystically-charged ciphers (equally wrong). Other hypotheses include 'Sailing Across The Ocean' and 'Saturdays And Thursdays Only'.

"Ozzy told me this himself," states Lindsay. "They had this song but no title. To close the issue they took the first letter of everyone's first name who was in the office at the time – Sharon, Arthur Sharp from Jet, Thelma, Ozzy's then-wife, and Ozzy himself – S.A.T.O. Simple as that."

Or is it? Bob Daisley is certain Lindsay has got it nearly right. "It was Sharon, Adrian – Sharon's then boyfriend who worked in the office, Thelma and Ozzy. The song lyrics I wrote about a particular Buddhist doctrine. It's based on one of the teachings which was titled 'A ship to sail across the sea of suffering'." Arthur or Adrian? Such is the heady brew of neological esoterica that fuels the cult of Ozzy…

With the record finished Lee took a well-deserved holiday to Lanzarote, blissfully unaware of the cogs turning silently in the inner workings of the machine. "I got back from Lanzarote and found a message on my answer machine saying I was no longer in the band. What a way to go, eh? Sharon had phoned my ex-wife to tell her," sighs the drummer resignedly.

"Bob got the same treatment. It got taken away from being a band to becoming just Ozzy. Randy was totally gutted. He phoned me and we spoke at great length. He wanted to leave and work with Bob and I but I persuaded him to stay. He was in a unique position and I told him so. I'm glad I did but of course I can't help thinking that if he had left he might still be alive. Things like that you can't even think of. At the time I was very glad he stayed."

Such a blow has naturally left a sharp imprint on Bob Daisley's memory too. He was staggered to discover that out of

Mini Madmen

the blue both he and Lee Kerslake had been fired. "It was very simple" he motions. "I got a phone call from Sharon and she just said 'You and Lee are out'." When asked if he knew of the reasoning behind such a decision Bob has no hard and fast theories but hindsight has naturally opened up a few avenues of thought.

"Ozzy was very keen on getting Tommy Aldridge into the band which is something I never understood. Tommy is a great drummer but Lee was his equal and actually much better suited to the band. Tommy was actually turning up to quite a few gigs too. I remember him being at the Brighton show. Sharon and Ozzy asked me to go along to see him play with Gary Moore at the London Marquee. Sharon said to me 'Isn't he a great drummer?'. I had to agree but I also made it clear what I thought. 'So is Lee,' I said 'And he's better for our band, too.' It was not the answer they wanted to hear but I could not see the sense in changing the band around for no gain. They kept on at me though but I kept making it clear that I was not going to agree. In the end I guess I stood my ground too much."

Tommy Aldridge bears witness to the same event. "I do remember Randy, Sharon and Bob coming to the Marquee Club and going out afterwards. I don't remember attending any of their shows, however that's not to say I didn't. I was working with Gary at the time and trying to establish more of a 'freelance' direction. This was shortly after my departing the Travers camp and was a bit disillusioned regarding the 'band' thing at the time. I was trying to maintain my 'independence'...I suppose until something came along that really struck my fancy."

Asked to expand upon the contrasting styles of the two drummers Daisley describes the differences as such. "Lee is more hard rock 'n' roll – a bit more like a bull in a china shop. Tommy is fancier than Lee but has got a pair of very fast feet. He's well known for his double bass drumming."

The situation also thoroughly perplexed Lindsay Bridgwater. "I simply didn't understand- not that it was my place to. Bob and Lee were the absolute backbone of that band and they were co-writers too. However, Ozzy had always wanted Tommy – it was no secret. The two have totally different styles; Tommy is a lot

Ozzy Osbourne

busier whereas Lee is just rock-solid. He could say a lot with very little."

With the benefit of hindsight, Bob Daisley also believes, that both replacements were American is significant. "Randy called me a few days later to say how sorry he was that I was no longer in the band which was good of him but then again I think they really were after an American band. In the end Lee and I had too much to say for ourselves I suppose. I guess Randy suggested Rudy Sarzo from his Quiet Riot days and Tommy was obviously first choice for Ozzy."

With these Machiavellian manouevres taking place behind the scenes, at centre stage the *Blizzard Of Oz* album was eating into the American Billboard charts and satisfied its appetite with over a million registered sales in a big double-platinum pie.

It was not only the unforeseen revolving door policy in the personnel department that grieved Daisley and Kerslake. "When *Diary Of A Madman* was released Lee and I were bloody angry. It was no longer Blizzard Of Ozz it was just Ozzy, and we were virtually erased. Our names are there but only in the smallest of fine print and only listed as songwriters. Rudy Sarzo and Tommy Aldridge were credited but never played a note on that record... it was recorded by Ozzy, Randy, Lee and myself but anyone buying the album would never have been able to figure that out. It really was insulting. Even the production credits changed. Lee and I were left out there too. I really could not see the point of that."*

Tommy Aldridge, quick to praise his predecessors, confirms that rather like embarrassing Russian political 'non-persons' airbrushed out of official photographs, the departing Brits were scheduled for retrospective revision.

Author's note: On the subject of credits. The bassist is credited as 'Bob Daisy' on writing credits in the sleevenotes for the 1997 'The Ozzman Cometh' compilation album. Typing error ? Maybe once – but eleven times! Must be a bass player thing as 'Trudy' Sarzo and 'Bill Susan' are also in evidence.

Mini Madmen

"Though I've never had the opportunity to tell him, Lee should be very proud of those records," he states for the record. "I remember someone (who shall remain nameless) trying to get me to re-record the drums. I declined saying I couldn't improve upon what he did. I didn't know it at the time but I was being approached not to 'improve' but only to 'replace' his performance. I didn't know why but can only imagine. By the way, the person who made this request is no longer associated with Ozzy."

Diary Of A Madman was released on November 7th 1981 peaking at Number 14 in the UK album charts. The very next week Black Sabbath's *Mob Rules* hit Number 12. To the eager fans, happy to fork out for both releases, the sheer level of quality evident on both records portrayed a keen sense of competition. Once again, both camps had come up with bona fide classics.

The true proving ground in terms of bulk sales and international status, though, was America. *Diary Of A Madman* made a big dent in the Billboard top twenty, running out of initial momentum at Number 16. *Mob Rules* would just scrape into the top thirty. Like two leviathans going mano-a-mano, the two products battled it out. When the dust settled and the soundscans were totted up, it was without question Ozzy, another two million sales under his title belt, hailed as the victor.

With a true Dunkirk spirit prevailing, Lee Kerslake did not have long to ponder on might-have-beens. Ossie Hoppie, the same man who had discovered his departure from Uriah Heep post-*Fallen Angel,* now found out that Lee was a free agent once again. Mick Box was straight on the telephone excitedly relaying plans to reform Uriah Heep. Once the drummer had established that certain people were no longer involved he jumped at the chance. His next action was to phone Bob Daisley. "Do you want to join Uriah Heep?" he inquired. "Not 'arf!!" came the reply. The circle had been closed.

The pair would retain their partnership for what would turn out to be Uriah Heep's 1982 renaissance album *Abominog*. The record pulled Mick Box's boys back from the brink and the fresh look Pete Goalby-fronted Heep found renewed international

Ozzy Osbourne

audiences and revitalized album sales. Also a member of the reforged Heep was erstwhile Heavy Metal Kids keyboard player John Sinclair, himself later to figure as a long-term player in the Ozzy story in later years. Daisley would stick with Heep for the follow up *Head First* effort in 1983 too, though in spite of this, Daisley's career with Ozzy was far from over. Indeed, it had only really just begun.

Diary Of A Madman arrived in the stores complete with the brand new band members' names emblazoned on it as a statement of intent: Ozzy Osbourne, Randy Rhoads, Rudy Sarzo and Tommy Aldridge. It was a fearsome combination.

Bassist Rudy Sarzo had been hand-picked for Ozzy by Randy Rhoads. The guitarist had known Sarzo since he had supplanted original Quiet Riot bass player Kelly Garni for the second Japanese release album, *Quiet Riot II*, released by CBS in 1979. As an aside Garni, the ousted partner, meantime kept it in the family by later joining Randy's brother Kelle Rhoads, act Emerald. Just previous to lining up for Ozzy's band, Sarzo had actually been working with Angel and also joining the fray was Don Airey. The keyboard player had been unable to tour with Ozzy up to that point or contribute to Diary as he was serving out a touring term with Rainbow. A well-timed telephone call secured his recruitment. "Ozzy phoned me up in November of 1981 and asked me to take over from Lindsay in the live show. I said I wouldn't do it if it meant playing offstage. He phoned back five minutes later and asked me to join the band as a full member." The man remembers being instantly struck by the unbridled power of the band that he had just joined. "When I heard Randy, Rudy and Tommy playing together I thought they sounded like Cream. Tommy did deservedly have a fantastic reputation at this point."

It would also be Don's first experience of working with Randy Rhoads outside the studio confines and in the live arena. "The way Randy played, needed a much different approach keyboard-wise to, say, working with someone like Ritchie Blackmore or Gary Moore. It had to be sparse, with sound FX, etc. Anything vaguely avant-garde he really liked. We'd play the gig tapes back in the bus, and if he went 'Wow!', I'd keep that bit in. He turned me on to a lot of diverse stuff – 18th century guitar music, obscure film soundtracks, records by pianists Katia and Marielle Labeque, Ravel and Debussy. I remember his favourite chord, which was the one in the film *Carrie*, when the hand comes out of the grave – we'd play that bit of the video over and over again."

Tommy Aldridge too has his own recollections of the first time the unit gelled as the new Ozzy Osbourne band. "I had never worked with Rudy Sarzo before but Randy had and Rudy was there on Randy's recommendation. I believe that Lindsay Bridgwater was present at this time as well. It was, I thought at the time, a relatively tight rhythm section. It worked well around Randy who I felt then and still do, was the catalyst. He was certainly my motivation for being there. Not to discount Ozzy of course, but my interest was predicated strictly on working with that guitarist. I only remember it to be very exciting working with Randy. The better I got to know Randy the more I realized just how very special he was. It was exciting to be part of that."

The new grouping faced an uphill struggle. Not only did they have to mentally lock as a band but quickly get down pat on a whole slew of material written and performed by those they had so recently supplanted. Aldridge enjoyed the challenge.

"As far as learning Lee's parts...some of it was necessary. First off...they're cool parts, some of them being 'thumbprint' parts. Meaning they need to played note-for-note. I was impressed with his playing on that record. I've kicked myself in the butt more than once for not being on that record. But again, I am the worst copy drummer but try to remain faithful to the music."

Bob Daisley's legacy also weighed heavy on his replacement Rudy Sarzo. In a '20 questions' interview for the infamous 'Metal Sludge' website on July 31st 2001, in which the bassist is asked to grade other musicians, Sarzo's admiration for his predecessor is clear. "Awesome bass player. I had the time of my life playing his bass lines live... let me tell you, his bass lines are world-class. So as a recording artist I definitely give him a ten.

Ozzy Osbourne

As for rock star appeal, oooh. You know he comes from a whole different '70s tradition. More of that very grounded, you know, type of bass player." Rudy finished by giving Daisley six points out of ten – losing marks due to lack of 'Glam' MTV appeal!

In the same 'Metal Sludge' interview Sarzo is also keen to verify the speculation that it was Randy Rhoads that secured the Ozzy position for him. When talking about the guitarist, Sarzo had this to say: "The fondest memory is actually the fact that if it wasn't for him, I wouldn't be here. He was completely, 100 percent responsible for me meeting Ozzy Osbourne. You know, the fact that he helped me through the early days. 'Cause, I mean, Sharon and Ozzy are wonderful people. But they can be pretty wacky! (laughs) And I got thrown into that, that, world, you know. It was like going on the biggest rollercoaster ride of your life, you know. I went from sleeping on the floor, on Kevin [DuBrow]'s floor in his apartment. We were sharing a, a....you know, I was living with him, at his place, and I didn't even have a bed. So I had a sheet. So, I was sleeping on this sheet, and I got a call to audition for Ozzy, and Randy really helped me out a lot. He's the one who told Ozzy, 'This is the guy.' So my fondest memory was that if it wasn't for him I'd... be playing conga drums in a Salsa band in Miami."

Quite incredibly, some 20 years after the event, that 'Ozzy insider' that Tommy Aldridge discussed had his wish come true. The March 2002 'Expanded' re-releases of both *Blizzard Of Ozz* and *Diary Of A Madman* would bear the most unexpected of re-issue updates. Nothing so minor has repackaging, remixing or remastering. On both albums both Daisley and Kerslake are eradicated for good – no credits, no photos and no sounds. Fans would be staggered to learn that the entire rhythm section had been excised and then re-recorded by Ozzy's present bassist Robert Trujillo and drummer Mike Bordin.

7
An Englishman's Castle

Launching in Towson, Maryland, on April 22nd 1981 Ozzy proceeded to pursue a mammoth 14-month globally encompassing tour. Ozzy's support bands for these US gigs were Brummie natives The Starfighters and pomp-metal outfit Magnum. The former of these acts was fronted by a notorious hard-drinking character named Steve Burton. More commonly known as 'Bertie', he had, as legend would have it, recently turned down an offer to join AC/DC as replacement for Bon Scott. That was not the only AC/DC connection as guitarist Stevie Young's obvious family resemblance betrayed him to be the cousin of Angus and Malcolm. The quintessentially British Magnum were Jet Records stablemates.

Initially the band was in the odd position in America of promoting the debut album almost a year after its recording. These inaugural Stateside shows, some supported by Def Leppard, ranged from crammed theatres packed to the gunwhales to gigs with attendances so poor that, according to later interviews given by Sharon Osbourne, the band sometimes had to fight to just get paid for their efforts. It would be during this period of dogged persistence that the Ozzy legend was kindled.

At the band's stop off in Las Vegas Randy Rhoads would be reunited with his old friend Kelly Garni. "We met up the night before the Vegas show on that very first tour and we had the best time ever" the bassist remembers fondly. Worryingly, however, the guitarist would reveal to Garni some of the more disturbing aspects of touring with Ozzy. "Randy was really bothered by the whole satanic thing. Y'know, he told me had guys coming up to him backstage with goats' heads and stuff which really scared him." Come showtime Garni and his partner received the best seats in the house. "Randy arranged it so that my date and I could watch the show from backstage. We sat on a road case in the wings just ten feet away from him. It was really funny because we were both pulling faces at each other. Afterwards we hung around to try and catch him again but they just got mobbed by

Ozzy Osbourne

fans so that was the last time we actually met. He would write me letters after that or phone now and then but often he was either tired or sick. Randy got sick a lot, he suffered from anaemia." A further extended bout of dates officially plugging *Diary Of A Madman* reaped another hit album and a constant stream of sold-out, hysterical gigs which featured an elaborate medieval castle stageset and a bizarre dwarf named 'Ronnie'. By now the *Blizzard Of Ozz* album was racking up sales of over 6,000 units a week.

The second leg of the American tour commenced at San Francisco's Cow Palace on the December 30th 1981. At that inauguration gig Randy Rhoads was presented with a notable award from *Guitar Player* magazine for 'Best New Talent'. Earlier Randy had picked up a similar award from the influential British *Sounds* rock weekly, being voted by fans as 'Best New Guitarist'. A brief respite from America was the welcome slot alongside Motorhead at the Port Vale 'Heavy Metal Holocaust' festival when Ozzy stepped in at the last minute to wryly supplant none other than a baulking Black Sabbath. Indeed, Motorhead would open for Ozzy in the States after both Def Leppard and UFO had enjoyed stints on the tour.

This trek was riddled with Ozzy outrages that outranked even his infamous biting-the-head-off-a-dove episode the year before. One famous episode included biting off the head of a bat tossed onstage at a concert in Des Moines on January 20th 1982. What Ozzy thought was a rubber toy actually hospitalized him as the dead animal carried the risk of a rabies infection. According to myth, the fact the creature was flesh and blood only became evident to Ozzy once he'd taken a bite which duly startled the bat into action.

On the road for this second round of dates was a guesting UFO, a valuable addition, being a major draw in their own right. UFO guitarist Paul Chapman was glad to meet up with Randy Rhoads again. The sheer size of the Ozzy show, though, would strike the Welshman as ambitious. "When we started the tour I thought the Ozzy production was too big for someone I didn't think was doing that well, what with the castle and the dwarf and

An Englishman's Castle

everything but as the tour got into gear their bet paid off. I got on fabulously with Randy straight away. He was a great guy, not really a party type person. I was endorsed by Washburn at the time and throughout the tour I kept having these guitars arriving. One day two acoustics turned up so Randy and I spent a good long time playing together. I remember I had just written 'Profession Of Violence' and he said the chords were really cool. I've always been slow at reading music but he was well up on it. He wanted to construct the chords for 'Profession' because I didn't know the name to one of the chords! He showed me how to build complex chords from major scales, using triads and compounding 3rd intervals. Consequently, the chord turned out to be an E7th, (inversion) starting on the third (G#), and not the root (E). That's when he showed me all about triads and chords, compound inserts, sevenths and ninths; his knowledge was quite unbelievable really. His grasp of scales was way ahead of its time. I mean, the song 'Diary Of A Madman' is a Hungarian minor scale." These reminiscences are not just a distant memory for Paul. "I teach now and my students of course want to know all about how the first two Ozzy albums were put together. I teach so much of Randy's stuff now."

Another character in Ozzy's entourage also evokes crystal clear memories for the UFO guitarist but for quite different reasons. Ozzy's stagehand and willing 'victim', dwarf John Allen, was introduced cruelly as 'Ronnie' prior to each ceremonial mock execution. Paul recalls Allen's diminutive stature provided no obstacle to his willingness to party. "He passed out once on our tourbus. I was the last one still awake and had to lock up. The thing is, it had been snowing constantly for about five or six hours while we carried on drinking inside. So, at about 4 a.m. I tried to wake him up but he was completely out cold in an alcoholic stupor. I put him over my shoulder while I tried to try to lock up at the same time. Suddenly he woke up and obviously being drunk and confused, not knowing where he was, he decided he didn't like being on my shoulder and jumped off. The problem was that he landed in a snowdrift that was deeper than he was tall so I lost him! There I am – drunk, searching for an even more drunk dwarf in a snowdrift in the middle of the night.

"I just couldn't see him and he panicked, not comprehending the swift change in body temperature I suppose, and started howling like a madman. It was pitch black and all I could hear was this screaming but I just could not find him. Well, although he was small he made a hell of a noise and by now lights were starting to come on in the hotel. I had visions of the police arresting me for 'dwarf abuse'! Anyway, I did find him and bravely rescued the little fella. I got him into the hotel lobby where he rather ungratefully started swearing very loudly at everyone!" Paul duly adopted UFO strategic manouevre Number 1. "I ran away!"

For Don Airey embarking on the American tour would also prove an unforgettable experience. He soon struck up a keen friendship and working relationship with Randy Rhoads. The keyboard player had also become aware of Randy's future aspirations to back out of life on the road in order to attain a music degree.

"It was very much in the air and we often talked about it" says Don. "He wasn't particularly enamoured of the rock 'n' roll lifestyle and had some pretty serious long-term musical goals. Mind you, this is not to say he couldn't create havoc with the best of them! If you ever saw soft furnishings and the like floating past your hotel window, that would be Randy just tidying his room up!"

Don was also witness to the lighter side of the young guitarist. "He had some very engaging traits. If you were in a restaurant or coffee shop with him and there was a lull in the conversation he'd just pull out his portable television, plug it into the nearest socket and just watch cartoons. He had a very infectious laugh and before long we'd all be watching and laughing along too. Then he'd order a round of Long Island ice teas and time would just fly! I know he collected a lot of train stuff in Europe. He was also an audiophile, very knowledgeable about speakers, record decks, etc and was always on the look out for additions to his system at home."

The camaraderie of the road though would be put under

An Englishman's Castle

severe strain by the explosion of adverse publicity surrounding Ozzy. On top of the regular round of meet and greets and the unceasing barrage of the press, Don found himself in the middle of a band that was the focal point for unwanted attention too.

"It was a frenetic time" he admits. "As there were so many journalists, photographers, radio DJs, competition winners and record company people continually joining and leaving the entourage, life on the tourbus became very difficult. Also there were the various religious organisations in individual towns trying to get us banned from their city limits. The Daughters of the American Revolution tried to stop us playing in Texas. The mayor of Odessa, Texas succeeded in exhorting his constituents to use their God given right as Americans to take a gun to this son of Satan (yes – Ozzy!). I got the distinct impression the FBI were harassing us through the local unions."

When time and energy would allow, band members would visit local clubs. Randy in particular was keen on jamming with any band on the night that would have him. Don has fond memories of one night when the group's long hair, combined with the guitarist's ready wit, nearly provoked serious trouble. "Tommy, Randy and I went to a club out in the sticks near Beaumont, Texas and sat in the corner listening to a very bad country band." Randy's boyish looks and blond mane obviously drew attention from the local good ol' boys as Don elaborates. "A lot of the rednecks were coming up and asking Randy to dance. Randy took it all very well and his put-downs to these guys had Tommy and me in stitches. We eventually made a hasty exit when one of them finally caught on to his wisecracks."

The singer would then stagger into a publicity disaster quite by accident. Ozzy was caught quite literally with his trousers down pissing on the Alamo! Ozzy was fortunate to get away with a class C misdemeanour. Arrested and booked only for public intoxication, which carried a maximum fine of $200, Ozzy evaded the count for which he could easily have been charged. The Alamo is categorised as a shrine and according to the letter of state law Ozzy, unaware, had actually been guilty of 'Desecration of a Venerated Object'.

Ozzy Osbourne

UFO were travelling to the San Antonio gig by bus when they heard an announcement on the radio. The DJ told his listeners the gig was in danger of being cancelled because "Mr. Osbourne is in jail at the moment!".

"All hell broke loose on that tour" sighs Paul Chapman "I'm pretty certain Phil went to jail on that tour too for mooning the Police Chief's daughter!"

With each successive show scaling renewed heights of excess some gigs still stand proud for Airey. Following Ozzy's national media 'splash' resulting from his spending the proverbial penny on the Texan holy of holies, Fort Alamo, the singer aired his grievances to an enthralled audience in San Antonio, Texas. Don remembers the content of Ozzy's ramble in detail.

"Ozzy gave a ten minute speech in the middle of the show that would have earned him a presidential nomination!" he enthuses. "Tommy Aldridge put a towel down as a pillow in front of the drums, lay down and went to sleep for the duration." Ozzy did not confine his outburst to the Alamo incident. Don catalogues other heartfelt topics Ozzy felt in need of sharing his views on with the crowd. "The importance of rock and roll, Peace and Love in the modern world, the effects of pollution on the planet, the effect Ronald Reagan was having on the planet, Ozzy for President, the price of food, the criminal justice system, you name it, he talked about it, and not in a shy way! It was marvellous."

A beachside Corpus Christi gig would go down in the annals of Ozzy folklore too, quite predictably for all the wrong reasons. UFO's bus arrived following a day off and the band stumbled off into the early morning Texan sunshine. Paul Chapman recounts the tale. "I had literally just stepped off the bus when I hear Ozzy shouting 'Hey, *Tonka*!' I looked around and saw him in this bar. It was totally empty except for Ozzy sitting at the end of the bar next to a cash register. Now this was at 8.30 in the morning so he must have been there all night. 'Come and have a Bloody Mary', he shouted over. 'Oh Lor', I thought but of course I joined him. So we had a drink and then he spotted Pete so then it was no stopping us. We had downed about six double Bloody Marys before Ozzy suggested we all go to this seafood restaurant for something to eat, his argument being we couldn't drink on an empty stomach. Well I was fucking plastered and just wanted to go to bed but somehow we made it to this restaurant where Ozzy just ordered absolutely everything off the menu – lobster, prawns, everything – and a bottle of Remy Martin! It was the middle of the afternoon by now and we were still drinking. Pete and I were wondering who was going to pay for all this because Ozzy had spent all his money earlier. Then I saw Sharon's head sticking around the edge of the door. We'd been caught like naughty schoolboys. Ozzy was literally dragged out by the scruff of his neck and we didn't see him again until the gig. Meantime we just about persuaded this waiter to cancel Ozzy's huge food order."

Upon arriving at their originally intended destination of the venue that evening UFO found much to their surprise that their dressing room had been relocated. "The roadies were more than a bit pissed off!" states Paul. "We had been put right on the other side of the arena." Seeking an explanation Chapman ventured off to find Ozzy and was met with an unexpected sight. "There was this huge black bouncer blocking the way to Ozzy's dressing room and yellow 'Do Not Cross' tape hung across the corridor. I showed this guy my pass but he told me nobody – but nobody – was getting past. Well, I could see past this guy and there was Ozzy, dressed up in his stage chainmail with a big pot of coffee – and he was jogging! Sharon had a stopwatch and was making Ozzy jog – very slowly I might add – gulp down some coffee, then jog back again on a circuit then have more coffee. It was intense!"

Sharon Osbourne's radical quick fix did not apparently produce the desired effect though. Paul spotted Ozzy just as the lights lowered for the start of the show. "Ozzy was walking down these steps holding this big black crucifix with mirrors on that he used. Well, he saw me and Pete and said 'Hello,' but as he did he tripped and fell down the stairs! Oh my God... The intro tape was running and Tommy was on his kit. Pete and I were thinking, 'fucking hell, he's broken his neck'. It was a long fall. But Ozzy got up and walked over to his mike for the start of 'Over The Mountain'. He starts to sing 'Over The…' He didn't reach 'Mountain'. It was like watching a cartoon. He got the first two words out then just fell over straight as a board backwards! The band was still playing and Sharon ran over frantically. Even the little dwarf John Allen ran up in his monk's habit and was fanning Ozzy with a towel. Ozzy was out stone cold." And the dastardly UFO duo? "We ran away!" Paul reveals. "We were seriously blamed for that whole day even though it wasn't our fault. The tour changed completely for us after that." The Corpus Christ audience received ticket refunds and the gig was later rescheduled at the close of the tour.

For Don Airey another landmark gig stays sharp in the memory purely for an artistic reason. "The other stand-out one was Knoxville, Tennessee, Randy's last gig, for no other reason than at this point the band was beginning to sound very cool."

Knoxville proved a welcome marker for Paul Chapman too. The UFO man had his home in Florida and was looking forward to a well-earned break with his family. UFO and Ozzy would split from the other acts and were scheduled to join Foreigner and Bryan Adams for two gigs at the Orlando Tangerine Bowl and the Miami Orange Bowl. However, Paul had promised to arrange a favour for Randy earlier.

"Randy had a really bad problem with his wisdom teeth and he really needed to see someone about it. His toothache was so bad his face had swollen up and he was in quite a bit of pain. Playing loud music wasn't helping him either as the vibrations got straight to the teeth. There was no dentist or doctor on the road with us so I said I would sort out a dentist for him when I got back home. It was pretty easy to do because I lived there and Randy really was in agony with his teeth so it needed to be sorted. We left Knoxville pretty early, our tour manager John Knowles got the bus packed while we were playing and then we were straight off. As we left Ozzy's intro music was on and I saw Randy walking up the ramp to the stage. 'See you at the hotel' I said. 'OK,' he replied. I'd previously arranged to meet Randy at the International Hilton so we could get his teeth problem fixed."

An Englishman's Castle

The next morning Paul had breakfast by the hotel pool and waited for Randy to arrive, looking through the yellow pages to find a local dentist. "I waited, and waited and waited. We swam in the hotel pool to kill some time. Well, of course this was my day off remember but by midday I was saying to my wife, 'where the fuck is he?'"

UFO's keyboard player Neil Carter had just got back to the hotel after picking up his wife Sue from the airport. When Paul set eyes on them in the lobby the first thing he saw was that both were weeping, openly and profusely. "Haven't you heard?" said Sue. "That's when they told me," says Paul. "I couldn't take it in. What was Randy doing in a plane? It didn't make sense."

Randy Rhoads died on March 19th 1982. Sharon Osbourne's friend Rachel Youngblood died in the same plane crash, as did the pilot Andrew Aycock.

Early that morning Aycock had taken Rhoads and Youngblood up in a small single-engined 1955 Beechcraft Bonanza F35 aircraft. There was talk that the plane, belonging to Jerry Calhoun, was taken by Aycock from its owner's hanger without permission. The band's bus, with the Osbournes and Rudy Sarzo still sleeping onboard, was parked near to a house by the airstrip.

There is some conjecture that Don Airey was taken for a flight prior to Rhoads and Youngblood. Airey witnessed the events unfolding as Aycock 'buzzed' the bus no less than three times before coming around for a fourth attempt. Crash investigators believed that on this last pass the aircraft, which was deemed to have been travelling at no more than ten feet off the ground and at speeds of some 140 mph plus, hit the back end of the bus with its left wing. The Bonanza's main body missed the bus, severed a pine tree and crashed into the garage attached to the house exploding on impact. The only substantial part of the aeroplane to survive the accident was the left wing which had hit the bus. Subsequent toxicology reports on Aycock showed traces of cocaine. Randy Rhoads' report was clean. Poignantly, the guitarist's autopsy makes mention of Rhoads' jewellery, a gold ring and a gold crucifix inscribed 'R.R.'. With Randy went a spirit that beckoned a new era of rock guitar. More significant though was that Ozzy had lost a dear friend and rare ally.

UFO's tour manager John Knowles hastily rescheduled UFO's plans. They were still to undertake the next day's gig and an evening soundcheck was put in place. For Chapman it would be an unpleasant experience.

"The atmosphere was ghastly. Behind me I had all of Randy's gear, his white Marshall stack. All of Ozzy's crew, all strong experienced guys, were just losing it. What made it especially eerie was the fact we were soundchecking at night in a stadium. Normally of course it's in the day but there we were with everyone's mind on Randy and everything we were playing, instead of being absorbed by the crowd as normal, was just drifting off into the night. We were all in tears. We just couldn't help it.

Next day when we played the actual gig Ozzy's crew were taking down his gear while we did our set. It was just devastating. We did the next day in Miami too then took a week off."

Somehow, within the maelstrom of recording, promotion and touring, material was also being compiled for a project that, although alluded to, has to date not been readily acknowledged as one of rock 'n' roll's great 'What if?'s – the Randy Rhoads solo album.

The guitarist had been embarking on a quest of self-improvement with the ultimate goal of striking out from the confines of rock 'n' roll. It is well known that Randy would seek out classical guitar tutors at every opportunity. Indeed, Ozzy often expressed his wish for his star guitarist to do his own thing. Lindsay Bridgwater confirms Randy's motives.

"Randy was working hard on a solo album," the keyboard player agrees. "Randy really was very classically influenced so we had an empathy there. We would often jam with him on guitar and me on piano. He felt the need to learn. We worked on a few things that ultimately were not to find themselves on the *Diary* album simply because they weren't suitable for Ozzy.

"It was actually rare to see Randy without a guitar. If he had lived to complete his own album it certainly would have been a revelation. Of that I have no doubt. There was one track in particular which I helped him transcribe. I wrote it down after he died because it was still fresh in my memory. I still have the manuscript."

Randy had been due to fly back to England to stay with his friend J.T. "Two weeks before he died he phoned to say he was coming back over, he was going to spend a week at my place. I had a 1958 Gibson ready for him."

Had Randy and J.T.'s fireside sessions resulted in anything more creative than just jamming? "We wrote a song together" J.T. affirms. "I've still got it. It's very typically Randy in style. I thought about using it for Budgie later on but the only person who can really finish it is Ozzy. It's an Ozzy song.

"I took the news of Randy's death very, very badly. In truth I have not been the same since, even though it happened nearly 20 years ago. God knows what he was doing in that plane, he was absolutely terrified of flying. But... Randy changed rock guitar forever, I think that is often overlooked. Ask any serious rock guitarist and they will tell you the same. The thing is, that what he played in private was a million times better than the Ozzy stuff. I know that sounds ridiculous but it's true – I've seen it. His mastery of the guitar was just unique."

Randy's life long friend Kelly Garni reveals just where Randy just might have been heading. "We spoke about forming a band together after he had done the Ozzy thing. Randy was planning on classical studies in England and after he was that really keen to do a heavy keyboard-orientated thing; we were both big Deep Purple fans, something like that or like a heavier Boston or Styx. That's the way he was thinking then."

Two decades later an Ozzy confidante would observe "You could see that Randy's influence had simply just stayed there with the band. That chugging rhythmic guitar style of 'I Don't Know' and 'Crazy Train' virtually defined the sound of Ozzy and none of the guitarists afterwards could really step too much out of that mould. Each new player had a dynamic new approach but they had to incorporate aspects of Randy's style. Randy had really defined what an Ozzy riff was. Everyone involved was very conscious of this and you could see it still there many, many years later – right up to 'No More Tears' that Randy style is still

8
Luck Of The Irish

Irishman Bernie Tormé is a talented guitarist with great character, renowned for some particularly wild axework and theatrics. Such showmanship brought him close to guitar-hero status whilst in Gillan.

Tormé first made his name as guitarist with Irish bands Wormwood and Urge, before relocating to London, forming Scrapyard in 1976. A hard rock trio of Tormé, bassist Bernie Hagley and drummer Roger Hunt, Scrapyard gigged solidly throughout the London area.

Hagley was to depart and the band were swiftly brought back up to strength with the addition of former Zzebra bassist John McCoy. However, this union lasted only a matter of months with Tormé striking out on his own as The Bernie Tormé Band. McCoy meanwhile soldiered on with Paul Samson on guitar as Scrapyard became McCoy.

Playing hard rock but with a punk image – Tormé having cut off his long hair to keep in vogue – the band managed to release two singles and contribute tracks to the punk compilation album *Live At The Vortex*. The Bernie Tormé Band were at this stage still a trio with the guitarist augmented by bassist Phil Spalding and drummer Mark Harrison, and, put in some British supports to Gillan, the headline act now featuring McCoy on bass. An album was recorded for Jet Records but remains unreleased. Disillusioned, Tormé took up his old colleague John McCoy's offer to hook up with Gillan. Spalding joined punk diva Toyah Wilcox's band followed by sessions for Mike Oldfield, Original Mirrors and Steve How and Steve Hackett's GTR. Harrison went on to The Nipple Erectors/The Nips and Dirty Strangers.

Tormé's ascent to guitar-hero status with Gillan was assured by his contribution to the albums *Glory Road* (1980) and *Future Shock* (1981). The guitarist locked in neatly into the band unit with his quirky rogue gypsy image proving a perfect foil for the veteran vocalist and the eccentric heavyweight McCoy. However, in spite of sell out tours, hit singles and numerous TV

Luck Of The Irish

appearances, the Gillan ship was financially leaky and it was this factor that prompted a split. Tormé drifted into the fold of veteran heavy rockers Atomic Rooster, but then Ozzy came calling.

"I'd spent from the previous September, a couple of months after I left Gillan," remembers Bernie, "till I got the call to join Ozzy, sorting out financing to complete the *Turn Out The Lights* album and bring in a producer on it. So, over that timescale I had managed to buy back the tapes from Ian Gillan's studio, got a publishing deal which financed the completion of the album at the Marquee Studios with Nick Tauber producing, and got it signed to record companies in both the UK and Germany for an April/May release." Bernie's own new band, the Electric Gypsies had a finalized roster of former Bethnal bass player Everton Williams, second guitarist Bob Andrews and drummer Mark Laff, the latter being alumni of Generation X.

Then David Arden turned up on the other end of Tormé's phone. "I had also sorted a UK tour that was due to start on April 20th," explains Bernie. "At the time of the phone call to join Ozzy we had never done a gig together. I had really worked my ass off to get the Electric Gypsies thing off the ground: if I had been offered the Ozzy situation a month or so after leaving Gillan, it might have been completely different. But at the time I was offered it, I had already taken a different route: I had already put an enormous amount of work, time, and my heart into getting out there and playing and promoting a record again."

There were other considerations to take into account too. "I also hadn't played on stage since the previous July, apart from doing a short Italian tour (during February, I think) with Rooster, which was, incidentally, a gas. On that tour I was standing in for John Cann, who hadn't wanted to tour when the other two (Vincent Crane and Paul Hammond) did. I agreed to do other stuff with them on a longer-term basis after the tour, but it was a very loose arrangement at that stage. It wasn't clear that there would be any subsequent touring or recording at all."

Don Airey was delegated to put together a rapid audition structure and recalls Bernie Tormé being at the forefront of his mind to handle the enormous task fate had dictated him. "It was a heartbreakingly awful time," the keyboard player confides. Nevertheless Don set about his task. "Bernie... was just what the circumstances dictated. I had seen Bernie with Gillan I think and thought he had the-off-the wall quality that Ozzy liked." Bernie thinks that besides Don's recommendation, Ozzy and Sharon may have been present at one of his earlier gigs too. "I was also told by Phil Banfield (Ian Gillan's manager) that Ozzy and Sharon had also been at an Aylesbury Friars warm-up gig for a Gillan tour in '80 or '81 and had seen me play. I had never met them at that time so I don't know how true that is. I never asked."

Tormé's diary records the necessary expedition of events over the next few days. "Randy died in Florida on Friday 19th, I was approached to go out to replace him on Monday 22nd, early afternoon as I remember" he observes. "I flew to Los Angeles on Friday 26th after a ticket cock-up on the 25th. I auditioned on the 27th and 28th, and was asked to do the gig on the 28th. We flew to New York on the afternoon of 29th, and I'm sure that the day of Randy's funeral was the morning of the 29th. I was there, auditioned, committed and in place before Randy was laid to rest. So the decision to carry on and approach me must have been made between Randy's death on Friday 19th and Sunday 21st. With the time difference and the need to track me down that would be just enough time to contact me on the 22nd. It must have been a very quick decision to ask me."

On paper the process looks to have been a whirlwind of activity with decisions being made with calculating expediency. The reality from Bernie's viewpoint was a multi-faceted emotional dilemma with implications for his long-term career. Over the years, the guitarist's own take on this traumatic period has remained unpublished. Indeed, interviewed for a previous book the guitarist asserts his then freely-given observations were twisted to such a degree that they ended up far removed from the truth. Naturally Bernie is keen once and for all to set the record straight regarding the circumstances of teaming up with Ozzy and the actual events. Bernie recalls the first telephone conversation:

Luck Of The Irish

"The gist of it was something like:
D: *'Hello Bernie, it's David Arden from Jet here, how are you?'*
B: *'Hello David I'm fine, how are you?'*
D: *'I suppose you've heard about the death of Randy Rhoads – Ozzy's guitarist, well the band are in the middle of a big US tour they need to complete. Can you go out and replace him?'*

"It was, as I remember, as blunt and short as that. I didn't understand what he was talking about at first, I hadn't even heard about Randy's death. This also probably makes me sound like a complete idiot, but I didn't know much about Ozzy's doings at that time, I hadn't been a great Black Sabbath fan and hadn't really followed his career. I hadn't heard *Blizzard Of Ozz* or *Diary Of A Madman*."

The call was such a shock to the system David Arden had to repeat his message before Bernie grasped exactly what he was being told. "It was a very difficult conversation to get dropped into out of the blue. They had a really huge problem, since everyone found it very hard to carry on. I asked when and for how long they would want me, and when he said 'from tomorrow for probably two months' I said no, I couldn't.

"I've got to say that I really felt for their position, I really would have liked to have helped them, it sounded just awful, but I could not see how. I said I couldn't do it because I had an album out the next month and a tour starting, and that I was committed to doing that."

But over the course of this initial conversation and subsequent other telephone exchanges Bernie Tormé began to realise the only answer David Arden would accept was 'Yes'. "David really presented it to me as if it was me or nothing, the tour would collapse and the world would come to an end, and while that was nice for my ego, it obviously wasn't the case. I was sure they could find someone else. I thought it was just the usual record company bullshit. I mean also this was not Ozzy or Sharon or even Don on the phone, none of whom I had ever even spoken to: it was all second or third hand, and I felt I was not getting anything like the full picture. I did feel that if it was all that important that I did it, Sharon or Ozzy or Don would have been on the phone.

"But David did make me feel that I would have liked to help them out if I could, but as I said I really didn't see how I could without destroying everything I'd been working for, and I was not going to do that. Again, fairly dumb, but I also didn't know how big Ozzy was in the US at that stage, I thought he was probably playing Agoras and suchlike, not stadiums."

As outlined previously Bernie's short but vitally important tenure with Ozzy has all too often been portrayed in ways at great variance with the truth. Naturally such accounts have not gone unnoticed by Bernie who maintains that the reason for the brevity of his stay and his initial acceptance of the position has never been adequately explained.

"There were three reasons why I did not want to get involved initially, apart from the fact that I thought it was logistically impossible from my end. Two of these reasons were probably unfair in retrospect, the third was something that was personally important to me, and meant I would only go as a stand-in to help them out of a jam.

"Reason one was that I had been signed to the Ardens and their record company Jet Records from the end of '77 till mid '79, (when I was in my punk band period). I had a certain amount of not very positive experience dealing with the Ardens at that time – although I don't include Sharon in that, I had never met her until I went to do Ozzy's thing. I was not keen to work for them again. This isn't to imply any dishonesty on their part – but it was just that you never knew what was going on, or where you stood, everything was done behind your back and you were the very last person to know about it, especially if it was bad news and concerned you. There are a lot of famous apocryphal stories about them. I don't know if any are true or not, and I don't really care; there are two sides to every story. But I found they were hard people for me personally to deal with, and I was not keen to do it again. So when David phoned me my immediate reaction was "Oh no, not them again. What do they want?."

The second reason Bernie baulked at the initial prospect, he believes may be incomprehensible to most. He simply did not want to tour in America again. Gillan's 1980 promotional jaunt to the States only held bad memories. "Most people hear the words 'American tour' and think wow, wouldn't it be great, hold me back!" The reality, as Bernie relates, was somewhat different. "It was one of the least enjoyable periods of my life, of all our lives in fact. As well as being a total disaster, it was absolute complete fucking hell. I got food poisoning and nearly died of it, and when I wasn't almost dying I felt like a total alien." The guitarist's creative environs in Britain were infused with the rich mixture of Punk, Glam and NWoBHM. His perception of America, though, shocked him. "At that time a kind of back-to-1974 time-warp still reigned supreme in a large part of America, mixed with a sizeable sprinkling of right-wing Christian intolerance. I spent my life avoiding getting beaten up." Bernie's shock of multi-coloured hair, pointed Cuban heels and deliberately torn black jeans exemplified his Romany ragamuffin punk image and in the UK had made him a focal point of the Gillan band. America had different ideas.

"Tommy Aldridge subsequently said to me on the bus, 'Boy, if you walked through Dallas lookin' like that you would *die*!' I felt like a Martian in Tesco's. So when David mentioned the words 'American tour' I thought '*oh* no, find someone else'. I'd like to say that I don't hold that view at all now, I love America. Satellite TV and MTV in particular, and time in general, changed it totally for the better."

There was a further overriding factor as to why Tormé felt reluctant to take up the offer. "The third reason, the most important one, and the one I still hold to was that I did not want to step into a dead man's shoes. The only reason I could see for doing it was to help out, help them to finish the tour. People are different and for me it's the most important thing that I treat people with respect. There's not a lot of it in the music business or the world, and that for me was the best way of my showing my respect. To a person, not to a guitar player. I don't expect anyone else to understand that, I couldn't really give a fuck if they do or not. I definitely don't expect them to agree with it, or to live by it, we're all different, we've all got different reasons: but for me it is important, and I tried to live by it. I don't think anyone did understand that."

David Arden's dogged tenacity eventually won the day. "I agreed on the third call," admits Bernie. "Following the previous telephone conversations I sat down and thought about it hard. I was so gobsmacked by David's call that I phoned a couple of people to ask what they thought. The consensus seemed to be that I ought to try to do it. Phil Banfield – Ian Gillan's manager – phoned me (David Arden had called him), and said I should do it, but I still couldn't see how. I felt in the circumstances I would like to help out if I could. I just couldn't imagine the hell Ozzy, Sharon and the band and all involved must have gone through. It must have been truly awful. Totally tragic for the families of the people killed. Horrific. I phoned David back and said I'd love to help but I really couldn't see how, since I couldn't afford to delay my album and tour and let people down. David started saying please think again, oh and by the way the money is..."

As much as Bernie would like to say the fiscal aspect of the offer held no bearing, he is brutally honest with himself. "Let me put this way, I was very hard up at the time. I'd as yet had no Gillan royalties, publishing or otherwise, and the sum David mentioned was probably more than I had earned in the previous six months. Times were very hard and the Tormé coffers were totally boracic. Black holes... I've never thought of myself as someone who does things just for money, you wouldn't be a musician if you did, but this definitely stopped me in my tracks and made me go 'hmmmmmm, maybe there is a way round... hmmmm'. Typical, terrible really. I was a rabbit trapped in the big-buck headlights." David Arden then told Bernie the gig was his. No auditions necessary because the band were familiar with his playing 2nd already knew, he could cut it.

Bernie was sceptical; "I found that very difficult to believe. I said to him the last thing I wanted to do was to go to Los Angeles for a gig I wasn't really after in the first place and waste at least a week having managed to reschedule all my shit, and then have the whole thing fall through. Well possible. In the music business

Luck Of The Irish

you never believe anything will happen until you've had the hangover. David was adamant, no auditions. I still didn't believe it."

Tormé then had a desperate dash to reschedule not only his plans but those of others who were relying on him at that point. The diplomat in him came to the fore as he managed to assuage his label boss Nick Raymond at Kamaflage/DJM and put back the release date of the Electric Gypsies album, and inform his band there would be a delay. In the circumstances, they proved extremely forbearing and understanding.

"My agent, Albert Samuel at Smash, was a quite a bit less happy, but agreed, though I had to agree to do the same gigs for a lot less money later in the summer. I talked to my band who were OK about it too."

A phone call was also put in to Phil Banfield who offered some sage advice. "He made the very practical suggestion that since there were, according to David, no auditions, and since I was having to move a lot of things around to do it, I should ask for a week's pay, cash upfront, before I left, just to protect myself and find out if I was being told the truth about the pay. That seemed like a good idea, since I was personally 100 percent certain there would at least be auditions, and that made everything else look a bit questionable too."

Bernie had one other proviso. "I also said I wanted to take a roadie, which he was also not happy about, but he agreed to, and that subsequently turned out to be a major mistake on my part. The guy got on the tits of the band and Ozzy's crew and I got a lot of grief for it, I wished afterwards I hadn't taken him."

Bernie got back in touch with David Arden, his welcome news relayed with a sting in the tail. "I said I could do it, I had managed to move things around, but it would have to be only a couple of months. He was really pleased, and confirmed it was only a couple of months till they finished the tour. I then said that I had been advised by Phil Banfield to require a week's pay cash up front to protect myself. There was a long silence at the other end of the phone, but he did agree. He didn't sound very happy about it. I was happy with his agreement, that made it sound as if the money amount was true, but as it eventually turned out, the big bucks spiel was all bullshit."

Bernie acknowledges that David Arden's persuasiveness and unwillingness to accept a negative answer won him over. "I was blagged into it by him making me feel that they really needed my help, the 'no-one else would do' shtick." He readily admits. "That appealed to my ego, even though it wasn't true, and I did want to help them out if I could. Temporarily. The money I was offered made it possible for me to do that, to move things around and keep people happy."

The following day Bernie travelled into the Jet offices in London to arrange shipping and carnets for getting his gear to America. He would also pick up copies of *Blizzard Of Ozz* and *Diary Of A Madman*. When he got home and put the albums on his record deck he was staggered.

"I was totally blown away, I loved the albums," he readily confesses. "Randy's playing, the songs, everything. Totally brilliant. Not what I expected at all. I also realised I was going to have to work very hard to try to get a handle on all of that material and the superb guitaring." At this stage Bernie still had no idea which songs made up Ozzy's live set and he still had not spoken to Ozzy or Sharon. "I spent all the next day (the 24th) playing the albums, trying to learn what I could, mostly just arrangements of songs, progressions and riffs. It was pretty hard to take in all of the details and nuances in a short space of time."

The adventure would get off to a false start before Bernie had even set foot on an aeroplane. "I was supposed to be going on the morning of the 25th: the week's pay – cash upfront – hadn't arrived. I phoned David who said it was being couriered across, and could I go to the airport and phone home to check it had arrived, otherwise I'd miss the flight. I sort of smelt the inklings of a rat, but I agreed."

Bernie and his roadie made it to the airport on schedule but would receive an unpleasant surprise when they attempted to pick up their tickets. Mistakenly only one-way tickets had been arranged and without being American citizens or green-card holders their flight would have been to no avail. U.S.

Luck Of The Irish

Immigration would have automatically turned the two men back on a return trip at the airline's expense.

An angry guitarist called home to relay the news to his wife. "She told me that the courier had indeed arrived, but only with a cheque for – well, for x pounds rather than xxxx pounds as promised. I was convinced at this stage the whole thing was indeed bullshit, so I phoned David at home and said 'Terrible mistake mate, one-way tickets and no cash. I'm going home, if you want me to go, sort it out.' He sounded a bit crestfallen, and said it would be sorted. I went home with absolutely no conviction that it would be, and very pissed off that I had rescheduled my album and tour for what looked like a waste of time." The farrago was finally put to rights by Jet and the procedure started for a second time.

"I didn't listen or learn any more music until the money in advance surprised me by arriving late that afternoon. Then I started work on it all for an hour or two again. I flew out on the 26th. I met Don Airey that night, only met the others the next day at the first auditions."

Coping with the grief of losing a dear friend the Ozzy band and organization had no inkling of the shenanigans Bernie Tormé had just endured simply to get him there.

As predicted Bernie arrived to find that contrary to David Arden's assurances, auditions were indeed taking place. Rudy Sarzo's brother Robert, later to make his name with Hurricane, was one of the applicants. Don Airey confirms this: "Rudy Sarzo's brother Robert auditioned. Gary Moore and Michael Schenker were asked but had said 'no'. Pat Travers had been very supportive on the phone, but his kind offer of help wasn't taken up. Pat had phoned a couple of times, very genuinely concerned on a personal level at what had happened."

Bernie Tormé was aware of the potential Pat Travers union too. "Pat was very keen to help, but when it came to it his management demanded silly stuff like equal billing and a lot of money." John Sykes, making a name for himself with The Tygers of Pan Tang, was also flown in for an audition. His services were requested once he had landed back in England but the axeman declined, eventually hooking up with Thin Lizzy.

UFO bassist Pete Way recalls the possibility of a union with Michael Schenker. "Ozzy called me asking for Michael's number. I think Peter Mensch was involved somewhere in there too. They never rehearsed together though. Y'know, Michael has been asked to play for everybody – Aerosmith, the Stones – everyone, but he's such an individual and not necessarily the person you really want in your band! Ozzy and Michael? It's just too different and wouldn't have worked. The thing with Michael is he's so fuckin' eccentric. I can say that because he's my best friend. Phenomenal, phenomenal guitarist but not right for Ozzy. Later Michael did have a few regrets though, he said to me he'd wished we'd have both done the Ozzy thing. Now that might have worked!"

There were other hopefuls as Bernie verifies. "I don't remember the names of the others, the names didn't mean much to me at the time, and I was very jetlagged and tired. I don't think I'd slept much since agreeing to go. I'd had a lot to sort out and think about." Bernie dutifully auditioned and then waited on the band and Sharon to come to a decision. After some discussion Sharon broke the news that the gig was definitively his. "I was really pleased, I really liked Ozzy and Don was a real nice guy. Tommy didn't really talk to me much, but it didn't matter, he was a real hero of mine and I was a bit overawed. Rudy was superb. But reality kicked in almost immediately, and this is all God's honest truth: Sharon then said the pay was x dollars a week, and I sputtered 'but, but, David said it was...'. Sharon replied, 'oh, he doesn't know what he's talking about'. I said 'oh...'."

Bernie then informed Sharon of his advance and was told it would be deducted from his weekly pay until the advance was cleared.

"I contemplated saying 'fuck it' and letting Robert do it, but I liked everyone and wanted to help and not kick them in the teeth, it was such a tragic situation. And I had never asked for the original salary in the first place, it's only money, after all. But it did leave a bit of a strange taste.

"Even at a glance it was very obviously heavy metal sideman

Luck Of The Irish

situation, it was not a band: that was clear by the fact that the rhythm section had changed, and that Tommy and Rudy hadn't played on the records up to that date. Basically it was Oz plus backing band. Of course there's no reason that it should be a band, it was just that I've never really had much desire to operate as a mercenary, a hired gun, its not what I get off on, I like bands."

The Ozzy band got back to work once more, with UFO still retained as openers, at the Leigh U. Stabler arena in Bethlehem, Philadelphia. If anyone noticed that date was April 1st the subject was not raised. Chalking up to experience the experience with the salary wrangle, the guitarist got down to work plotting the set with Don Airey. "Initially Don spent quite a few hours teaching me the songs we auditioned on: he helped me a lot," he confirms. "Since he doubled a lot of Randy's licks and solos, he knew what Randy played. This was both a blessing and a curse, since it meant I had to really stick to a fairly exact game plan, and not play it the way I really would have liked. I would have preferred not to do that, I did not want to imitate. But that seemed to be what Ozzy initially wanted. He seemed very paranoid about my not playing stuff exactly like Randy, and honestly even if the notes were exactly the same, I wouldn't, probably couldn't play it identically, ever. But I could understand why he felt like that, I just didn't find it much fun or easy to do initially."

With just two days rehearsal behind them the band set out to re-launch the tour in Bethlehem, PA. Bernie's first opportunity to perform the entire set came with the gig soundcheck. Learning the show was more than enough to contend with, and practical teething problems with sound and guitars had to be taken into account also. It was to be another equipment issue that brought home to him the very reason of his being there in a way he could never have envisaged.

"My gear hadn't arrived for that gig: I had one Strat I brought from the UK, one I'd bought in Los Angeles, and a hired plank with a Fender sticker and strings on from SIR in New York. I needed at least three since three or four tracks were de-tuned for Ozzy's voice. Really for safety I needed four, but my other was

Ozzy Osbourne

still in transit, so I prayed I wouldn't break a string on the detune. Luckily I didn't."

Bernie's out-of-reach guitars were not specially customised but they were trusted and familiar. "They were just very good instruments, their tremmy arms didn't make 'em go out of tune. They were older, worn in."

Instruments and the power that fed them raised further difficulties. "I've never been much of a one for guitar technology, I like the classic Strat Tele and Les Paul sounds too much. Strats are my fave, because you can get more sounds out of them. Ozzy didn't like Strats at all, he was a Gibson man. I had nightmares with my sound on that tour incidentally, the amps never sounded right, a bit weedy, but there was bugger-all I could do about it. No-one on the crew knew why."

These sound problems were not an 'Ozzy' problem though, more an Anglo-American mismatch, as Bernie outlines. "I had sounded dire in the US when I toured it with Gillan too. I only found out later that I needed a voltage regulator/stabiliser. British Marshalls, especially old ones, don't like the unevenness in US power, which is multiplied in the amp due to US power being 110 volts, and that's even more of a problem if you have a big show, huge PA and a huge lighting rig drawing lots of power." And then came the horrifying realization that something else was missing from the equation.

"My pedals also hadn't arrived, and a Strat directly into an unsouped Marshall superlead sounds a bit like a distorted banjo," Bernie states. Still cased up with his guitars in the gear cases there was only one set of pedals available at such short notice- and they belonged to Randy Rhoads.

"I really did not want to use them, it seemed like desecration," Bernie sighs. "A guitarist's gear is very personal. It's part of them. I used Randy's pedals for the soundcheck. I could just about deal with that. At that time mine were being flown from Los Angeles to New York, some of the crew were trying to get them from La Guardia or wherever in time for the gig. It didn't happen, and the situation came up, 8000 people in, and I either had to use Randy's pedals or no gig. No one was happy about it,

Luck Of The Irish

me probably least of all, I hated doing it, and again it left me feeling depressed about the situation. I felt that really this was a gig that someone else ought to be doing, not me."

The first gig without Randy. In Bernie's words: "The first gig. That's unforgettable. Very mixed emotions and mixed up memories about that. Everyone was under a great amount of stress, looking at it in retrospect it must have been the make or break as to whether it would carry on or not. Ozzy was very supportive, very helpful for the whole gig, took a lot of pressure off me. It was not the same situation as Brad's (*3). I suppose with Brad they were really putting him on the spot, with me on that first gig they must have been more concerned with what was going on in their own heads and hearts. They probably really were not that concerned with me, just so long as I didn't make a total balls of it."

With the full gamut of emotions on overload the very last thing Bernie Tormé, already dealing with unfamiliar guitars and pedals that had a life of their own, was a further set of technical difficulties outside of his control to contend with. "I was pretty scared, I wasn't really at all sure of what I was doing, and in that stage setup that was not a good way to be. The onstage sound was absolutely crap. I could hardly hear a note I played, I had set up my three amps and five cabs back of the stage behind the portcullis, and they may as well have been back in England, I couldn't hear a fucking thing without standing close to it. Mind you that may have been a blessing. I couldn't hear Don or Rudy at all."

What the guitarist could register though was not exactly beneficial in attempting to construct a cohesive aural platform on which to work. "All I could hear was Ozzy wailing like the back end of Concorde, and Tommy's snare, no bass drum, no hi-hat, no toms" he reveals. "A very uphill journey sound-wise, and the most difficult thing was not getting totally lost on stuff like 'Believer' or 'Steal Away The Night', which I had problems remembering at all at the start." With the gig in full flow Bernie's focus was shifted away from getting through the show as Randy's chorus pedal repeatedly turned itself off and on. "It didn't scare me, I'm not scared of that sort of shit, sometimes it just happens. Something trying to say something. But because I didn't feel good about using the pedals, it was a bit freaky. Some of the crew noticed it too."

As the tightly-rehearsed show raged around him Bernie's peripheral vision began to digest the strangest of surroundings with the show and the antics of the dwarf all registering. "I made it, but it was all just approaching OK, nowhere near good. I didn't think I did much of a good job that first show, but the bootlegs of it were much better than I expected. It sounded OK." With the gig over Bernie informed the others of his pedal problems. "They seemed to think I was crazy, they said if it happened it must have been condensation on the switch. Maybe it was, but I've been using pedals now for 33 years, it's never happened, me any other time."

Some encouragement came from a welcome and respected source. "Tommy said afterwards that I must have had the biggest balls in the world to do that gig, but the worst thing I could do was hit some bum notes, so fucking what, I hit a few, probably more than a few, but I got through it with no disasters. But what Ozzy and the band did that night really needed the biggest balls in the world. I am very proud of having helped them to get through that gig. I am glad I had a chance to do that."

Watching side-stage Paul Chapman could not quite believe what he was seeing. "I had known Bernie for quite some time and it was very weird watching him up there. I was standing next to the monitor desk with Sharon and I'm not ashamed to say we were both crying. What was uncanny was that Bernie looked like Randy – the hair, the clothes, everything. Randy used to wear these purple waistcoat kind of things and they had dressed him up the same. I just thought, *Jesus Christ, they've tried to clone him*. It was bizarre. I tell you, I'm sure Bernie won't mind me saying this – he was losing it. He was so nervous. I really felt for him. Somehow, God knows how, he managed to pull it off and put on a good show. Amazing."

9
Hair By Sarzo Of Cuba

With his first taste of fire out of the way Bernie attempted to settle into the touring routine. However, despite his guitar style remaining intact, his trademark image would be in for a battering of the first order.

"The first and only time in my life that I have ever been in a band and been told what clothes I had to wear and that I had to have my hair cut. Hence in any of the pictures of me with Ozzy I've got this ridiculous retro, pudding-bowl, un-Tormé-like wig / hat on. Dreadful. Sharon demanded it and since no hairdresser was around Rudy Sarzo did it! Rudy, you're a great bass player, I love what you do, but never take up hairdressing.

Anyone who knows me or the bands I've been with over the years would probably agree that while I've often looked like a total cunt, I've always had a pretty strong visual image. Its part of what you try to express as a performer. If I'd wanted to be told what to wear I would've joined an Irish Showband years ago. It seemed to me to be pantomime, plastic and a bit corporate, and I thought Ozzy's music and the band were so strong that it was unnecessary. It was a bit like having my mum telling me what to wear again, very weird, and a bit sad in the circumstances, like clinging on to something that really didn't matter at that point anyway."

As Paul Chapman has already pointed out the style gurus would have designs on Bernie's wardrobe too. "Because I was six foot, quite a bit bigger than Randy, I was also told to wear Rudy's spare clothes. Rudy was approximately my build. Didn't feel quite right to me: I think the fact that a different person to Randy was playing should have been made clear, and no attempt should have been made to make the actor less important than the role. It was a bit like a soap opera when one actor dies or leaves and someone comes in and wears the same clothes and says the same things: that didn't seem right to me, it seemed creepy. It seemed to me to be a denial of something. The production and show was no way as important as Randy's death and absence, and trying to make it look as if not much had happened seemed to me to be out of balance. And that is not a judgement of anyone, because there was a lot of paranoia and even panic floating around at the time, and paranoia and stress are not conducive to making the most balanced choices. I don't think it was the right choice, but I can see how it happened."

On the positive side, however, Bernie Tormé had least reconciled himself with the fact that he was playing alongside some of the greatest rock musicians in the world. Of his fellow band members Tormé has only the greatest respect. "Tommy was a real hero of mine. I was aware of the things he did with Black Oak and I'd heard his solo and I just loved his playing. I get off on drummers, and he's one of the best. I wish I'd been able to hear more of him on stage. He's such a great player. Rudy Sarzo I didn't know, but he was absolutely awesome, great bass player, solid and clever. Don Airey I was obviously aware of with Rainbow and various other bands, but actually working with him you released how brilliant he is, he underplays his ability for the benefit of the song and the other players. Total opposite to me! Great to play with." Bernie recalls Don as being quite a linchpin in the live show. "The keyboard interplays were pretty much left intact, which left me struggling to keep up with Don on a few occasions. It was good discipline, but it did not leave me playing to my strengths, which is very much doing it off the top of my head. That's when I feel I'm best."

Bernie got on with the task in hand but describes what should have been a process of gradual easing of pressure as operating in reverse. "For me the first few gigs were all a bit one step forward followed by two steps back. The only part of the set that I could relax on was the guitar solo bit – I'd been doing that for years with Gillan, I could have done it in my sleep. So I did my routine, I can't remember if I did the very hokey Hendrix play- with-the-teeth thing that night or the night after, but anyway, because I was relaxing I probably played for two, maybe three minutes. I needed it for my sanity. The audience dug it, lighters up everywhere. After the gig that night or the next night Sharon came up to me and said the guitar solo was too long, it had to be more like

Hair By Sarzo Of Cuba

Randy's, under 60 seconds. That was hard work – because I wasn't Randy.

"They were very worried and paranoid at that stage, very understandably so, but it made it very difficult for me. Maybe they thought I was trying to make a name, score points or something, maybe they thought I was a bit too '60s Strat/bluesy, not 'classical' like Randy. I don't know what they thought.

"I was just relaxing at the guitar break truck stop, after driving at about 200 miles an hour on a very twisty road with no idea of what was coming next. Anyway it was their show, so they called the shots, but I felt it to be an added stress, I needed that bit to catch my breath."

A lack of communication, whether deliberate or otherwise, put both Bernie and Sharon Osbourne into an awkward unclear situation, not, their making. Bernie describes the moment the two parties realised he had never wished to be involved long-term. "Again, David Arden did not appear to have passed on my lack of desire for the long-term gig to Sharon or the band, who appeared not very happy when I said that I had to get back after a couple of months. Sharon especially, understandable since she was manager, didn't seem too happy with that."

The guitarist would also be surprised when talk turned to future plans. "Ozzy discussed writing with me, which obviously would have been only in a long-term situation. Then Sharon started talking about extra gigs in Alaska and Hawaii, which were as I remember four or so months away. This freaked me, but obviously they were not going to change stuff around to suit me. I think Sharon found it ridiculous that I wanted to go back and do my own crummy tour!

I was also always really uncomfortable about the fact that there was no mention of Randy's death during the show: I know that Ozzy couldn't have done it without breaking down, and that alone made it impossible, but I would have been far happier if it had been mentioned. Having come from Gillan, and having had a bit of a name in the UK, the possible reverse situation would cross my mind, if I had been killed and someone had replaced me and the band had continued touring within two weeks. In those circumstances I would have liked a mention, so its absence in Randy's case always made me very uncomfortable. I know Ozzy couldn't have done it, but I wish it had been possible."

It's a familiar scenario in the rock world – outright hostility from the fans to any new recruit, especially one that has been deemed to have unjustly taken the place of a perceived hero. Randy Rhoads – a genuine hero, not a product of media myth, had been cruelly taken and here was a relative nobody occupying his space. The fans had bought their tickets to see Ozzy and Randy after all but the expected antipathy swiftly gave way to respectful appreciation. "The audiences were just great, very supportive, you couldn't ask for better" outlines Bernie. "I personally got no shit at all, or none that I was aware of, which was not the case when I joined Ian Gillan, where there was a lot of the 'we want Blackmore' shit initially."

Paul Chapman backs this up. "Bernie got accepted pretty well. Poor guy – I really felt for him. I couldn't have done it, I tell you. At Madison Square Garden he was so incredibly nervous. The gig was packed out too, an element of morbid curiosity, I suppose... but Bernie, I have to say, did a fantastic job. People forget that, they think 'Oh, Bernie, that guy who stood in for Randy,' but they forget the fact that he's a great soulful guitarist. Not many I know could have stood that kind of pressure."

Musically, as others in this book have testified, the complexities and structure of the songs demanded respect. Bernie records the task he had in front of him. "I was continually terrified I was going to get lost, and because of the sound it could well have taken till the beginning of the next song to find out where I was! So I really only started getting into enjoying specific songs with which I felt at ease and more confident. 'Mr. Crowley' was probably first, then 'Flying High Again'. I loved 'Over The Mountain', but that scale in the beginning of the first verse was a nightmare at first. Out of seven gigs I probably got it right twice! I never really got into 'Revelation Mother Earth', 'Goodbye To Romance', 'Believer' or 'Steal Away'. I got to love 'Crazy Train'. Initially I found that really quite hard. I majorly hated 'Iron Man'. Beyond me why anyone likes that. My kids love it!"

In spite of the intensity of the songs and the production Bernie still manages to put this light-hearted observation on his onstage surroundings. "Tommy was a half a mile away up the great pyramid of Cheops, Don was like the house elf occasionally sticking his head out the castle window to empty the slops, I couldn't see him or hear him. Rudy would be thundering away in his own world on the other end of the football pitch going through the book of heavy metal bass-player poses. Other than that it was keep rolling at all costs and stay out of Ozzy's – and the dwarf's – way! Occasionally Ozzy communicated by pulling my hair or looking in panic at me because I probably had this what-the-fuck-happens-next expression on my face, but he was mostly really tied up with the audience, it was a full-on show.

"I had to regiment myself to do the shows, there was no choice in the circumstances. I did loosen up as time went on, but I did need to know what Randy had done to begin with. Knowing that, on some tracks I had started to go away from it, doing my own bits in places. I suppose 'Mr. Crowley' was the first track that I tried to stamp some identity on, but I was never really happy with the hammer-on solo, I'd have liked to have built on that. I am much more of a free-form player than Randy was, playing the same thing tends to bore me a bit, and then I don't play quite as well, quite on top of it. I need to be on the edge to play well, and with repetition or a formula I'm not on the edge. Some people shine at that, but it's not my strong point. Randy was definitely out of classical and Spanish, and amazing at it too. That was not my school."

Contending with more than most could endure, Bernie's senses were assailed when Ozzy pulled the same hair-pulling trick on the Irishman as he had on Randy night after night. Problem was, no-one had deigned to tell Bernie what was coming… "All I thought was 'Aaaaaargh! What the fuck's happening?!?' It's a strange thing that I didn't try to sock him or something, that's probably what you would normally do if someone pulls as hard as they can on your hair. I suppose I must have realised it was not serious, but the initial thing was that it was."

Ozzy Osbourne

Understandably though, the overwhelming thoughts were of Randy and a sense of unreality at dealing with the practicalities of getting through the shows and ultimately the tour. A musician lives for that moment onstage, that brief burst of artistic freedom and fulfillment of ego, but in the straitened emotional circumstances of this tour the work ethic quashed any such luxuries.

"I don't think that enthusiasm or euphoria came into it when I was there," Bernie says unashamedly. "It was get the job done and do it as best you can, I think, for everybody in the band. I don't think they really wanted to play at all at that stage. But if you play you sometimes get lost in it, you forget, and if that happened they probably looked up and expected to see Randy. It must have been hard."

For obvious reasons the outlandish excess and vivacity one would normally associate with Ozzy Osbourne was conspicuous by its absence. The sheer weight of losing Randy threatened to turn Ozzy's tourbus into a mobile bunker. "Ozzy's dressing room was not exactly a barrel of laughs," Bernie says sombrely. "Sharon didn't allow any alcohol (or other recreational substances obviously) at all in the dressing room, or on the bus for that matter. Not even a can of beer. It was like an old people's church outing or something. *Not* very rock 'n' roll. No one was very happy, that's obvious in the circumstances. Rudy sat and practiced with his Roland bass synthesizer in one room, doing awesome Stanley Clarke impressions – slapping from hell – really stunning stuff, while Ozzy and Sharon sat in the other room and moaned about him making a racket. It was all pretty grim. I understand they had a lot on their minds, but I couldn't deal with it, it was a wasteland that dressing room, about as inviting as a night on the Siberian tundra.

"I had a bit of a brain problem about all of the 'not being allowed to': I was Irish, I was 30 – Randy had died the day after my 30th birthday – and I could not quite mentally accept being treated like I was a 10-year-old. I'm from Dublin, and it's part of my culture that I like a drink. It was like trying to deprive a Rasta of his ganja. I couldn't spiritually connect with the source without my Guinness... I found it all a bit tense. I have a total aversion to being told how to live my life, that is not what I got into playing rock 'n' roll for. I don't get fucked-up, I don't let people down onstage, but I don't regard it as part of any gig being told how to live offstage."

With alcohol strictly off the agenda Bernie sought solace elsewhere. In dire need of a watering hole and lighter company Don Airey suggested the guitarist introduce himself to some fellow-travellers. "Don told me to go down and say hello to UFO in their dressing room, must have been the second or third gig or so. Pete, Paul, Phil, all of them, they were all great, gave me a few cans of beer, made me feel at home and human: a few beers and a bit of a laugh, it was all I needed, it saved my sanity for quite a few days. I love them to death, great bunch."

It must be remembered that although Ozzy was topping the bill, UFO were far from a support band – they were onboard more as special guests. The band's support in certain areas of America approached that of an arena headlining band, a reputation built on a steady upward climb of album sales topped by the awesome live outing *Strangers In The Night*. With these Ozzy dates UFO were promoting the sleeker and more radio-friendly sound of *The Wild, The Willing And The Innocent*. The band's capacity for intoxication and subsequent offstage tomfoolery was already legendary. "I got on well with them, loved watching them too, tottering about the stage." Bernie remarks fondly. "Great band, really entertaining, right up my street."

With Bernie in place merely to plug a gap, the race to find a permanent replacement was feverish. Over in California Brad Gillis was pushing his band Ranger. Although history records that Ranger would evolve into the multi-platinum success story of Nightranger, at the time Gillis and his colleagues were finding it tough going.

"We had spent a couple of years getting demos together and playing around the Bay Area honing our live show", he relates. "It was kind of a problem, getting a record deal, because we were a little heavier than normal, with songs like 'Don't Tell Me You Love Me' and 'Can't Find Me A Thrill'. I actually started another band called The Almeida All Stars. We were playing locally

Ozzy Osbourne

around the Bay Area and we were doing Ozzy, Blue Oyster Cult and Bad Company tunes around the night club circuit, trying to keep myself busy, keep my chops up. Meanwhile, Nightranger kept trying to get a record deal. We were actually doing two of Ozzy's songs at that time".

Brad became aware of the tragedy of Randy's death in the same way as most Americans. "I'd heard on the radio that a plane crashed and Randy Rhoads was killed. That totally blew me away." It was all the more poignant for Gillis as, not only being an aspiring rock guitarist, he had, been a fan. Brad had caught the Ozzy show at the 'Day In The Green' outdoor festival in Oakland a matter of weeks beforehand. "In the back of my mind, I thought 'Gee... I wonder who they're going to replace him with?' Anyway, I'm doing this All Stars gig, doing my Ozzy tunes and this guy came in, a friend of mine, checking me out."

The friend was Preston Thrall, brother of the renowned guitarist Pat Thrall. "Pat Thrall played with Tommy Aldridge in the Travers set-up. Tommy Aldridge was of course playing drums with Ozzy Osbourne at the time. Anyway, there's the connection. After the show that night, Preston comes up and said 'Man, I should let my brother know you would fit right in and to get a hold of Tommy about landing you the gig with Ozzy'. I thought 'Sure, like *that's* going to happen.' I said 'Well, go ahead and we'll see what happens.' That was on the Friday night."

Unbeknown to Brad, wheels were set in motion immediately upon Preston Thrall's recommendation. "Sunday morning, I get a phone call, early in the morning, waking me up and there is this English lady saying, 'Bradley?' I'm like, 'Yeah...?' She says, 'This is Sharon Arden, Ozzy Osbourne's manager, and we'd like to know if you'd want to fly to New York to audition for the band?' I'm going 'w*ho is this?*'"

The guitarist had quickly but wrongly surmised he was the victim of a prank call. "She says, 'No, it's Sharon. Would you like to talk to Ozzy?' I said 'Yeah! Put Ozzy on the phone!' This Englishman's voice says, 'Hello Bradley?' and you know when you talk long distance, or at least back in '82, there was a delay in the phone line? I could tell it was long distance."

Hair By Sarzo Of Cuba

Reality sank in and the full enormity of the telephone call was beginning to strike home. Gillis concluded he really was in conversation with Ozzy Osbourne.

"After speaking with him after a minute or so he says, 'Get a piece of paper and a pencil and I want you to write down the songs that I want you to learn.' All of a sudden, I started believing that it was Ozzy and I started trembling. I thought, *oh my God, this is for real!* I got a piece of paper and he named all the songs and said, 'Would you be available to fly out on Tuesday?' Here it was Sunday morning and I said, 'Oh yeah. Sure. I don't know if I can learn 19 songs by Tuesday...' He says, 'No, no, no, learn what you can. Come on out and you can work out here'.

"Sure enough they send me a ticket to fly me out on Tuesday. I ended up getting all the albums because back then, there were no CDs! I found all the songs and started learning the material".

By the next Tuesday as planned Gillis found himself in New York. He had been told that Bernie Tormé was deputizing but assumed he would be pitched into a cattle-call audition process. He was wrong; the night of his arrival Ozzy Osbourne was playing at the prestigious Madison Square Garden with a reluctant guitarist who in all honesty just wanted to go home. The gig Randy had so looked forward to but never got to see. "Oh, how I wished I would've done that gig..." recalls an awestruck Gillis. With the enormity of the situation bearing down on him, the guitarist joined the entourage. However, his first impression left him a little disconcerted.

"A limo driver had picked me up at the airport and took me to the Helmsley Palace Hotel" he remembers. "I went to check in and there's no room under my name! Ooops... they gave me a one-way ticket and I had $150 in my pocket, and the room was $135... So... I had to pay cash for it. That left $15 in my pocket!" Maybe this was all an elaborate hoax after all.

Understandably concerned, he duly checked in awaiting some recognition of his arrival. "There was no-one around from the Osbourne entourage because they were all at Madison Square Gardens. I basically just went to my room and waited. Sure enough, about midnight I get a phone call from the road manager saying, "Hey! Come on up and meet Ozzy." I thought, "Wow, this is it... Cool." I went up to the penthouse and there were press, media, radio, and rock stars everywhere!"

This initial impression reinforced, Brad surmised that he was about to be put through his paces in a tough process of elimination. "It pretty much looked like there were about 20 or 30 long-haired musician/guitar player types in there, auditioning for the gig. I was thinking; 'oh, great. Competition.' A big auditioning process. I met Larry McNinny, the road manager, and said 'You know I had to pay for my own room!' and he handed me five crisp $100 bills and said 'This should keep yuh happy.' I said, 'Yeah, that'll work'."

With at least his fiscal worries now set at ease, the guitarist laughed and asked the obvious question. "'How many people here are auditioning?' He replies, 'No, no, it's just you, Brad. If you can't cut the gig, then we'll send you home and get somebody else.' Well, no pressure there!"

Then came Brad's first meeting with Ozzy himself. The urgency of the situation dictated that the pair got down to business without delay. "I went downstairs and grabbed my red Strat from my room and came back up to the suite.

"He said, 'What song do you want to play?' I said, 'Well... 'Flying High Again' and so he sang it and I played my guitar, no amp at all. I came to the solo, played all the solo parts and he jumped up, gave me a big hug and said, 'Bradley, I love you. Pull me through!' The mood in the room lifted immediately to one of sheer relief. Not just for the guitarist either, he had already got a sense of the anguish his new employer was enduring. "He was having a hard time, you know, going through the tragedy of losing Randy Rhoads."

Now officially 'in', Brad Gillis then set about applying his craft to his new-found surroundings. "I hung out for four or five days on the road around the New York area, sitting in my room every day, with a live Randy Rhoads tape that the sound man had recorded a few weeks before Randy's death, so I could check out all the segués between songs."

Bernie Tormé describes the moment he surmised a successor

was waiting in the wings. "I think someone had told me about Brad initially, and he came up to me and said hello when we were having breakfast someplace, maybe Rhode Island, maybe New Haven. I know I baled out just after Madison Square Garden, because we were staying at the Helmsley Palace in New York at the time. I really was not enjoying it, and I think I was aware of Brad being carried as an insurance policy at that point. I think they were very worried that I would just say 'fuck it' and leave, because that's what was said I had done in Gillan, coupled with my lack of enthusiasm for the long-term gig. Of course there was no way I would have done that.

"Initially I think I felt a bit unhappy about him being there, but really it was par for the course in the situation, and after I saw him playing somewhere backstage I realised that this could lead to a situation that made everybody happy."

Tormé is quick to praise Gillis: "we never jammed, I think we did a bit of twiddling around together backstage, his four-note hammer-ons blew me away; he, like Randy, was much better at those than I was at that time. He was a nice guy. He obviously had not been around the block too many times. Bright-eyed and bushy tailed! Very straight and to the point, which I liked. A good guitarist."

With Brad Gillis in place and Bernie Tormé treading the boards, there were however still other names under consideration as Don Airey confirms. "Ray Gomez played with us in New York, and maybe Earl Slick was in there somewhere." Bernie Tormé confirms; "I was told by Don after the Madison Square Garden gig on the 5th that he had auditioned Earl Slick at the venue on the afternoon of the gig. They didn't let me go to the venue to soundcheck because of this, which really pissed me off majorly at the time."

Oblivious at the time to the media circus surrounding the Ozzy circus Ray Gomez relays the tale from his standpoint. "One morning, I got a call from a writer, a guy who wrote for a New York magazine. It was a very strange thing. He asked me if I would like to play Madison Square Garden with Ozzy Osbourne!"

As if this wasn't enough his friend then dropped a further

bombshell "You'll have about 36 hours to do it he said. Apparently Ozzy wanted a change. I think Rudy, maybe someone else, strongly suggested to call me." It was actually Tommy Aldridge who put the word in.

"I suggested the call to Ray," says the drummer. "I do remember Rudy and I getting together with Ray at some point. It's a bit sketchy actually!"

The guitarist's retained knowledge of his pre-Ozzy collusion with Sarzo and Aldridge is more than a bit fuzzy too. "I think I hung out with Rudy and Tommy more so than jammed. We almost played on a couple of occasions. Could've been for a project called Taxi, I think." Whatever the circumstances of previous liaisons or proposed projects, Ozzy's rhythm section had good cause to suggest Gomez.

Born in Casablanca of Moroccan descent and having been touted as a jazz guitar child prodigy in Spain, Ray Gomez was much in demand behind the scenes during the '70s. An attempt at forming an ill-fated 'supergroup' with future Ozzy drummer Carmine Appice and ex-Yes man Bill Bruford had faltered, but studio credits with John Lennon, Stanley Clarke, Herbie Hancock and Narada Michael Walden had bolstered his reputation.

Striking out on the solo trail Gomez launched a 1980 album, *Volume,* which was involved in a CBS promotion alongside the debut Joe Perry Project album. Upon their release in Britain, buyers purchasing either record were entitled to a free cardboard guitar at the point of purchase.

The album featured Rick Derringer, Axis and Black Sabbath drummer Vinnie Appice, as well as mystic funk icon and drum phenomenon Narada Michael Walden on percussion. Will Lee and Blackjack's Jimmy Haslip supplied bass. By the time of *Volume's* release Gomez had already established an enviable reputation among fellow musicians. Don Airey confirms that Ray Gomez was under serious consideration for the Ozzy post and simply describes the guitarist as "a wonderful player".

The possible inclusion of Gomez was not as outlandish as it seemed at first. "All the rock guys knew of the fusion players"

Hair By Sarzo Of Cuba

Ray states. "I'm a rock/blues/fusion guy so it would have worked no problem. Also, I was told that Randy used to really like my playing a lot. That was very nice to hear."

Next came the meeting. "I was asked to call the Waldorf Astoria hotel in New York. I spoke to Sharon and she invited me to dinner with Ozzy and Rudy. We just hung out really. Ozzy was, erm...out there. I don't know if he actually ate – there was some brandy on the table for sure! It was a surreal event."

Ray recalls the practicalities of the issue. "I was asked to learn a full set of high energy material in basically 24 hours. I said I'd give it a shot but it was tight. The playing style was not much of a problem – it was just transmitting that balls-to-the-wall rock sound. The energy and the sound of what I was doing was similar. It was not a loose blues gig; there were a lot of structured riffs to learn. It was all pretty much arranged."

As it transpired the Ozzy camp weighed up the risks and opted for Gillis. "They worked it out with Brad," relates Ray. "It was a tough thing but I think it just settled. In the end I think there was no guarantee it would work, the risk was too great. I did start learning songs though just in case."

The actual Madison Square Garden gig itself would become a permanent fixture in Bernie Tormé's memory not due to the scale of the occasion but because of a near-fatal incident involving Sharon Osbourne. With the show about to commence, the band members were positioned behind swift-drop Kabuki curtains behind their own castle gate portcullis. Ozzy was underneath the central pyramid awaiting his grand entrance.

Bernie takes up the tale. "So, I'm trapped in the portcullis, the intro music is playing. They had a Kabuki curtain hanging up. I've had no soundcheck due to massed guitarists being auditioned before the gig – including Earl Slick – so I'm not a happy camper."

With the intro tape still rolling, a foolhardy individual in the audience launched a maroon onto the stage. The device bounced off the boards and hit Sharon Osbourne foursquare in the neck and exploded on impact.

"Bang and flash," recollects Tormé. "I haven't seen Sharon,

who has just come out of the pyramid. So we're about ten seconds to Kabuki drop, 30 seconds to portcullis lifting time, and I see three or four crew carrying a prostrate Sharon about three feet in front of my portcullis with blood pumping from her throat. They carry her off. Man, I thought she was dead. The show starts. 'Over The Mountain'... I spent the entire show looking at Ozzy wondering if he knew his missus might be dead when he came off stage. He knew nothing about it. But there was no time to say or do anything till the show was over, it was such a tight show."

(Thankfully, Sharon, although her injuries required stitches, was relatively unharmed.) "It looked worse than it was. And Madison Square Garden was a great show incidentally, I really enjoyed it, even with the above having gone down. I played OK too."

As the tour rumbled on Brad Gillis had imposed upon himself an intensive and perfectionist regime. "I was inside my room... oh geez... 12 hours a day just playing my guitar and learning all the riffs. On the fifth day Ozzy came up to me. 'Let me know when you're ready 'cause Bernie wants to go home.' he said." Brad told Ozzy he was.

It had taken only four gigs: Bethlehem, Boston, New Haven and New York Madison Square Garden for Bernie to convince himself beyond doubt that he could assist Ozzy no more. He called Ozzy and Sharon in their hotel room the day after the Madison Square Garden gig and requested a meeting in his room.

"I said that I didn't feel I was the right person to do the gig, I wasn't enjoying it, and I wanted them to find an alternative, and as soon as they had, I wanted out. I found it very difficult to verbalise a precise reason why I did not want to stay, I still do, it was just a lack of happiness with the overall vibe, that's always difficult to justify." Bernie believes that Sharon, no doubt having seen this conversation as somewhat inevitable, took the news better than Ozzy.

The discussion then got a little 'odd': "Sharon said something strange about it being understandable because it was not my type of music. I've still got no idea what she was talking about, maybe she was just trying to grease the wheels and not hurt Ozzy, maybe she was remembering the Punk band I had had on Jet in '77... I've no idea really.

"It was a bit bizarre, funny even, 'cause I loved the music, it was right up my street, a bit like Gillan with tunes and fewer keyboard solos. Very close to my ideal stuff. Anyway, I dorked a bit at that, and then thought that I would grease the wheels and agreed. Not really my kind of music? What the fuck, there didn't seem to be much to be gained in arguing the point at that stage. It was a bit like we were speaking a different language. Ozzy probably thought I wanted to go off and study ukulele or something, funny in retrospect. Apart from that they were very understanding and kind."

The meeting closed with due thanks on both sides and a touch of characteristic modesty from the singer. "Ozzy said that he was very grateful to me, he said that I had really saved the tour and his career. He was just great about it, really appreciative. It was very nice of him to say that, but looking back it obviously was not true. Ozzy's pretty indestructible, and people love him to an unbelievable extent. That was so obvious at the gigs, that's what kept him going, and if it hadn't been me it would have been someone else, maybe a few days later, whatever, but the fact is the thing was going to carry on, that had been decided before I was even asked."

Three further gigs would follow: Providence, Buffalo and Rochester. Glen Falls was scheduled but cancelled. "Having told them I wanted to leave, everything seemed to go into very slow motion. They didn't seem to want to audition Brad and make the jump for ages. It was almost as if while I was prepared to stay they went around auditioning everyone possible, but after I decided I wanted to walk the plank they got temporary regrets, cold feet, whatever, wanted to hang on to the devil they knew. Brad was hanging around for quite a few days. I really had to almost talk Don into giving him a try. I suppose the band were not keen to go through all of the shit of someone new again. Don tried to talk me into staying."

Ozzy Osbourne

Unbeknown to Bernie his successor had been decided upon much earlier although, as Brad admits, the learning curve was vertiginously steep. "I only had a chance to play six or seven songs at the soundcheck with the band, before my first gig in Binghampton, New York, sold out with 7,000 people." Brad recollects nostalgically. "All the other songs, I'd never even played with the band before that first night."

Bernie Tormé backs this up and concedes that he had been asked to wait side-stage just in case. Nobody need have worried; "the band eventually auditioned Brad just before the Binghampton gig, they were happy, and I stayed for the first gig in case he didn't cut it on stage. It was quite a little gig, no stage show, and he was excellent, closer to Randy than me. More West Coast technique than Irish/British filth. Perfect."

Fortunately the American newcomer's debut gig came without the added burden of a Bernie Tormé-style image makeover. "When Brad did his first gig I think he cracked that one and wore a white boiler-suit!" Bernie laughs.

Besides his fashion statement Brad's first test under fire was particularly memorable. "That was quite an experience. I screwed up on one song called 'Revelation, Mother Earth'. I went into the fast part too soon and Ozzy looked at me with that evil look like '*You screwed up!*' I caught myself and got back into place and finished out the night, and did well!"

With the gig wrapped and a huge weight lifted from many shoulders by Brad's performance that night, Ozzy would bid farewell to Bernie Tormé. "Ozzy came up to me and asked me how much money would help me set up my band and tour in the UK. He had mentioned something about it beforehand, but I hadn't really taken it seriously. I said I really didn't know, and he asked if some big bucks would help. I was totally gobsmacked, and said yes, of course."

The singer took Bernie to the coach that provided the on-the-road base for the tour's accountant and promptly requested a cheque made out to Bernie for said big bucks. "The guy looked at Ozzy and literally said 'but you can't do that', recalls a staggered Tormé. "Ozzy repeated it, getting a bit pissed off, and the

Hair By Sarzo Of Cuba

guy wrote me the cheque. I could not believe it. What a gentleman. I then asked him if I could buy the blue-green Strat off him, which Ozzy had paid for in Los Angeles as a spare. It cost about $2000, a 64 L series. He just told me to take it as a present. Unbelievable."

Bernie Tormé flew home on April 14th. Randy Rhoads had been dead for just 26 days.

Seven gigs, a fortnight out of his life, all held in a maelstrom of raw emotion he'd never known. Bernie tries to summarise: "I really don't think I was the right guy for them to ask. I was really uncomfortable about replacing Randy; it seemed to me that what I was doing didn't show sufficient respect from me for him as a person or for his death. People are different, and I could not get away from feeling that at the time, and I still couldn't. It may not have bothered many, but it did bother me. In contradiction to that I was very glad to help Ozzy and the band get over what has to have been one of the most difficult points in their careers, if not in their lives. And I was very proud as a gunslinger to be asked, and to pull it off. But the only way I could personally reconcile the irreconcilable was to be temporary, and I probably used a lot of peripheral shit to justify that, the way you do. Looking back on it, none of that peripheral stuff was very important after all, it could all have been put on hold."

Misconceptions regarding the terms and conditions of his tenure, added to a liberal sprinkling of plain old bad journalism, would hound Bernie during and after his experience with Ozzy and the guitarist feels he was treated unfairly for not persevering. "I got quite a lot of shit at the time back in the UK for not carrying on, both in the press and personally. People seemed to think I was being bigheaded and arrogant for not carrying on, but that was a load of bollocks. It was like, how dare a humble worm like me say no to the great Ozzy. But it wasn't at all like that. Obviously it would have been a better career move to stay, I had no illusions about that, but I just couldn't do it, it wasn't for me in the great scheme of things."

Contact between the Osbournes and Tormé since has been fleeting although Ozzy has in various interviews freely voiced his admiration for Bernie since and his praise has been unqualified.

"I met Ozzy again a couple of times in the '80s, not too long after, at Liverpool when Pete Way was playing bass…and again at a drinking club in North London! I bumped into Sharon about a year ago at a *Kerrang!* magazine do, I went up and said hello. I think she thought she'd seen a ghost, she seemed very nervous. Nice to see her again, though."

With a little under a year's worth of touring with the Ozzy Osbourne band stretching before him, Brad Gillis soon got into his stride. "I started touring and did better and better every night," the guitarist maintains. "I got more comfortable with the material and learned how to swing my guitar neck back and forth and play at the same time – Rudy taught me that. After about two weeks of touring and playing, we did a live broadcast from Memphis, Tennessee, the 'King Biscuit Flower Hour – Live Ozzy Osbourne' and that's when the whole country was able to hear me, the fans and my friends back home. That's when I started getting a little respect. I kicked butt that night. I played very well and after that, things went smooth."

10
Way To Go

Taking over from Don Airey on keyboards came the familiar figure of Lindsay Bridgwater, recalled for service with Ozzy for the second time.

Don Airey would go on to make his mark as a sessionman extraordinaire. By 1985 he was back helping out Gary Moore for his *Out In The Fields* record. Lindsay Bridgwater found work with Budgie, who were buoyed by their signing to RCA Records and the strength of their album *Nightflight*. Budgie hit the road with vigour, Bridgwater assuming keyboard duties, most notably for a successful string of shows in Poland during 1982. The keyboard player would then be re-summoned to the Ozzy camp.

Bridgwater admits that he got off on the wrong foot with Brad Gillis. "It was never going to be the same experience again after Randy Rhoads had gone. Brad was doing a great job but I admit I initially approached this new band in the wrong way. I was still carrying too many memories of Randy. I remember starting to show Brad some pieces and he turned to me and said something like 'No, you've got to play them this way'. I was really resentful because Randy had showed me those parts... too territorial. Although I admitted my actions were immature, the thing is the memories of Randy and me working out those parts was still with me. Brad did a fantastic job all round but Randy could never really be replaced by anyone."

Bridgwater would view his 1982 Ozzy campaign in a different light to his erstwhile tenure. "I wanted to be more involved this time around simply because I loved the music. Coming in to fill Don's place was odd because he was a star in his own right and had been more forthright in his approach and so had made it easier for me second time around. He actually took the keyboard role to another plane altogether. So, I kind of felt the need to co-ordinate everybody which of course I could fulfil because I had been once around the block already. I think for that second time I became more of an integral part of the rhythm section, part of the machine. Gradually I came to the fore. I even would go out and take my bow at the end of the evening!"

"I loved the *Diary* album, personally" states Lindsay Bridgwater. "For a musician to listen to it gives a different perspective of course, but it truly is a wonderful record. I was only sorry we never got to play more songs from it."

There would be another new face in the entourage too. That of the renowned UFO bassist Pete Way. Recently having split away from his immediate post-UFO project Fastway, a union with ex-Motorhead guitarist 'Fast' Eddie Clarke, Way clambered onboard for Ozzy's European dates. His reputation preceded him – Way's larger-than-life persona had, apart from Phil Lynott, probably added more charisma to the role of bassman than anyone else in rock.

Since the age of 16 Way had been recklessly cavorting across UFO stages displaying postures and poses that hardened yoga instructors can only dream of, often in states of chemical inebriation that would have the Surgeon General reeling. Despite all this, Way laid claim to having played a major hand in crafting some of British heavy metal's greatest recordings – *Phenomenon*, *Obsession*, *Lights Out* and, of course, *Strangers In The Night*. All this would be pulled off whilst wearing some of the most outrageous custom striped or diamond-backed stage uniforms known to man. He began the mental sweepstake among fans at UFO gigs – *who will fall over first?* Way, Mogg or Tonka? Very often it would be all three.

Way believes he first hooked up with Ozzy backstage at an early UFO show in Birmingham but would cement their friendship at the Nomis rehearsal studios upfront of the debut Blizzard Of Ozz dates in 1980.

"Ozzy is the same character as I am, essentially" reckons Way. "So, when we got to Nomis and found the Ozzy band there we just had a great, great time. Ozzy is such a great, great man. He shares the same love of rock 'n' roll as I do, so we clicked instantly. It was an odd combination of bands in there at the time and at any one time you would see the pool table with The Clash, Elvis Costello, UFO and Ozzy's band on it. Actually, I spent a lot of the time in a daze thinking 'Fuckin' hell – I'm drinking with the God of rock n' roll'!

The camaraderie set in place at Nomis would be rekindled two years later. Way had sensationally quit UFO over musical differences, notably concerning the *Mechanix* album. Fastway seemed a good bet but Way received a rude awakening one day with a knock at the door.

"There was a lawyer standing there from Chrysalis Records telling me I could not sign to CBS. They placed an injunction on me so I was stuck. I'd enjoyed working with Eddie, I'd co-written the Fastway album, rehearsed the songs and CBS had put in big money but I couldn't do a thing. I had to sign off on everything."

Between the rock and the hard place, Way was saved by a phone call.

"It was Ozzy. Out of the kindness of his heart he simply said 'Come and play bass with me.' So that's what I did. I didn't expect a salary or anything. I think Sharon was interested because I had proven writing skills with UFO which may have come in handy later. I was just relieved. The God of rock 'n' roll had taken pity on a poor destitute bass player!"

Pete believes Ozzy's call to arms was purely altruistic. "Maybe Ozzy thought I looked better naked than Bob Daisley? I dunno, I was the wrong man for that band. I'm not an Ozzy player and really, the only reason I was there because both Sharon and Ozzy have a big heart. The very last thing Tommy Aldridge needed to deal with was me – not that he made it easy for me though. In truth I didn't play the Ozzy songs very well. Brad was a great guitar player – very, very underrated. He's a very talented man and a nice guy too.

I tried hard but we had just one day's rehearsal for me to learn the songs and the rest of it was catch-up in hotel rooms with Lindsay. He was a cool guy, focused on the job of teaching me but Tommy, well, I guess he resented having a junkie for a bass player and who can blame him? At the time I thought that he could have given me more of a chance, I could really have used his coaching, but looking back I guess I can see it more through his eyes."

Stylistically, too, Pete maintains the pieces simply didn't fit. "Onstage I would just be doing my best but I was struggling. I was totally addicted to heroin at the time. My style is more Sid Vicious than Geddy Lee, I'm not precious about the craft, I'm into the rock 'n' roll. Anyway, it was enough for me to share the same stage as Ozzy. Just seeing him working the crowd. That was just awesome."

Bridgwater's overriding memories of his second term of Ozz duty with Pete Way are ones of musical achievement and friendship. "Brad had got comfortable in the role very quickly. He really had developed his own niche and was excelling at it. Pete, having come in at what seemed like very short notice, was doing his very best in a very short space of time. He was a lovely guy, very professional. I never really understood this thing about him being the wild man. I suppose he must have been because even Ozzy said to me once 'if you think I'm wild, you should see Pete in action.'

"All I ever saw of him though was the perfect gentleman. We would often spend nights in hotel rooms going through the songs piece by piece. Pete really wanted to get it right. The songs were a lot more complex with more time changes than he had been used to with UFO. With the way Randy wrote, being so brimful of ideas, there were probably as many riffs in one Ozzy song than on an entire album from another band."

Way was in fact becoming the centre of frantic activity at probably the lowest physical ebb of his life. The bassist had ignited a blitzkrieg of activity by his baling out of UFO and after the Fastway fiasco the press were now eager to learn of any inevitable Ozzy/Way shenanigans. To top it all, Pete found the time to produce albums for two tearaway acts, The Cockney Rejects and Twisted Sister. All this whilst dealing with a major habit.

Way, even after all these years, is still keen to express his thanks to Ozzy and Sharon for the lifeline they threw him in 1982. "Sharon was fantastic. I wish she was looking after me now – although I don't think I'd marry her!" he laughs. "I totally admire that woman for everything she's done – not just for

Way To Go

Ozzy but for rock 'n' roll in general. She's the Hillary Clinton of rock. Sharon totally took the stress off Ozzy. They've both got great vision and, although you hear about all the business side with them, really the reason they do it is because they just have a great love of rock 'n' roll.

"The thing I learnt is that they really look after the people who matter. If you're there for them they'll return the favour one hundred times over. Ozzy rides greatness. He really does. He's like me in one sense – we're both sentenced to play rock 'n' roll. I'm just totally honoured I got the chance not just to drink with him but play with him. I had a totally awesome time and they paid me very, very well for the privilege."

With the closure of the European dates Way took his own path, creating one of rock 'n' roll's most suitably titled bands – Waysted. Debuting with the 1983 opus *Vices* [sic], Waysted, fuelled by the band leader's full-blown smack addiction, proceeded to somehow stumble through a succession of quality albums.

11
Enter Jake

Turning a problem into an opportunity, Ozzy solved his dilemma of delivering another album under contract to Don Arden and simultaneously delivered a hammer blow to Black Sabbath. The *Speak Of The Devil* live record, titled *Talk Of The Devil* outside of America and recorded September 26th and 27th at the Ritz venue in New York, would, in terms of media print alone, squash Sabbath's own live offering *Live Evil*.

Delivered in November of 1982 *Speak Of The Devil's* ace up the sleeve was breathtakingly audacious and oh, so simple. Ozzy had cut an entire double album of Black Sabbath songs served up so raw the veins were still pumping and the nerves still twitching when the meat hit the taste buds.

In contrast Iommi and Dio bickered publicly over mixing minutiae and the results of their labours lumbered out in January of 1983. Not only that but Ozzy had stolen a march and got to the church first. As a newly shaven-headed Ozzy took to the live circuit once again, *Live Evil* plateaued at Number 37 in America.

Tommy Aldridge records some swipes in his direction as part of the fallout. "I did hear that after doing the live album of Sabbath material that I recorded with Ozzy, Butler and Iommi weren't impressed with the performance. That was certainly their prerogative as it was their material. I've always been hired to play the way that I play and not try to 'copy' someone else. With the greatest respect to Bill Ward, I chose to play those songs, while still trying to faithfully represent them, in my own style. I think they were maybe a little offended by that. That's unfortunate but...you gotta like what you like."

The crafting of the live album, though, was apparently not a spontaneous decision as discussions with Randy Rhoads' confidant Kelly Garni revealed. "Randy spoke to me about this, it was a big ticker for him. Ozzy had wanted Randy to do an album of Black Sabbath songs but Randy really didn't want to do it. He objected because he was actually really bothered by playing that stuff. I'll never forget when I saw him play live with Ozzy he

Enter Jake

warned me that he was going to be playing some Black Sabbath numbers. I can quote him word for word – 'OK, Don't laugh, we do a couple of Black Sabbath songs.' He hated telling me that, he had this embarrassed grin on his face and he was looking down at the floor all embarrassed. Well, I did laugh at him!"

With Gillis re-prioritizing Nightranger, to subsequent huge success it must be said, the Ozzy band was in need of fresh blood. Enter Jake E. Lee.

Jake E. Lee (or, to give him his real name Jakey Lou Williams) had been raised in West Virginia by his American Naval officer father and Japanese mother. In later life the Williams family had relocated with the military to Imperial Beach, California. His musical upbringing had centred upon a regime of enforced piano lessons but his elder sister would lure the young Jake into the big bad world of rock 'n' roll with her album collection. Sadly for Jake, his sister would lose her life in a motorbike accident. At school Jake had been an outsider, his untypically long hair and obsession with guitar playing setting him apart from the other kids. His first band, Teaser, named after the Tommy Bolin album, was conceived at the Mar Vista High School. Legend has it Lee would be expelled from school for a series of misdemeanours including punching a teacher who objected to the loudness of his guitar playing by pulling the plug on his guitar amp.

As Teaser elevated themselves from school gigs to dates on the local San Diego club circuit Lee would strike up a rapport with Enforcer guitarist Warren De Martini. Another encounter was with one Stephen Pearcy, lead singer of Mickey Ratt. The late '70s found Lee experimenting with a number of jazz-rock-fusion bands and whilst pursuing this avenue the guitarist would audition for a new band which Jerry Goodman, violinist with the Mahavishnu Orchestra, was assembling. Lee didn't get the job. Before long Jake, shifting base to Hollywood, was in the ranks of Pearcy's band which in time had evolved into simply Ratt. Club gigs at such infamous venues as The Roxy, The Whiskey and The Troubadour ensued but Lee would decamp, suggesting his friend De Martini as an able substitute.

Ozzy Osbourne

Lee had a fleeting tenure with the Greg Leon Invasion. The band was centred on guitarist Greg Leon who had claims to fame with early incarnations of both Dokken and Dubrow, but Jake would soon take a career sidestep, as Rough Cutt frontman Paul Shortino relates;

"Almost all the members of Rough Cutt were in Ratt at one point. We were rehearsing at the Starwood Club when it was closed down." The incarnation of Rough Cutt that Jake would join numbered Shortino, guitarist Bob Dalilis, bassist Joe Cristo (an ex-Ratt man), keyboard player Claude 'Steel' Schnell and drummer Dave Alfred. "Dave said he knew a guitar player who would be great for the band" records Paul. "Jake had just quit Ratt and was looking for a new project. Dave asked him to jam with us and the next thing you know, Jake is in the band!"

With former Rainbow and Black Sabbath man Ronnie James Dio taking Rough Cutt under his wing for both production and career guidance, the band entered the studio to demo. Two songs from these sessions, 'A Little Kindness' and 'Used And Abused', would surface on the 1983 Backhouse compilation *L.A.'s Hottest Unsigned Rock Bands*.

"Jake's style of guitar was so different from a lot of players out there. Jake has great vibrato and technique and is a great showman," Shortino opines. "Ronnie was thinking of using him for his record. We were playing the Hollywood club circuit at the time and Jake had heard Ozzy was looking for a guitar player. Jake asked Wendy Dio if she could get him an audition for the

---

Author's note: The 2000 release 'Before And Laughter 'supposedly includes Jake E. Lee-era Ratt material but this is hotly disputed by the guitarist who claims he never recorded anything with Ratt beyond rehearsal tapes. The debut self-financed Ratt single 'Dr. Rock' does not feature Jake.

Author's note: After two Invasion mid-'80s albums and brief sojourns with Rough Cutt, Marshall Law and – allegedly – Dio, Leon was still plugging away in 1997 with Wishing Well.

Enter Jake

spot and she did. Jake got the gig and the rest is history. He was offered a great spot with a 'rock legend'. It was a great move for his career. In my heart, we parted as friends and I could only wish him good fortune."

Managed by Wendy Dio's Niji organization, Rough Cutt's future held promise. A collection of strong riff heavy songs and the characteristic vocal chimes of Paul Shortino made the band an exciting proposition. With such an obvious talent Lee's obvious next step would be Dio itself. Lee and Ronnie worked up material for what would eventually emerge as the debut Dio record *Holy Diver* before Irishman Vivian Campbell took the reins.

Jake E. Lee's enrolment into the Ozzy stable came courtesy of another player who had already featured significantly in the Ozzy timeline – original bass player Dana Strum. "I got a call from Sharon and Ozzy's attorney Fred Ansis," relates Strum who felt at the time he was being treated with kid gloves. "I was treated very nicely. Sharon had done her best to make all of the past bad vibe just go away. As it stood she knew that I was 'unpaid' in a sense."

The call came out of the blue; Strum recalls that hearing of Randy's death he cried himself to sleep and felt a heavy burden of misplaced guilt. The memories that came flooding back of earlier times at the Le Parc were now being put sharply into focus.

Strum was soon to find himself back in familiar territory. "Sharon put me onto Ozzy who asked if I had any great guitarists up my sleeve. Mike Jensen, a long-time Ozzy PR man, got me involved in the pitch to do a Los Angeles guitar round-up. It felt like time had stood still."

Strum's enthusiasm took over and he got to work. "I thought that George Lynch was the guy and called him." This is when George learnt that his manager at the time of Ozzy's first guitarist auditions had never brokered the subject of Dana and Ozzy's interest in him.

"I worked with each guy on the phone," Strum recalls. "I could prep them for what was to be a fill-in spot to keep Ozzy on tour as well as to go on and write. Ozzy was very concerned that any new guy could be a good riff writer as well." Once worked out and ground rules established, the bass player set up studio sessions in North Hollywood.

Strum was not originally slated to play at the session but having organised the whole event and being a bass player Ozzy got the jam rolling.

"Ozzy said to me – 'Get up there. You know you want to,' Strum remembers. "So we – George, Ozzy, Tommy and me – jammed to 'Crazy Train, and 'I Don't Know' and some more fun shit. It was the second wave!" Decisions were made and Strum was instructed to deliver the good news.

"I was told that George had got it. I was even told to tell him he had it and that he was going to England or on the road. George had quit his job and was into doing it big time."

"George Lynch was on fire," he exclaims. "A great player. But, the other stand-out guy was Jake. He was late and with a girl in tow but nonetheless he was damn good. He played a number of styles that shocked me. From his background you just would never have thought…"

It was a delicate situation. George Lynch had not only believed he had got the gig but had been told so.

Strum takes up the story. "It was a good bit late and no-one in the room was thinking other than George had got it. That included George and his then wife Christy who was also there. Then Jake showed up; Ozzy and Sharon liked his image and vibe, the whole Crüe/ Ratt type thing. Jake played very well and the night got very odd… I was told that George might not be the guy. Ozzy, Sharon and Tommy kinda seemed to fancy Jake and his whole trip and vibe."

Tommy Aldridge confirms this rapid decision change "Jake was the guy. Jake's playing was – and is – unique and he really was the only one that could really do the job. It's unfortunate that we didn't find him sooner."

George Lynch was far from amused to find out he had lost out. "George was shocked, very pissed and very upset." Strum recalls. "This was the *worst* thing for him."

Enter Jake

Strum was facing the *déjà vu* of acting as ringmaster once again. "Hook-up master to Ozzy again – how strange that was!"

His previous experience with Ozzy had rekindled Strum's natural drive to organise and involve himself to the fullest. He still felt he had responsibilities.

"I was a bit worried that Jake would not have the songs or riffs to bring to the party so myself, Jake and Ron Mancuso (Modern Design's guitarist) spent a few nights working things out. We put down what would later become three of the riffs for songs on the *Bark At The Moon* album. It was a trip but more than that, a way to secure Jake a gig and write some Ozzy stuff from afar. We actually swore Jake to secrecy. Jake was the right guy for the gig and we just wanted to give him the best shot, plus Ron and I still loved the music. Money? What money?"

Matters got deeper than even the music. "I got very involved with Jake," Strum confides. "I even discussed with him his name change, organised the PR shots and set up an article with the LA magazine *Music Connection* titled 'From Nothing to the US Festival.' I spoke with Jake a lot during the making of *Bark At The Moon*. I even arranged to rent a car for Jake and his girlfriend Sharon. I would regret that – the car was totalled!"

Jake was immediately flown to England to begin rehearsals with the Ozzy Osbourne band for the European leg of the *Speak Of The Devil* tour.

Taking over Pete Way's mantle would be the relatively unknown figure of Don Costa. If Pete Way was 'wild', Costa was, according to the media, virtually a basket case.

He'd paid his musical dues with a proto-version of W.A.S.P. upfront of stints with Hollywood acts Dante Fox and Damien. Soon the press were releasing lurid tales of Costa's exploits, the most memorable being that the bass player would take a cheese grater onstage to shred his knuckles and belly with, inviting girls in the audience to lap up the blood. It was perfect Ozzy fare.

Whatever the realities of Costa's onstage exploits, behind the scenes his apparent primeval nature continued apace. "Our sound engineer Chuck Weissner would record every gig for us on tape so the band could listen back to it later that night" records

Lindsay. "Jake in particular was very aware of whose shoes he was filling and really was keen to get everything just right. Jake had enormous ability and great flair but he was always willing to listen and learn."

One night the keyboard player got more than he bargained for though. "So, one night Don Costa was listening to a tape on the bus. I said to him 'Is that a tape of last night?'. He looked up and said to me 'Yeah, Wanna listen?'. So I listened but it wasn't a tape of the concert. It was an *in flagrante delecto* recording he had made of his previous night's conquest with this girl screaming and howling in ecstasy! 'No, you idiot, I meant the show!' I said.

"'Yeah right, OK…' I thought. Don was a big hit with the ladies and virtually every night would get at least one, often more, back after the show. What they did not know was that he had a tape recorder under his bed and recorded every one of them for posterity! I think he had rather an interesting little audio library accumulating."

"In many ways Don was a typical never-been-out-of-America kind of guy" Lindsay Bridgwater observes. "I remember one occasion, we were in Paris driving around the Arc de Triomphe. Someone was telling him about how inside the monument there is a flame kept perpetually burning in honour of the French soldiers that had died in the two world wars. Don, quite genuinely, said 'They have wars over here too?' A thousand years of European history had simply passed him by…

"The thing you have to remember about Don Costa was that underneath all the madness he was a great player," maintains Lindsay. "I don't know why he went. Was he pushed or did he fall? Sometimes it felt like not a case of if but when. I think in the time I worked for Ozzy over three years we had eight different line-ups. The whole band was in a constant state of flux."

Costa would briefly hit the limelight post Ozzy with M-80, a union with guitarist Niki Buzz. After just one album Costa decamped, never to be heard of since.

The Ozzy Osbourne band would, in sheer terms of numbers, peak in 1983. The band were invited to perform at the gargan-

Enter Jake

tuan US Festival in San Bernadino to over 400,000 people – Jake E. Lee's American concert debut.

The U.S. tour would see the Ozzy bandwagon helter-skeltering at an alarming speed, visiting many cities twice performing in open amphitheatres. Demand for tickets in New York was so great the band played the Palladium twice in one night. Public acclaim, though, did little to dispel the cloak of suspicion surrounding Ozzy, as Bridgwater elaborates.

"Ozzy certainly eclipsed Black Sabbath for attracting the religious zealots out of the woodwork. It was odd for me because in between times I was playing organ in church. It didn't affect me, I just saw through it all. Ozzy though, it did get to. Sharon had to keep him on the rails. I don't think I could have summoned the strengths Ozzy found to get through all that side of things. His professionalism was there at all times, he kept his stamina and energy up while being in the eye of a hurricane really. It must have been bloody hard work being Ozzy. The outside world had a very distorted view of us whereas in actual fact it was just five blokes getting on with business. That tour was hardly the orgy on wheels many might have supposed."

The band, on a second leg supported by Def Leppard, had grown in stature so rapidly that by the time a return to New York was made it would not be the Palladium but the packed 17,000-capacity Nassau Coliseum that welcomed them.

That same year Bob Daisley received a surprise telephone call. "It was Ozzy," says Bob. "He was in a jam and needed a writer for his next album *Bark At The Moon*. It must have been a bit humbling for him to call I suppose. Well, in spite of everything we had remained friends and so I took up the offer. The album led to a full world tour with America and Japan. I like Tommy Aldridge as a bloke. He was good to work with, a great, great live drummer but I still didn't believe he was right for the band. That should have been Lee there. In fact this showed up in the studio too because we used to get the drums down a lot faster with Lee.

"I thought Jake E. Lee did a phenomenal job filling Randy's shoes, though. He had started off trying to make his mark under this huge shadow cast by Randy and really did well. The pressure really was on him but he stuck to it and did it in his own style too which greatly impressed me. We wrote quite a bit together."

One unused song Jake E. Lee brought along for use on the album was entitled 'The Rapture'. Written when still a teenager, Lee had the song worked up although Ozzy apparently could not find a suitable vocal melody to tag onto it.

Whilst still in the employ of Ozzy the bassist was thrown in at the deep end for an intensive fortnight with a mutual friend of both Daisley and Ozzy when he guested for Gary Moore's live band temporarily. "I did the *Emerald Aisles* video" laughs Bob. "Five days to learn 14 songs from scratch and then be filmed playing them! That was a tough one but we pulled it off. Fantastic shows and Gary was a really nice bloke. Of course he knew the score with Ozzy but said to me 'If ever you're not with Ozzy give me a call!'. Well, later I did make that call and I stayed with Gary off and on for quite some time."

Following the *Moon* sessions Aldridge would find himself replaced by the legendary moustachioed figure of Carmine Appice. The drum stool position was, Spinal Tap-like, becoming more like a game of musical chairs. Daisley succinctly wraps up the occupancy for the next term. "They let Tommy do the album, then fired him – got Carmine Appice in then fired him halfway through the tour and got Tommy back in!"

Bark At The Moon hit the racks in December of 1983. The album needed to fare well as back in the parallel universe of Black Sabbath their latest release *Born Again* had tested fans' loyalty to near breaking point and won through. Having taken a battering both from the press and their embittered ex-frontman Ronnie James Dio, the band had been forced into a radical tactical manouevre to regain advantage by spectacularly enrolling Deep Purple star Ian Gillan as their new frontman. Besieged on two fronts now – Dio's *Holy Diver* had demonstrated Ronnie's solo pedigree as well as a personal fan loyalty, Black Sabbath simply had to deliver.

Opinion was sharply divided but sales in their homeland were not. *Born Again*, with the ink of the media's review hardly dry,

Enter Jake

quite bizarrely gave Black Sabbath their highest charting album since 1973. Nevertheless *Bark At The Moon* would provide Ozzy completists with the challenge of attaining both the European and American versions, the two territorial variants differing in both artwork and song content. The US version has the Ozzy logo in yellow and red whilst the Euro outing is in yellow and blue. The track 'Spiders' replaces 'Slow Down' for America and vice versa for the rest of the world. Strangely 'Forever' was retitled 'Centre Of Eternity' for the US market. If fans were not confused enough, the two pressings came with completely different track orders.

A 12" single of the title track was released in the UK upfront to promote the album. This release too proved collectable as a limited run silver vinyl edition with an unreleased tongue-in-cheek track 'One Up The B Side' and the American album track 'Slow Down'.

Bark At The Moon fared well, gaining a foothold inside the Billboard top twenty. In the UK the title-track single, backed by a video in which Ozzy is garbed in full-blown Hollywood werewolf disguise, gave him his biggest solo single success to date.

1983 was also notable for an Ozzy recording that would largely go unnoticed by fans but, by didn't, of association, prompt a media furore a decade later. Ozzy had donated a lead vocal track to the song 'Shake Your Head (Let's Go To Bed)' for the Was (Not Was) album *Born To Laugh At Tornadoes*. Apparently unbeknown to Ozzy, he had replaced an earlier session singer's track that Don Was had felt was lacking the correct feel – that of Madonna. Underneath Ozzy's vocal Madonna is still quite audible.

The track would resurface in the '90s on the compilation *Hello Dad, I'm In Jail*, Ozzy's track still in place but Madonna's contribution supplanted, surreally, by that of actress Kim Basinger.

12
Carmine Feel The Noise

Next in line for recruitment into Ozzy's band was the highly respected figure of drummer Carmine Appice, a man as well-known for his trademark moustache as his undeniable percussive abilities. For the first time Ozzy was inviting a 'name' artist into the fold.

Appice had came to prominence some two decades earlier with the pioneering rockers Vanilla Fudge. Bassist Tim Bogert, having been impressed with a drummer he had seen playing a gig at New York's Headliner Club, took his band-mates to see the guy play and the trio quickly invited the aspiring Appice to work with them.

With Appice in the group a record contract with Atco would follow after Shangri-La's writer/producer George 'Shadow' Morton had caught a live version of The Pigeons' new take on the Supremes' 'You Keep Me Hangin' On' after being invited down to a gig by manager Phil Basille. Morton cut the track with the group and emerged with the deal from Atco's Ahmet Ertegun and the song was released as the group's first single in the spring of 1967. Just prior to its release the group had formally adopted the name Vanilla Fudge. The group's eponymous debut album appeared later in the year and was supported by gigs with Mitch Ryder, Blue Cheer and The Yardbirds as the record began to shoot up the charts in America. *Vanilla Fudge* also made something of a minor impact in Europe as well.

In February 1968 the second album, *The Beat Goes On*, appeared and Atco then re-issued the 'You Keep Me Hanging On' single (with a new B-side) which reached Number 6 in the States as the buzz on Vanilla Fudge kept on growing. The band's third album, *Renaissance*, was issued not long afterwards as the quartet continued a hectic touring schedule that saw them play date after date in North America and also venture over to Europe. They broke the American West Coast opening up for Hendrix; they would also play support on British outfit Cream's farewell American tour in the autumn of 1968.

Carmine Feel The Noise

In December that year the Fudge played a show in Boston opened by the embryonic Led Zeppelin, which led to a lengthy and often picaresque friendship between the two bands. In February 1969 the *Near The Beginning* album would feature only four songs, including a side-long live recording of 'The Break Song'. One last album, *Rock And Roll*, appeared in September 1969 before Appice and bassist Bogert left to link up with guitarist Jeff Beck and with boogie band Cactus. Other '70s gigs included KGB and Rod Stewart, with whom he co-wrote 'D'Ya Think I'm Sexy?' He was in the midst of a run of drum clinic master classes in Europe when the world of Ozzy collided with his.

Carmine expands upon how he landed the position with the Ozzy Osbourne band. "I was in the south of France doing some drum clinics and a friend of mine called me and told me Ozzy had fired Tommy and I should call Sharon in London as they needed someone fast. So, I called Sharon and I went to London straight from France and had a meeting and a play. No audition – just to hang out. After few days Ozzy and Sharon told me I was in and we were in business."

Implanting Appice into the band necessitated some long distance learning sessions, as Carmine reveals. "I went to England to rehearse but in order to get my work visa I had to leave. So, I ended up writing charts for the show and practicing in LA at my house listening to a tape of Ozzy live with Tommy on drums. In actual fact I had only two days of real rehearsing with the band in England."

Musically, an outsider might believe interpolating Ozzy's material with Appice's established trademark sound might be difficult for the drummer to accommodate.

"My style was a little heavier, less notes and funky overtones. Tommy plays a bit faster and maybe not funky at all. Hard to describe the difference. I originated my own style." When asked if any adaptation to his recognised style took place to fit the Ozzy material Carmine has this to say.

"Maybe a little...but Lee, the original drummer of the Ozzy band played like me so the songs were already in my style so I think Tommy had to adjust more than Bob did. I just played whatever happened each night. I had light cues worked out for different parts of the solo but each solo was a little different."

The drummer records his impressions of his band members with obvious respect. "All the other musicians were top of the line, all of them, the best in their field. I thought Jake was great. Even in Rough Cutt he was great. He had a great feel and he was a killer on stage. I know that Sharon and Ozzy were pushing Jake's image hard to break the Randy thing – Jake just went along and played great and got on with the business of playing. Jake's a unique player. He had a great stage presence and for me the way he played chords using his thumb differently was unique.

"I struck up a friendship with Jake as we were the only two American guys in the band and my roadie André was the third American so we had some things in common. At the time it was my first bus tour and I couldn't sleep on the bus so we would both stay up all night watching movies on the bus together."

Appice's rhythm partner Bob Daisley too comes in for praise. "Bob was better than ever. Bob has got a great groove and sound. He's an easy-going guy, flows with any situation. He comes up with melodic bass lines that become hooks for the song. He doesn't overplay. Bob Daisley is the meaning of the saying 'fat bottom groove'..."

Conversely Daisley has this take on Carmine. "Carmine was very clever on the drums – too clever sometimes!" he laughs. "He would put a lot of funk stuff in but in general he was more like Lee than Tommy in style. Carmine would do a lot of drum clinics in the afternoons before a gig so when we played live we could hear all these extra little fancy bits creeping in!"

The European dates, with San Francisco's highly respected Y&T as opening act, would peak with a gargantuan Metal festival in Dortmund, Germany. Featuring the cream of the Heavy Metal world – Iron Maiden, Judas Priest, Def Leppard, The Michael Schenker Group etc. many thought Ozzy's was the festival's finest hour.

"The Dortmund Festival really stands out," confirms Appice.

Carmine Feel The Noise

"It was televised and the band was great. The audience went nuts. I had a great solo that night too which was televised all over Europe."

Carmine's tenure would be interrupted abruptly. The departure was so swift it would actually come mid-tour with a reinstated Tommy Aldridge waiting in the wings. "I left the band because Sharon fired me," Carmine readily admits. "She said I was too big a name and they wanted more of a back-up player. At the time I was doing a lot of press for the tour and I was doing master classes at music stores five times a week and receiving lots of press for it. Sharon didn't like that. I was also getting mentioned too much on MTV. J.J. Jackson would say "Here are the Ozzy concert dates with the Legendary Carmine Appice on drums." Sharon didn't like it. In fact she told me I needed to start my own band – so I did. I started King Kobra straight after Ozzy."

Appice maintains the band knew the score before taking him on. "I talked to Sharon and Ozzy before I joined and told them I did get a lot of press in the US and that I did clinics and Master Classes while I was on tour which generated a good amount of press.

"That same year Ozzy was in *Oui* Magazine in the US. Everyone was in it. Besides Ozzy there was Motorhead, Mötley Crüe, Joe Perry and me. We all had five-ten pages in the mag and we were on a calendar, each on a different month. My issue sold over 3 million copies and *Oui* gave me a big party and an award for the issue. So I talked about press, bringing up that mag and all. I also ran a drum contest that was covered by press and national TV in the US and MTV. So, I guess at the time I joined nobody cared but afterwards in the US it got... weird!"

The omnipresent Daisley had seen the writing on the wall. "Tommy Aldridge turned up for the show in Dallas, his hometown. I could see exactly what was going to happen. Within a few days Carmine had been fired. We did a day's rehearsal with Tommy and then carried straight on as if nothing had happened."

Another casualty, albeit unexpected, was Lindsay Bridgwater. "I had done the European dates in the beginning of 1983 with

Ozzy Osbourne

Jake and Don." He relates. "We actually spent quite some time working through the songs. Both Jake and Don were very professional and had done their homework so it was only really topping and tailing to get the songs just right for the road. I didn't have to teach them anything really."

Bridgwater would commence the American dates but would not complete the full run. "I left halfway through the US tour. I took it on the chin really but I was very sad to leave. Don completed the tour." Tommy Aldridge's own last Ozzy gig would come soon after at the Brazilian 'Rock In Rio' event in front of 300,000 South American fans.

The album ballad 'So Tired' would have two shots at the British charts. Originally launched in March 1984 it sank, oddly, without trace. Revamped less than two months later and bolstered by a welcome inclusion of three live tracks – 'Bark At The Moon', 'Suicide Solution' and 'Paranoid', recorded in Salt Lake City, Utah on March 18th, an Ozzy Osbourne logo textile patch and another limited 12" coloured vinyl (this time gold), it hit the top twenty.

After his second Ozzy experience Lindsay Bridgwater was inducted into a potentially exciting band unit led by erstwhile Mott The Hoople and Bad Company guitarist Mick Ralphs. Anticipation was high and although an album, *Take This* issued in 1983, actual circumstances around the group were less than stable. The band was scheduled to tour but these plans would wither away leaving a clutch of London gigs as a legacy.

"Mick put a lot of his own money into the project," Lyndsay recounts. "We were all put on retainers. The band was hot to trot but sadly it all fell apart when Mick joined Dave Gilmour's band."

Years later Bridgwater would again tread the rock 'n' roll boards as part of Denny Laine's band for touring in Poland and Russia. In 1984 the keyboard player put in a worthy six-month spell with the musical *Blood Brothers*. Occasionally the inkling for rock still drags him back into the arena, as witnessed by a recent live sojourn with the regrouped cult '60s act Quatermass. These days Bridgwater's preoccupations are mainly in the classical field. "I'm rediscovering my classical roots actually," he states. "Most of the '90s has been spent with the London Philharmonic Orchestra. I have an absolute passion for Covent Garden but I keep my feet on the ground with a London blues band too."

And, there is of course the suspended question that Lindsay cannot avoid, one that has been passed into Ozzy folklore and handed down in less than hushed tones by successive band members down the years. Is he the man Ozzy got to stand on one leg for the entire duration of a show?

"Ah…er..it was a wind up. I think that could well be me" he offers, somewhat sheepishly. "In Ozzy's world it was all a bit surreal at times and I probably am guilty of losing my powers of judgement at times. There was an occasion when I put my hand in my pocket to discover Ozzy had peed in it! And, of course, I famously had my eyebrows shaved off too. I endured quite a bit of teasing initially because I was young and sensitive back then. I think the incident in question got exaggerated hugely though. I'm not sure if I even did stand on one leg at all but, yes, the roadies had told me they had an earthing problem onstage. They explained to me that I would be OK if I just kept the one leg off the ground in order to avoid forming a circuit and getting electrocuted! I don't think I actually did it although the memory is a bit fuzzy so possibly I did. I do recall thinking that this must be another bloody wind-up."

Ultimately Bridgwater is philosophical yet generous about his tenure with the Ozzy band. "I wanted more for sure, but it just wasn't my time" he muses. "In truth I never really seized the opportunity that Ozzy gave to me. There are no regrets, no rancour, no bitterness. Just lots of very pleasant memories. Ozzy actually sent me a letter much later saying thanks for the good times. I have very fond memories too, so I was very happy to receive that."

Latterly, whilst performing harpsichord in a live performance at the Vatican for the Pope's 80th birthday celebrations Bridgwater would be struck by the world of irony his particular wheel of fortune had circumscribed.

13
Casting The Net

Ozzy knew exactly who was next in line to occupy his drum stool. He had been tipped off by Mötley Crüe's Tommy Lee, a man boasting equal repute for his renowned drumming abilities as for his often-aired media excesses. If Tommy Lee was suggesting a candidate then Ozzy was to take it seriously. Doubly so, as it turned out, as Ratt's drummer Bobby Blotzer had put forward the same man himself – Randy Castillo. However, fate was to dictate otherwise.

"I was living in Albuquerque at the time" Castillo elaborates. "I had been learning to ski and, of course, on only my second attempt I crashed and burned in a major way. When I got the call I had my right leg fully plastered up to the knee and suspended in the air. It was actually both Tommy Lee and Bobby Blotzer that called me at four in the morning. They were at a party in LA and they passed the phone over to Ozzy. Imagine, it's four in the morning, my leg is in plaster and Ozzy is giving me all these compliments on my drumming so when I told him… The timing was the worst for me. I just couldn't believe it. Ozzy was speechless when I told him I had broken my leg 'I'm fucking cursed!' he said. So, there I am thinking that it's all over but Ozzy says 'Come down to LA anyway, I want to meet you.' Randy flew out the very next day.

Nevertheless auditions to pull in a new drummer were held in Los Angeles to which Randy Castillo – complete with a broken leg – attended.

"When I got out of the car the first thing I see is a line of drummers waiting for their audition. So, of course they see me with my crutches and my broken leg so you can picture what these guys are thinking. 'That guy hasn't got a hope!' I was taken to meet Ozzy straight away and we clicked at once. But then I have to play. I tried but with my left foot in plaster I couldn't even hit the bass drum. My foot was swelling. It felt like it was about to explode. Ozzy was really desperate for a drummer though and he needed one then. The good thing was though that we had become almost instant friends, I really liked him straight away."

Kiss sticksman Eric Singer would also try out and, as Bob sheepishly admits, "apparently I was the one who said Eric wasn't good enough! Eric told me this many years later but I don't even remember him being there." (Daisley would later work with Singer in Black Sabbath, among other projects). Sandy Gennaro of Blackjack and Pat Travers were also among the hopefuls who nearly secured the position (coincidentally Gennaro had replaced Tommy Aldridge in the Travers band in 1980).

Another face was even more familiar as Daisley recounts. "Bill Ward came down too. Not for an audition but just for the crack. He came down and we said, 'fuck it, let's play'. We had a good time with Bill. That was a good session." The welcome diversion of Ward's jam could not allay the very real work at hand though. Bob recalls just how gruelling the auditioning process was and how his normal conciliatory nature was lost toward the end. Each candidate had four tracks to run through- 'Over The Mountain', 'Crazy Train', 'I Don't Know' and 'Flying High Again'.

"Jake and I were doing the auditions while Ozzy watched. It was drummer after drummer, day after day after day. After the first twenty or so it got a bit of a chore. Up until then we had been very professional, very polite, telling the unsuccessful applicants 'thank you, we'll let you know' or 'you're not quite what we're looking for' but it was disheartening going through four songs with a drummer who you knew, after a few seconds, wasn't good enough."

With patience at a low ebb Bob concedes the latter auditionees fell foul of his and Jake's frustration. "If they didn't get the fill intro to the first song 'Over The Mountain' right we would just stop them right there and say 'Sorry – Next!'. It got that frustrating."

It was with some degree of relief that Fred Coury was finally chosen. Earlier in life the young Coury had in fact nearly railroaded himself from his chosen destination of rock 'n' roll to the world of sport. He had been attending hockey training school but the impact of his first ever gig in Toronto featuring a line-up of The Who, Heart and The J Geils Band had captured his imagination and kindled a new ambition. "I went home and told my Mom I wanted to be a rock 'n' roll star" he laughs. His ma replied "That's sweet" and Fred Coury was on his way.

Coury, still only 18, had only previously plied his trade with Chastain, appearing on their 1985 release 'Mystery Of Illusion'. Hooking up with Chastain had been on personal recommendation from renowned bassist Billy Sheehan to Mike Varney, Shrapnel Records boss. It would be Varney who would put Coury up for the Ozzy position.

At this stage, enter Ozzy's Mr. Fixit, Dana Strum, once again. This time, though, his instincts for a good Ozzy man would fail him.

"I was practicing eight hours every day learning all the Ozzy and Black Sabbath songs I could in time for the audition" states Fred. "I would just go in there and play and play and play, all to try and get the Ozzy gig. One day I came out of the studio and I saw this guy who I recognized. 'Wow, it's that Dana Strum guy!' I thought. This was like the first real rock star I had ever met. He was there doing pre-production for some other band and asked me what I was doing so I told him that I was trying out for the Ozzy gig. *Give it up,* he said. *You're not gonna get it. I know the guy who's gonna get it.* I was crushed. It just destroyed me."

Come the day of the audition Fred sensed all was not well. Fred knew the owner of Mates Rehearsals where the try-outs were taking place. As he went in his acquaintance told him, prophetically, "I have a feeling you're the guy." Lifting his confidence somewhat his friend's portent then fell flat as the reality of the situation dawned. "Everyone wanted Randy Castillo. He was the guy." he confides. "Everyone knew it was Randy's gig but he turned up with a broken leg in this big plaster cast. Well, he played and was still great but he had this cast on. What could they do? In the end I was the first runner up so I got the gig."

The youngster, aware of Randy's position within the camp, still had to go through with the audition. He hadn't spent time on

Casting The Net

those gruelling learning sessions to give up now. A sarcastic yet truthful observation from Bob Daisley jangled his nerves a bit more to add to the tension. "Bob told me that I was born the year after he first started playing bass guitar. That made me feel, uh, just great!"

Fred listened as drummer after drummer were put through their paces. "I noticed that Ozzy never sang with them. When it was my turn I did a few songs and then Ozzy wanted to sing! I was actually having a ball because, believe it or not, this was the very first time I had played with monitors. I would hit the drum and hear it come back at me. I'd never heard that before! The mix was great and it made a world of difference."

The eager teenager was keen to show the by now weary auditioning team just how much he had learnt. "I suggested this Ozzy song, or that Sabbath song because of course I knew all of them. I had learned every damn Ozzy song – every one! Every time I suggested a song to play they didn't know it so I would start them off and we would try them out. It was surreal. We were there for about an hour and when I finished I turned round and there was every other drummer all standing at the back of the room. I was blessed that day."

The new team of Ozzy, Jake, Bob and Fred would then enter the studio in London. Bob Daisley has cause to recollect this period well; "I was writing lyrics sitting at home in my garden," he muses. "Ozzy would send me a backing track with any old stuff on it. The tapes would have all Ozzy's phrasing and vocal melody ideas down and then I would put lyrics in to fit, to make the songs make sense. During this writing period Ozzy and I had a falling out though. The record company wanted to hear how the songs were sounding so we went into a studio. I put the bass on the demos but, as I said, Ozzy and I fell out, we really locked horns."

However, a later contact would set the pattern for the next few years. "Ozzy called me again less than six weeks later wanting some lyrics for *The Ultimate Sin*" Bob confides. "Of course, I ended up doing it. I did some demos and wrote the lyrics for *The Ultimate Sin* album which was a bit of an odd one because I don't think anyone in the band really liked it. I know Ozzy doesn't rate it – he calls it 'The Ultimate Din'! Ozzy and I had a verbal fallout though and Ozzy told me that we could not work together. So be it, I thought, and left."

Daisley soon got to work again with Gary Moore but this port in a storm proved less of an attraction than the prospect of another call from the Black Sabbath family – this time for the mothership.

"I was called in for the *Eternal Idol* album. I played all the bass on that record although Dave Spitz gets a credit too. Haven't I been here before?" he laughs. "I put down the bass and wrote a lot of the lyrics too because although Ray Gillen was a fantastic singer he wasn't a great writer. They then got rid of Ray and got another guy – Tony Martin – to completely re-record the vocals note for note perfect. They asked me to join the band but I was too secure with Gary Moore who was doing very well. Besides, the whole Black Sabbath thing was looking a little shaky."

Coury too would move on after laying down his demos. Shortly after, Fred was flicking through *Circus* magazine when he spotted his name. "It said I had worked with Ozzy on pre-production. How cool is that? It looked great on my resumé!" The drummer would get another surprise just as Cinderella was getting into gear. "I picked up the phone one day and it was Ozzy calling from out of the blue. 'Best of luck with the new band,' he said. The nice thing was he really meant it and he had taken the trouble to call me after he had heard about Cinderella. That was awesome. Sharon and Ozzy treated me so well during that time I worked with them. They're very awesome people."

As for Dana's advice? "I kinda proved him wrong in a way I think though, but it bugged me for nearly 15 years!" confesses Fred. "Then recently Cinderella and Slaughter played together and he remembered and apologized to me!"

Next occupant of the drum stool would be Jimmy DeGrasso. His tenure would be brief, lasting from March until April 1985. The veteran bassist Neil Murray would be on hand for a few days too at this juncture, just prior to re-joining Whitesnake; post-

Casting The Net

Ozzy, DeGrasso would of course make his name with Alice Cooper and Megadeth.

Randy Castillo, now minus his plaster cast, would be waiting in the wings. "Ozzy had been using Fred Coury, for about a month I think, and by this stage they were rehearsing in Scotland. I was back in Albuquerque resting up when I got another call from Ozzy. He asked if my leg had healed and then if I still wanted the gig. It was all very quick, Ozzy wanted me on a plane the next day and had arranged the tickets. What was unbelievable, though, was that as I was making my travel plans the phone rang again. It was Steve Vai inquiring if I was available to join David Lee Roth's band! Shortly after David Coverdale calls wanting me to join Whitesnake so the whole day just got totally crazy. I'd said yes to Ozzy though and I really wanted that gig bad so next day I was there. I ended up staying for eight fantastic years too."

In June of 1985 future Ozzy bassist Phil Soussan had chosen to take up an offer from none other than Jimmy Page. These sessions, it would transpire, it became the basis for Page's collaboration with former Free singer Paul Rodgers and the band known as The Firm. Soussan was involved with the band prior to the inclusion of eventual incumbent Tony Franklin and during this period would work with former Uriah Heep drummer Chris Slade and Rat Scabies of The Damned.

"Phil Carlo at Swansong called me to tell me that Jimmy had wanted me to jam with him. Chris Slade came by and played for one day but although he would end up eventually being the guy Jimmy wasn't sure. We played with Rat and that line-up lasted quite some time." Soussan had previously come to public attention with the Swansong-signed Wildlife, a classy melodic hard rock act whose inaugural line up comprised of brothers Chris and Steve Overland, bassist Nigel Widowson, keyboard player Mark Booty and drummer Richard Plumb. Widowson was supplanted by Bob Skeat whilst Plumb lost his spot to former Hotline drummer Pete Jupp.

The veteran Bad Company drummer Simon Kirke had replaced Jupp who joined Samson for their 1983 album. By early

Ozzy Osbourne

1984 Kirke was out and replaced by Jeff Rich, formerly with Judie Tzuke. This last incarnation of Wildlife also saw the inclusion of former Cuddly Toys and Reflex bassist Phil Soussan. Promise was high but ultimately Wildlife would founder. Teaming up with Robin George in 1984, however, would turn out to be a good move.

During the mid-'80s the then fledgling Channel 4 TV station was bravely testing the early evening with a weekly heavy metal show dubbed *ECT*. Often disastrous live performances, set in a pseudo sci-fi panorama, by bands such as Rock Goddess, Warlock, Madam X and Rogue Male made for strangely compulsive viewing. One such performance by Robin George's band would catch the eye of someone just a little more influential than the average viewer.

Phil Soussan takes up the story. "I'd been with Robin for almost a year and for various reasons it really was time for me to move on. We had just done the live TV show *ECT* and it was actually really good. Afterwards I went back home and got a phone call from Lynn Seagar who worked for Sharon Osbourne. She told me there was someone who wanted to talk to me and next thing I know I'm talking to Ozzy on the phone! Well, Ozzy told me he had just watched the show and he wanted to meet up to discuss something. He was in Spirals Bar, a place I knew well. So we arranged to meet that night. I did warn him though that I was with a few friends and they would be coming along with me."

The friends were the noted guitarist Lawrence ('Florence') Archer latterly of Wild Horses and Stampede (and later of UFO) and the Scottish singer Fin, of erstwhile Ozzy bassist Pete Way's chaotic act Waysted. This troupe set out for their destination by way of a few other drinking establishments and before long the bass player's phone was ringing again. "It was Ozzy," Phil relates. "He was a bit angry too. 'I'm still fucking waiting!' he said."

Soussan hurried up his colleagues and they eventually made it to Spirals where a worse-for-wear Ozzy was indeed waiting, albeit less than patiently.

Casting The Net

"Ozzy was with Lynn. We had a good long conversation even though he was pretty drunk," the bassist recalls. "He spoke about fame and fortune and that he really wanted me to join the band and record the next album." The young bass player was already aware that both Bob Daisley and Fred Coury had vacated. "I knew Randy Castillo was involved so I was definitely up for it." Soussan and Castillo actually already knew and respected each other from the drummer's days working with Lita Ford. Indeed Soussan and Ford had even dated on occasion. The Ozzy offer seemed like a logical and profitable step up.

However, as is seemingly typical in any scenario involving Ozzy, matters took a bizarre turn before the night was out. "This guy that Lawrence knew turned up at completely the wrong time. His name was Dominic, Dominic Dibbs I think, and he was eccentric to say the least. Unbelievably, he would tell people that he was the reincarnation of Ozzy Osbourne come back to earth- this being even though of course Ozzy was still very much alive. The thing was, he did actually look like Ozzy too. He would wear the clothes and the eye make-up and say he was Ozzy. Well, there I was talking to Ozzy when Dominic comes in! The two of them sat facing each other having a real go at each other. They were having this contest trying to see who could eat the most rose petals!!" This consumption of flowers in an attempt to determine who indeed was the 'real' Ozzy did not resolve the issue though. "They then had a big altercation – the real Ozzy Osbourne and the reincarnation of Ozzy arguing! We were pissing ourselves!"

Phil Soussan left the surreal world of Spirals Bar that night not knowing quite what to make of it all. As it would turn out it was indeed to signal the inception of a rollercoaster time with Ozzy. The next day would give him a foretaste of what was to come.

"Sharon phoned me up," Phil states. "She told me everything that Ozzy had said the night before was a load of rubbish and that I was not being asked to join the band. It had all been a big mistake." Chalking his episode in Spirals up to experience, a few weeks elapsed before Soussan paid a weekend visit to Brighton,

Ozzy Osbourne

staying the weekend with friends, his host being his Swansong Records colleague Phil Carlo. As coincidences go the next one would take some beating.

"This was about three weeks after first meeting Ozzy." Soussan remembers. "I had walked into a shop in Brighton and, quite unbelievably, there was Ozzy." The singer was quite taken aback. "He was as surprised as I was I think. In fact he even asked me if I was following him! It was a seaside joke shop and Ozzy was stocking up on an industrial quantity of those little glass stink bombs. He loved to torment people with those."

Randy Castillo confirms Ozzy's predeliction for stink bombs. "Ozzy is one of the all-time great practical jokers" the drummer laughs. "He always has a stink bomb in his pocket and he throws them out onstage when other bands are in the middle of a set."

It emerged that Ozzy's band was rehearsing just up the street. The conversation did not take long to get around to the subject of that previous inebriated offer. "Well, now he was sober and he asked if I would like to come up and have a play – that night! I quite literally ran to get back to London, grab my guitar and get back down to Brighton. I also had to learn a tape too before going along that night."

Phil soon was made aware of the situation with the band. "They had been trying some American guy but it wasn't working out. Anyway, we played and they ended up keeping me around for quite a while." (The 'American guy' was in fact former Steeler member Greg Chaisson. The band had rehearsed up in Scotland with Chaisson for a fortnight.)

Phil would then bump into Ozzy tour manager Jimmy Ayres when the pair travelled back up to London. "Well, he told me straight that the band were unsure about me because I played with my fingers and not a pick. They liked me but didn't like the fact I used my fingers. It was just a style of playing I had fallen into really. I could play fine with a pick and told Jimmy so. He replied that, in his opinion, he thought I would get the job if I used a pick. It was odd, though, because none of the band had ever mentioned this."

One wonders if this was because the reliable Bob Daisley used

Casting The Net

a pick. It is a point Geezer Butler has mentioned previously in interviews. Phil Soussan believes it is simply down to the nature of the songs.

"Yes, Bob uses a pick but it's the songs. In general they are a lot more aggressive than Sabbath, less pedantic. Sabbath have this kind of dull pounding style. It's about definition and speed with Ozzy." The young bassist's next session with Ozzy's band proved a revelation.

"I started playing as normal and then later I said 'Shall I use a pick?' and the whole mood changed! 'A pick? Oh yeah!' It was just what they wanted but they hadn't told me. A few days later, my birthday in fact, Ozzy came to me and said 'Happy Birthday – by the way, you've got the gig if you want it.' I actually told him I'd think about it but of course very quickly afterwards said 'Yeah, sure, great!' I was in. It was all very surreal how it turned out from delivering Randy for his audition to a few weeks later being on the chopping block myself."

Barry Evans, previously bass tech for Neil Murray in Whitesnake, was assigned to Phil – apparently Neil had occupied the bass slot just prior to Phil's induction – and the new band set about putting down a series of basic demos on a four-track recorder as pilots for the next album. "We were rehearsing songs for the album without the vocals at first," admits Phil. "Bob Daisley was still writing the lyrics while we were sorting out the music."

In spite of these delays the demos would be accepted and for *The Ultimate Sin* the esteemed Ron Nevison was picked as producer. Nevison had made his name with such seminal works as UFO's mighty live opus *Strangers In The Night* and as producers go, Nevinson was very definitely in the A league. However, things would not turn out as the band imagined.

"When he arrived it was obvious he had not given the tapes a listen at all," recalls a miffed Soussan. "It was actually pretty insulting and we were rightly pissed off. Well, he went away and listened to the tape but when he came back he had the nerve to say he wasn't going to record the album unless he could hear a single. He actually seriously suggested we try having a go at 'Born To Be Wild'!* You can imagine Ozzy's reaction. It really was quite amazing but Nevison was being serious. We actually kicked around a few suggestions for cover versions until Randy and I were asked if we had any songs."

As it turned out the band's newest recruit did indeed have a song. "I'd had this song that I had written at the end of Wildlife. I had the music, melodies and a title and then Chris Overland came in and added some lyrics to it. It became 'Shot In The Dark' he says. "Ozzy didn't think the lyrics were appropriate so I rewrote them and we sped it up quite a bit too and Ozzy put his ideas in too and it ended up great."

The Ozzy band retired to the Townhouse Studios to start proceedings for the album recording but encountered problems from the off. "It was very, very difficult working with Ron," Phil states emphatically. "The truth of it was we thought he was just bloody lazy. The band and the producer fought about a lot of things.

Nevison wanted to spit the album out; for the band, though, the process was like pulling teeth. The atmosphere in the studio was so adversarial that it did succeed in unifying the band and made us a tighter unit. I even had to go back and re-record all my bass parts because they weren't recorded correctly in the first place."

One wonders just why, in such an apparently hostile atmosphere, Nevison's services were maintained but, as Phil states, the producer had status. "He had been very lucky and had been involved in some pretty big albums around that time. He was the hot guy and it was felt he could be an asset. Sharon did mention, however, that she was not afraid to do whatever she would have to do."

With relationships in the studio straining, matters would take a turn downward to a new low. "I know Ozzy was insecure about the album because it was the first one he had done without Bob Daisley," Soussan records. "What really got to us, though, was when we found out that Nevison actually wanted Randy and me out. He went to Sharon and told her the rhythm section has to go! He also said that Jake didn't take direction very well! Sharon, bless her, in her own particular manner, told Ron to sack the singer too and start his own band!"

Ironically Ozzy did cut 'Born To Be Wild' – in 1992 as a duet with Miss Piggy!

14
Tapping In

With Ozzy's band in a constant state of flux from year to year, it would be quite remarkable that the next player to enter the fold would tenaciously hold on to his position for a marathon 15 years. Keyboard player John Sinclair is not what one would call a high profile figure – mainly operating hidden from view sidestage – but still fulfilling the same valuable role as occupied by Don Airey and Lindsay Bridgwater.

John's first footsteps into the world of rock 'n' roll came with his appearance on a solo album by Larry Page on the now highly collectable Penny Farthing Records. The ambitious ivory tickler was just 19.

From there, in the grand tradition of British rock upward career moves, Sinclair answered a *Melody Maker* advert and found himself working with Jackie Lynton. A well-known and much loved figure on the blues-rock scene, Lynton had strong connections with perennial boogie rockers Status Quo and the young keyboard player undertook his first major touring schedule as their support player.

A series of Jackie Lynton gigs at London's Marquee Club would dictate his next port of call. A mysterious hooded figure in the audience would turn out to be Gary Holton, lead singer of the boisterous bovver band The Heavy Metal Kids on a less-than-innocuous mission to check out Sinclair's skills.

Holton's sense of theatrics was in keeping with his character both on and offstage. The savvy Londoner had, as a youngster, played the Artful Dodger in the West End stage performance of *Oliver!* and that persona of the likeable cheeky ne'er-do-well had stayed with him. Holton's band, The Heavy Metal Kids, were popular in the London area and would stage-manage fights as part of their live set, and found themselves on the nation's television screens courtesy of a BBC documentary on youth violence. The only flaw in Holton's plan was that in 1973 when he launched the band, Punk hadn't yet happened and The Heavy Metal Kids were somewhat out on a limb.

Ozzy Osbourne

Two albums with Danny Peyronel had preceded Sinclair's term and following the sophomore effort, *Anvil Chorus,* The Heavy Metal Kids had reportedly split. The group duly regrouped but minus Peyronel who had taken up a high profile position with UFO thus leaving a vacancy to be plugged by Sinclair. Although original guitarist Cosmo was in the frame, upon Sinclair's induction he would later make way for a new face in the form of Barry Paul.

Sinclair would record the 1977 Mickey Most-produced Kids' album *Kitsch*. The keyboard player would, however, break away from anarchic Kids, journeying to America to earn his crust with session work. Lee Kerslake, whom he had met when the Kids supported Uriah Heep on tour, would often stay over when Uriah Heep hit the States.

Meantime chirpy frontman Gary Holton embarked on a solo career which saw a brief tenure in The Damned in late 1978 and a European-only released album. Holton would also hit the British charts in 1984 with his version of 'Catch A Falling Star', The singer had found fame as a TV actor alongside Jimmy Nail, portraying the blue-collar Romeo and Cockney carpenter Wayne in the ITV series *Auf Wiedersehen Pet*. Sadly, at the height of his acting career, Holton died in tragic circumstances in 1985 during filming of the second series.

A stint in Lion and more work with Lee Kerslake followed before the keyboard player found himself inducted, a world more bizarre than any rock 'n' roll adventure – Spinal Tap.

Reality and the movies collided; Christopher Guest (Nigel Tufnel in Tap) had been fishing for genuine rock 'n' roll stories to spice up the film and a Uriah Heep American Air Force base gig stood head and shoulders above the rest. The band's promoter had put the gig in as a last minute stop-gap when a previously scheduled date had fallen through, and *This Is Spinal Tap* would immortalise the tale into one of the movie's most cringe-inducing moments of pathos. Bob Daisley has vivid memories of the event too. "We turned up at this gig and they had written this huge sign in glitter on the hall." The portent of doom must have been striking as the band members read the herald 'The Uriah

Tapping In

Heep show - sold more records than Abba!' "It happened exactly the same as the movie – as soon as we started to play all their air traffic control commands started to come out of the sound system."

Daisley still has hysterics when relaying the tale of a hard rock band's worst nightmare. "The whole audience was in uniform and all the women looked like Dolly Parton." Uriah Heep opened with a steaming Metal riff and were met with stony silence. Besides inspiration for storylines John Sinclair would contribute 'keyboards and musical styling' for which he is credited in the movie. He also appeared in the pilot to the movie. The keyboard player was then asked to commit to filming of the actual movie but found himself between a rock and a hard place with Uriah Heep.

This presented Sinclair with a dilemma. Uriah Heep had just completed the *Head First* record, an important stepping stone on from the rejuvenation given the band by *Abominog*. However, Bob Daisley had left the fold for another term with Ozzy and Trevor Bolder had stepped in on bass. With a world tour imminent, Sinclair's loyalty had to remain with his band rather than an uncertain movie career.

In 1986 Sinclair found himself back in the UK. Unbeknown to the keyboard player a good friend at the rock 'n' roll security company, Artist Services, had mentioned Sinclair's abilities to Ozzy's tour manager Jimmy Ayers. His former Uriah Heep colleague Bob Daisley, in and out of the Ozzy set-up for years now, had also suggested the same name on a few occasions.

The Ultimate Sin was wrapped by the time Sinclair became involved and after a quick audition the keyboard player was invited on board – a stay that would last 15 years.

Sinclair's task was the same as Bridgwater's and Airey's – to add colour and depth to songs such as 'Perry Mason', 'No More Tears' and of course 'Mr. Crowley'. Being out of sight from the main show apparently held no qualms for him.

With the album cut and laid to rest the band geared up for what would turn out to become a monstrous world tour. "We began rehearsals at a big warehouse near the Ace café off the

Ozzy Osbourne

North Circular Road. We set up the whole stage in there and had full production rehearsals. I remember one day Vince and Tommy from Mötley Crüe came by to see us" recollects Phil Soussan. The infamous Crüe singer and Soussan would immediately hit it off, in the future leading eventually to a working collaboration in the future. For now, though, the Ozzy band was primed and ready to roll.

"Then we went straight out and played our first gig in Dublin," Phil Soussan reminisces. The bassist has vivid memories of the opening night, his debut as a public member of the Ozzy Osbourne band. "The Irish crowd was nuts – they went ballistic. The album had just come out and was shooting up the charts. After the show it was just incredible. I've never been so exhausted after a gig. I was just drained, physically tired. I couldn't hear for two days after that gig. At the time I didn't think it was that loud but it must have been. After the gig everyone else was running around but I just sat at the hotel with a hot chocolate. Not very rock 'n' roll but I was beat."

The musician's head was swimming with the enormity of it all. "I was nervous but not in the manner of stage fright or anything. I just wanted to prove my point and make a good impression. It was very taxing, there was a lot to remember musically and we had done no warm-up shows. Randy and I also had some very big shoes to fill so the pressure was on big time. That early on we couldn't take anything for granted. We thought we had done a good job but I do remember actually looking around for approval after the show. It was a big sense of relief really, the same I'm sure for Randy."

The Ultimate Sin, in spite of production upheavals and what is now reflected upon to be a fairly nondescript set of songs by Ozzy's previous high standards would nevertheless prove to be a steadfast hit. The catchy 'Shot In The Dark' single had given the band a bona fide hit and, as such, the album a good initial impetus. Not only did it climb high in the charts internationally but it kept on selling making the world tour ever more drawn out as new legs were added to fulfill demand.

The era in which the album was launched was at the height of

Tapping In

the Los Angeles Glam rock renaissance as spearheaded by Mötley Crüe, Hanoi Rocks and Dokken. Ozzy himself would not go unaffected by this focus on image. At the time the singer's flowing sequinned silver cloaks and designer bleached hair seemed the norm for an international rock star.

"We were all into it," Phil Soussan readily admits with no hint of shame. "Those cloaks were actually Ozzy's idea. He'd been to a Diana Ross concert and had seen her in a glittering coat. He called Fleur Thiemeyer, our stageclothes designer and said, 'get me a glittering silver coat just like Diana Ross'. I think everyone at the time thought it looked quite good. Ha Ha! The whole band at that point was quite glammed up actually."

Phil would find guitarist Jake E. Lee a hard character to fathom. "Jake was a great guitarist no doubt. He had the showmanship, the stage presence, charisma and the right look too," he recognizes. "He was a genuine loner though. I travelled on the same bus as him throughout that whole tour and must have had at the most three conversations with him."

Metallica would open up for Ozzy for the first two American legs of the tour. "At the start Metallica nearly got thrown off the tour because of a barney Ozzy got into with Lars Ulrich over an altercation between my bass tech, Barry, and Lars... but it didn't last. We all got on pretty well," says Soussan. The untimely death of bassist Cliff Burton led to Blue Oyster Cult stepping into the breach before a final spree with Queensryche rounded off the jaunt.

In the UK the multi-platinum and then red hot Ratt, one of Jake E. Lee's previous acts, would act as openers with Leicester's Chrome Molly fulfilling support duties for three gigs. Australian dates were scheduled in but aborted when Ozzy lost his voice due to nodal growths on his vocal cords. Doctors ordered a strict regimen of silence for two weeks.

The Ozzy Osbourne band would also find themselves playing a special one-off gig in the capital city. Not at Hammersmith Odeon or Wembley arena, though, but at the rather less salubrious surroundings of H. M. Prison Wormwood Scrubs! A captive audience at last…

For security reasons the band would even have to rehearse within the confines of the jail. With the multitude of gigs that have drifted into the misty annals of time, Phil Soussan has good reason to have the memory of this particular event etched on his brain. "We had found ourselves locked up in a prison having rehearsals with some of the inmates on several occasions, one guy I think called T.J. was really cool, he was a guitar player who had had a tragic turn of events in life and found himself behind bars for 25 years."

Another inmate and willing helper would make an impression but for another reason entirely. "While we were rehearsing one other older inmate would make us endless cups of prison tea. At one point Randy asked what his crime had been and we were told that he had poisoned his entire family – wife, kids, the lot."

One wonders how Ozzy was feeling at the prospect of performing a gig to some of Britain's most hardened criminals. Ozzy's period of incarceration at Her Majesty's pleasure whilst a truculent teen banged up for minor misdemeanours paled in comparison to the sentences being endured by the majority of the inhabitants of Wormwood Scrubs. Phil recalls the gig itself.

"The day of the gig we were locked in this big hall with 300 hardcore lifers and only about ten guards... halfway through the set this big guy jumps up on stage and sticks his shoe on his head and starts dancing around. This was the guy that had tried to decapitate a cop in the Brixton riots... all of a sudden I realised that if they was a riot here we would have been toast."

Ozzy would pop up in some unexpected places too. The 1986 teen horror flick *Trick Or Treat* included both Ozzy and Kiss mainman Gene Simmons in extended cameo roles – Ozzy ironically portraying the anti-rock 'n' roll Reverend Aaron Gilstrom.

Back on the open road and with the world tour winding ever onwards Phil Soussan was feeling ill at ease within the camp. "There were days when I never really knew whether I was in the band or not. I was young though, only 24-25 and naïve enough to just go along with it. I never really felt there was a unified focus within the band despite Randy and me being tight. You got the impression that it was our privilege to be there, which of

Tapping In

course it actually was, but we were there for all the right reasons. Musically as a band we were very strong."

As strong as they were, the Ozzy Osbourne band and their organization could not control everything, however. The stage centrepiece, a monolithic green Ozzy statue that descended to reveal the real, flesh-and-blood Ozzy to the awaiting masses would prove temperamental. "It got stuck in the air once," Soussan laughs. "When they finally got it going only two of the three motors started lowering it with the net result that the whole thing started to tip over! Ozzy was carrying a cordless microphone that was switched on and all you could hear over the music was Ozzy yelling across the arena, 'Help! Help! Get me out of this fuckin' thing! Aaarrrggh!!!' And all that from the Prince of Darkness."

Randy Castillo recalls the same incident, the drummer being a little too close to the unfolding scenario for comfort. "This bright green, fork tongued Ozzy monster got caught in my drum riser as Ozzy was being lowered down to stage level. The crowd must have been wondering what the hell was happening. Was this part of the show – Ozzy screaming for help? Everyone in the place could hear it. It was a bad situation because my drum tech had to get up there and kick the monster off my riser. He was scared of heights and if he had fallen… It was a long way down. Ozzy was white as a ghost afterward, probably the only time I've seen Ozzy in fear of his life. We were all laughing later but it was a serious moment."

As the tour reached Japan tensions within the band would come to a head. "Sharon asked me to take Ozzy out for a drink in Tokyo," Phil recollects. "Well, of course he got plastered. At one point we ran into some of the crew who ran away from us like we had some terribly contagious disease. They were the smart ones!" The battle-hardened crew obviously made a wise decision, for "we ended up in Japanese Beatle bar with the owner bringing us litre bottles of saki. Every time Ozzy looked away I would pour it under the table to stop him drinking it but the guy would then come out with another one! All this to Japanese renditions of 'Lucy In The Sky With Diamonds', 'I Want To

Ozzy Osbourne

Hold Your Hand' and other favourites!

We finally left and I tried to drag Ozzy back to the hotel despite his resistance. At one point he wanted to sit down at a roadside soup kitchen and have yet another drink. He slipped off the seat and cut his arm. When we got back to the hotel a very pissed-off Sharon took delivery of her husband. All I heard when the door slammed was crashing and yelling, fighting and banging. The next morning the two of them were sitting in the hotel lobby – dark glasses, bruises, black eyes and hair missing. It was funny!"

Ozzy's reluctant drinking partner's amusement at the sight of two of the rock world's most esteemed figures in such a state of dishevelment did not last for long though. "I was told, in front of everyone, that I was fired."

Naturally the musician took this quite literally. "I guess they held me responsible. I went upstairs and started to pack my bags but then they changed their minds."

With *The Ultimate Sin* breaking the million sales mark in America alone (it would eventually go double platinum) and giving Ozzy huge international sales patterns too, the climax of such a successful world tour would turn out unintentionally to be a muted affair. Originally the band were scheduled to close in Tyler, Texas but public protest had forced the cancellation of this event. Therefore the original penultimate gig in Corpus Christi would end up being the final show.

Phil Soussan: "The last night of the tour was a great anti-climax. There were no parties – it was just like any other gig." Of course, being Ozzy, even this dampened atmosphere could not go unmarked. The bass player recalls an odd character forcing his presence upon Ozzy over breakfast that day.

"It was about 9.30 in the morning in a crowded hotel coffee shop with all of us quietly eating breakfast. This guy jumps up next to Ozzy with a bible in his hand and starts chanting 'Behold Satan!!' over and over again." According to Soussan Ozzy simply turned to their uninvited guest and said dryly "Look, I'm not Satan. I'm just trying to eat me scrambled eggs."

Returning to London with the Tokyo incident a distant

Tapping In

memory, practicalities for the next album became paramount. "Sharon and Tony Martell, head of CBS, had pulled me aside at our platinum album party in New York to tell me that they wanted me to start writing for the next album. I took a room in Sharon's Maida Vale offices, converted it into a studio, and spent the next four months writing before going on to LA in the beginning of 1987 so we could start getting some songs into shape."

Once in California the elements of friction that had been developing around Jake began to seriously hinder progress. "Randy, John Sinclair and I would show up at rehearsal at midday as arranged and basically wait for Jake. This happened every day. Jake simply never showed. He had brought a new car and was working on that all the time. His roadie Spike would be there but for days Jake just would not arrive. I don't think that for a long time Ozzy knew about this because he was spending a lot of time promoting the *Tribute* album."

Finally the errant guitarist did come to the rehearsal studio. "He showed up in the evening after we had been waiting for him all day," Phil says resignedly. "So, he arrives and the first thing he says is 'I need a sleep'. So he takes a nap! After he woke we tried to find a practical solution to this so we asked him what time he wanted to rehearse. 'Four,' he said. So, next day we were there at four and he arrived at eight and told us he was too tired to do anything! This, unbelievably, went for about three months. Well, of course, word eventually got back and Ozzy and Sharon laid down the law. If he wasn't there by one o'clock the next day he was fired."

Trying to keep the peace Phil telephoned Jake in an endeavour to instil some enthusiasm and drop a strong hint that he really was required to attend the next day's session. His conciliatory efforts received an unexpected reply.

"As a favour I told him that he really needed to be there tomorrow and he had to be there on time," the bassist muses. "He told me in no uncertain terms that he ran this band and that was that. I've actually never seen him since." The next day Phil and Randy were instructed to meet up with Ozzy at the Westwood Marquee Hotel and from there went onto a Mexican restaurant.

Ozzy Osbourne

During their four hour stay Sharon was elsewhere informing Jake he was no longer part of the band. Another era came to an end.

"I've heard that Jake kind of holds me responsible for his dismissal" opines Soussan. "I've never spoken to him to this day but I find it odd he thinks I had something to do with it. He credits me with too much power there I think."

15
Next!

With Jake E. Lee scrubbed from the team sheet an earnest quest for a replacement was soon set in motion with Soussan and Castillo proving to be any budding wannabe's first line of redoubt. "We got through loads of guitarists, hundreds and hundreds. Auditioning really is a hell of a task," affirms the bassist. All the budding applicants had three songs to learn – 'Crazy Train', 'Mr. Crowley' and 'I Don't Know'. Phil was delegated the task of sifting through a mountain of audition packages. Quite an endeavour as the Los Angeles grapevine had rapidly spread word of the hottest job in town. Among those who elevated themselves to the possibles listings were Steve Fister, who both Randy and Phil knew from previous jam sessions, Jake E. Lee's old Rough Cutt sparring partner Amir Derakh, Vinnie Moore, Chris Impelliterri, Joe Holmes and Nick Nolan. "A lot of the G.I.T. people" Phil laughs. "I think we must have seen them all."

Mitch Perry of MSG and Steeler was also a contender. "Mitch was in there too although I think he might have said something wrong which cost him his chance," according to Soussan.

As Phil Soussan confirms, one potential candidate who would make it into the chosen few was Steve Fister. The young six stringer had already made his mark by working with the former Detective and Silverhead vocalist Michael Des Barres and with hoary Psych rocker pioneers Iron Butterfly.

When the call to arms for the Ozzy position came Fister was working up his first solo album in collusion with the erstwhile Dave Lee Roth sibling partnership of Gregg and Matt Bissonette. Another project being pitched to record companies had Fister in alliance with former Ted Nugent singer Derek St. Holmes.

Steve describes how he got to hear about the try-outs. "At that time, you had a 'network' of friends, musicians, cocktail waitresses, music writers, record company people, etc." he explains. "You just had to call and hang out, to find out who was looking for a guitar player. I had heard through that grapevine that Ozzy was looking for a new guitarist. So, I called a friend of mine at Jet Records for info about the auditions. I got an address to send a promo pack. I thought at least I'll get a shot at the gig. I learned 'Shot In The Dark' and another one. You also had to look the part, very important! In the next few weeks I waited for a call."

The musician's wait would prove to be frustrating. Not only did he not get a call back but he had to endure the uninhibited glee of those who did receive an invitation.

"I guess every guitar player in the LA area was up for the gig. It seemed like anyone who owned a guitar and hung out at the Rainbow Bar and Grill got an audition," Steve says with feeling. However, the guitarist had the foresight to apply for another opening at the same time which, as a coincidence would have it, would land him at his originally intended destination. "During that time I heard Lita [Ford] was also looking for a guitar player. I heard that she had been through 80 or more players. While waiting for the Ozzy call I got a call to audition for Lita."

Lita Ford, often dictated by way of sheer talent as being the top ranking in the girl guitar league, had carved her name with pride as part of the original all girl teen brat pack The Runaways. It was Lita, who admits to having attended her first Black Sabbath concert at the tender age of 13, who lent The Runaways their metallic sheen.

The lady in black records just how the presence of Ozzy Osbourne had shaped her entire career. "My cousin took me to see Black Sabbath at the Long Beach Arena. It was my first ever gig and it totally changed my life!" she gushes. "The band's music was just so awesome, really dark and powerful. I remember Ozzy being hunched over with all his crosses – and all that hair! It wasn't just the music, it was the whole atmosphere the band created. The smell struck me too – thousands of kids smoking pot!"

The teenaged Lita left that night with her life's mission clearly laid out in front of her. "Seeing Black Sabbath was an inspiration. It gave me my whole want for rock 'n' roll and made clear to me exactly what I wanted to do."

The Runaways had forced Lita into the American popular cul-

Next!

tural consciousness but the band's flame flickered all too briefly. Squabbling tore the band apart leaving a cult legacy of proto-Riot Grrrl teen spirit to be picked up by later generations.

Now flying solo, Lita's seductive looks and supreme guitar skills had propelled her to the forefront of the hard rock scene again. The opening 1983 salvo of *Out For Blood* was a mean statement of intent it proving that girls could shred too, and, provided the impetus needed for the follow-up 1984 outing *Dancin' On The Edge* to chart on both sides of the Atlantic. Drums on the *Dancin'* opus had been handled by Randy Castillo.

Gearing up for the launch of what would be her greatest commercial endeavour, the million selling *Lita* album, her business affairs at this juncture were coincidentally handled by the intuitive figure of Sharon Osbourne.

Such was the Metal queen's regency at the time of the auditions, the domain into which Steve Fister entered. "I went to Leeds rehearsal in North Hollywood to play for her," Steve records. "I had learned four tunes. I remember there were three guys ahead of me, one of which was Scott Sheets from Pat Benatar's band. The holding room looked like a waiting room at a maternity hospital! Lots of raw nerves! I went in and played, and Lita asked me to hang around."

His wait would, not as expected, be ended by Lita Ford though. "Half an hour later Ozzy and Sharon walk in! We played the songs again for them. In the last three weeks I could not have bought an audition with him, and there I am playing Lita tunes with him sitting three feet in front of me!"

One can only imagine what state Steve Fister's frayed nerves were in at this point. Further protracted waiting ensued. "After we played, Lita went into the office with Sharon, and I just hung out with Ozzy. Lita had introduced me as having just worked with Michael Des Barres. Ozzy was really nice, telling stories and such. Funny and friendly. Fun to be around. The next day, I was officially hired on with Lita. As the rehearsals progressed I was made the 'musical director' in charge of rehearsing the band, making the set lists etc."

Steve's fate had been dictated by the fact that both Ozzy and

Lita were hungry for a new guitarist at the same juncture. Phil Soussan had recommended Steve for the Ozzy gig but his style of playing was deemed more suitable for Lita Ford's band. "Over the years I've played with both Phil and Randy on various sessions, gigs and jams. Phil told me that after he reviewed my package, they wanted to audition me for Ozzy." The Osbournes had other ideas though, and Lita's need was as great as Ozzy's.

Steve soon found himself in at the deep end in his new band environment. It would, as history confirms, prove a fruitful relationship. "At that time Lita did lots of press and didn't have a lot of time. So I was appointed to run the rehearsals, pace the show, (always subject to her approval, but she gave me lots of room) write endings for the tunes, write the guitar harmony parts. Lita was cool, she let me play a lot of solos on the gig, we did a lot of harmonies and trade-offs, and on some tunes she would just sing and I'd play all the guitar." And so as Lita Ford claimed her man, the hunt for an Ozzy guitar slinger continued apace.

Meantime in the thick of the action in the Ozzy camp the Soussan/Castillo rhythm section-cum-judging panel developed their own system for weeding out the no-hopers. "We had secret signals. If Randy dropped a drumstick that meant he was telling me the guy was no good and likewise for me if I 'accidentally' dropped my pick. It worked out fine because nobody got really upset but then we had this one guy who was just racing around the studio like a lunatic, running up and down and spinning around. He was obviously not right for the job because he wasn't a brilliant player but he was just so entertaining to watch I lost my concentration. Of course what I wasn't seeing was Randy dropping sticks behind me. In the end he threw a stick straight into the back of my head to force my attention. 'Sorry, I dropped my stick' he said! He had dropped about eight sticks before resorting to that move."

The bassist recalls another memorable candidate. "There was also some Swedish guy who was very good but didn't make it in the end. Actually, the reason he didn't make it was because he tried to tell us that we were all playing in the wrong keys which really pissed us off! When we played 'Flying High Again' with

Next!

this guy Ozzy sang the first line with an appropriate change: 'Got a crazy feeling I don't understand, get this cunt away from me.' We cracked up!"

There was another high-calibre applicant who very nearly made the grade, Kramer Guitars endorsee Jimi Bell. The young guitarist had made an impression with his act Joined Forces, opening for Joan Jett. Indeed, Bell's playing had prompted both Kramer and Seymour Duncan to grant full endorsements and put the musician forward for a movie slot. Bell, alongside a cameo by Joan Jett, would wind up in the Michael J. Fox film *Light Of Day*. It was Kramer Guitars who sent Bell's video to Sharon Osbourne, hence securing the audition. As Jimi relates he made it past the first hurdle. "From that point they flew me out to LA for auditions. The audition itself was a great experience for me. You had to play with Phil and Randy first. Sharon was there for my audition. She was a wonderful woman and was very nice to me. After I was done, they said they wanted Ozzy to hear me play. So about a day later, I auditioned with Ozzy."

Come the day of final reckoning, Bell was just as nerve ridden as his predecessors at the trials. Witnessing Ozzy manifest his disdain for one unlucky soul who had stepped up before him did little to dampen his fears. "There was one person before me and he was butchering the 'Flying High' solo. Ozzy was standing behind him pretending to stab and strangle him. Of course this scared me because I was next to audition!*"

Fully committed, though, Bell duly took his turn. "As I started to play, Ozzy started to get into my playing. When ever I played a solo, he knelt down in front of my amp and listened. Some of the songs I played were, 'I Don't Know', 'Crazy Train', 'Suicide Solution', and a jam. When I was done, they were very impressed. They sat me down and Sharon said, 'Well, it's between Zakk and yourself'.

The Osbournes invited Bell out for a meal that evening, an event during which Bell would experience Ozzy's wicked sense of humour at first hand. "While eating, I asked Ozzy if he wanted my tomatoes my from salad. He replied, 'No!' So about a minute later while eating, he reached his hands into my salad and snatched the tomatoes. It was a funny experience to have Ozzy reaching into your plate like that!" he laughs. "Then we went back to Ozzy's place. While I was there a Black Sabbath video came on TV and Ozzy grabbed his daughter Aimee and said, 'Look, Aimee, there's daddy with his old band!' That night, Phil and Randy took me out to the Troubadour Club in LA where they met up with Chris Impelliterri and Blackie Lawless. The next day I flew home waiting to hear the results."

Then came Zakk Wylde, suggested by the rock photographer Mark Weiss. "Zakk, or Zachary Wylant (real name Jeffrey Weilandt) as he was known then, was flown in and I picked him up at the Hyatt," remarks Phil. "He was there hanging out with another good friend, Adrian Vandenberg. He was totally wide-eyed, just a laughing kid. We took him down to rehearsals and it was just so refreshing. Not only was he a really nice guy, really friendly but he could really play. The other really great thing about him was that he arrived and said Let's go!', plugged himself into a Marshall and let rip. After Randy and I had been wasting time with all those jokers taking two hours to set up massive rack systems it was great to see just raw enthusiasm."

Zakk Wylde, it appears, was just glad to be given the opportunity. "He was so genuine. Zakk was having a blast and I don't think he realized how right he was for the job." recalls Phil. "He even got his albums out to get autographed. He said 'I'll probably never see you guys again'. He was the right guy for the job though. Ozzy liked him too because he reminded him of Randy, the enthusiasm and even the look to a degree."

Another close contender was Terrif man and former Randy Rhoads guitar pupil Joe Holmes – although his day would come later on down the line. Of the other hopefuls Vinnie Moore and Chris Impelliterri would persevere with their solo careers whilst Amir Derakh would completely re-invent himself for the Nu-Metal age scoring platinum success in the millennium with Orgy.

Meantime, one of the final contenders pipped to the post by Zakk would not find his efforts had been in vain. Whilst

---

*Author's note: Soussan believes this was the 'Swedish guy'.

Next!

awaiting auditions Bell had shared the same hotel as Zakk and the pair had often jammed together. "We got along really great. I knew later that he respected my playing because he mentioned it at a guitar clinic that he was doing."

Much as Steve Fister had been manouevred over into the employ of Lita Ford so Jimi Bell would find there was other Black Sabbath – related work in need of his guitar skills. "After finding out they went with Zakk, I received a call from Geezer Butler who told me Sharon had recommended me for his new band. From there I flew to England to work with Geezer where Gloria Butler made me feel very much at home."

The band Geezer was assembling at the time was led up front by former Persian Risk and Ghost vocalist Carl Sentance. "I loved his singing and thought he was a great guy. He looked like a young Roger Daltrey at the time" conveys the guitarist. Also involved were Robert Plant's erstwhile keyboard player Jezz Woodruffe and the highly rated drummer Gary Ferguson.

In the throes of working up this new endeavour Geezer and Jimi managed to find time to catch a break, the Black Sabbath bassist instilling some English culture into the American with a visit to the medieval stronghold of Warwick castle. Along with Butler's eldest son Biff (now a fine musician in his own right) a younger member of the Osbourne clan was along for the ride too. "We all went up to the castle lookout tower where we stayed for a while. It was getting dark so we decided to go back down. As we headed down the stairs we didn't realize that there were no lights in the tower. It had a spiral staircase all the way down. So Geezer grabbed Biff and I took Aimee and carried her step by step to the bottom as I leaned into the circular wall of this old tower." The American guitarist was already envisaging his name in headlines next to that of Ozzy's, like he had always dreamed of but, this time for all the wrong reasons.

"At this point, it was pitch dark and I started to pray, 'Oh my God, please don't let me fall with Ozzy's daughter in my arms!' This would be the end of me!" Aimee and Jimi arrived safely on the ground. Geezer's proposed band project would record demos and videos but ultimately stalled. Sentance, after a term as a theatre actor, would later find his services in demand fronting Swiss rock institution Krokus.

16
Eyes Closed To Success

In May of 1987 with Zakk Wylde on board the Ozzy band set to work on the next record. The band spent a good portion of 1987 ensconced in the hurricane-lashed Music Farm – soon dubbed the Beetle Farm – working up songs which would eventually surface on *No Rest For The Wicked*.

One insider portrays the strengths Zakk brought to the team. "With Zakk in the band things got a lot noisier, that's for sure," he laughs. "There were absolutely no doubts about Zakk at all, he was just so confident and totally into it. To tell the truth his playing was pretty awe-inspiring and a bit of an inspiration to us all. I've seen it all, but when he started playing guitar my jaw just dropped. Amazing stuff straight from the top of his head."

Zakk's resemblance to Randy had not passed unremarked either. "He was a pretty Randy-ish type figure. Randy's influence was with us all the time and Zakk seemed to fit into that. When he first joined the band he was very much up on classical music. He would set up his music stand and simply practice for hours and hours – he's changed a lot!"

Phil Soussan was again asked to contribute to the songwriting process but this would eventually lead to his opting out of the band. "I was writing songs for the album as requested but we were having difficult negotiations over the publishing arrangements. It's quite a normal thing in this game but it's also important for a writer to hang on to his ???????????? because publishing for a writer eventually becomes his pension. This went on for about three months and basically I didn't want to sell so I quit."

Soussan's term of engagement would come to a close in March 1988. "I didn't want to leave, I had friends there but it was time to move on. Randy Castillo thought I was an idiot and told me so. We had loads of arguments afterwards about it although we are still great friends to this day."

The bassist's next port of employ would again, just as with Ozzy, come along in the form of a coincidence. "Randy Castillo and I went on a long holiday to Tahiti. We met Billy Idol on the beach there which led to me appearing on his next record. Randy was supposed to join Billy's band too but didn't in the end."

Fred Coury, now firmly ensconced in Cinderella with 6 million record sales behind him, happened to find himself meeting up with Ozzy once more just prior to of recording for the *No Rest For The Wicked* album. "I was actually in an elevator in this apartment block saying goodbye to a friend when Ozzy kinda 'kidnapped' me and took me to his room. So there I was, sitting with Ozzy and the comedian Sam Kinison having a real good time. Ozzy was just sitting there listening to old Black Sabbath records and I was just thinking to myself 'This is the coolest!' I was flipping out.

"So, anyway, Ozzy asks me 'Fred, What do you think of Mike Inez?' I replied that I didn't know who he was. Nowadays he's a very good friend but then I didn't know him. Ozzy says 'He's my new bass player.'

"Then Ozzy asks me 'What do you think of Bob Daisley?' so I tell him the truth which is that Bob is by far the best bassist I've ever played with in my life".

Two days later Fred received a surprise visitor at his door. "It was Bob Daisley," says Coury. "He came round to say thank you! I don't know how much influence I had with Ozzy just by saying what I did that night but it was a really nice thing for Bob to do. I guess Ozzy must have told him. He came to my room just to tell me that. Cool!"

Bob relates yet another saga in his life with Ozzy Osbourne. "I did the *No Rest For The Wicked* record, writing lyrics and music and playing bass. I also wrote and performed fretless bass on a track that didn't make the album called 'The Liar'. It came out later on a 12" single. Geezer did the tour I think."

Daisley would also record the *Odyssey* album with Swedish guitar maestro Yngwie Malmsteen – the Scandinavian's biggest selling album to date. He would then be once again absorbed by the Black Sabbath camp when, alongside Ozzy, he played on drummer Bill Ward's solo album *Ward One – Along The Way*. Inevitably it would not be Daisley's last tenure with Ozzy either.

In October, 1988 Ozzy served up *No Rest For The Wicked*.

Eyes Closed To Success

The album sessions had begun with Roy Thomas Baker but would be completed by Keith Olsen. With the sanitized *Ultimate Sin* having, despite the odds, racked up larger sales than anticipated, the new album needed to be something special.

Ozzy fans had nothing to fear, with Zakk Wylde Ozzy had found a foil every bit as arresting as his predecessors. Randy had the vision and Jake the groove but Zakk rudely observed no precedents. The lead single *Miracle Man* proved to be a well aimed swipe at American TV evangelists. Ozzy seemingly delighted at bloodying the noses of the likes of Jimmy Swaggert and his crucifix-wielding cronies who had hounded him over so many road miles.

The Japanese really went to town in an exercise of marketing zeal. Besides the regular release, the record was offered repackaged as *The Bible Of Ozz* boasting an extra two tracks, a heavyweight belt buckle, an Ozzy logo patch, a Zakk patch and a book, the whole thing cased in packaging designed to give a Biblical appearance.

If there was one overriding factor about *No Rest* it was that riffs ruled. 'Tattooed Dancer', 'Devil's Daughter' and the unhinged lunacy of 'Crazy Babies' rode riffs that seasoned rodeo veterans would have difficulty hanging on to. Somehow though Ozzy not only maintained his grip but would perform the feat with a nonchalant ease. Of course the album itself could never fully hope to capture Wylde's untamed approach but it gave the youngster enough leeway to prime his audience. *No Rest For The Wicked* was more a statement of intent – *Zakk's here. Keep your heads down, the management accepts no responsibility.*

Zakk's zeal in stamping his authority knew no parameters. If he was rockin' he was unstoppable until the curtain dropped. Ample evidence for this can be found in this eyewitness account from a backstage vantage point at London's Hammersmith Odeon. "Zakk had got up on top of this pile of cabs for his solo spot. Unfortunately he had ripped the back of his trousers open so all I could see right in front of me was this dirty great pair of balls! It was not a pretty sight. Anyway, Zakk didn't care one bit – he just got on with the show so I had just had to stand with

Ozzy Osbourne

Zakk's balls swinging in front of me! He was soloing like there was no tomorrow with his hair swinging, his balls swinging and the kids just loving it."

Among those staying low in the trenches at this time was Tony Iommi. 1988 had been a grim year for Black Sabbath. So dull had Iommi's star dimmed that in April a well-executed *Kerrang!* magazine April Fools hoax ran with an 'exclusive' story related to plans for top Welsh crooner Tom Jones to join the band, the combination revealing their intention to record a concept album and undertake a tour based upon the dual subjects of bullfighting and Welsh mining.

Taken outside of the context of an olde-English jape the story had an unpleasant ring of truth to it. Iommi, now on singer number eight since Ozzy's 1979 departure – Walker, Dio, Gillan, Donato, Keel, Hughes, Gillen and now Tony Martin, could not replace the original frontman. True, Dio's era had been artistically edifying but Gillan's tenure had been like watching two beached whales battling for space in a stagnant rockpool. Iommi's last effort, 1987's *Eternal Idol,* had undergone an all too public nightmare involving three producers, two singers and even the quick fix of Bob Daisley's depping to get it into the stores, by which time fans had simply had enough. The fact that *Eternal Idol* was in fact a fine album meant little. The record company heeded a media sensing a giant-killing – and Black Sabbath were ignominiously dropped.

That year Black Sabbath put in a low-key appearance at an Oldbury working men's club, performing for charity in an atmosphere of stale pints and sticky carpets. The present author witnessed one of the strangest ever Black Sabbath line-ups for this one-off gig comprising Iommi, Martin, drummer Bev Bevan and keyboardist Geoff Nichols handling bass duties.

Meanwhile Ozzy imperiously announced a touring line-up of Zakk Wylde, Randy Castillo and his old Black Sabbath cohort Geezer Butler on bass. The resulting world tour would be a triumph. Not only did Ozzy nick Iommi's bass man he would also (artistically and metaphorically speaking) nick his ex-ladyfriend too when he hooked up with Lita Ford for a monster hit single.

Eyes Closed To Success

It was plain to see who was winning this round.

1988 would be the year that Ozzy Osbourne scored his biggest American hit single. What made the success of 'Close My Eyes Forever' the more remarkable though was that the track came together by happy accident, was initially resisted as a single choice by all the powers that be, and to top it all was a duet with Lita Ford.

Ford: "It was a total accident. My band and I were in a North Hollywood recording studio trying to find some more songs for the *Lita* album. We needed one or two more songs to complete the record." The pressure of wrapping up an album was relieved in true Ozzy Osbourne style as he and Sharon arrived, bringing along a new-found friend. A strong but silent type with jet black hair, Ozzy's companion would make an immediate impression on Lita.

"It was a life-size inflatable gorilla from the San Diego zoo!" Lita howls at the memory of it. "Those things are big – and this was actual size. I had just moved apartments and Sharon and Ozzy had brought me this gorilla as a housewarming gift. You should have seen this fucking thing. It was huge! So anyway, a couple of bottles of wine were opened and we started to play pool. Eventually Sharon got bored and left. At the studio there was this little room set off with guitars, keyboards and stuff so we got drunk and before we knew it we were writing a song. Ozzy has this great sense of melody, he's very inspired by The Beatles, and he's just a great singer. People often don't appreciate that about him. We carried on, completely drunk, until we had finished. By that time it was daylight. We were pretty sloshed."

The finished song, although a ballad, was far from stereotypical. "Ozzy's idea for the lyric was this vision of him standing on a mountain looking over the entire world but with his eyes closed, still able to see everything," Lita reveals. "Isn't it amazing what alcohol can do?"

Sharon Osbourne was far from happy though. "Sharon was very upset with both me and Ozzy for staying out all night" Lita confides. "But hey, we had a song!"

A song was not the only thing Lita had. "I had to drive home

– drunk – with a gorilla!" she laughs. "So, there I am in my black jeep with Ozzy's life-size gorilla in the passenger seat with his seat belt on to keep him from falling out driving home thinking, 'oh God please don't let me get pulled over'. And, of course, I was pulled over. Even a drunk woman can do a lot by just batting her eyelids so I said 'I live just over there, please let me go, officer'. What could he do? Ozzy Osbourne, a gorilla and Lita Ford. Who would make that up?"

The Mike Chapman produced *Lita* album would be Ford's biggest album of her career. Kick-started by the bouncy single 'Kiss Me Deadly' just missing out on a US top ten slot but securing a heavy MTV rotation which brought Lita's bodacious curves to the masses. The songwriting calibre was high (Nikki Sixx had co-written 'Falling In And Out Of Love'), the guitar quota was high and even higher were the hormone levels of the teenage male population of America. The album had it all and its *tour de force* had not even been unleashed yet.

"The radio hit on 'Close My Eyes Forever' even before anyone else," Lita admits. "Nothing was planned at all. It started to take off without any record company involvement. People everywhere were playing that song. One day the news must have finally sunk in because a guy from the record company called and said "Lita, you're gonna have to do a video of that song".

This snowballing momentum would be questioned from an unlikely source though. "Sharon was against it at first," says Lita. "She was very keen to promote Ozzy and me as completely separate artists. I think she thought we should leave it, not do it right now and try another track. The problem was the song kept on growing." This opinion that Lita and Ozzy should be marketed as distinct separate entities even dictated the perception given out to the TV viewer from the promotional video. "We did it in an old train station but it looks like we are not even in the same room. That's the way it was shot. Although we were in reality together the video looks like we're not. I was on ground level and Ozzy was on this shelf type thing. We're never actually together in the video."

Divisive videos aside 'Close My Eyes Forever' duly delivered

Eyes Closed To Success

top ten on the Billboard charts and gave the Americans a refreshed look at the world of Ozzy Osbourne. The ballads had always been there, right from the Black Sabbath fave 'Changes', but obscured by the insanity of decapitated doves, bats' heads, tortured dwarves, tattooed werewolves and vampire fangs. Now Ozzy's more heartfelt renderings would be given more credence and acceptance, opening up new markets later demonstrated by the acceptability of mainstream tracks such as 'Mama, I'm Coming Home'.

"The fans made it a hit," Lita reckons. "They wanted it and they forced it to happen, both my fans and Ozzy's fans. It wasn't the record company or anybody else – just the fans."

With Lita now a platinum media darling and Ozzy sharing the same management stable a joint tour seemed inevitable. It was not to be, however.

"I was very excited. We were riding high with a big hit single and then they put out Vixen on tour with Ozzy instead of me!" Lita says unable to hide her indignation. "Ozzy and I had this huge hit, all over radio and MTV, and they put fucking *Vixen* on!! Like, what's the whole idea? Don't get me wrong – I love Vixen, nothing against them as female artists – God knows we have to stick together in this game – but where's the logic? I just could not see the sense. I was very, very hurt."

Lita Ford did manage just one show with Ozzy. "I did my hometown show at Long Beach Arena with Ozzy but I didn't get to see them or speak to them the entire day. I was ready to jam, I always am, but nothing happened. Strange." Ozzy and Lita would never get to sing 'Close My Eyes Together' live.

Lita Ford still has trouble reconciling those times. "Sharon was wonderful and I loved her. Ozzy was wonderful too. I mean, he was out there on occasion but he was a great, great guy and a fantastic singer too. You gotta love him. Sharon worked really hard for me, made me a platinum artist and she's one of the best people I've ever known but at the end it was a weird situation. We had the big hit but it just wasn't promoted for some reason. It would have been great for both our fans to see us do that song together live."

Ozzy Osbourne

On August 12th and 13th, 1989, Ozzy played the Moscow Music Peace Festival. This gargantuan display of *perestroika* featured heavyweight acts such as Bon Jovi, The Scorpions and Mötley Crüe. The bill was filled out with small club bands but Ozzy was a world-wide name and the crowd just went crazy when it was his turn to play.

The following year, Ozzy aided his old mucker Bill Ward on his inaugural solo outing. Released on the independent Chameleon label, the album would witness Ozzy donating lead vocals to two tracks 'Jack's Land' and 'Bombers (Can Open Bomb Bays)'. Unfortunately, due to the nature of its release, the album received little attention and those not quick off the mark enough at the time to purchase it were disappointed. A re-release is projected but with the two Ozzy-fronted songs excised. Ozzy would also turn up in a more unlikely combination with comedian Billy Connolly and boxer Frank Bruno the same year delivering 'The Urpney Song' for inclusion on the *Dreamstone* cartoon series.

With the gap widening between product, a stopgap release was hastily convened. No new material was as yet on the table so mobile recording studios attended some of the last gigs of the tour. These tapes would be issued as the mini album *Just Say Ozzy*, a record which would only serve to mystify fans and critics alike. Featuring four Ozzy numbers and renditions of Sabbath's 'War Pigs' and 'Sweet Leaf', it did at least capture the Wylde/Butler combination in flow but achieved little outside of that. Puzzled fans were far from impressed and *Just Say Ozzy* snuck timidly into the gutter of the Billboard rankings before just as hastily sneaking out again.

In a *Metal Forces* magazine interview Geezer Butler had this to say about the record. "It's just one of those record company things, and the record company pointed out we hadn't released anything for about 14 months, and the new album won't be out for about a year, and they wanted some product. It was kind of like 'What haven't we done?' Ha Ha. The record company took over at that point. It's just to shut them up really."

Having scored his biggest American hit to date and found

Eyes Closed To Success

renewed fan fervour by showcasing to the rock world yet another guitar protégé, Ozzy would deal the media yet another shot in the dark. Only this time it was a parting shot. Ozzy was not going out on the road anymore. There would be 'No More Tours'.

17
Nailing It Down

The Ozzy, Wylde, Butler and Castillo line-up would remain in force for recording what would, eventually, turn out to be the *No More Tears* album. However, Butler would then make a hasty exit leaving the bass role vacant. This gap would be plugged by Terry Nails, a man pivotal in the crafting of the album but often neglected by biographers.

Nails had forced his presence onto the Californian club scene with Killerwatt. Session duties then ensued which led to a project with Quicksilver Messenger Service guitar legend John Cipollina.

Nails would also work with some of the early Bay area Punk bands with live production. During this period some of Nails' clients were booked to open for no less than the Sex Pistols, leading to a friendship between Nails' and Pistols guitarist Steve Jones.

Another colleague, bass player Mike Varney of The Nunns, would hook Nails up with his next assignment, Tommy Tutone.

"I still have a hard time believing I even got that gig," confesses Nails. "I was actually a professional skateboarder at the time and my playing hand was in a cast due to a skateboarding accident and I was only able to play with one finger of my fretting hand, it was really bizarre. Tommy said he really liked my playing because I didn't over-play!" A six year tenure with Tutone was broken by relocating to Los Angeles and an endeavour with drummer Matt Sorum and guitarist Danny Stag. The bassist readily admits that at this juncture in his life he had also instigated a re-evaluation when it came to traditional rock 'n' roll recreation.

"Most of my time was taken up by just getting sober, which I'm glad to say I still am. And that's how I got hooked up with Jonesy and where I met Ozzy. We were all trying to do the same thing. I must say that we were all in pretty fabulous shape at the time. I could barely remember where I lived, I'm not sure whether Jonesy actually had a place and Ozzy was really fed up and pretty damn unhappy with the way his life was going. A very lovely crew we were..."

It would be a colourful and notorious crowd Nails was hanging with at the time. Both he and Jones, whilst performing together as a band, would also be temping off and on with The Cult. "Steve and I and the guys were doing gigs with The Cult and actually played a couple of gigs as temporary members. Me and Steve and our drummer Pete Kelly – awesome drummer, real powerhouse, with Ian and Billy, talk about fun! Wow! It was a real hoot. Steve and Billy sounded great together. It was like playing with family because Billy, Ian, Steve and myself spent a lot of time together when we weren't playing. Besides us, there was another part of the gang that included Charlie Sexton, Julian Lennon, Mickey Rourke, James Caan and Mickey's brother Joey, oh yeah, and Randy Castillo when he was in town, which wasn't that often 'cause he was out on tour so much. Later on Phil Soussan was part of that group also. We all hung pretty tight back in those days cause we all had bikes and we all rode together."

It would be Castillo who put in the invite to try out with Ozzy. "I was out sort of club-hopping one night on my bike with my teenage daughter Willia, when I ran into Randy coming out of a club we were just going into. He came over to us while I was parking the bike to say hello and asked me what I was doing tomorrow. I told him I didn't have anything planned, so he said 'do you want to do some playing with us?'.

Now you gotta understand something about Randy – he loves to play and is always playing with somebody, so I wasn't sure just who the 'us' he was talking about was. So I said 'sure, who are we playing with?' He told me Geezer and Ozzy had a tiff and that Geezer had split and they needed someone to fill in for him till he came back, which he didn't do till years later.

"Needless to say, I was pretty stunned, I mean after all playing with Ozzy was probably one of the best gigs, if not the best gig in the country as far as I was concerned. The next morning Sharon Osbourne called me and told me where the studio was and asked me if I needed anything and thanked me for helping them out. She was so nice it just blew me away, and that's how I got hooked up with Ozzy.

"There is one other person that might have recommended me and that's Bill Ward, the drummer for Black Sabbath. I worked with him for a while when he was getting ready to do his solo album... That was a lot of fun too. Bill's a great guy."

A somewhat nerve-jangled Nails arrived at Frank Zappa's rehearsal complex, Joe's Garage, the next day. "Geezer had walked either earlier that day or maybe the evening before. It may have just been a case of being in the right place at the right time. When I got to the studio the next day the equipment that Geezer was using was still set up and plugged in, so I think it was pretty much spur-of-the-moment."

Fortunately for the new enlistee his friend put him at ease. "When I got there I went in and got set up straight away. I think the only person there was Randy, which made things a bit easier 'cause we were pretty good friends already. Everyone filtered in fairly soon afterwards."

Then came the bombshell. "Someone, I think it was Zakk, suggested that we warm up with a Black Sabbath song. Well I figured I was screwed right then and there because I had to admit to everyone including Ozzy that I didn't know any Black Sabbath songs because I never really listened to them. 'Well, there goes that gig' I thought, but all Ozzy and the guys did was laugh. Everything started out pretty good as Randy and I started going through a bunch of old songs that we grew up listening to like Blue Cheer's version of 'Summer Time Blues' and some other stuff." Indeed, the new band unit gelled quickly enough to reap some cast iron results from this early union.

"We took a short break and I came back into the room early to warm up" Nails explains the sequence of events. " I was just kinda playing this heavy sort of groove when Randy came in and started playing this thuggish type of drum beat with me, then Zakk came in and started playing also and the thing just sorta took off by itself. Then I noticed Ozzy standing there with this little memo tape recorder in his hand recording what we were doing. He then walked up to the mike and started making up lyrics on the spot, something about a hellraiser, and that's how

Nailing It Down

the song 'Hellraiser' got started."

The streak of good fortune was about to be abruptly curtailed though in spectacular and embarrassing fashion. "Everything was going really good until we started working on 'Zombie Stomp'. It was at that point that I somehow completely fried and I do mean *fried*, Geezer's amp. It kinda sounded like a series of gigantic nuclear farts.

"Zakk told me later on that he had listened back to the rehearsal tapes months later and that he was rolling on the floor laughing when he heard it. At the time I was just thinking, 'shit! How am I gonna pay for this now?'

"Needless to say that cut everything short for the day. When we left I didn't know whether I was coming back or not, but I thought what the heck, at least I got to play with them once and, hell, it was really a lot of fun."

A couple of days later Nails received a telephone call from Sharon Osbourne asking if he would mind coming back in to play some more.

"Mind? Would I mind coming in and playing more bass? I thought; sure, I'd love to. How much do I have to pay you? I told her I could probably manage it and asked when and where and she said tomorrow at the same place. She then asked what kind of equipment I would like them to rent for me – since I had obviously just ruined Geezer's rig – and I said that I'd like to ruin, I mean…use my own if that was OK. So they arranged to have my stuff picked up the next day."

The bassist found himself in the midst of a long, drawn-out process that the *No More Tears* album sessions had stagnated into. The recording and writing was becoming protracted, ebbing and flowing with each new personality's arrival and departure. Nails got the impression the team had reached stalemate and needed a pick-me-up.

"Why? I don't honestly know. There seemed to be a lot going on behind the scenes that I just wasn't a party to. Ozzy seemed to be doing really good for a while and then sort of fell off, if you know what I mean. I don't really mean to be telling stories out of school, but I just don't know how else to put it.

Ozzy Osbourne

"From what I had been told, they had been in the studio for over a year trying to get the songs for the album worked out and were at a sort of stalemate with the whole thing when I came into it. After that things started to move pretty fast. Ozzy told me that if Geezer didn't come back that he wanted me to take his place and I did for a while. I think that the bringing in of someone new to the project changed the vibe enough to get things going again. But then again, who knows? It could have been the weather for all I know."

Despite the turbulence Terry Nails was quick to recognise the calibre of the players involved. "One of the things I remember most is how blown away I was by Zakk's playing. He was just fucking amazing! Zakk was a complete madman. A really great guy and an insane guitar player. One of the best I've ever seen, completely one with his instrument. Someone who would constantly push the limits and make everyone a better player because of it. Randy is a great drummer and a good friend, rock solid player. Ozzy? What can I say about him? I love Ozzy, it's that simple."

Randy Castillo describes how, although the sessions were drawing out much longer than expected, the title track for the album had come together spontaneously. "The song 'No More Tears' came together as if by magic. Mike Inez was just jamming a bass riff at rehearsal and then Zakk from out of nowhere started laying down this monster of a riff that was just like 'Wow!' So John starts to put down a keyboard pattern and this thing is growing and we're all getting excited because you know when you've got a song that's special. I don't think we got it nailed that day but we got straight back to it. Funny thing was when we tried to recapture that spark in the studio we hit a brick wall. I had put the chorus in but the song had kinda stalled. Ozzy had actually got bored of the whole thing and was having a sleep in the control room but suddenly he gets up and just starts singing this incredible vocal. Straight away all the magic came pouring back and the song is finished. Just like that! Ozzy is great at that kind of thing. He has a real gut instinct for what it takes to make something work."

Nailing It Down

With the album taking so long to commit to tape and a myriad of players involved, the goals appeared to have been temporarily lost. As so often happens in studio scenarios such as this the attention to detail clouded the initial nature of the songs, as Nails clarifies when discussing the original demo takes.

"I'd say that they were a lot more ballsy when they were recorded the first time. They had a spontaneity and energy that seemed to be lacking on the later album. I don't mean all the songs, just certain ones like 'Same Old Desire', 'I Don't Want To Change The World' and 'Zombie Stomp'. To me the songs sounded like they had been rehearsed too many times."

The actual recording process would be far from smooth though. "When we did the demos – the stuff that you hear on the *No More Tears, The Demo Sessions* CD – we had this guy who did a good job for us, but he kinda fucked things up for himself when we started the album the first time.

"It seems that he had a bass player friend that he wanted to get to do the bass on the album and he started trying to manipulate the situation. He ended up finding himself out of a gig as well as probably being a contributing factor to the reason I found myself out of a gig as well. At least that's what the other guys told me they think happened.

"From what I understand the guy actually came in played and Ozzy was so unhappy with the situation that he decided to scrap the whole project till a later date."

With *No More Tears* requiring salvage Bob Daisley's literary skills would be in demand again. Having assembled the Mother's Army band with another Ozzy veteran drummer ,Carmine Appice, alongside former Deep Purple, Rainbow and Yngwie Malmsteen colleague Joe Lynn Turner and Nightranger guitarist Jeff Watson, a familiar call interrupted proceedings.

Nonetheless things did not work out according to plan. "Typically I got a call from Ozzy asking me to leave for Los Angeles the next day. I think I made it a few days later and started recording straight away. I wrote all of the lyrics for all of the songs on *No More Tears* and they were accepted" he states. "We even shook on it. Then they changed their minds. All the song titles stayed the same but they got in different lyric writers to redo them all."

On hand during this period of revision would be none other than Lemmy of Motorhead, a man whose lyric-writing abilities are often buried in the volume of the music that they complement. Terry Nails: "It was great to have Lemmy involved 'cause he's just fun to work with and very professional. He wrote most of the lyrics for the album. Ozzy would give him an idea about what he wanted and Lemmy would come back the next day with a finished lyric sheet and that's what you hear on the album. Lemmy had been a friend of mine for a while so it was just that much more comfortable in the studio. Besides, I love Motorhead."

One of those tracks Lemmy is credited for, 'Hellraiser', would be included not only on the Ozzy product but rather cheekily on Motorhead's own 1992 *March Or Die* opus. Nails is unequivocal; "their version of 'Hellraiser' was by far the best…" Ozzy returned the favour to Lemmy by lending his distinctive vocal tones to another *March Or Die* track 'I Ain't No Nice Guy'.

Did any of Nails' lyrics end up on the finished record? The bassist is not credited on the sleeve notes. "Let me put it this way, some of the songs were very different when I first came in and the way they sounded after I came in is the way they got recorded on the album," he says gingerly. "Don't get me wrong, I knew what I was dealing with when I got into it and I didn't expect anything, although it would have been nice to get a thank you on the album. Aside from that, they took care of me very, very well. I sure would have liked to have done the album but that's not the way the cards played out. It sure was fun while it lasted though…"

As for the eleventh-hour re-induction of Daisley on bass, Nails has this to offer. "I'm not surprised that Bob got the call to do the album. That seems to be the way things went. Nobody ever seemed to know what was going to happen next, including Ozzy. Bob was definitely the right man for the job, he's simply a great player."

Nailing It Down

The story does not end for Terry Nails there though. Besides his ongoing involvement with Steve Jones the bassist was also busying himself with a side venture, Bone Angel. This band unit was fronted up by former Alien and Four Horsemen vocalist Frank C. Starr and included ex-Dio and Rough Cutt guitarist Craig Goldie with Impelliterri man Mark Bistany on drums.

"We did a couple of gigs under the name Hardluck and then Craig and Mark got busy with other projects so we asked Randy [Castillo] to come in and play." Castillo would induct guitarist John Lowry into the fold. It was this unit that would witness a second term of studio involvement with Ozzy.

The bass player unfolds the scenario. "Just before the album came out a year or so later, Ozzy and – Zakk, I think – were at loggerheads over publishing on the album. Neither of them was about to budge on the issue, so Ozzy said 'fuck it' and decided to start all over again from scratch and asked the Bone Angel guys to come in and start writing a new album. So we did – for about a week – until he was able to work things out with Zakk and then that was it."

To promote the album Epic undertook the unprecedented move of releasing to radio a promotional sampler entitled *The No More Tears Demo Sessions*. Backed up by an interview narrative with Ozzy, the disc contained working versions of 'I Don't Want To Change The World', 'Desire', 'Time After Time', 'Won't Be Coming Home' and 'Mrs. J'.

The penultimate track would, with a change of lyrics, evolve into 'S.I.N.' whilst 'Mrs. J' is a Zakk Wylde acoustic guitar showcase. It is not only the music and the rarity of this disc that makes it a highly prized item as a print of an original painting by Ozzy himself graces the cover.

The *No More Tears* album itself barged into the Billboard top ten during October of 1991. Fans found it, on the whole, a more introspective, even gloomier, work than previous fares. Highlights would be the comparatively upbeat 'Mr. Tinkertrain' and the maudlin title track itself. 'I Don't Want To Change The World' would soon become locked into the live set and the ballad 'Mama, I'm Coming Home' gave the man a further hit single to add to the trophy collection.

October 1991 would be made doubly special for those keeping an eye on behind-the-scenes machinations in the Black Sabbath camp. When Butler had baled out of the *No More Tears* sessions he had naturally gravitated towards Tony Iommi. That very same irresistible natural pull, though, was drawing in another star – Ronnie James Dio.

Butler had earlier jammed with Dio at a show on one of his *Lock Up The Wolves* tour dates, an event which immediately sparked rumours that changes were afoot in the Sabbath tribe. With the pipe of peace passed between Dio and Butler, big chief Iommi needed little persuasion. Both Black Sabbath and Dio had weathered the storms of lacklustre product and consumer indifference in recent years and the *Heaven And Hell* and *Mob Rules* glory days beckoned brightly. Fans had grown tired and even scathing of the game of musical chairs Black Sabbath had turned into whilst Dio's support had slowly ebbed away after two spectacular opening albums. Past recriminations were thrown aside as the triumvirate reunited. To round off the package Vinnie Appice stepped up to the drum stool too.

As Ozzy was laying down his spurs Black Sabbath had just laid down the gauntlet.

Ozzy in relaxed times with Black Sabbath.
Photo by: Jørgen Angel

Black Sabbath. Tony trades his moustache with Bill for the day.
Photo by: Jørgen Angel

Black Sabbath live.
Photo by: Jørgen Angel

Ozzy bears his cross with Black Sabbath.
Photo by: Jørgen Angel

Badaxe 1979, Dana Strum on right.

*Rare home snaps of Randy and Budgie's J.T.
Photo's supplied by: John Thomas*

Randy's friend J.T. of Budgie supporting Ozzy in 1980.
Photo supplied by: John Thomas

Bernie Tormé, Electric Gypsy
Photo supplied by: Bernie Tormé

Bernie Tormé, Gillan guitar hero.
Photo supplied by: Bernie Tormé

Bernie Tormé, onstage with Ozzy.
Photo supplied by: Bernie Tormé

Bernie Tormé, onstage with Ozzy.
Photo supplied by: Bernie Tormé

*Ozzy, Brad Gillis and that white jumpsuit.
Photo supplied by: Brad Gillis*

*Carmine Appice and Ozzy.
Photo supplied by: Carmine Appice*

A newly shorn, pensive Ozzy does press for his new band. 1983.
Photo by: Jørgen Angel

A glammed up 'Ultimate Sin' era Ozzy. 1986.
Photo by: Matt Sampson

Ozzy flying high again.
Photo by: Jørgen Angel

Ozzy and Jakey Lou Williams (a.k.a. Jake E. Lee).
Photo by: Jørgen Angel

*Bob Daisley recording Bill Ward's solo album.
Photo supplied by: Bob Daisley*

*Bone Angel. L-R: the late Frank Starr and Randy Castillo (RIP), bassist Terry Nails and guitarist John 'Johnny 5' Lowery.
Photo supplied by: Terry Nails*

*Opposite page:
Denmark greets Ozzy. Don Costa on bass in background.
Photo by: Jørgen Angel*

Phil Soussan live with Vince Neil.
Photo supplied by: Phil Soussan

Dana Strum with Slaughter.
Photo supplied by: Dana Strum

Phil Soussan today.
Photo supplied by: Phil Soussan

18
Vai-able Options

No More Tears. No more tours? Hardly. Ozzy limbered up for a last-hurrah offering to the collective press that the time had come to hang up his crucifixes and become the family man. This last round of farewell dates saw Ozzy flanked by Zakk Wylde, Mike Inez on bass and Randy Castillo. The familiar, if usually discreet, personage of keyboard player John Sinclair was not involved, having been enticed away, albeit with the Osbournes' blessings, to join The Cult for their 'Sonic Temple' arena shows.
Selective dates on the *No More Tours* campaign would be captured on tape for a subsequent double album *Live And Loud*.

On November 15th Ozzy wound up the tour with a date at Costa Mesa in California. By all accounts this was to be the last ever Ozzy Osbourne show. Winding their way across America too, Black Sabbath had been vainly plugging their reunification-with-Ronnie album *Dehumanizer*. The combining of Dio, Iommi, Butler and Appice was anticipated to give a much needed shot in the arm to Sabbath's then rather limp standing.
In the early '80s the Dio version of Sabbath had truly given Ozzy a run for his money but the unrestrained excellence in songwriting evident on those past albums was generally felt to be lacking.

Neutered by a dearth of solid songs and a somewhat hamfisted attempt at what was originally an inspired album cover-concept of Geezer's, *Dehumanizer* emerged in June 1992 with a less than convincing fanfare. Broken down into its components the album, on paper, could not fail but only rarely did it sparkle. The performances were exemplary and the required heaviness was evident. The missing ingredient was the majestic X factor abundant on *Heaven And Hell* and *Mob Rules*.

Although sales of the record were solid they were far from spectacular. The album just scrambled into the US top 50 and, with the media focussing on Ozzy's farewell tour, the rug had been well and truly pulled from under Sabbath's feet once again.

Negotiations were held to climax the grand finale of Ozzy's tour with a clutch of Black Sabbath songs performed by the

Ozzy Osbourne

original members – Ozzy, Tony, Geezer and Bill – to round off the evening. Black Sabbath in turn were invited to support Ozzy. Exactly what Ronnie James Dio said when he heard this offer has sadly remained unrecorded but the result was plain enough. Unable to quell his pride or his anger he walked out, leaving Sabbath without a singer.

Black Sabbath did open up for Ozzy for those gigs with the unexpected but crowd-pleasing face of ex-Judas Priest man Rob Halford leading the way. The fellow-Brummie had known Iommi since the mid-'70s when the Sabbath guitarist had Judas Priest signed up as one of his agency acts.

A 20-year, 20-million selling reign with Judas Priest had demonstrated to the world that Halford's tungsten-lined vocal cords had inhuman capabilities and had inspired legions of less than convincing copyists. To the Heavy Metal cognoscenti Halford was a god and right now Sabbath required a large dose of divine intervention. With just days to memorize the entire Black Sabbath set, Rob Halford pulled the band from the brink of disaster to an achievement that ranks high in Metal's pantheon.

Ozzy's set climaxed with the original foursome cranking out 'Black Sabbath', 'Fairies Wear Boots', 'Iron Man' and 'Paranoid'. And then, a fearsome fireworks display signalled the closure of Ozzy's onstage career.

In 1993, with Ozzy officially out to pasture, word filtered through that retirement was not all that Ozzy had maybe thought it to be and he had a hankering for the bright lights once again.

Ozzy poked his head above the parapet by lending his vocals to Irish act Therapy?'s take on 'Iron Man' for a Black Sabbath tribute *Nativity In Black*. His colleague Geezer Butler would also figure on the same album as part of the Bullring Brummies, led by the ubiquitous Rob Halford.

There was even a projected album title, *X-Ray* being bandied about and deeper rumblings that Ozzy's new compadre was to be one of the most stellar names in metal, Steve Vai. Having just

*Quote from carmineappice.net

Vai-able Options

come off the adulation afforded to his *Sex And Religion* album Vai was hot property. Indeed, Vai's profile was at such a peak there was a very real possibility of the proposed venture going out under a different title.

"We thought about a name... maybe a one-off for Ozzy," confirms the guitarist. "Ozzy had been working on a CD with his band and they finished about half of it. They then decided to pair Ozzy up with various people to write some additional stuff. My name came up and Ozzy came to see me play while I was on tour in Europe with Aerosmith. We got together after that tour and hit it off very well. We wrote and demoed for about 15 or so songs."

With the introduction of new blood it was determined that a familiar face might provide the right grounding to see the project through. Daisley – who else?

"I got a call from Sharon in 1994," Bob Daisley relates. "I was in the middle of the Mother's Army project at the time. Anyway, I then found myself in the studio with Ozzy, drummer Deen Castronovo and Steve Vai. What had happened was that someone had decided to re-create the atmosphere and sound of the first two albums. That's why they got Steve in, who was of course a well-known and genuine guitar hero. They had apparently tried working with someone else on bass but then the suggestion was made that if they were really trying to capture that particular sound then they should get me back."

Although Steve Vai was a musician of unquestionable repute, the leap of imagination required to transport Vai's skills, displayed on work with Roth, Whitesnake and Alcatraz, is quite wide when one considers the sheer heaviness required for Ozzy's music. More importantly did the guitarist catch wind of any attempt to recapture past glories and the quest for a 'Randy Rhoads' aura?

"It was a very creative process. I obviously approach things differently from Randy but there was a great vibe for sure. Yes, it was much different. Everything was tuned down to C and I was using an octave divider on a lot of stuff. Very, very heavy."

Vai recalls the sessions with Ozzy with obvious fondness. "Working with him was a complete pleasure and a blast. He is one of the most unique and interesting people I have ever met. Sort of like the Godfather of Metal. You would never believe how funny he is. Just the way he talks and explains things and the extraordinary stories he would tell constantly were historical delights. He's pure rock music and he's not in the least bit stupid or anybody's fool. He knows exactly what he wants and there is an honesty and realness to him that is undeniable. He has no circuit breaker between his head and his mouth and he speaks what he is feeling the moment he feels it. He acts the same around his musicians as he does with his family. He's very real. It was refreshing to have the opportunity to work with him for three months and it's an experience in this business I will cherish and remember for ever. After working with him I know why his fans are so loyal and why they feel the way they do about him. They have good reason to."

The course of events, however, did not pan out as Daisley, and probably Vai, envisaged. Daisley: "We went to New York to rehearse at the Sony studios. We were actually getting on great, doing some great work, but right in the middle of this we were told that Sony had pulled the plug on the project. Frankly, I did not believe it. I could not have imagined Sony cancelling a project that had two top-selling artists involved."

The guitarist saw things differently. "We liked working together and felt like we should make a whole record together but the record company ended up feeling that he should take some of the best stuff from what we had done and complete the CD he started with his band. It was not a money issue. I would almost consider working for free to work with Ozzy. He's... Ozzy! Like I said, the record company felt that he should finish what he started and I believe the new producer, Michael Bienhorn, was not very keen on working with me."

Steve got back to what he knew best and rapidly set to work on his next solo venture *Alien Love Secrets* leaving fans of both camps wondering just what might have been. Meantime, Bob Daisley felt his assumptions had been proven correct and explains the pattern of events after Ozzy had parted ways with Vai.

Vai-able Options

"Deen Castronovo was gutted and he was wondering what to do. I told him that in my opinion this whole thing was a ploy to get Steve out of the picture and that we would get a call in a few days, time saying it was all on again but with another guitarist. The very next day that call came saying 'we still want you and Deen'. Well, that was OK but they kept me hanging on for months. It ended up with us in London working with these outside songwriters!"

The experience of hit songwriters Mark Hudson (Aerosmith) and Jim Vallance (Bryan Adams' writing partner) was brought to bear on the endeavour but Bob Daisley is scathing. "It was bloody ridiculous. They wanted to get back the original sound and were asking these songwriters to come up with those kind of songs when one of the blokes that had written them was just sitting there playing bass! I got fed up and left. I think Geezer took over again."

The acquaintance struck up in the earlier aborted Ozzy/Vai project would signal another venture that Daisley is proud of. "Steve Vai was doing a track for a Hendrix tribute called *In From The Storm*. The whole thing was being produced by Eddie Kramer. Steve recommended Kramer to get me in, which was nice of him. We had quite a band with Steve, myself, Paul Rodgers from Free and Tony Williams on drums who is sadly no longer with us. A great session."

In early 1995 Wylde was beckoned back into the Ozzy camp to complete the *Ozzmosis* record. The album included contributions from Rick Wakeman, re-forging a link back to the keyboard maestro's assistance afforded to Black Sabbath during the '70s. With Daisley gone it would be Geezer Butler handling bass chores and Castronovo on drums. The only evidence of Steve Vai's involvement was a co-write credit on the cut 'My Little Man'. The stability Ozzy sought was not to transpire, though. Wylde was being courted by the leviathan that was Guns N'Roses and, although virtually impotent for the past few years, the spell woven by the Axl Rose-led supergroup had proved highly attractive.

The comeback tour would not even attempt to gloss over the

Ozzy Osbourne

fact that Ozzy had changed his mind. Dubbed the 'Retirement Sucks' tour, the band was slated to include Wylde in the line-up. However, the guitarist's public dalliances with Guns N'Roses and the indecision surrounding any commitment ignited a further round of auditions.

During periods of inactivity Geezer and Castronovo convened GZR with Fear Factory vocalist Burton C. Bell and Midlands guitarist Pedro Howse for the uncompromisingly raw *Plastic Planet* album.

19
Skol?

Joe Holmes first made his presence felt as founder member of an act assembled on the reputation of ex-Angel vocalist Frank Dimino in the mid-'80s following the disintergration of singer's first post-Angel act, The Ruffians. Moving to Portland, Oregon, Dimino put a new group together entitled Terriff featuring guitarist Joe Holmes, bassist Emil Lech Brando and drummer Tom Cosmo. Demos were recorded before Dimino, frustrated at the lack of progress, moved back to Los Angeles. Dimino and his former Angel colleagues Punky Meadows and Barry Brandt united again in late 1985 in an attempt to resurrect the band.

Lech promptly joined Sound Barrier before stints with Joshua and Driver; Holmes meanwhile joined theatric Metal act Lizzy Borden before quitting that band to recreate Terriff. This second version of the band numbered Holmes, Cosmo, bassist Mike Davis and vocalist Dana Freebarin. But Terriff folded once more when in October, 1990, Holmes landed the plum job of Dave Lee Roth's lead guitarist.

Fred Coury recalls being asked his advice on the Terriff man at the time. "The owner of Mates Rehearsals had known Joe for years and years so that's how I got to know him too. Joe is a truly fantastic guitarist and a really nice guy too. Anyway, someone from the Roth organization, I think it was Pete Angelus, called me to tell me they were looking for another guitarist. Then Dave himself got on the phone and said 'You seem to know everyone. Who's a really hot guitarist?' We had a talk about styles and I said 'Well, there is only one guy – Joe Holmes'. Two weeks later I saw that he was in the band."

By the close of the nationwide tour Holmes had bailed out. Roth would struggle visibly without him. The Nile Rodgers produced *Your Filthy Little Mouth*, with Steve Hunter and Terry Kilgore supplying guitars, was released in early 1994 and failed to capture the sparkle of previous outings.

However, during 1995 before Joe Holmes secured the position Ozzy, unbeknown to most, would try out another guitarist.

Ozzy Osbourne

The unheralded Rock City club in Nottingham was, one night early in 1995, honoured with a clandestine Ozzy gig, but this was no average warm-up. The man on guitar was Alex Skolnick. Skolnick had made his mark as a quite electrifying player with his early work for Bay Area Thrash-metallers Testament before a leap to the more refined, if no less heavy, environment of Savatage. Indeed, the guitarist had carved out such a name for himself that he was already being revered by fans of both bands as the hottest guitarist to go through the ranks of either. The surprised Rock City audience lapped it up and we were collectively of the opinion that the throng had witnessed the debut of Ozzy's new right-hand man. The gig was intense to say the least and Skolnick had seemed at ease throughout, Ozzy being happy to introduce him to the crowd by name repeatedly. It was not to be though. An anonymous Ozzy insider sheds some light.

"Yeah, I was there at that gig," he confirms. "And it was Alex. I was actually quite surprised when we came to rehearsal. Alex was a really nice guy, really into it. He really thought that after that show in Nottingham he had got the gig but it just didn't work for some reason. I remember him being quite shocked. One minute he was there the next he wasn't and we just carried on as normal." Catching up with Alex himself puts the whole thing into context. "In seven years you're the first person that's contacted me about that gig!" the guitarist says by way of introduction, illustrating just how easily other accounts of Ozzy's career have wiped the slate of this incident. Post-Savatage Skolnick was pursuing his own jazz rock endeavour Exhibit A. "I had left Testament in 1992. In 1991, I started playing with different artists and realized I wanted to stretch out musically. I recorded with Primus bassist Les Claypool then toured with bassist Stuart Hamm, both in 1991. In 1993 I recorded with bassist Michael Manring on his album *Thonk*. In '94 I recorded with Savatage on their album *Handful Of Rain*, and toured the US and Japan with them. I also had my own band, but it wasn't having much luck getting a record deal. Towards the end of 1994, I was one of three guys called in to audition for the Spin Doctors and came in second."

Skol?

Meanwhile, in New York Ozzy had tried run-throughs with Ritchie Kotzen of Poison and Warren De Martini of Ratt fame. Neither exactly slouches on the guitar but obviously the Ozzy 'X' factor was to be found elsewhere and Deen Castronova thought he knew just the man. Alex, then just arriving home to Berkeley, California, from guitar clinic demonstrations in Texas, records just how eager the Ozzy camp was to establish contact. "There were a lot of messages on my answering machine. The first one said 'Alex, this is Deen Castronova. I'm playing drums with Ozzy. We need a guitar player. I think you'd be perfect. Give me a call as soon as you can.' He left his hotel number. Apparently he had called just when I'd left town a week earlier. The next message was also from him, trying to reach me again. Then there was a message from someone at Sharon Osbourne's office, and another message from Dean. I wondered if the next message would be from Ozzy! By the time I called Dean had checked out of his hotel, so I called Sharon's office. I was informed that they didn't have a guitarist yet, and that I should expect a call from Sharon. She called a short time later and asked if I'd like to come to London." Skolnick mailed Ozzy's office video footage of Savatage in Japan and Testament recordings. In return a rather large parcel winged its way from the Osbournes to Alex. Inside was a copy of every Ozzy album and a list of 20 tracks to learn – most of the *Live And Loud* album plus two from *Ozzmosis* including 'Perry Mason'. "I was told to expect a call in a few weeks, when Ozzy finished his vocals in the studio. It was hard to keep it a secret, but I held it in. A few weeks later I got a call early in the morning from the office asking if I could be on a plane to London the next day. And off I was."

Once in London Alex was put through his paces with a formal audition. It would prove a somewhat intimidating process. "Dean filled me in on all the details. Yes, this was an audition, but I was highly recommended and they liked the materials I had sent so I had a very good shot. I also met a couple of guitar techs who were co-ordinating the auditions. I was told to make sure I'm in tune, don't waste any time and be prepared to launch from one song right into the other!" Alex had his instructions and the assembled collective waited on the appearance of Ozzy. "I guess it went really well. I had been told to be ready to play as soon as Ozzy walked in. So he comes in, waves hello to everyone, gets behind the mic and asks what I want to play. We launch into 'I Don't Know.' and during the solo, Ozzy is staring at me from behind dark glasses. It was a bit intimidating. But he starts slowly nodding his head, and gives the thumbs-up sign. We finish the song and a second later he calls out the next song, 'Crazy Train'. During the solo, he has the same reaction. As soon as we're done he looks at me and says 'Great! Can you come back at noon tomorrow?' 'Sure,' I said. He left and everyone in the room started cheering. 'Was it OK?' I asked? 'Are you kidding?' said Dean. "That was awesome. I can't believe he asked you back after just a couple of songs! That's unheard of. Way to go!"

Indeed, Alex's audition had proven so positive, an immediate live test was deemed necessary. The guitarist would be quite taken aback to learn that he would be playing a full-blown gig within days. "I got back to the hotel and was told that it went so well that they've decided to book an unannounced show at Rock City in Nottingham. So the next day, we played ten songs. It had much more of a feel of a rehearsal than an audition. Sharon was there, as were the kids. A couple of days later, we moved to a rehearsal studio in Birmingham. We did a few rehearsals, but they were without Ozzy, just instrumental. I remember he had come down with a bad cold and almost had to cancel the show, but he got well just in time for the gig." Ozzy, happy to introduce Alex by name at that gig, had seemingly found his man. As an eyewitness the present author can confirm that not only did the crowd warm to Ozzy's new candidate, but that Skolnick seemed in his element. Ozzy was beaming smiles and apostrophised Alex's presence with named introductions on a number of occasions throughout the show. For Skolnick the gig made an indelible mark on the memory. "It was absolutely amazing. Definitely one of the loudest gigs I've ever played; I didn't wear ear plugs because I was afraid it would affect my performance. My ears rang all night! All the songs felt like I imagined, but with even more of an intensity. I really liked playing the Sabbath tunes too.

Skol?

Even though it was short, it was still a great experience and I wouldn't trade it for the world."

Ozzy's band for the day featured Alex, Geezer Butler on bass, John Sinclair on keyboards and Deen Castronovo on drums. The Nottingham Rock City crowd thought they had just been privileged to see Ozzy's new line-up for the forthcoming tour.

It never happened; Alex takes up the story from his vantage point. "It is a mystery. After the show, Ozzy gave me a big hug, and said 'Alex, you've got the gig.' Guys in the crew were thanking me, saying they haven't heard it sound that good since they could remember, and they could finally go home. One of them said he hadn't seen Ozzy look so happy in a long time. Also I had figured out a way to play the multiple guitar harmonies in 'Mr. Crowley' live, and someone said 'Man, when you played that, we were all floored. Even Randy didn't do that.' I had been in London a total of about ten days. I flew back home the day after the show. Even though Ozzy said I was hired, I knew enough not to count on anything happening until contracts were signed and an itinerary received (even then, nothing is certain!). A short time later, I was informed I wasn't doing the tour. It was a little disappointing, but I think it worked out for the best. There was no detailed explanation. I asked Sharon if there was anything I could have done differently. She said absolutely not, it was fabulous and I could have worked out great.

"But the fact was they had someone who they felt better fit the group right now, who turned out to be Joe Holmes. I made it clear I would have loved to have stayed on, but I understood that they had to make the decision that they felt was best. I said they could still call me anytime I'd be happy to work with them again. That's still true. But I guess it wasn't meant to be and I'm just thankful for the opportunity I had, short as it was!"

After his fleeting tenure with Ozzy Alex got down to his music in serious fashion. "In retrospect, everything seems to have turned out for the better. I had always had a secret desire to go back to school and get my music degree (inspired by Randy), and perform and study improvisational music, from John Coltrane, The Brecker Brothers, Weather Report, Miles Davis and John McLaughlin. I always knew of the risks of being more of a 'jazz' artist, but decided that if nothing else, I could play in small clubs, continue my studies, get my musicianship to the highest possible level. So immediately after the Ozzy experience, I enrolled myself in school and started working as a jazz and world music guitarist in clubs, restaurants and private events. A few years ago, I moved to New York to complete my studies at New School University, one of the top music programs in the country. Since moving here, I've been busy as a sideman, session guitarist, composer and leader of my own groups."

Holmes meanwhile, courtesy of a tip-off from Deen Castronovo, had entered the world of Ozzy Osbourne. The opening had been created when Zakk Wylde reportedly had found himself on the receiving end of a tempting offer from Guns N'Roses. Unable to decide firmly which camp to settle in and with a series of conflicting signals to contend with, in the end the decision was made for him. As it transpired the Guns N'Roses post would evaporate into thin air leaving Wylde temporarily high and dry.

Auditioning in Los Angeles, Holmes kept quiet about having had Randy Rhoads as a guitar tutor, fearing it would jeopardise his chances. He still got the gig and Ozzy's new band of Holmes, Butler, Sinclair and Castronovo hit the road.

Joe Holmes was the antithesis of the six-foot blond-maned Zakk Wylde. Blessed with an incredible degree of control and fluidity to his playing style he would soon find favour with Ozzy fans. From the audience the initial perception of Holmes was of a slight dark-haired figure, lost in his own world, faithfully churning out a structured but dynamic regime that had Ozzy purists reeling in admiration. Opening dates for the 1995 world tour started in Chile. Following a handful of gigs Castronovo was out (though he later turned up as a member of AOR stalwarts Journey) and Randy Castillo, pulled from his act Juice 13, was back on the drum stool.

Between Ozzy tenures Castillo had actually issued his own record with the band Red Square Black. Castillo had been joined in Red Square Black by John Lowery from the days of Bone

Skol?

Angel. The album, ahead of its time, being an almost Industrial Pop Rock act, was issued by Zoo Records but poorly promoted.

The subsequent *Ozzmosis* album proved to be Osbourne's most successful for nearly a decade, debuting in the American Billboard album charts at Number 4 and selling over 127,000 copies in its first week of release. Midway through the 'Retirement Sucks' dates, Geezer returned home and Mike Inez, on his second Ozzy call-up, took the position.

A third single was lifted from *Ozzmosis* in the form of 'I Just Want You' with an accompanying video. The single was timed perfectly to coincide with an American tour commencing in May. Ozzy's band for this jaunt was made up of Joe Holmes, Robert Trujillo of Suicidal Tendencies and former Faith No More drummer Mike Bordin.

In August Ozzy co-headlined the Monsters of Rock festival with Kiss, the third time he had appeared at the event. Dates promoting the album would continue throughout the year with a further run of American shows, winding up in Honolulu on November 11th. With major name rock acts struggling to fill stadiums nationwide, Sharon Osbourne's next venture would seemingly fly in the face of all logic but would illustrate just what a shrewd player she undoubtedly is.

'Ozzfest' would signal the debut of a concept many felt ambitious in the extreme. The event arrived in two massive outdoor shows on October 26th in Phoenix, Arizona and the following day in San Bernadino, California. Backing up Ozzy for these gigs were Slayer, Fear Factory, Coal Chamber and Neurosis.

In March 1997 the *Ozzfest Live* album and video arrived in stores on the short-lived Red Ant label. Live cuts from all the bands appearing on the day were topped off with Ozzy's 'Perry Mason'. The Ozzfest concept solidified its standing with its first proper run of dates stretching through the summer of 1997. Headlined quite spectacularly by a Black Sabbath line-up of Ozzy, Tony Iommi, Geezer Butler and stand-in Mike Bordin on drums, the show saw Ozzy doubling up appearing with his own band too. Other featured artists were Pantera, the newly controversial ticket of Marilyn Manson, Type O Negative, Machine

Ozzy Osbourne

Head and Fear Factory. A secondary stage was occupied by the Osbourne – managed Coal Chamber, Powerman 5000, Downset, Vision Of Disorder, Slo Burn and feisty feminine metal Swedish-style in the shape of Drain (aka Drain STH in the US).

An unqualified success all round, the only potential fly in the ointment surfaced on June 5th in East Rutherford, New Jersey, after Marilyn Manson's antics prompted local authorities to try and ban the show in its entirety. The Osbournes threatened to counter-sue and the show went ahead.

Ozzy would also unite in the studio with one of the major Ozzfest attractions, Type O Negative, cutting a version of 'Pictures Of Matchstick Men' for shock-jock Howard Stern's movie *Private Parts*.

With no new product in the pipeline the welcome compilation album *The Ozzman Cometh* saw a release on November 11th. No ordinary cash-in collection, *The Ozzman Cometh* dug up archive Black Sabbath basement demo versions of 'Fairies Wear Boots', 'Behind The Wall Of Sleep', 'War Pigs' and 'Black Sabbath' with a previously unused Ozzy track 'Back To Earth'. With no new material as such, the album still made platinum status. The year rounded off with the realization of a dream that had kept the rock world salivating since the all-too-brief 1985 Live Aid performance.

Black Sabbath would be one of the bona fide 'legends' reunited for a one-off performance to realize Bob Geldof's vision.

Although Sabbath's Live Aid gig had fired earnest discussions about a reunion which had taken many years to reach fruition, the plain truth was that Ozzy, in terms of commercial success, simply didn't need Sabbath. Not only had Ozzy outgrown Black Sabbath, he had eclipsed them. Negotiations ebbed and flowed behind the scenes for many years but it seemed to the outside world that it was not business concerns that brought Black Sabbath back together but an honest healing between four friends.

In early December the original Black Sabbath – Ozzy Osbourne, Tony Iommi, Geezer Butler and Bill Ward joined forces for two blockbusting shows in their hometown of

Skol?

Birmingham. The gigs, held at the cavernous National Exhibition Centre, would be captured for historical record on the *Reunion* album.

The Black Sabbath resurrection would re-commence in late May, 1998, with a full scale European tour taking in Germany, Hungary, Austria, Italy, the Czech Republic, Poland, Sweden, Finland and Norway. Ozzfest too was back, bigger and better for 1998, spanning the United States from its inception in New Jersey on July 5th to its grand finale in Washington DC on August 2nd. On June 20th Ozzfest had reached the UK and the Milton Keynes National Bowl. Black Sabbath and Ozzy would be joined by such contemporaries as the Foo Fighters, Korn, Limp Bizkit and scores more.

Reunion would issued in October, just two days after Ozzy's infamous appearance on the notorious *South Park* cartoon. *Reunion* gave Black Sabbath something they had been lacking for 18 years – a platinum album. Not only would the CD satisfy fans' desire for live material but it would also offer up two brand new studio recordings in 'Psycho Man' and 'Selling My Soul'. Before October was out Ozzy and Black Sabbath had put in an appearance on the *The Late Show With David Letterman*, performing 'Paranoid'. It had been 23 years since the last Sabbath TV showing. The year signalled another personal landmark for Ozzy, a lifelong and vocal fan of The Beatles, with his vocal inclusion on the title track of Ringo Starr's *Vertical Man* album.

So much for retirement. 1999 would see no let-up. By late May Ozzfest had recommenced with the added tag of 'The Last Supper'. Was this an indicator that these were in fact to be the last ever Black Sabbath shows or a clue to the more theologically inclined that this was merely a portent of yet another resurrection? For this run of shows John Sinclair, too, would find himself deputizing with Black Sabbath.

Kicking off on May 25th at the Coral Sky Amphitheatre in West Palm Beach, Florida, and running through until the closing date in California at the suitably titled Devore Blockbuster Pavilion in late July, Ozzfest, grossing a gargantuan $19.4 million, would yet again defy all trends and come out on top as one of the most heavily attended touring packages of the year. By now the whole shebang was regarded not so much as a trend-defying, nostalgic touring package, more a proving ground for new talent.

That same month was significant to Randy Castillo, having leap-frogged onto the bandwagon of yet another major act supplanting the errant Tommy Lee in Mötley Crüe.

Castillo has cause to recall the events surrounding the switch. Just as Tommy Lee had persuaded Ozzy to enlist Randy, now Ozzy and Sharon paid back the same favour. "Yeah, it was Ozzy and Sharon that called me about the gig with Mötley. That's the kind of people they are, always pulling favours for friends and looking out for people. They had put in some kind words with Nikki Sixx and then called me. I called Nikki and we spoke for over an hour, just discussing the kind of music we both liked and then he says 'Do you want the gig?' I said 'Don't you want to see me play first?' and of course Nikki says 'I've seen you play hundreds of times. We know you can play. You're the guy we want.'

"So Nikki got off the phone to talk to Vince and Mick then calls me back ten minutes later. 'Dude, you've got the gig'. Simple as that."

Within weeks Randy Castillo was ensconced onstage with Mötley Crüe for their 'Maximum Rock' world tour.

For Ozzy, 1999 would also be marked with a guest appearance for the famed Yes keyboard player Rick Wakeman. In an ambitious move Wakeman re-convened his leviathan *Journey To The Centre Of The Earth* saga that had reigned supreme among pomp in the '70s recording a sequel, *Return To The Centre Of The Earth*. Amongst an all-star international cast Ozzy contributed lead vocals to the track 'Buried Alive', which also surfaced as a single.

As 2000 drew in, and with a lull in Ozzy's activities, Holmes, Trujillo and Bordin founded a fresh act, Mass Mental, fronted by ex-Dub War vocalist Benji. As for Ozzy, he was soon back in the public eye collaborating with Wu Tang Clan on the track 'For Heaven's Sake' and putting in a cameo in the *Little Nicky* comedy.

Ozzy announced his drummer for the 2000 Ozzfest series to

Skol?

be Roy Mayorga. However, within weeks drummer Brian Tichy, a man with a diverse CV stretching across the spectrum from Zakk's Pride & Glory to a recent stint with Foreigner, was on the drum stool. Launched on July 2nd in Palm Beach, Florida, the event still retained Ozzy as overall headliner despite several murmurings that the event would carry on without Ozzy at the helm. The supporting line-up was as stellar as ever.

Rumours toward the tail end of 2000 saw internet reports on KNAC's website which had Ozzy's new band slated as Zakk Wylde returning on guitar, a reinstatement of Geezer Butler on bass and the amazingly newsworthy inclusion of erstwhile Mötley Crüe drummer Tommy Lee.

The projected album would not actually transpire and the band that initially set to work could not be more different. Joe Holmes was still holding down the guitarist slot, Rob Trujillo had kept his place and on drums was the young Brooks Wackerman of Suicidal Tendencies, Trujillo's old band. Pre-production for a new album began in earnest but soon faltered when the band and slated producer Toby Wright simply didn't gel.

The band would morph once again with the now heavily-bearded (not to mention self confessed heavily-beered) Zakk Wylde regaining his place on guitar and Tim Palmer landing the job as producer. When it did appear, however, on October 16th 2001, *Down To Earth* swiftly broke the Billboard Top 5. Both fans and media readily agreed that Ozzy had lost none of his bite or fervour for aggressive rock and that *Down To Earth* hosted some of his finest vocal and songwriting accomplishments to date.

Surreally Ozzy, and the rest of the Osbourne clan, made it into the top rankings of the TV ratings with their 'fly on the wall' docu-soap *The Osbournes*. Ozzy also belatedly received his personal star on Hollywood's walk of fame and yet another round of Ozzfest dates stretched far into the future… Retirement still sucked.

Postscript

Just how has Ozzy Osbourne stayed the course? Our anonymous insider provides a fitting finale:

"Ozzy is the same performer now that he ever was. Offstage he can be very quiet and unassuming. He's a very thoughtful person too, very articulate, which is something the public don't see. He has an intense interest in history which he loves to share with people and he paints a lot too. The other thing of course is that he is a family man. It's a whole different side to him the public don't see because all they want after all is Ozzy the product not Ozzy the man.

Onstage he is someone else of course. There are always the two Ozzy characters. It's never false though, it's the show but it is him as well and it just kicks in as soon as he gets on stage. Everyone is very understanding of how the whole thing works on the road too. He actually has a very strong personality as he has to in order to deal with it. You see, everyone else in the organisation and the band can get on with it, do their work and have a great time as part of this character world built around Ozzy but he has to deal with it in his own head. I think he has suffered with it in the past but he has been able to do that now for a long time because he knows his own person very well."

When asked just when Ozzy might just one day really, truly, once-and-for-all retire the same source counters with a quote from Ozzy. "I asked him this once. Ozzy just looked at me and said "What else can I do? Go and grow fucking marrows?"

The Ozzy Osbourne Solo Discography

(Album tracklistings same for different territories unless listed)

1980
Albums:
BLIZZARD OF OZZ, Jet JETLP 234 (UK) **7 UK**
I Don't Know / Crazy Train / Goodbye To Romance / Dee / Suicide Solution / Mr. Crowley / No Bone Movies / Revelation Mother Earth / Steal Away (The Night)
BLIZZARD OF OZZ, Jet JZ36812 (USA) **21 USA**
Singles/EPs:
Crazy Train / You Looking At Me, Looking At You, Jet JET 197 (7" single promotion release)
Mr. Crowley / You Said It All (Live), Jet JET 7003 (7" single) **49 UK**
Mr. Crowley / You Said It All (Live) / Suicide Solution (Live), Jet 8Z8-37640 (USA 12" picture disc single)
Mr. Crowley / You Said It All (Live) / Suicide Solution (Live), Jet 12 EXP 37640 (USA 12" single)
Mr. Crowley / You Said It All (Live) / Suicide Solution (Live), Jet JET 12003 (UK 12" single) **46 UK**
Crazy Train / Steal Away (The Night), Jet ZS6 02079 (USA 7" single)

1981
Albums:
DIARY OF A MADMAN, Jet FZ 37492, **14 UK, 16 USA**
Over The Mountain / Flying High Again / You Can't Kill Rock 'n' Roll / Believer / Little Dolls / Tonight / S.A.T.O. / Diary Of A Madman
Singles/EPs:
Over The Mountain / I Don't Know (Live), Jet JET 7017 (7" single)
Over The Mountain / I Don't Know (Live), Jet JET 12017 (12" single)
Flying High Again / I Don't Know (Live), Jet ZS5 02582 (USA 7" single)
Flying High Again / 'Diary Of A Madman' montage, Jet AS 1317 (USA 12" promotion)

1982
Albums:
SPEAK OF THE DEVIL, Jet ZX 2 38350 (USA) **14 USA**
Snowblind / Symptom Of The Universe / Black Sabbath / N.I.B. / Fairies Wear Boots / War Pigs / Sabbath Bloody Sabbath / Iron Man / Children Of The Grave / Paranoid / The Wizard / Sweet Leaf / Never Say Die
SPEAK OF THE DEVIL, CBS 40AP2481-2483 (JAPAN)
TALK OF THE DEVIL, Jet JETDP 401 (UK) **21 UK**

Ozzy Osbourne

<u>Singles/EPs:</u>
Little Dolls / Tonight, Jet (7" single)
Mr. Crowley (Live) / I Don't Know (Live), CBS (7" single free with Japanese 'Speak Of The Devil' album)
Symptom Of The Universe (Live) / N.I.B. (Live), Jet P 7030 (UK 7" single)
Symptom Of The Universe (Live) / Iron Man (Live) / Children Of The Grave (Live), Jet JET 12030 (UK 12" single)
Paranoid (Live) / Symptom Of The Universe (Live), Jet 810 (HOLLAND 7" single)
Never Say Die (Live) / Paranoid (Live), Jet ZS4 03534 (USA 7" single)

1983
Albums:
BARK AT THE MOON, Epic EPC 25739 (UK – Logotype in blue & yellow) **9 SWEDEN, 24 UK**
Rock 'n' Roll Rebel / Bark At The Moon / You're No Different / Now You See It (Now You Don't) / Waiting For Darkness / So Tired / Spiders / Forever
BARK AT THE MOON, CBS Associated QZ 38987 (USA – logotype in red & yellow) **19 USA**
Bark At The Moon / You're No Different / Now You See It, Now You Don't / Rock 'n' Roll Rebel / Centre Of Eternity / So Tired / Slow Down / Waiting For Darkness
BARK AT THE MOON, Epic 25KP1026 (JAPAN)
BARK AT THE MOON, Jigu KJPL-055 (KOREA – Different cover)
<u>Singles/EPs:</u>
Bark At The Moon / One Up The B Side, Epic A 3915 (UK 7" single) **21 UK**
Bark At The Moon / One Up The B Side / Slow Down, Epic TA 3915 (UK 12" single)
Bark At The Moon / One Up The B Side / Slow Down, Epic WA 3915 (UK 12" silver vinyl single)
Bark At The Moon / Spiders, CBS Associated ZS4 04318 (USA 7" single)
So Tired / One Up The B Side, CBS Associated ZS4 04383 (USA 7" single)
So Tired / Bark At The Moon (Live), Epic EPCA 4452 (UK 7" single)
So Tired / Waiting For Darkness / Bark At The Moon (Live) / Suicide Solution (Live) / Paranoid (Live), Epic TA 4452 (UK gold vinyl 12" single)
So Tired / Forever (Live), Epic (UK 7" single) **20 UK**
So Tired / Bark At The Moon (Live) / Waiting For Darkness / Paranoid (Live), CBS Associated DA 4452 (USA 7" double single)

1984
Albums:
THE OTHER SIDE OF OZZY, CBS 28AP 2982 (JAPAN)
Mr. Crowley / I Don't Know / Suicide Solution / You Looking At Me Looking At You / You Said It All / Bark At The Moon / One Up The 'B' Side / Spiders

The Ozzy Osbourne Solo Discography

/ Paranoid / Suicide Solution
Singles/EPs:
Prince Of Darkness / You Looking At Me, Looking At You / One Up The B Side, CBS 20AP 2887 (JAPAN 7" single)

1986
Albums:
THE ULTIMATE SIN, CBS Associated 0Z 40026 (USA) **6 USA**
Secret Loser / The Ultimate Sin / Thank God For The Bomb / Never Know Why / Lightning Strikes / Shot In The Dark / Killer Of Giants / Fool Like You / Never
THE ULTIMATE SIN, Epic ZK 40026 (UK) **8 UK, 4 SWEDEN**
Singles/EPs:
Shot In The Dark / Rock 'n' Roll Rebel, Epic QA 6859 (UK 7" single) **20 UK**
Shot In The Dark / Killer Of Giants / Rock 'n' Roll Rebel, Epic TA 6859 (UK 12" single)
Shot In The Dark / You Said It All (Live), CBS Associated ZS4 05810 (USA 7" single)
The Ultimate Sin / Lightning Strikes, Epic A 7311 (UK 7" single) **72 UK**
The Ultimate Sin (Live) / Never Know Why (Live) / Thank God For The Bomb (Live), CBS Associated 9Z9-40532 (USA 12" picture disc)

1987
Albums:
TRIBUTE, CBS Associated ZX2 40714 (USA) **17 SWEDEN, 13 UK, 6 USA**
I Don't Know / Crazy Train / Believer / Mr. Crowley / Flying High Again / Revelation Mother Earth / Steal Away The Night / Suicide Solution / Iron Man / Children Of The Grave / Paranoid / Goodbye To Romance / No Bone Movies / Dee
TRIBUTE, Jigu KJPL-0528 (KOREA. Single album)
Singles/EPs:
Crazy Train (Live) / Crazy Train (Studio), Epic 650943 7 (UK 7" single)
Crazy Train (Live) / Crazy Train / I Don't Know, Epic 650943 6 (UK 12" single)
Crazy Train (Live) / Crazy Train (Studio), CBS Associated ZS4 07186 (USA promotion 7" single)
Crazy Train (Live) / Shot In The Dark, CBS Associated ZS8-08463 (USA 7" single)

1988
Albums:
NO REST FOR THE WICKED, CBS Associated ZK 44245 (CD USA) **13 USA, 23 UK, 18 SWEDEN**
Miracle Man / Devil's Daughter / Crazy Babies / Breaking All The Rules / Bloodbath In Paradise / Fire In The Sky / Tattooed Dancer / Demon Alcohol
NO REST FOR THE WICKED, CBS Associated OZ 44245 (LP USA)

Ozzy Osbourne

BIBLE OF OZZ, Sony 49DP5210-2 (JAPAN)
Singles/EPs:
The Ultimate Sin / Bark At The Moon / Mr. Crowley (Live) / Diary Of A Madman, Epic 652875 6 (UK 12" single)
Miracle Man / Crazy Babies, Epic 653063 0 (UK 7" single)
Miracle Man / The Liar / Crazy Babies, Epic 653063 8 (UK 12" single)
Crazy Babies / You Said It All (Live), CBS Associated ZSK 1345 (USA 7" promotion single)

Ozzy featured on the following LITA FORD single A side.

Close My Eyes Forever / Under The Gun, RCA 8899 (USA 7" single)
Close My Eyes Forever / Under The Gun / Blueberry, RCA PT49410 (USA 12" single)

1989
Albums:
BEST OF OZZ, Sony 25DP 5396 (JAPAN)
Over The Mountain / Secret Loser / Goodbye To Romance / Shot In The Dark / Mr. Crowley / Bark At The Moon / Crazy Train / Centre Of Eternity / Diary Of A Madman / The Ultimate Sin
Singles/EPs:
Hero / You Said It All (Live) / Devil's Daughter / Fire In The Sky, CBS Associated ZAS 1512 (USA 12" promotion single)

1990
Albums:
TEN COMMANDMENTS, Priority DIDP 072766 (USA)
Flying High Again / Crazy Train / Diary Of A Madman / Shot In The Dark / Thank God For The Bomb / Bark At The Moon / Tonight / Little Dolls / Steal Away (The Night) / So Tired
JUST SAY OZZY, CBS Associated 6Z 45451 (LP USA) **69 UK**
Miracle Man / Bloodbath In Paradise / Shot In The Dark / Tattooed Dancer / Sweet Leaf / War Pigs
JUST SAY OZZY, CBS Associated ZK 45451 (CD USA)
Singles/EPs:
War Pigs (Live) / Breaking All The Rules, CBS Associated ZSK 1948 (USA promotion CD single)

1991
Albums:
NO MORE TEARS, Epic Z46795 **25 SWEDEN, 17 UK, 7 USA**
Mr. Tinkertrain / I Don't Want To Change The World / Mama, I'm Coming Home / Desire / S.I.N. / Hellraiser / Time After Time / Zombie Stomp / A.V.H.

The Ozzy Osbourne Solo Discography

/ Road To Nowhere
NO MORE TEARS, Sony SRCS 5580 (JAPAN)
Singles/EPs:
No More Tears / S.I.N., Epic 657440 7 (UK 7" single) **32 UK**
No More Tears / S.I.N. / Party With The Animals, Epic 657440 2 (UK CD single)
No More Tears / S.I.N. / Don't Blame Me / Party With The Animals, Epic 657440 5 (UK CD single)
No More Tears / S.I.N. / Party With The Animals, Epic 657440 6 (UK 12" picture disc single)
Mr. Tinkertrain, Epic ZSK 4605 (USA promotion CD single)
Mama, I'm Coming Home / Don't Blame Me / I Don't Know / Crazy Train, Epic 6576170 (UK 12" single) **46 UK**
Mama, I'm Coming Home / Don't Blame Me / Party With The Animals, Epic 45K 74265 (USA CD single) **28 USA**
I Don't Want To Change The World / Mama, I'm Coming Home / No More Tears, Epic XPR 1745 (UK 12" promotion single)

1992
Albums:
THE NO MORE TEARS DEMO SESSIONS, Epic ZSK 4643
I Don't Want To Change The World / Mama, I'm Coming Home / Desire / Time After Time / Won't Be Coming Home / Mrs. J / Interview
Singles/EPs:
Road To Nowhere / Party With The Animals, Epic ZSK 4493 (USA promotion CD single)

1993
Albums:
LIVE AND LOUD, Epic Z2K 48973 **44 SWEDEN, 22 USA**
Paranoid / I Don't Want To Change The World / Desire / Mr. Crowley / I Don't Know / Road To Nowhere / Flying High Again / Suicide Solution / Goodbye To Romance / Shot In The Dark / No More Tears / Miracle Man / War Pigs / Bark At The Moon / Mama, I'm Coming Home / Crazy Train / Black Sabbath / Changes
LIVE AND LOUD, Epic 473798 1 (UK double vinyl album)
LIVE AND LOUD SAMPLER, Epic ZSK 5247 (Promotion)
Singles/EPs:
Changes / No More Tears, Epic 35-74986 (UK 7" single)
Changes / No More Tears / Desire / Changes (with audience), Epic 659340 2 (CD single)
Changes / No More Tears / Desire / Changes (with audience), Epic 659340 6 (UK 12" single)

Ozzy Osbourne

1995
Albums:
OZZMOSIS, Epic 481022 1 (UK LP) **22 UK, 4 USA**
Perry Mason / I Just Want You / Ghost Behind My Eyes / Thunder Underground / See You On The Other Side / Tomorrow / Denial / My Little Man / My Jekyll Doesn't Hide / Old L.A. Tonight
OZZMOSIS, Sony SRCS 7776 (JAPAN CD)
BEST BALLADS, (1995) (RUSSIA)
See You On The Other Side / Mama I'm Coming Home / Revelation (Mother Earth) / Killer Of Giants / Time After Time / Ghost Behind My Eyes / You're No Different / Fire In The Sky / Tonight / Old L.A. Tonight / So Tired / Goodbye To Romance / Road To Nowhere / Close My Eyes Forever
OZZTORY 1- HARD & MELODIOUS SIDE, Sony XDCS 93189 (1995) (JAPAN Promotion)
Intro / Crazy Train / Mr. Crowley / Over The Mountain / Flying High Again / Bark At The Moon / Centre Of Eternity / Secret Loser / Shot In The Dark / Miracle Man / Breaking All The Rules / I Don't Want To Change The World / No More Tears
OZZTORY 2- BALLAD & MELODIOUS SIDE, Sony (1995) (JAPAN Promotion)
Mama / I'm Coming Home / Time After Time / Road To Nowhere / The Liar / So Tired / Tonight / Goodbye To Romance / Dee
Singles/EPs:
Thunder Underground / Perry Mason / Tomorrow / I Just Want You, Epic XPCD 741 (UK promotion CD single)
See You On The Other Side / Ghost Behind My Eyes / I Just Want You / Old L.A. Tonight, Epic SAMP 3143 (GERMANY promotion CD single)
Perry Mason (Edit) / Living With The Enemy, Epic 662639 7 (UK 7" picture disc) **23 UK**
Perry Mason (Edit) / Perry Mason (Album version) / Living With The Enemy / The Whole World's Falling Down, Epic 662412 2 (GERMANY CD single)
Perry Mason (Edit) / Living With The Enemy / The Whole World's Falling Down, Epic 662639 2 (UK CD single)
Perry Mason (Album version) / No More Tears / I Don't Want To Change The World / Flying High Again, Epic 662639 5 (UK CD single)

1996
Albums:
GREATEST HITS, D.O.G. Entertainment DOG 1009 (PORTUGAL)
Perry Mason / Mr. Tinkertrain / Miracle Man / No More Tears / Bark At The Moon / Crazy Babies / The Ultimate Sin / Never Know Why / I Just Want You / Believer / Mr. Crowley / Thunder Underground / Over The Mountain / Forever

The Ozzy Osbourne Solo Discography

Singles/EPs:
See You On The Other Side (Edit) / See You On The Other Side (Album version) / Voodoo Dancer / Aimee, Epic 662778 2 (UK CD single)
See You On The Other Side (Edit) / Voodoo Dancer / Living With The Enemy / Perry Mason (Edit), Sony SRCS 7962 (JAPAN CD single)
I Just Want You (Single edit) / Aimee / Mama, I'm Coming Home, Epic 663570 2 (UK CD single)
I Just Want You (Single edit) / Voodoo Dancer (Demo) / Iron Man (with THERAPY?), Epic 663570 5 (UK CD single)
I Just Want You (Album version) / Aimee (Demo) / Voodoo Dancer (Demo), Epic 663570 6 (UK etched 12""single)

1997
Albums:
OZZFEST LIVE, Ozz Records RA7000-2
Perry Mason (Live)
THE OZZMAN COMETH, Sony EK 67980 (USA) **13 USA**
THE OZZMAN COMETH, Epic 487260-2 (EUROPE) **21 SWEDEN, 68 UK**
Black Sabbath / War Pigs / Goodbye To Romance / Crazy Train / Mr. Crowley / Over The Mountain / Paranoid (Live) / Bark At The Moon / Shot In The Dark / Crazy Babies / No More Tears (Edit) / Mama, I'm Coming Home / I Don't Want To Change The World (Live) / I Just Want You / Back On Earth / Fairies Wear Boots / Behind The Wall Of Sleep / 1988 Interview
THE OZZMAN COMETH, Sony SRCS 8507-8 (JAPAN)
Black Sabbath / War Pigs / Goodbye To Romance / Crazy Train / Mr. Crowley / Over The Mountain / Paranoid (Live) / Bark At The Moon / Shot In The Dark / Crazy Babies / No More Tears (Edit) / Mama, I'm Coming Home / I Don't Want To Change The World (Live) / I Just Want You / Back On Earth / Fairies Wear Boots / Behind The Wall Of Sleep / 1988 Interview / Walk On Water / Pictures Of Matchstick Men
Singles/EPs:
Fairies Wear Boots / Behind The Walls Of Sleep / Interview, Sony (JAPAN promotion CD single)
Back On Earth / Walk On Water / I Just Want You, Sony 665049-2 (UK CD single)

2000
Albums:
DOWN TO EARTH, Sony, **4 UK, 4 USA, 1 SWEDEN**
Gets Me Through / Facing Hell / Dreamer / No Easy Way Out / That I Never Had / You Know... (Part 1) / Junkie / Running Out Of Time / Black Illusion / Alive / Can You Hear Them?

Ozzy's Black Sabbath Discography

1970
Singles/EPs:
Evil Woman (Don't Play Your Games With Me) / Wicked World, Fontana TF 1067 (1970) (UK)
Evil Woman (Don't Play Your Games With Me) / Wicked World, Fontana 5267977 (1970) (NEW ZEALAND)
Evil Woman (Don't Play Your Games With Me) / Wicked World, Fontana 6059 002 (1970) (GREECE)
Evil Woman (Don't Play Your Games With Me) / Wicked World, Vertigo 6059 002 (1970) (UK)
The Wizard / Evil Woman (Don't Play Your Games With Me), Vertigo 6059 005 (1970) (FRANCE)
Paranoid / The Wizard, Vertigo 6059 010 (1970) (UK) **4 UK**
Paranoid / The Wizard, Warner Bros. WB 7437 (1970) (USA)
Paranoid / The Wizard, Phillips SFL 1300 (1970) (JAPAN)
Paranoid / Rats Salad, Vertigo 6059 014 (1970) (FRANCE)
Iron Man / Electric Funeral, Warner Bros. 7530 (1970) (CANADA)
Albums:
BLACK SABBATH, Vertigo VO 6 (1970) **8 UK, 23 USA**
BLACK SABBATH / The Wizard / Behind The Walls Of Sleep / N.I.B. / Sleeping Village / Warning / Evil Woman (Don't Play Your Games With Me)
PARANOID, Vertigo 6360 011 (1970) **2 GERMANY, 1 UK, 12 USA**
War Pigs / Paranoid / Planet Caravan / Electric Funeral / Fairies Wear Boots /Iron Man / Hand Of Doom / Rat Salad

1971
Singles/EPs:
Paranoid / Rat Salad / Electric Funeral, Vertigo 6276 004 (1971) (MEXICO)
Albums:
MASTER OF REALITY, Vertigo 6360 050 (1971)
5 GERMANY, 5 UK, 8 USA
Sweet Leaf / After Forever / Children Of The Grave / Embryo / Lord Of This World / Into The Void / Solitude / Orchid

1972
Singles/EPs:
Tomorrow's Dream / Laguna Sunrise, Vertigo 6059 061 (1972) (UK)
Tomorrow's Dream / Laguna Sunrise, Warner Bros. WB 7625 (1972) (USA)
Tomorrow's Dream / Laguna Sunrise, Vertigo SFL-1744 (1972) (JAPAN)
Paranoid / Wicked World / Evil Woman (Don't Play Your Games With Me),

Ozzy's Black Sabbath Discography

Vertigo 6276 003 (1972) (PORTUGAL)
Snowblind / St. Vitus Dance / Tomorrow's Dream / Supernaut, Cashbox KS 130H (1972) (THAILAND)
Albums:
VOLUME 4, Vertigo 6360 071 (1972) **8 UK, 13 USA**
Wheels Of Confusion / Tomorrow's Dream / Snowblind / Changes / Supernaut / FX / Laguna Sunrise /Under The Sun /Cornucopia / St Vitus Dance

1973
Singles/EPs:
Children Of The Grave (B-Side) / Roadhouse Blues (STATUS QUO) (A Side), Vertigo DJ005 (1973) (Split single with STATUS QUO - Promotion release)
Sabbath Bloody Sabbath / Changes, WWA WWS 002 (1973) (UK)
Sabbath Bloody Sabbath / Changes, Warner Bros. WB 7764 (1973) (USA)
Sabbath Bloody Sabbath / Changes, Vertigo SFL-1833 (1973) (JAPAN)
Sabbath Bloody Sabbath / Changes, Vertigo 6165001 (1973) (GERMANY)
Sabbath Bloody Sabbath / Looking For Today / Sabbra Cadabra, Warner Bros. S 2695 (1973) (USA)
Paranoid / Black Sabbath / Changes / Tomorrows Dream, Vertigo 6276 009 (1973) (AUSTRALIA)
Sabbath Bloody Sabbath / Killing Yourself To Live, Cashbox KS 235 (1973) (THAILAND)
Albums:
SABBATH BLOODY SABBATH, WWA WWA 005 (1973)
49 GERMANY, 4 UK, 11 USA
A National Acrobat / Sabbath Bloody Sabbath / Who Are You? / Killing Yourself To Live / Spiral Architect / Fluff / Looking For Today / Sabbra Cadabra

1974
Singles/EPs:
Iron Man / Electric Funeral, Warner Bros. WB 7802 (1974) (USA)

1975
Singles/EPs:
Paranoid / Iron Man, Warner Bros. GWB 0312 (1975) (USA)
Sabbath Bloody Sabbath / Rats Salad / Fluff / Paranoid, Vertigo 6299 003 (1975) (BRAZIL)
Albums:
SABOTAGE, NEMS 9119 001 (1975) **7 UK, 28 USA**
Hole In The Sky / Don't Start (Too Late) / Symptom Of The Universe / Megalomania / Am I Going Insane (Radio) / The Writ / Supertzar / Thrill Of It All

Ozzy Osbourne

1976
Singles/EPs:
Am I Going Insane (Radio) / Hole In The Sky, NEMS 6165 300 (1976)
Am I Going Insane (Radio) / Hole In The Sky, Vertigo SFL-2060 (1976) (JAPAN)
It's Alright / Rock 'n' Roll Doctor, Vertigo 6079 100 (1976) (HOLLAND)
Gypsy / She's Gone, Vertigo 6079 102 (1976) (HOLLAND)
Gypsy / She's Gone, RTB 554008 (1976) (YUGOSLAVIA)
She's Gone / It's Alright, Vertigo 6832 187 (1976) (SPAIN)
Albums:
WE SOLD OUR SOULS FOR ROCK'N'ROLL, NEMS 6641 335 (1976) **21 SWEDEN, 35 UK, 48 USA**
Black Sabbath / The Wizard / Warning / Paranoid / Wicked World / Tomorrow's Dream / Fairies Wear Boots / Changes / Sweet Leaf / Children Of The Grave / Sabbath Bloody Sabbath / Am I Going Insane (Radio) / Laguna Sunrise / Snowblind / NIB
TECHNICAL ECSTASY, Vertigo 9102 750 (1976) **33 SWEDEN, 13 UK**
Back Street Kids / You Won't Change Me / Rock 'n' Roll Doctor / It's Alright / All Moving Parts (Stand Still) / She's Gone / Dirty Women / Gypsy

1977
Singles/EPs:
Paranoid / Snowblind, NEMS NES 112 (1977) (UK)
Paranoid / Evil Woman (Don't Play Your Games With Me), Immediata 103.466 (1977) (GERMANY)
Paranoid / Tomorrow's Dream, NEMS SRS S10.044 (1977) (HOLLAND)

1978
Singles/EPs:
Never Say Die / She's Gone, Vertigo SAB 001 (1978) **21 UK**
Never Say Die / She's Gone, Vertigo 6079 103 (1978) (GERMANY)
Never Say Die / Hard Road, Vertigo 6837 512 (1978) (FRANCE)
Hard Road / Symptom Of The Universe, Vertigo SAB 002 (1978) (UK) **33 UK**
Hard Road / Symptom Of The Universe, Vertigo 6079 104 (1978) (GERMANY)
Paranoid / Snowblind, NEMS NES 121 (1978)
Paranoid / Tomorrow's Dream, NEMS 26550 (1978) (BELGIUM)
Paranoid / Sabbath Bloody Sabbath, Arabella 102.280 (1978) (FRANCE)
Albums:
NEVER SAY DIE, Vertigo 9102 751 (1978) **37 SWEDEN, 12 UK**
Swinging The Chain / Never Say Die / Hard Road / Shock Wave / Johnny Blade / Junior's Eyes / Air Dance / Break Out / Over To You

Ozzy's Black Sabbath Discography

1980
Albums:
LIVE AT LAST, NEMS BS001 (1980) **26 SWEDEN, 5 UK**
Tomorrow's Dream / Sweet Leaf / Cornucopia / Wicked World / Killing Yourself To Live / Snowblind / Children Of The Grave / War Pigs / Paranoid / Cornucopia

During Ozzy's solo career the following Black Sabbath Ozzy era singles were released:

Paranoid / Tomorrow's Dream, NEMS 79800 (1979) (HOLLAND)
Paranoid / Snowblind, NEMS BSS 101 (1980) (UK) **14 UK**
Paranoid / Snowblind, NEMS 110 6104 (1980) (GERMANY)
Paranoid / Snowblind, NEMS 7 RECORDS MS 454 (1980) (AUSTRALIA)
Paranoid / Snowblind, NEMS SP06-5 (1980) (JAPAN)
Paranoid / Snowblind, SVKS 3019 (1980) (YUGOSLAVIA)
Hard Road / Symptom Of The Universe, Vertigo SFL-2355 (1980) (JAPAN)
Paranoico / Rats Salad, NEMS 16S0090 (1981) (SPAIN)
Paranoid / Iron Man, NEP 1 (1982) (Limited edition picture disc)
Paranoid / War Pigs / Iron Man / Black Sabbath, That's Original TOF 101 (1986)
Paranoid / Iron Man / War Pigs, Castle CD 3-5 (1988) (3" CD single)
Paranoid / Iron Man, Old Gold OG 9467 (1990)
Paranoid / Sabbath Bloody Sabbath / Electric Funeral, Old Gold 6129 (1991) (UK CD single)
Paranoid / Tomorrow's Dream / Iron Man / Laguna Sunrise / Black Sabbath, Castle CGC 6022 (1991) (UK CD single)
Paranoid / Black Sabbath / Iron Man / Blue Suede Shoes, Burning Airlines PILOT 49 (2001) (HOLLAND 'Black Mass' CD ROM EP)

1998 Black Sabbath reunion:
Singles/EPs:
Psycho Man (Radio edit) / Psycho Man (Danny Saber remix edit), Epic SAMPCS 5513 (1998) (UK Promotion release)
Paranoid (Live) / Psycho Man (Danny Saber remix) / Psycho Man (Radio edit), Sony ESC 666599-2 (1998) (GERMANY)
Selling My Soul (Danny Saber Remix edit) / Selling My Soul (Album version), Sony ESK 41767 (1998) (USA promotion release)
Albums:
REUNION-LIVE, Epic 491954-9 (1998) **41 UK, 11 USA**
War Pigs / Behind The Wall Of Sleep / NIB / Fairies Wear Boots / Electric Funeral / Sweet Leaf / Spiral Architect / Into The Void / Snowblind / Sabbath Bloody Sabbath / Orchid / Lord Of This World / Dirty Women / Black Sabbath / Iron Man / Children Of The Grave / Paranoid / Psycho Man (Studio) / Selling My Soul (Studio)

Ozzy Osbourne

Black Sabbath Compilations Featuring Ozzy Osbourne

Some may contain songs featuring other vocalists.

ATTENTION VOL. 1, Fontana 6438 057 (1975)
Paranoid / Sleeping Village / Warning / Evil Woman / Iron Man / The Wizard / Behind The Wall Of Sleep / NIB
ATTENTION VOL. II, WWA WWA 101 (1975)
Sweet Leaf / Black Sabbath / Rat Salad / Electric Funeral / After Forever / War Pigs / Fairies Wear Boots
THE ORIGINAL, NEMS (1976)
Paranoid / N.I.B. / Changes / Sabbath Bloody Sabbath / Black Sabbath / War Pigs / Laguna Sunrise / Tomorrow's Dream
STARGOLD, NEMS 0084.501 (1976)
Black Sabbath / Evil Woman / Warning / N.I.B. / Changes / Sabbath Bloody Sabbath / Laguna Sunrise / Tomorrow's Dream / Sweet Leaf / Children Of The Grave / Lord Of This World / Solitude / War Pigs / Paranoid / Planet Caravan / Iron Man
GREATEST HITS, NEMS NEL 6009 (1977)
Paranoid / N.I.B. / Changes / Sabbath Bloody Sabbath / Iron Man / Black Sabbath / War Pigs / Laguna Sunrise / Tomorrow's Dream / Sweet Leaf
ROCK LEGENDS, Vertigo 6321 120 (1978) (AUSTRALIA)
Back Street Kids / Rock 'n' Roll Doctor / Dirty Women / Never Say Die / Shock Wave / Air Dance / Johnny Blade
ROCK HEAVIES, Vertigo 9198 623 (1980) (GERMANY)
Back Street Kids / Rock 'n' Roll Doctor / Dirty Women / Never Say Die / Shock Wave / Air Dance / Johnny Blade
BEST OF BLACK SABBATH, NEMS (1983) (picture disc)
THE BEST, Starcall STAR 301 (1983) (AUSTRALIA)
Paranoid / N.I.B. / Iron Man / Supernaut / Sabbath Bloody Sabbath / Changes / Sabbra Cadabra / Children Of The Grave / Tomorrow's Dream / Wicked World / Sweet Leaf / Snowblind
HAND OF DOOM, Victoria JS9016/4 (1984) (SPAIN Box Set release)
Black Sabbath / The Wizard / Behind The Walls Of Sleep / N.I.B. / Sleeping Village / Warning / Evil Woman (Don't Play Your Games With Me) / War Pigs / Paranoid / Planet Caravan / Electric Funeral / Fairies Wear Boots /Iron Man / Hand Of Doom / Rat Salad / Sweet Leaf / After Forever / Children Of The Grave / Embryo / Lord Of This World / Into The Void / Solitude / Orchid / Wheels Of Confusion / Tomorrow's Dream / Snowblind / Changes / Supernaut

Ozzy's Black Sabbath Discography

/ FX / Laguna Sunrise /Under The Sun /Cornucopia / St Vitus Dance
30 ANOS DE MUSICA ROCK-SALVAT, Vertigo 8222971 (1984) (MEXICO release)
Back Street Kids / You Won't Change Me / It's Alright / Gypsy / All Moving Parts / Rock 'n' Roll Doctor / She's Gone / Dirty Woman
THE BLACK SABBATH COLLECTION, Castle CCSLP 109 (1985)
Black Sabbath / The Wizard / Warning / Paranoid / War Pigs / Iron Man / Tomorrow's Dream / Fairies Wear Boots / Changes / Sweet Leaf / Children Of The Grave / Sabbath Bloody Sabbath / Laguna Sunrise / Snowblind / N.I.B.
MASTERS OF ROCK, Teal MMTI 1384 (1986) (SOUTH AFRICA)
Paranoid / N.I.B. / Changes / Sabbath Bloody Sabbath / Iron Man / Black Sabbath / War Pigs / Laguna Sunrise / Tomorrow's Dream / Sweet Leaf
THE KINGS OF HELL, Alldisc 26.008 (1987) (ARGENTINA)
The Wizard / War Pigs / Changes / Sabbath Bloody Sabbath / Sweet Leaf / Paranoid / Solitude / Black Sabbath / Cornucopia / Tomorrow's Dream / Laguna Sunrise
BLACKEST SABBATH, Vertigo (1989)
Black Sabbath / Paranoid / Iron Man / Children Of The Grave / Snowblind / Sabbath Bloody Sabbath / Hole In The Sky / Rock 'n' Roll Doctor / Never Say Die / Lady Evil / Turn Up The Night / Sign Of The Southern Cross (Live) / Heaven And Hell (Continued) (Live) / Children Of The Sea (Live) / Digital Bitch / Trashed / Seventh Star / Born To Lose / Lost Forever
BLACKEST SABBATH, Vertigo 838 818-2 (1989) (UK version)
Black Sabbath / Paranoid / Iron Man / Snowblind / Sabbath Bloody Sabbath / Hole In The Sky / Rock 'n' Roll Doctor / Never Say Die / Lady Evil / Turn Up The Night / Sign Of The Southern Cross (Live) / Heaven And Hell (Live) / Children Of The Sea (Live) / Digital Bitch / Seventh Star / Born To Lose
BACKTRACKIN', Knight (1990)
Paranoid / Iron Man / Black Sabbath / Killing Yourself To Live / Snowblind / Sweet Leaf / Into The Void / Electric Funeral / Sabbra Cadabra / St. Vitus Dance / Fairies Wear Boots / Supertzar / Children Of The Grave / Sabbath Bloody Sabbath / N.I.B. / Symptom Of The Universe / Planet Caravan / War Pigs / Rat Salad / Am I Going Insane (Radio) / Megalomania / The Wizzard / Cornucopia / Hole In The Sky
BACKTRACKIN', Masterpiece TRK CD 103 (1990) (UK Version)
Paranoid / Killing Yourself To Live / Snowblind / Sweet Leaf / Into The Void / Electric Funeral / Sabbra Cadabra / St. Vitus Dance / Fairies Wear Boots / Sabbath Bloody Sabbath / Symptom Of The Universe / Planet Caravan / War Pigs / The Wizard / Cornucopia
THE BLACK SABBATH COLLECTION VOLUME II, Castle CCS CD 199 (1990)
THE OZZY OSBOURNE YEARS, Essential ESB CD 12 (1991)
Black Sabbath / The Wizard / Behind The Wall Of Sleep / N.I.B. / Evil Woman / Sleeping Village / Warning / War Pigs / Paranoid / Planet Caravan /

Ozzy Osbourne

Iron Man / Hand Of Doom / Fairies Wear Boots / Electric Funeral / Sweet Leaf / After Forever / Embryo / Lord Of This World / Solitude / Into The Void / Wheels Of Confusion / Tomorrow's Dream / Changes / Supernaut / Snowblind / Cornucopia / St. Vitus Dance / Under The Sun / Sabbath Bloody Sabbath / A National Acrobat / Sabbra Caddabra / Killing Yourself To Live / Who Are You / Looking For Today / Spiral Architect / Hole In The Sky / Symptom Of The Universe / Megalomania

THE OZZY OSBOURNE YEARS, Essential ESB 142 (1991) (Vinyl Version)
Black Sabbath / The Wizard / Behind The Wall Of Sleep / N.I.B. / Evil Woman / Sleeping Village / Warning / War Pigs / Paranoid / Planet Caravan / Iron Man / Hand Of Doom / Fairies Wear Boots / Electric Funeral / Sweet Leaf / After Forever / Embryo / Lord Of This World / Solitude / Into The Void / Wheels Of Confusion / Tomorrow's Dream / Changes / Supernaut / Snowblind / Cornucopia /

THE MASTERS OF HEAVY METAL, Castle CHC 7022 (1991)
Paranoid / Killing Yourself To Live / Snowblind / Sweet Leaf / Sabbath Bloody Sabbath / Symptom Of The Universe / Planet Caravan / War Pigs / Into The Void / Electric Funeral / Sabbra Cadabra / St. Vitus Dance / Fairies Wear Boots / The Wizard / Cornucopia

THE BLACK SABBATH STORY, Castle CHC 7028 (1991)
Black Sabbath / N.I.B. / Paranoid / War Pigs / Iron Man / Children Of The Grave / Orchid / Lord Of This World / Snowblind / Tomorrow's Dream / Sabbath Bloody Sabbath / Sabbra Cadabra / Symptom Of The Universe / Am I Going Insane (Radio)

IRON MAN, Spectrum 550720-2 (1994)

1970-1983 BETWEEN HEAVEN AND HELL, Rawpower RAWCD 104 (1995)
Hole In The Sky / Into The Void / Sabbath Bloody Sabbath / N.I.B. / Paranoid / War Pigs / Iron Man / Wicked World / Supernaut / Back Street Kids / Never Say Die / Neon Knights / Mob Rules / The Dark – Zero The Hero / Black Sabbath

UNDER WHEELS OF CONFUSION, Essential ESF CD 419 (1996)
Black Sabbath / The Wizard / N.I.B. / Evil Woman / Wicked World / War Pigs / Paranoid / Iron Man / Planet Caravan / Hand Of Doom / Sweet Leaf / After Forever / Children Of The Grave / Into The Void / Lord Of This World / Orchid / Supernaut / Tomorrow's Dream / Wheels Of Confusion / Changes / Snowblind / Laguna Sunrise / Cornucopia (Live) / Sabbath Bloody Sabbath / Killing Yourself To Live / Hole In The Sky / Am I Going Insane (Radio) / The Writ / Symptom Of The Universe / Dirty Women / Back Street Kids/ Rock 'n' Roll Doctor / She's Gone / A Hard Road / Never Say Die / Neon Knights / Heaven And Hell / Die Young / Lonely Is The Word / Turn Up The Night / Sign Of The Southern Cross / Falling Off The Edge Of The World / The Mob Rules (Live) / Voodoo (Live) / Digital Bitch / Trashed / Hotline / In For The Kill / Seventh Star / Heart Like A Wheel / The Shining / Eternal Idol

Ozzy's Black Sabbath Discography

ROCK GIANTS, Spectrum 554 103.2 (1997) (GERMANY)
Sabbath Bloody Sabbath / The Wizard / Sweet Leaf / Electric Funeral / Into The Void / Wheels Of Confusion / Paranoid / Iron Man / Am I Going Insane / Killing Yourself To Live / Snowblind / Hole In The Sky / Laguna Sunrise / War Pigs

THE BEST OF BLACK SABBATH, Castle RAW DD145 (2000)
Black Sabbath / Wizard / N.I.B./ Evil Woman (Don't Play Your Games With Me) / Wicked World / War Pigs / Paranoid / Planet Caravan / Iron Man / Electric Funeral / Fairies Wear Boots / Sweet Leaf / Embryo / Children Of The Grave / Lord Of This World / Into The Void / Tomorrow's Dream / Supernaut / Snowblind / Sabbath Bloody Sabbath / Killing Yourself To Live / Spiral Architect / Hole In The Sky / Don't Start (Too Late) / Symptom Of The Universe / Am I Going Insane / Dirty Woman / Never Say Die / Hard Road / Heaven And Hell / Turn Up The Night / Zero The Hero

THE SINGLES, Castle Music CMKBX002 (2000) (UK singles box set)
Evil Woman / Wicked World / Paranoid / The Wizard / Tomorrow's Dream / Laguna Sunrise / Sabbath Bloody Sabbath / Changes / Never Say Die / She's Gone / Hard Road / Symptom Of The Universe

STAR PROFILE, All Stars (2000)
Black Sabbath / Warning / N.I.B. / War Pigs / Iron Man / Paranoid / Sweet Leaf / Orchid / Lord Of This World / Solitude 1/ Wheels Of Confusion / Changes / Fluff 1/ Sabbath Bloody Sabbath

Other Ozzy Osbourne Recordings

1980

QUARTZ
Singles/EPs:
Stoking The Fires Of Hell / Circles, MCA 642 (1980)
Recorded in 1977 when Tony Iommi was producing the debut album for Birmingham Heavy Metal band Quartz. Not only did Iommi produce the track 'Circles' but Queen guitarist Brian May contributed guitar parts and Ozzy played harmonica. Inexplicably the song was left off the album, possibly for contractual reasons, only surfacing as the B-side to the 1980 single 'Stoking The Fires Of Hell'. Quartz guitarist Geoff Nichols would later join Black Sabbath first as a bassist then as long-term keyboard player.

1983

WAS (NOT WAS)
Albums:
BORN TO LAUGH AT TORNADOS, CBS 592 (1983)
Ozzy originally recorded vocals for the track 'Shake Your Head (Let's Go To Bed)' in 1983 as companion to Madonna. The two did not meet in the studio, Madonna having put her vocals down in an earlier session. Later Don Was would remark that Ozzy's vocal was intended to completely replace Madonna's efforts although her lines are still clearly audible. Years later when Was (Not Was) intended to release a compilation album *Hello Dad, I'm In Jail*, Madonna requested that her vocals be removed. Actress Kim Basinger re-recorded the lines.

1988

LITA FORD
Albums:
LITA, RCA (1988)
Ozzy's biggest singles chart success would come with his duet with Lita Ford on her 'Close My Eyes Forever' track. The song was co-written by Ozzy.

1989

GARY MOORE
Albums:
AFTER THE WAR, Virgin 0777 7 86107 2 4 (1989)

Other Ozzy Osbourne Recordings

Ozzy provided backing vocals for two songs, 'Speak For Yourself' and 'Led Clones', for his friend Gary Moore's 1989 album *After The War*. The latter track was a shameless dig at the Zeppelin-soundalike band Kingdom Come. Both Bob Daisley and Don Airey also appear on the album.

MAKE A DIFFERENCE FOUNDATION
Albums:
STAIRWAY TO HEAVEN – HIGHWAY TO HELL, Mercury 842 093-2 (1989)
Ozzy and band deliver a version of Jimi Hendrix's 'Purple Haze' for the Make A Difference Foundation album. The record was compiled of cover versions recorded by artists who had been 'touched' by drug or alcohol problems.

1990

BILL WARD
Albums:
WARD ONE – ALONG THE WAY, Chameleon D2-74816 (1990)
Ozzy lends lead vocal to his friend Black Sabbath drummer Bill Ward's *Ward One – Along The Way* album. Ozzy can be heard on 'Jack's Land' and 'Bombers (Can Open Bomb Bays)'. Both Zakk Wylde and Bob Daisley also contribute to the record.
   Now deleted, there are plans to re-release the album albeit minus the Ozzy tracks.

MIKE BATT & THE LONDON PHILHARMONIC ORCHESTRA
Singles/EPs:
The Urpney Song, Adventure ADVTS 102 (1990)
Ozzy, champion boxer Frank Bruno and renowned 'Big Yin' Scottish comedian Billy Connolly all add their distinctive vocals to this track which featured as part of the soundtrack to the *Dreamstone* children's TV show.

1991

DWEEZIL ZAPPA
Ozzy and Dweezil Zappa recorded an off-the-wall interpretation of the Bee Gees dance classic 'Stayin' Alive' intended for use on Zappa's *Confessions* album. For contractual reasons the Ozzy tapes were resigned to the vaults although Zakk Wylde's guitar solo did thankfully stay put.

INFECTIOUS GROOVES
Singles/EPs:
Therapy, Epic ESK 4238 (1991)
Ozzy features as guest vocalist on the track 'Therapy' by Robert Trujillo's

Ozzy Osbourne

post Suicidal Tendencies act Infectious Grooves. The single, from the album *The Plague That Makes Your Booty Move... It's The Infectious Grooves* was only issued as a promotional release.

ALICE COOPER
Albums:
HEY STOOPID, Epic EK 46786 (1991)
Ozzy joins an all star cast that featured on Alice's 1991 album, featuring on the anti suicide anthem 'Hey Stoopid'.

1992

WAS (NOT WAS)
Singles/EPs:
Shake Your Head (Let's Go To Bed), Phonogram WASX 11 (1992)
The 1992 version sees Madonna's vocal replaced by actress Kim Basinger. Ozzy's vocals remain intact.

MOTORHEAD
Albums:
MARCH OR DIE, Epic NK 48997 (1992)
Lemmy had collaborated as lyric writer with Ozzy for the *No More Tears* album, gaining a credit for the track 'Hellraiser'. Not only do Motorhead offer their own take on 'Hellraiser' but Ozzy himself came into the studio to put vocals on the track 'I Ain't No Nice Guy'.

1994

THE MUPPETS
Albums:
KERMIT UNPIGGED, BMG 78400-10004-2 (1994)
Ozzy duets with Miss Piggy on a rendition of Steppenwolf's seminal 'Born To Be Wild'. Ironic, seeing as producer Ron Nevison could not persuade Ozzy to cut the track for himself on the *Ultimate Sin* album.

THERAPY?
Albums:
NATIVITY IN BLACK, Sony 66335 (1994)
If not the first, then without doubt the finest Black Sabbath tribute album to emerge to date. Ozzy pairs up in an unlikely union with alternative Irish rock act Therapy? for a version of 'Iron Man'. The album also found Bill Ward and Geezer Butler in alliance with fellow Brummie, Judas Priest frontman and one-off live Black Sabbath singer Rob Halford and Wino from the Sabbath-fixated Doom band Obsessed, billed as the Bullring Brummies for 'The

Other Ozzy Osbourne Recordings

Wizard'.

Others paying homage are Megadeth with 'Paranoid', Faith No More ('War Pigs'), Al Jourgensen's 1,000 Homo DJs ('Supernaut'), C.O.C. ('Lord Of This World'), Sepultura ('Symptom Of The Universe), Ugly Kid Joe ('N.I.B.'), White Zombie ('Children Of The Grave'), Biohazard ('After Forever') and Iron Maiden singer Bruce Dickinson in league with Godspeed ('Sabbath Bloody Sabbath').

1996

BEAVIS & BUTTHEAD
Albums:
BEAVIS & BUTTHEAD DO AMERICA, Famous Music GEFD 25002 (1996)
Ozzy united with the MTV cartoon Metal pranksters for the song 'Walk On Water', part of the soundtrack to the *Beavis & Butthead Do America* movie.

1997

TYPE O NEGATIVE
Albums:
PRIVATE PARTS, Warner Bros. 9 46477-2 (1997)
A union between one of the '90s most successful Gothic Metal acts Type O Negative and Ozzy on Status Quo's '60s hit 'Pictures Of Matchstick Men' for the soundtrack to notorious shock jock Howard Stern's autobiographical *Private Parts* movie.

1998

RINGO STARR
Albums:
VERTICAL MAN, Mercury 558400 (1998)
An avid fan of The Beatles, Ozzy was no doubt thrilled to donate a lead vocal track to the title song on Ringo Starr's *Vertical Man* album. Ozzy was in good company for this record, others in the studio numbered Paul McCartney, George Harrison, Steven Tyler, Scott Weiland, Alanis Morissette and Brian Wilson.

SOUTH PARK
Albums:
CHEF AID – THE SOUTH PARK ALBUM, (1998)
When the *South Park* gang decided to record an album Ozzy was the obvious choice, not only for his cartoon manifestation to bite the head off Kenny, but to provide vocals to the track 'Nowhere To Run'. Other musicians featuring

Ozzy Osbourne

on this track are DMX, Ol' Dirty Bastard, Crystal Method and Fuzzbubble.

BUSTA RHYMES
Albums:
EXTINCTION LEVEL EVENT, Elektra 62211 (1998)
Ozzy features on 'This Means War', actually a radical remake of 'Iron Man', by rapper Busta Rhymes. The song would also feature on the Black Sabbath tribute *Nativity In Black Volume Two*.

1999

COAL CHAMBER
Albums:
CHAMBER MUSIC, Roadrunner (1999)
An act at the time managed by Sharon Osbourne. Hot Nu-Metal band Coal Chamber's version of Peter Gabriel's 'Shock The Monkey' benefitted greatly from Ozzy's involvement on guest vocals.

RICK WAKEMAN
Albums:
RETURN TO THE CENTRE OF THE EARTH, EMI 556763 (1999)
Rick Wakeman, noted for both his adventurous solo career and of course as keyboard player with prog legends Yes, is an old acquaintance of Ozzy. Wakeman performed on both Black Sabbath's *Sabbath Bloody Sabbath* and on Ozzy's *Ozzmosis*.
Return To The Centre Of The Earth was an ambitious attempt to rekindle the glories of Wakeman's all conquering '70s concept pieces. With narration from Star Trek's Patrick Stewart and vocal guest slots for Bonnie Tyler and Justin Hayward, the record certainly gave Rick's many fans cause to celebrate. Ozzy is featured on the song 'Buried Alive'.

TONY IOMMI
Albums:
IOMMI, Divine Recordings P2 27857 CD (2000)
Both Ozzy and Bill Ward grace the track 'Who's Fooling Who' from Tony Iommi's debut solo album. The Black Sabbath guitarist had previously attempted to go solo with the *Seventh Star* album although this would subsequently be shoe-horned into the unwieldy 'Black Sabbath featuring Tony Iommi' tag. Initial recordings for this project were laid down during 1996 working with a band of *Seventh Star* frontman Glenn Hughes, the omnipresent Don Airey and erstwhile Judas Priest drummer Dave Holland. These sessions would be abandoned but to the amazement of those involved, would soon surface on the bootleg market cheekily dubbed *Eighth Star*.
The 'Iommi' recordings would, in the main, feature contemporary guest

Other Ozzy Osbourne Recordings

artists such as Henry Rollins, Billy Corgan of the Smashing Pumpkins, Skin of Skunk Anansie, Dave Grohl of the Foo Fighters and Pete Steele of Type O Negative. The 'old school' concessions are former Black Sabbath bassist Lawrence Cottle, Queen guitarist Brian May, Cult singer Ian Astbury and a surprise inclusion of Billy Idol. According to quotes from Iommi himself Ozzy asked to be included on the album.

The Ozzy Sidemen Discographies

DON AIREY
Don's discography, which covers a wide range of styles, would in full warrant a book of its own. Included here are the most important rock releases.

BABE RUTH:
KIDS STUFF, Capitol EST 23739 (1976)
Oh, Dear What A Shame / Welcome To The Show / Since You Went Away / Standing In The Rain / Sweet, Sweet Surrender / Oh Doctor / Nickelodeon / Keep Your Distance / Living A Lie

COLOSSEUM II:
STRANGE NEW FLESH, Island (1976)
Dark Side Of The Moog / Down To You / Gemini And Leo / Secret Places / On Second Thoughts / Winds
ELECTRIC SAVAGE, MCA (1977)
Am I / Intergalactic Strut / Put It This Way / All Skin And Bone / Rivers / The Scorch / Lament / Desperado
WARDANCE, MCA (1977)
War Dance / Put It That Way / Major Key / Castles / Fighting Talk / Quasar / Inquisition / Star Maidens / Mysterioso / Last Exit

GARY MOORE:
BACK ON THE STREETS, MCA (1978)
Don't Believe A Word / Back On The Streets / Parisienne Walkways / Fanatical Fascists / Flight Of The Snow Moose / Hurricane / Song For Donna / What Would You Rather Bee, Or A Wasp

BLACK SABBATH:
NEVER SAY DIE, Vertigo 9102 751 (1978) **37 SWEDEN, 12 UK**
Swinging The Chain / Never Say Die / Hard Road / Shock Wave / Johnny Blade / Junior's Eyes / Air Dance / Break Out / Over To You

STRIFE:
BACK TO THUNDER, Gull GULP 1029 (1979)
Shockproof / Let Me Down / Feel So Good / Sky / You Are What You Are / Red Sun / Fool Injected Overlap / Weary Traveller

RAINBOW:
DOWN TO EARTH, Polydor POLD 5023 (1979) **17 SWEDEN, 6 UK**
All Night Long / Eyes Of The World / Since You've Been Gone / No Time To Lose / Love's No Friend / Lost In Hollywood / Danger Zone / Makin' Love

The Ozzy Sidemen Discographies

COZY POWELL:
OVER THE TOP, Ariola ARL 5038 (1979) **34 UK**
Theme 1 / Killer / Heidi Goes To Town / El Sid / Sweet Poison / The Loner / Over The Top
TILT, Polydor POLD 5047 (1981) **58 UK**
Cat Moves / Sunset / Living A Lie / Hot Rock / The Blister / The Right Side / Jekyll & Hyde / Sooner Or Later

MSG:
MICHAEL SCHENKER GROUP, Chrysalis CHR 1302 (1980) **8 UK, 100 USA**
Armed And Ready / Cry For The Nations / Victim Of Illusion / Bijou Pleasurette / Feels Like A Good Thing / Into The Arena / Walking Out From Nowhere / Tales Of Mystery / Lost Horizons

RAINBOW:
DIFFICULT TO CURE, Polydor POLD 5036 (1981) **9 SWEDEN, 3 UK**
Difficult To Cure / I Surrender / Spotlight Kid / No Release / Viellacht Das Machsterzeit / Can't Happen Here / Magic / Freedom Fighter / Midtown Tunnel Vision
STRAIGHT BETWEEN THE EYES, Polydor POLD 5056 (1982) **7 SWEDEN, 5 UK, 30 UK**
Death Alley Driver / Stone Cold / Bring On The Night / Power / Dream Chaser / Tite Squeeze / Tearin' Out My Heart / Eyes Of Fire / Miss Mistreated / Rock Fever

GARY MOORE:
CORRIDORS OF POWER, Virgin V 2245 (1982) **30 UK**
Don't Take Me For A Loser / Always Gonna Love You / Wishing Well / Gonna Break My Heart Again / Falling In Love With You / End Of The World / Rockin' Every Night / Cold Hearted / I Can't Wait Until Tomorrow
ROCKIN' EVERY NIGHT – LIVE IN JAPAN, Virgin ZIDCD1 (1983)
Rockin' Every Night / Wishing Well / I Can't Wait Until Tomorrow / Nuclear Attack / White Knuckles / Rockin' And Rollin' / Back On The Streets / Sunset
DIRTY FINGERS, Jet (1984)
Hiroshima / Dirty Fingers / Bad News / Don't Let Me Be Misunderstood / Run To Your Mama / Nuclear Attack / Kidnapped / Really Gonna Rock / Lonely Nights / Rest In Peace
RUN FOR COVER, Ten DIXP 16 (1985) **6 SWEDEN, 12 UK**
Out In The Fields / Empty Rooms / Run For Cover / All Messed Up / Reach For The Sky / Military Man / Nothing To Lose / Once In A Lifetime / Listen To Your Heartbeat / Out Of My System

ALASKA:
THE PACK, Music For Nations MFN (1985)
Running With The Pack / A Woman Like You / Where Did They Go? / Schoolgirl / S.O.S. / Help Yourself / Miss You Tonight / The Thing / I Really Wanna Know

Ozzy Osbourne

PHENOMENA:
PHENOMENA, Bronze 207044 (1985) **30 SWEDEN**
Kiss Of Fire / Still The Night / Dance With The Devil / Phoenix Rising / Believe / Who's Watching Who / Hell On Wings / Twilight Zone / Phenomena

ZENO:
ZENO, Parlophone PCSD 102 (1986)
Eastern Sun / A Little More Love / Love Will Live / Signs On The Sky / Far Sky / Emergency / Don't Tell The Wind / Heart On The Wing / Circles Of Dawn / Sent By Heaven / Sunset

HELIX:
WILD IN THE STREETS, Capitol EST 2046 (1987)
Wild In The Streets / Kiss It Goodbye / Long Way To Heaven / Never Gonna Stop The Rock / Dream On / What Ya Bringin' To The Party / High Voltage Kicks / Give 'Em Hell / Shot Full Of Love / Love Hungry Eyes / She's Too Tough

WHITESNAKE:
1987, Liberty EMC 3528 (1987) **8 SWEDEN, 8 UK, 2 USA**
Still Of The Night / Bad Boys / Give Me All Your Love / Don't Turn Away / Looking For Love / Crying In The Rain / Straight From The Heart / Is This Love / Children Of The Night / Here I Go Again
SLIP OF THE TONGUE, EMI EMD 1013 (1989) **11 SWEDEN, 10 UK, 10 USA**
Slip Of The Tongue / Cheap 'n' Nasty / Fool For Your Lovin' / Now You're Gone / Kitten's Got Claws / Wings Of The Storm / The Deeper The Love / Judgement Day / Slow Poke Music / Sailing Ships

DON AIREY:
K2, 121 Records (1988)
K2 Overture / Sea Of Dreams Part I / Sea Of Dreams Part II / Voice Of The Mountain / Song For Al / Balti Lament / Ascent To Camp 4 / Can't Make Up Your Mind / Summit Push / Close To The Sky / Blues For J.T. / Julie If You Leave Me / Death Zone – Whiteout / Song For Al / Take Me Home

FASTWAY:
ON TARGET, GWR GWCD 22 (1988)
Dead Or Alive / Change Of Heart / A Fine Line / Two Hearts / You / Let Him Rock / She Is Danger / Show Some Emotion / These Dreams / Close Your Eyes
BAD BAD GIRLS, Legacy LLCD 130 (1990)
I've Had Enough / Bad, Bad Girls / All Shook Up / Body Rock / Miles Away / She Won't Rock / No Repair / Death Of Me / Cut Loose / Lucky To Lose / Big Beat No Heart

GARY MOORE:
AFTER THE WAR, Virgin (1989) **3 SWEDEN, 23 UK**
After The War / Speak For Yourself / Livin' On Dreams / Led Clones /

The Ozzy Sidemen Discographies

Running From The Storm / This Thing Called Love / Ready For Love / Blood Of Emeralds / Dunlace / The Messiah Will Come
STILL GOT THE BLUES, Virgin (1990) **1 SWEDEN, 13 UK, 83 USA**
Movin' On / Oh Pretty Woman / Walking By Myself / Still Got The Blues (For You) / Texas Street / All Your Love / Too Tired / King Of The Blues / As The Years Go Passing By / Midnight Blues / That Kind Of Woman / Stop Messin' Around

GRAHAM BONNET:
HERE COMES THE NIGHT, President PCOM 1114 (1991)
Something About You / Here Comes The Night / Long Time Gone / Only One Woman / Please Call Me / A Change Is Gonna Come / I'll Go Crazy / I Go To Sleep / Look Don't Touch / Eyes Of A Child / Don't / What She Says, You Hear It Means

GLENN TIPTON:
BAPTISM OF FIRE, Atlantic 7567 82974-2 (1997)
Hard Core / Paint It Black / Enter The Storm / Fuel Me Up / Extinct / Baptism Of Fire / The Healer / Cruise Control / Kill Or Be Killed / Voodoo Brother / Left For Dead

TEN:
BABYLON, Frontiers (2000) **100 GERMANY**
The Stranger / Barricade / Give In This Time / Love Become The Law / The Heat / Silent Rain / Timeless / Black Hearted Woman / Thunder In Heaven / Valentine

SILVER:
SILVER, AOR Heaven (2000)
Silver / Pretender / Sister Love / Marianna / Christine / She Was Mine / Walk The Stage / Sergei's Revenge / Brother Kill Brother / The Writer / Far Behind / No More Tears / Silverous

Don's partner on guitar for the *Silver* album is erstwhile Ozzy colleague Bernie Tormé.

COMPANY OF SNAKES:
HERE THEY GO AGAIN – LIVE, (2001)
Intro / Come On / Walking In The Shadow Of The Blues / Trouble / Kinda Wish You Would / Rough 'n' Ready / Don't Break My Heart Again / Moody's Blues / Slow 'n' Easy / Sweet Talker / Ready And Willing / Would I Lie To You? / Ain't Gonna Cry No More Today / Silver On Her Person / Lovehunter / Is This Love? / Since You've Been Gone / Here I Go Again / Wine, Women And Song / Fool For Your Lovin'
BURST THE BUBBLE, SPV (2002)
Ayresome Park / Labour Of Love / Ride Ride Ride (Run, Run, Run) / Burst The Bubble / Sacrificial Feelings / What Love Can Do / Little Miss Happiness / Hurricane / Kinda Wish You Would / Days To Remember / Back To The

Ozzy Osbourne
Blues / All Dressed Up / Can't Go Back / She / Ayresome Park – Reprise

TOMMY ALDRIDGE

BLACK OAK ARKANSAS:
IF AN ANGEL CAME TO SEE YOU, WOULD YOU MAKE HER FEEL AT HOME?, Atco 7008 (1972) **93 USA**
Gravel Roads / Fertile Woman / Spring Vacation / We Help Each Other / Full Moon Ride / Our Mind's Eye / To Make Us What We Are / Our Eyes Are On You / Mutants Of The Monster
RAUNCH N' ROLL – LIVE, Atco 7019 (1973) **90 USA**
Gettin' Kinda Cocky / When Electricity Came To Arkansas / Gigolo / Hot Rod / Mutants Of The Monster / Hot And Nasty / Up
HIGH ON THE HOG, Atco 7035 (1973) **52 USA**
Swimmin' In Quicksand / Back To The Land / Movin' / Happy Hooker / Red Hot Lovin' / Jim Dandy / Moonshine Sonata / Why Shouldn't I Smile? / High 'n' Dry / Mad Man
STREET PARTY, Atco 101 (1974) **56 USA**
Dancing In The Streets / Sting Me / Good Good Woman / Jail Bait / Sure Been Workin' Hard / Son Of A Gun / Brink Of Creation / I'm A Man / Goin' Home / Dixie / Everybody Wants To See Heaven "Nobody Wants To Die" / Hey Y'All / Brink Of Creation
AIN'T LIFE GRAND, Atco 111 (1975)
Taxman / Fancy Nancy / Keep On / Good Stuff / Rebel / Back Door Man / Love Can Be Found / Diggin' For Gold / Cryin' Shame / Let Life Be Good To You

RUBY STARR:
SCENE STEALER, Capitol 11549 (1975)
Maybe I'm Amazed / Morning Glory / That's It / I'll Meet You Half Way / Love On Ice / Who's Who / Be My Baby / Mass Transit / Fistful Of Love / Drift Away

BLACK OAK ARKANSAS:
X-RATED, MCA MCF 2734 (1975) **99 USA**
Bump 'n' Grind / Fightin' Cock / Highway Pirate / Strong Enough To Be Gentle / Flesh Needs Flesh / Wild Men From The Mountains / High Flyer / Ace In The Hole / Too Hot To Stop
LIVE! MUTHA, Atco 128 (1976)
Jim Dandy / Fancy Nancy / Lord Have Mercy On My Soul / Fever In My Mind / Hey Y'All / Rebel / Taxman / Hot And Nasty
BALLS OF FIRE, MCA MCF 2762 (1976)
Ramblin' Gamblin' Man / Fistful Of Love / Make That Scene / I Can Feel Forever / Rock 'n' Roll / Great Balls Of Fire / Just To Fall In Love / Leather Angel / Storm Of Passion / All My Troubles

The Ozzy Sidemen Discographies

PAT TRAVERS:
HEAT IN THE STREET, Polydor POLD 5005 (1978) **99 USA**
Heat In The Street / Killer's Instinct / I Tried To Believe / Hammerhead / Go All Night / Evie / Prelude / One For Me And One For You
GO FOR WHAT YOU KNOW – LIVE, Polydor POLS 1011 (1979) **29 USA**
Hooked On Music / Gettin Betta / Go All Night / Boom Boom (Out Go The Lights) / Stevie / Makin' Magic / Heat In The Streets / Makes No Difference
CRASH AND BURN, Polydor POLS 1017 (1980) **20 USA**
Crash And Burn / Can't Be Right / Snortin' Whiskey / Born Under A Bad Sign / Is This Love / The Big Event / Love Will Make You Strong / Material Eyes
RADIOACTIVE, Polydor 2391 499 (1981) **37 USA**
New Age Music / My Life Is On The Line / (I Just Wanna) Live It My Way / I Don't Wanna Be Awake / I Can Love You / Untitled / Feelin' In Love / Play It Like You See It / Electric Detective

GARY MOORE:
DIRTY FINGERS, Jet 241 (1984)
Hiroshima / Dirty Fingers / Bad News / Don't Let Me Be Misunderstood / Run To Your Mama / Nuclear Attack / Kidnapped / Really Gonna Rock / Lonely Nights / Rest In Peace

LITA FORD:
DANCIN' ON THE EDGE, Vertigo VER 13 (1984) **96 UK, 66 USA**
Gotta Let Go / Dancin' On The Edge / Dressed To Kill / Hit 'n' 'Run / Lady Killer / Still Waitin' / Fire In My Heart / Don't Let Me Down Tonight / Run With The $

VINNIE MOORE:
MIND'S EYE, Roadrunner RR 9635 (1986)
In Control / Saved By A Miracle / Lifeforce / Mind's Eye / Journey / Daydream / Hero Without Honour / NNY / Shadows Of Yesterday

M.A.R.S.:
PROJECT:DRIVER, Roadrunner (1987)
Nations On Fire / Writings On The Wall / Stand Up And Fight / Nostradamus / Unknown Survivor / Fantasy / Slave To My Touch / I Can See It In Your Eyes / You And I

WHITESNAKE:
SLIP OF THE TONGUE, EMI EMD 1013 (1989) **11 SWEDEN, 10 UK, 10 USA**
Slip Of The Tongue / Cheap 'n' Nasty / Fool For Your Lovin' / Now You're Gone / Kitten's Got Claws / Wings Of The Storm / The Deeper The Love / Judgement Day / Slow Poke Music / Sailing Ships

MANIC EDEN:
MANIC EDEN, CNR Music (1994)
Can You Feel It / Gimme A Shot / Fire In My Soul / Do Angels Die / Pushing

Ozzy Osbourne

Me / Dark Side Of Grey / Keep It Coming / When The Hammer Comes Down / Ride The Storm / Can't Hold It

HOUSE OF LORDS:
DEMONS DOWN, Victory Music 383 480 002-2 (1992)
O Father / Demons Down / What's Forever For / Talkin' Bout Love / Spirit Of Love / Down, Down, Down / Metallic Blue / Inside You / Johnny's Got A Mind Of His Own / Can't Fight Love

MOTORHEAD:
MARCH OR DIE, WTG/Epic NT48997 (1992) **42 SWEDEN, 60 UK**
Stand / Cat Scratch Fever / Bad Religion / Jack The Ripper / I Ain't No Nice Guy / Hellraiser / Asylum Choir / Too Good To Be True / You Better Run / Name In Vain / March Or Die

STEVE FISTER:
AGE OF GREAT DREAMERS, 2nd Degree SD-202 (1999)
Tribal Stomp / True Grit / Age Of Great Dreams / Tell Me Something Good / Road To Paris / White Light / Weird Blues / Turn It Out / JB Meets JB / Meat And Three / Rocket Town

THIN LIZZY:
ONE NIGHT ONLY, SPV 085-21992 CD (2000)
Jailbreak / Waiting For An Alibi / Don't Believe A Word / Cold Sweat / The Sun Goes Down / Are You Ready / Bad Reputation / Suicide / Still In Love With You / Cowboy Song / The Boys Are Back In Town / Rosalie / Black Rose

TED NUGENT:
FULL BLUNTAL NUGITY, Spitfire (2001)
K.L.S.T.R.P.H.K./ Paralyzed / Snakeskin Cowboys / Wang Dang Sweet Poon Tang / Free For All / Yank Me, Crank Me / Hey Baby / Fred Bear / Cat Scratch Fever / Stranglehold / Great White Buffalo / Motorcity Madhouse

CARMINE APPICE

This discography chronicles Carmine's rock appearances. He has also appeared on numerous pop album sessions and enjoyed a lengthy tenure with Rod Stewart.

VANILLA FUDGE:
VANILLA FUDGE, Atlantic 587 086 (1967) **31 UK, 6 USA**
Ticket To Ride / People Get Ready / She's Not There / Bang Bang / Illusions Of My Childhood (Parts I-III) / You Keep Me Hangin' On / Take Me For a Little While / Eleanor Rigby
THE BEAT GOES ON, Atlantic 587 100 (1968) **17 USA**
Sketch / Variation On A Theme From Mozart's Divertimento No. 13 in F / Old Black Joe / Don't Fence Me In / 12th Street Rag / In The Mood / Hound Dog

The Ozzy Sidemen Discographies

/ I Want To Hold Your Hand – I Feel Fine – Day Triupper – She Loves You / The Beat Goes On / Beethoven's Für Elise And Theme From Moonlight Sonata / The Beat Goes On / Voices In Time: Neville Chamberlain – Winston Churchill – F.D. Roosevelt – Harry S. Truman – John F. Kennedy / Merchant / The Game Is Over / The Beat Goes On
RENAISSANCE, Atlantic 587 110 (1968) **20 USA**
The Sky Cried / When I Was A Boy / Thoughts / Paradise / That's What Makes A Man / The Spell That Comes After / Faceless People / Season Of The Witch
NEAR THE BEGINNING, Atco 228 020 (1969) **16 USA**
Shotgun / Some Velvet Morning / Where Is Happiness / Break Song
ROCK N' ROLL, Atco 228 029 (1969) **34 USA**
Need Love / Lord In The Country / I Can't Make It Alone / Street Walking Woman / Church Bells Of St. Martins / The Windmills Of Your Mind / If You Gotta Make A Fool Of Somebody

CACTUS:
CACTUS, Atco 2400 020 (1970) **54 USA**
Parchman Farm / My Lady From South Of Detroit / Bro. Bill / You Can't Judge A Book By The Cover / Let Me Swim / No Need To Worry / Oleo / Feel So Good
ONE WAY... OR ANOTHER, Atco 40216 (1971) **88 USA**
Long Tall Sally / Rockout, Whatever You Feel Like / Rock n' Roll Children / Big Mama Boogie / Feel So Bad / Song For Aries / Hometown Bust / One Way... Or Another
RESTRICTIONS, Atco 40307 (1971)
Restrictions / Token Chokin' / Guiltless Glider / Evil / Alaska / Sweet Sixteen / Bag Drag / Mean Night In Cleveland
OT' N' SWEATY, Atco K 50013 (1972)
Swim / Bad Mother Boogie / Our Lil Rock 'n' Roll Thing / Bad Stuff / Bringing Me Down / Bedroom Mazurka / Telling You / Underneath The Arches

JAN AKKERMAN:
TABERNAKEL, Atco 7032 (1973)
Britannia / Corananto For Mrs. Murcott / The Earl Of Derby, His Galliard / House Of The King / A Galliard By Anthonie Holborne / A Galliard By John Dowland / A Pavan / Javeh / A Fantasy / Lammy – I Am – Asleep, Half Asleep, Awake…/ She Is / Lammy, We Are / The Last Will And Testament / Amen

BECK, BOGERT, APPICE:
BECK, BOGERT, APPICE, Epic EPC 65455 (1973) **28 UK, 12 USA**
Superstition / Black Cat Moan / Lady, Oh To Love You / I'm So Proud / Livin' Alone / Sweet Sweet Surrender / Why Should I Care / Love Myself With You
LIVE IN JAPAN, Epic (1975)
Superstition / Lose Myself With You / Jeff's Boogie / Going Down / Boogie / Morning Dew / Sweet, Sweet Surrender / Livin' Alone / I'm So Proud / Lady / Black Cat Woman / Why Should I Care / Plynth / Shotgun (Medley)

Ozzy Osbourne

KGB:
KGB, MCA (1976)
MOTION, MCA MCF 2773 (1976)
Woman, Stop Watcha' Doin' / I Only Need A Next Time / My Serene Coleen / Lookin' For A Better Way / Lay It All Down / Treading Water / Goin' Thru The Motions / Je T'Aime / Determination

TOMMY BOLIN:
PRIVATE EYES, Columbia 581612(1976) **98 USA**
Bustin' Out For Rosey / Sweet Burgundy / Post Toastee / Shake The Devil / Gypsy Soul / Someday Will Bring Our Love Home / Hello Again / You Told Me That You Loved Me

PAUL STANLEY:
PAUL STANLEY, Casablanca NBLP7123 (1978) **40 USA**
Tonight You Belong To Me / Move On / Ain't Quite Right / Wouldn't You Like To Know Me / Take Me Away (Together as One) / It's Alright / Hold Me, Touch Me (Think Of Me When We're Apart) / Love In Chains / Goodbye

LES DUDEK:
GHOST TOWN PARADE, Columbia 35088 (1978)
Central Park / Bound To Be A Change / Gonna Move / Friend Of Mine / Does Anybody Care? / Down To Nothin' / Tears Turn Into Diamonds / Falling Out / Ghost Town Parade

EDDIE MONEY:
PLAYING FOR KEEPS, Columbia CK 36514 (1980)
Trinidad / Running Back / The Wish / Get A Move On / When You Took My Heart / Satin Angel / Let's Be Lovers Again / Nobody Knows / Million Dollar Girl

CARMINE APPICE:
CARMINE APPICE, WEA 99196 (1981)
Have You Heard / Keep On Rolling / Paint It Black / Blue Café / Sweet Senorita / Drum City Rocker (Ballad Of Drum City) / Hollywood Heartbeat / Be My Baby / Am I Losing You / Drums, Drums, Drums

TED NUGENT:
NUGENT, Atlantic 32028 (1982) **51 USA**
No, No, No / Bound And Gagged / Habitual Offender / Fightin' Words / Good And Ready / Ebony / Don't Push Me / Can't Stop Me Now / We're Gonna Rock Tonight / Tailgunner

TIM BOGERT:
MASTER'S BREW, Takoma TAK-7105 (1983)
Let Him Know / Devotion / Don't Leave Me This Way / Slow Dancin' / Trouble

The Ozzy Sidemen Discographies

D.N.A.:
PARTY TESTED, Boardwalk NB36002-1 (1983)
Doctors Of The Universe / Intellectual Freedom For The Masses / Rock 'n' Roll (Part 2) / The Song That Wrote Itself / Party Tested / The Recipe For Life / What About

VANILLA FUDGE:
MYSTERY, Atco 90149-1 (1984)
Golden Age Dreams / Jealousy / Mystery / Under Suspicion / It Gets Stronger / Walk On By / My World Is Empty / Don't Stop Now / Hot Blood / The Stranger

JEFF BECK:
FLASH, Epic EPC 26112 (1985) **27 SWEDEN, 83 UK, 39 USA**
Ambitious / Gets Us All In The End / Escape / People Get Ready / Stop, Look And Listen / Get Workin' / Ecstasy / Night After Night / You Know, We Know

KING KOBRA:
READY TO STRIKE, Capitol 12386-1 (1985)
Ready To Strike / Hunger / Shadow Rider / Shake It Up / Attention / Breakin' Out / Tough Guys / Dancing With Desire / Second Thoughts / Piece Of The Rock
THRILL OF A LIFETIME, Capitol 12473 (1986) **27 SWEDEN**
Second Time Around / Dream On / Feel The Heat / Thrill Of A Lifetime / Only The Strong Survive / Iron Eagle (Never Say Die) / Home Street Home / Overnight Sensation / Raise Your Hands To Rock / Party Animals
KING KOBRA III, Rocker NRR26 (1988)
Mean St. Machine / Take It Off / Walls Of Silence / Legends Never Die / Redline / Burning In Her Fire / Perfect Crime / It's My Life / No. 1

PINK FLOYD:
A MOMENTARY LAPSE OF REASON, EMI 1003 (1987) **3 USA, 3 UK**
Signs Of Life / Learning To Fly / The Dogs Of War / One Slip / On The Turning Away / Yet Another Movie / Round And Around / New Machine Part 1 / Terminal Frost / New Machine Part 2 / Sorrow

TED NUGENT:
LITTLE MISS DANGEROUS, Atlantic 252388-2 (1986) **76 USA**
High Heels In Motion / Strangers / Little Miss Dangerous / Savage Dancer / Crazy Ladies / When Your Body Talks / Little Red Book / Take Me Away / Angry Young Man / Painkiller

BLUE MURDER:
BLUE MURDER, Geffen (1989) **45 UK**
Riot / Sex Child / Valley Of The Kings / Jelly Roll / Blue Murder / Out Of Love / Billy / Ptolemy / Black Hearted Woman
NOTHIN' BUT TROUBLE, Geffen 24419 (1993)
We All Fall Down / Itchycoo Park / Cry For Love / Runaway / Dance / I'm

Ozzy Osbourne
On Fire / Save My Love / Love Child / Shouldn't Have Let You Go / I Need An Angel / She Knows

MOTHER'S ARMY:
MOTHERS ARMY, FEMS (1993)
Mothers Army / Darkside / Dreamtime / One Way Love / Second Nature / Memorial Day / Get A Life / By Your Side / Voice Of Reason / Anarchy / Save Me / Mothers Army (Reprise)

Mother's Army included Bob Daisley

MARTY FRIEDMAN:
TRUE OBSESSION, Shrapnel 1100 (1996)
Rio / Espionage / Last September / Rock Box / The Yearning / Live And Learn / Glowing Path / Intoxicated / Farewell / Thunder March (Demo version)

GUITAR ZEUS:
GUITAR ZEUS, (1996)
Dislocated / This Time Around / Safe / 4 Miles High / So Long / Nobody Knew / Guitar Zeus Part 1 / Killing Time / Where You Belong / Days Are Nights / Time To Set Alarms / Under The Moon & Sun / Guitar Zeus Part 2 / Where You Belong / Under The Moon & Sun

Bob Daisley performs bass on 'Guitar Zeus'.

GUITAR ZEUS II – CHANNEL MIND RADIO, Polygram (1997)
Stash / Code 19 / Perfect Day (Interlude) / Gonna Rain / Interlude In E Major / Even Up The Score / Out Of Mind / Nothing / Trippin' Again / Dead Wrong / Doin' Fine / My Own Advice / Where You Belong / GX Blues

Zakk Wylde performs guitar on 'Guitar Zeus II'

GUITAR ZEUS:
GUITAR ZEUS JAPAN, Sony SRCS-1001 (2000)
Days R Nites / This Time Around / Safe / Dislocated / Angels / Couldn't Be Better / Black White Horse / Goodnite / Moon & Sun / Occupants / Snake / Killing Time / Days R Nites

KING KOBRA:
THE LOST YEARS, Cleopatra (1999)
Mean Street Machine / Fool In The Rain / Young Hearts Survive / Your Love's A Sin / #1 / Walls Of Silence / Lonely Nights / Redline / Perfect Crime / Overnite Love Affair / Poor Boy (You Are My Life)

KING KOBRA:
HOLLYWOOD TRASH, MTM Music 0681-37 (2001)
Do It / Bitch / The Gift / Hollywood Trash / Jessy / The Edge / Watch What You Think / Angels / Blaze / Freedom / Ready To Strike / Take It Off / Here Comes The Night

The Ozzy Sidemen Discographies

MIKE BORDIN

FAITH NO MORE:
FAITH NO MORE, Mordan (1985)
We Care A Lot / The Jungle / Mark Bowen / Jim / Why Do You Bother? / Greed / Pills For Breakfast / As The Worm Turns / Arabian Disco / New Beginnings
INTRODUCE YOURSELF, Slash (1987)
Faster Disco / Anne's Song / Introduce Yourself / Chinese Arithmetic / Death March / We Care A Lot / R N' R / The Crab Song / Blood / Spirit
THE REAL THING, Slash 828 217 1 (1989) **38 SWEDEN, 30 UK, 11 USA**
From Out Of Nowhere / Epic / Falling To Pieces / Surprise! You're Dead / Zombie Eaters / The Real Thing / Underwater Love / The Morning After / Woodpecker From Mars / War Pigs / Edge Of The World
LIVE AT THE BRIXTON ACADEMY, Slash (1991) **20 UK**
Falling To Pieces / The Real Thing / Epic / War Pigs / From Out Of Nowhere / We Care A Lot / Zombie Eaters / Edge Of The World / The Grade / The Cowboy Song
ANGELDUST, Slash (1992) **18 SWEDEN, 2 UK, 10 USA**
Land Of Sunshine / Caffeine / Midlife Crisis / R.V. / Smaller And Smaller / Everthing's Ruined / Malpractice / Kindergarten / Be Aggressive / A Small Victory / Crack Hitler / Jizzlober / Midnight Cowboy
KING FOR A DAY– FOOL FOR A LIFETIME, Slash (1995) **5 UK, 31 USA**
Get Out / Ricochet / Evidence / The Great Art Of Making Enemies / Star A.D. / Cuckoo For Caca / Caralho Voador / Ugly In The Morning / Digging The Grave / Take This Bottle / King For A Day / What A Day / The Last To Know / Just A Man
ALBUM OF THE YEAR, Slash 828 901-2 (1997) **11 SWEDEN, 7 UK, 41 USA**
Collision / Strip Search / Last Cup Of Sorrow / Naked In Front Of The Computer / Helpless / Mouth To Mouth / Ashes To Ashes / She Loves Me Not / Got That Feeling / Paths Of Glory / Home Sick Home / Pristina

GEEZER BUTLER

Geezer Butler of course appeared on all of the Black Sabbath albums that featured Ozzy. In addition the bassist performed on the following non Ozzy albums.

BLACK SABBATH:
HEAVEN AND HELL, Vertigo 9102 752 (1980) **25 SWEDEN, 9 UK, 28 USA**
Lonely Is The World / Heaven And Hell / Children Of The Sea / Wishing Well / Lady Evil / Neon Knights / Die Young / Walk Away
MOB RULES, Mercury 6V02119 (1981) **30 SWEDEN, 12 UK, 29 USA**
The Sign Of The Southern Cross / Mob Rules / Slipping Away / Turn Up The Night / Voodoo / Country Girl / Over And Over / Falling Off The Edge Of The World / E5150
LIVE EVIL, Vertigo SAB 10 (1983) **15 SWEDEN, 13 UK, 37 USA**

Ozzy Osbourne

Children Of The Sea / Black Sabbath / Paranoid / Neon Knights / Iron Man / Children Of The Grave / E5150 / Heaven And Hell / Voodoo / Sign Of The Southern Cross / War Pigs / Mob Rules / NIB
BORN AGAIN, Vertigo VERL 8 (1983) **7 SWEDEN, 4 UK, 39 USA**
Disturbing The Priest / Stonehenge / Zero The Hero / Trashed / The Dark / Born Again / Hot Line / Digital Bitch / Keep It Warm
DEHUMANIZER, IRS EIRS CD 1064 (1992) **13 GERMANY, 12 SWEDEN, 28 UK, 44 USA**
Computer God / After All (The Dead) / TV Crimes / Letters From Earth / Masters Of Insanity / Time Machine / Sins Of The Father / I / Buried Alive
CROSS PURPOSES, IRS (1994) **33 GERMANY, 41 UK**
I Witness / Cross Of Thorns / Psychophobia / Virtual Death / Immaculate Deception / Dying For Love / Back To Eden / The Hand That Rocks The Cradle / Cardinal Sin / Evil Eye
CROSS PURPOSES LIVE, PMI 7243 491314 3 9 (1995)
Time Machine / Children Of The Grave / I Witness / Into The Void / Black Sabbath / Psychophobia / Wizard / Cross Of Thorns / Symptom Of The Universe / Headless Cross / Paranoid / Iron Man / Sabbath Bloody Sabbath

<u>G//Z/R:</u>
PLASTIC PLANET, Rawpower RAWCD 105 (1995)
Catatonic Eclipse / Drive Boy, Shooting / Giving Up The Ghost / Plastic Planet / The Invisible / Séance Fiction / House Of Clouds / Detective 27 / X13 / Sci-clone / Cycle Of Sixty

<u>GEEZER:</u>
BLACK SCIENCE, Eagle EAGCD001 (1997)
Man In A Suitcase / Box Of Six / Mysterons / Justified / Department S / Area Code 51 / Has To Be / Number 5 / Among The Cyberman / Unspeakable Elvis / Xodiak / Northern Wisdom / Trinity Road

Both the G//Z/R and GEEZER albums include Deen Castronovo.

RANDY CASTILLO

<u>LITA FORD:</u>
DANCIN' ON THE EDGE, Vertigo VER 13 (1984) **96 UK, 66 USA**
Gotta Let Go / Dancin' On The Edge / Dressed To Kill / Hit 'n' 'Run / Lady Killer / Still Waitin' / Fire In My Heart / Don't Let Me Down Tonight / Run With The $

<u>BRET MICHAELS:</u>
LETTERS FROM DEATH ROW, ULG 17769 (1998)
Party Rock Band / Human Zoo / The Last Breath / I'd Die For You / Times Like These / Little Willy / The Devil Inside / A Letter From Death Row / Sounds Of Sex / "69" / Angst Mary / Steel Bar Blues

The Ozzy Sidemen Discographies

MÖTLEY CRÜE:
NEW TATTOO, Motley 8120 (2000)
Hell On High Heels / Treat Me Like The Dog I Am / New Tattoo / Dragstrip Superstar / 1st Band On The Moon / She Needs Rock 'n' Roll / Punched In The Teeth By Love / Hollywood Ending / Fake / Porno Star / White Punks On Dope

DEEN CASTRONOVO

WILD DOGS:
WILD DOGS, Shrapnel 1003 (1983)
Life Is Just A Game / The Tonight Show / The Evil In Me / Born To Rock / Never Gonna Stop / Two Wrongs / Take Another Prisoner / I Need A Love / You Can't Escape Your Lies
MAN'S BEST FRIEND, Shrapnel 1012 (1984)
Livin' On The Streets / Not Stoppin' / Woman In Chains / Beauty And A Beast / Believe In Me / Rock's Not Dead / Endless Nights / Ready Or Not / Stick To Your Guns
REIGN OF TERROR, Music For Nations MFN80 (1987)
Metal Fuel (In The Blood) / Man Against Machine / Call Of The Dark / Siberian Vacation / Psychoradio / Streets Of Berlin / Spellshock / Reign Of Terror / We Rule The Night

TONY MACALPINE:
MAXIMUM SECURITY, Squawk VERH 44 (1987)
Autumn Lords / Hundreds Of Thousands / Tears Of Sahara / Keys To The City / Time And The Test / Kings Cup / Sacred Wonder / Etude 4 Opus 10 / Vision / Dreamstate / Porcelain Doll

DR. MASTERMIND:
DR. MASTERMIND, Roadrunner RR 9605-2(1988)
Domination / The Right Way / Man Of The Year / The Villa (2631) / We Want The World / Control / Abuser / Black Leather Maniac / I Don't Wanna Die

MARTY FRIEDMAN:
DRAGON'S KISS, Roadrunner RR 9529-2 (1988)
Saturation Point / Dragon Mistress / Evil Thrill / Namida (Tears) / Anvils / Jewel / Forbidden City / Thunder March

CACOPHONY:
GO OFF!, Roadrunner RR 94991(1988)
X Ray Eyes / E.S.P. / Stranger / Go Off! / Black Cat / Sword Of The Warrior / Floating World / Images

NEAL SCHON:
LATE NITE, Columbia 45106 (1989)
Le Dome / Late Nite / Softly / The Theme / I'll Be Waiting / I'll Cover You /

Ozzy Osbourne
Rain's Comin' Down / Smoke Of The Revolution / Inner Circles / Steps / Blackened Bacon

BAD ENGLISH:
BAD ENGLISH, Epic EPC 463447-2 (1989) **39 SWEDEN, 74 UK, 21 USA**
Best Of What I Got / Heaven Is A 4 Letter Word / Possession / Forget Me Not / When I See You Smile / Tough Times Don't Last / Ghost In Your Heart / Price Of Love / Ready When You Are / Lay Down / The Restless Ones / Rockin' Horse / Don't Walk Away
BACKLASH, Epic EPC486569-2 (1991) **21 SWEDEN, 72 USA**
So This Is Eden / Straight To Your Heart / Time Stood Still / The Time Alone With You / Dancing Off The Edge Of The World / Rebel Say A Prayer / Savage Blue / Pray For Rain / Make Love Last / Life At The Top

JOEY TAFFOLLA:
INFRA-BLUE, Shrapnel 1050 (1991)
Infra-Blue / Six String Souffle / Wrecking Ball / Mississippi Mud / Kraken-Z-VIP / B.M.W. / V Jam No. 5 / Violation / A Place In The Sun / Crankenstein / Romans 10:9

HARDLINE:
DOUBLE ECLIPSE, MCA MCD10586 (1992)
Life's A Bitch / Dr Love / Rhythm From A Red Car / Change Of Heart / Everything / Takin' Me Down / Hot Cherie / Bad Taste / Can't Find My Way / I'll Be There / 31.91 / In The Hands Of Time

VON GROOVE:
VON GROOVE, Chrysalis (1992)
Once Is Not Enough / Better Than Ever / Can't Get Too Much / Once In A Lifetime / Every Beat Of My Heart / House Of Dreams / C'Mon, C'Mon / All The Way Down / Arianne / Slave To Sin / Love Keeps Bringing Me Home / Smaug / Sweet Pain

PAUL RODGERS:
HENDRIX SET, Victory Music 480014 (1993)
Purple Haze / Stone Free / Little Wing / Manic Depression / Foxy Lady

TONY MACALPINE:
PREMONITION, Roadrunner RR8965-2 (1994)
Opus 28 "18 / The Violin Song / Ghost Of Versailles / Tower Of London / Rusalka / Rondeau Partita "2 / Gila Monster / The Czar / Maestro Di Cappella / Inflection / Opus 23 "3 / Animation / Winter In Osaka

G//Z/R:
PLASTIC PLANET, Rawpower RAWCD 105 (1995)
Catatonic Eclipse / Drive Boy, Shooting / Giving Up The Ghost / Plastic Planet / The Invisible / Séance Fiction / House Of Clouds / Detective 27 / X13 / Sci-clone / Cycle Of Sixty

The Ozzy Sidemen Discographies

STEVE VAI:
ALIEN LOVE SECRETS, Epic 478586-2 (1995) **39 UK**
Mad Horsie / Juice / Die To Live / The Boy From Seattle / Ya Yo Gakk / Kill The Guy With The Ball – The God Eaters / Tender Surrender
FIREGARDEN, Epic 485062-2 (1997) **41 UK**
There's A Life In My House / Crying Machine / Dyin' Day / Whookam / Blowfish / Mysterious Murder Of Christian Tierra's Lover / Hand On Heart / Bangkok / Fire Garden Suite / Deepness / Little Alligator / All About Eve / Aching Burger / Brother / Damn You / When I Was A Little Boy / Genocide / Warm Regards

STEVE VAI:
7th SONG: ENCHANTING GUITAR, Sony 85182 (2000)
For The Love Of God / Touching Tongues / Windows To The Soul / Burnin' Down The Mountain / Tender Surrender / Hand On Heart / Melissa's Garden / Call It Sleep / Christmas Time Is Here / The Wall Of Light / Boston Rain Melody

STEVE VAI:
FLEX-ABLE LEFTOVERS, (1998)

JAMES MURPHY:
CONVERGENCE, (1996)
Since Forgotten / Convergence / The Last One / Vision / Touching the Earth / Red Alert / Deeper Within / Shadow's Fall / Tempus Omnia Revelant

GEEZER:
BLACK SCIENCE, Eagle EAGCD001 (1997)
Man In A Suitcase / Box Of Six / Mysterons / Justified / Department S / Area Code 51 / Has To Be / Number 5 / Among The Cyberman / Unspeakable Elvis / Xodiak / Northern Wisdom / Trinity Road

GEORGE BELLAS:
TURN OF THE MILLENNIUM, Shrapnel (1997)
Turn Of The Millennium / Ripped To Shreds / Everlasting / Relentless / Voyage In Time / Forever In Time / Future Music / Eternity / Survive / Monolith / Lightyears
MIND OVER MATTER, Shrapnel (1998)

JAMES MURPHY:
FEEDING THE MACHINE, Diehard (1999)
Feeding The Machine / Contagion / No One Can Tell You / Epoch / Deconstruct / Odyssey / Through Your Eyes (Distant Mirrors) / Race With Devil On Spanish Highway / Visitors / In Lingua Mortua

JOURNEY:
ARRIVAL, Columbia 69864 (2001)
Higher Place / All The Way / Signs Of Life / All The Things / Loved By You

Ozzy Osbourne

/ Livin' To Do / World Gone Wild / I Got A Reason / With Your Love / Lifetime Of Dreams / I Live And Breathe / Nothin' Comes Close / To Be Alive Again / Kiss Me Softly / We Will Meet Again

DON COSTA

<u>M-80:</u>
M-80, Roadrunner (1984)
Face Cracker / Get Out Of Town / Supply And Demand / Frying Pan (Into The Fire) / Hollywood Chills / Stop In The Name Of Love

FRED COURY

<u>CHASTAIN:</u>
MYSTERY OF ILLUSION, Roadrunner RR 9742 (1985)
Black Knight / When The Battle's Over / Mystery Of Illusion / I've Seen Tomorrow / Endlessly / I Fear No Evil / Night Of The Gods / We Shall Overcome / The Winds Of Change

<u>CINDERELLA:</u>
LONG COLD WINTER, Mercury 834 612-2 (1988) **38 SWEDEN, 30 UK, 10 USA**
Bad Seamstress Blues / Fallin' Apart At The Seams / Gypsy Road / Don't Know What You Got (Till It's Gone) / The Last Mile / Second Wind / Long Cold Winter / If You Don't Like It / Coming Home / Fire And Ice / Take Me Back
HEARTBREAK STATION, Vertigo 848 018-2 (1990) **42 SWEDEN, 36 UK, 19 USA**
The More Things Change / Love's Got Me Doin' Time / Shelter Me / Heartbreak Station / Sick For The Cure / One For Rock 'N' Roll / Dead Man's Road / Make Your Own Way / Electric Love / Love Gone Bad / Winds Of Change

<u>ARCADE:</u>
ARCADE, Epic EK 53012 (1993)
Dancin' With The Angels / Nothin' To Lose / Calm Before The Storm / Cry No More / Screamin' S.O.S. / Never Goin' Home / Messed Up World / All Shook Up / So Good...So Bad.../ Livin' Dangerously / Sons And Daughters / Mother Blues
A/2, Epic EK 57586 (1994)
Angry / The Move / So What / Get Off My Back / When I'm Gone / Welcome / Kidnapped / Chain To Me / Room With A View / Your Only Age / Hot Racin'

<u>CINDERELLA:</u>
LIVE AT THE KEY CLUB, Deadline CLP 0593-2 (1998)
The More Things Change / Push, Push / Hot And Bothered / Shelter Me /

The Ozzy Sidemen Discographies

Nightsongs / Somebody Save Me / Heartbreak Station / The Last Mile / Coming Home / Falling Apart At The Seams / Don't Know What You've Got / Nobody's Fool / Gypsy Road / Shake Me

BOB DAISLEY

CHICKENSHACK:
UNLUCKY BOY, London 632 (1973)
You Know You Could Be Right / Revelation / Prudence's Party / Too Late To Cry / Stan The Man / Unlucky Boy / As Time Goes Passing By / Jammin' With The Ash / He Knows The Rules

WIDOWMAKER:
WIDOWMAKER, Jet 2310 432(1976)
Such A Shame / Pin A Rose On Me / On The Road / Straight Faced Fighter / Ain't Telling You Nothing / When I Met You / Leave The Kids Alone / Shine A Light On Me / Running Free / Got A Dream
TOO LATE TO CRY, United Artists UAG 30038 (1977)
Too Late To Cry / The Hustler / What A Way To Fall / Here Comes The Queen / Mean What You Say / Something I Can Do Without / Sign The Papers / Pushin' And Pullin' / Sky Blues

RAINBOW:
ON STAGE (LIVE), Polydor 2657 016 (1977) **25 SWEDEN, 7 UK**
Over The Rainbow / Catch The Rainbow / Mistreated / Still I'm Sad / Kill The King / Man On The Silver Mountain / Blues / Starstruck / 16th Century Greensleeves
LONG LIVE ROCK N' ROLL, Polydor POLD 5002 (1978)
18 SWEDEN, 7 UK
Long Live Rock 'n' Roll / Lady Of The Lake / L.A. Connection / Gates Of Babylon / Sensitive To Light / The Shed / Rainbow Eyes / Kill The King

URIAH HEEP:
ABOMINOG, Bronze BRON 538 (1982) **34 UK**
Too Scared To Run / Chasing Shadows / On The Rebound / Think It Over / Hot Night In A Cold Town / That's The Way It Is / Running All Night (With The Lion) / Hot Persuasion / Prisoner / See Your Soul
HEAD FIRST, Bronze BRON 545 (1983) **46 UK**
The Other Side Of Midnight / Lonely Nights / Sweet Talk / Love Is Blind / Rool – Overture / Red Lights / Rollin' The Rock / Staring Through The Heart / Weekend Warriors

GARY MOORE:
VICTIMS OF THE FUTURE, Ten 205 914 (1984) **15 SWEDEN, 12 UK**
Teenage Idol / Victims Of The Future / Shapes Of Things / Empty Rooms / Murder In The Skies / All I Want / Hold On To Love / Law Of The Jungle
RUN FOR COVER, Ten DIXP 16 (1985) **6 SWEDEN, 12 UK**

Ozzy Osbourne

Out In The Fields / Empty Rooms / Run For Cover / All Messed Up / Reach For The Sky / Military Man / Nothing To Lose / Once In A Lifetime / Listen To Your Heartbeat / Out Of My System
WILD FRONTIER, Ten DIXG 56 (1987) **2 SWEDEN, 8 UK**
Over The Hills And Faraway / Wild Frontier / Take A Little Time / The Loner / Friday On My Mind / Strangers In The Darkness / Thunder Rising / Johnny Boy / Crying In The Shadows

BLACK SABBATH:
THE ETERNAL IDOL, Vertigo VERH 51 (1987) **66 UK**
The Shining / Ancient Warrior / Born To Lose / Lost Forever / Hard Life To Live / Scarlet Pimpernel / Glory Ride / Eternal Idol

YNGWIE MALMSTEEN:
ODYSSEY, Polydor POLD 5224 (1988) **7 SWEDEN, 27 UK, 40 USA**
Rising Force / Hold On / Heaven Tonight / Dreaming / Bite The Bullet / Riot In The Dungeons / Déjà Vu / Crystal Ball / Now Is The Time / Faster Than The Speed Of Light / Krakatau / Memories

GARY MOORE:
AFTER THE WAR, Virgin (1989) **3 SWEDEN, 23 UK**
After The War / Speak For Yourself / Livin' On Dreams / Led Clones / Running From The Storm / This Thing Called Love / Ready For Love / Blood Of Emeralds / Dunlace / The Messiah Will Come
STILL GOT THE BLUES, Virgin (1990) **1 SWEDEN, 13 UK, 83 USA**
Movin' On / Oh Pretty Woman / Walking By Myself / Still Got The Blues (For You) / Texas Street / All Your Love / Too Tired / King Of The Blues / As The Years Go Passing By / Midnight Blues / That Kind Of Woman / Stop Messin' Around
AFTER HOURS, Virgin CDV 2684 (1992) **4 UK**
Cold Day In Hell / Don't Lie To Me (I Get Evil) / Story Of The Blues / Since I Met You Baby / Separate Ways / Only Fool In Town / Key To Love / Jumpin' At Shadows / The Blues Is Alright / The Hurt Inside / Nothing's The Same

MOTHER'S ARMY:
MOTHERS ARMY, FEMS (1993)
Mothers Army / Darkside / Dreamtime / One Way Love / Second Nature / Memorial Day / Get A Life / By Your Side / Voice Of Reason / Anarchy / Save Me / Mothers Army (Reprise)

VERTEX:
VERTEX, Blue Dolphin 7001 (1996)
Follow / One Like A Son / Synthetic Flesh / F.T.W. / Time And Time / Is Justice Your Peace / Fight / Ain't Gonna Be / Mother Mary / Core (Version 1.2.0.)

The Ozzy Sidemen Discographies

STREAM:
NOTHING IS SACRED, USG CD USG 1022-2 (1998)
Chasin' The Dragon / Snake Eyed Moon / Rock Bottom / Camouflage / Fade To Black / Bed Of Fire / Blood For Gold / Far From The Maddening Crowd / The Other Side / Still Believe (Touch Of A Stranger)

MOTHER'S ARMY:
PLANET EARTH, USG 1018-2 (1998)
Circle Of Hands / Cradle To The Grave / Misery Me / Planet Earth / For The Moment / Seas Of Eternity / The Child Within / One Common Law / Mother Earth
FIRE ON THE MOON, USG 1027-2 (1998)
N.D.E. / Way Of The World / A Day In The Night / Fire On The Moon / Do What I Like / Common Ground / No Religion / Moruroa Atoll / The Code / The Lonely / Another Dimension

BRAD GILLIS

NIGHTRANGER:
DAWN PATROL, Boardwalk EPC 25301 (1982) **38 USA**
Don't Tell Me You Love Me / Sing Me Away / At Night She Sleeps / Call My Name / Eddie's Comin' Out Tonight / Can't Find Me A Thrill / Young Girl In Love / Play Rough / Penny / Night Ranger
MIDNIGHT MADNESS, MCA (1983) **15 USA**
(You Can Still) Rock In America / Rumours In The Air / Why Does Love Have To Change / Sister Christian / Touch Of Madness / Passion Play / When You Close Your Eyes / Chippin' Away / Let Him Run
SEVEN WISHES, MCA MCF 3278 (1985) **10 USA**
Seven Wishes / Faces / Four In The Morning / I Need A Woman / Sentimental Street / This Boy Needs To Rock / I Will Follow You / Interstate Love Affair / Night Machine / Goodbye
BIG LIFE, MCA DMCF 3362 (1987) **28 USA**
Big Life / Color Of Your Smile / Love Is Standing Near / Rain Comes Crashing Down / The Secret Of My Success / Carry On / Better Let It Go / I Know Tonight / Hearts Away
MAN IN MOTION, MCA 6238 (1988) **81 USA**
Man In Motion / Reason To Be / Don't Start Thinking (I'm Alone Tonight) / Love Shot Me Down / Restless Kind / Halfway To The Sun / Here She Comes Again / Right On You / Kiss Me Where It Hurts / I Did It For Love / Woman In Love
GREATEST HITS, MCA DMCG 6055 (1989)
(You Can Still) Rock In America / Goodbye / Sister Christian / The Secret Of My Success / Rumours In The Air / Sing Me Away / When You Close Your Eyes / Sentimental Street / Restless Kind / Eddie's Comin' Out Tonight
LIVE IN JAPAN, MCA MCAD-10024 (1990)
Touch Of Madness / When You Close Your Eyes / Man In Motion / Don't Start Thinking (I'm Alone Tonight) / Let Him Run / Goodbye / Reason To Be

/ Four In The Morning (I Can't Take Any More) / Sister Christian / Don't Tell Me You Love Me / Halfway To The Sun / (You Can Still) Rock In America

BRAD GILLIS:
GILROCK RANCH, Food For Thought CDGRUB27 (1993)
Stampede / Honest To God / Opus Winfrus / Monster Breath / Slow Blow / Mr. Lollipop / If Looks Could Kill / Lions, Tigers And Bears / Shades Of Pomposity

This debut solo album also includes Carmine Appice.

NIGHTRANGER:
FEEDING OFF THE MOJO, Semaphore 50 528-422 (1996)
Mojo / Last Chance / Try (For Good Reason) / Precious Time / The Night Has A Way / Do You Feel Like I Do / Tomorrow Never Knows / Music Box / Longest Days / Tell Me I'm Wrong / So Far Gone
NEVERLAND, Sony (1997)
Forever All Over / Again Neverland / As Always I Remain / Someday I Will / My Elusive Mind / New York Time / Walk In The Future / Slap Like Being Born / Sunday Morning / Anything For You / I Don't Call This Love
ROCK MASTERPIECE COLLECTION, MCA Victor (1997) (Japanese release)
Don't Tell Me You Love Me / Sing Me Away / Night Ranger / (You Can Still) Rock In America / Sister Christian / When You Close Your Eyes / Rumours In The Air / Sentimental Street / Four In The Morning / Goodbye / The Secret Of My Success / I Did It For Love / Touch Of Madness (Live) / When You Close Your Eyes (Live) / Don't Tell Me You Love Me (Live) / (You Can Still) Rock In America (Live)
ROCK IN JAPAN '97, Zero Corporation (1997) (Japanese release)
Neverland / Touch Of Madness / My Elusive Mind / Sing Me Away / Someday I Will / Brad Gillis Guitar Solo / Rumours In The Air / Jeff Watson Guitar Solo / Eddie's Comin' Out Tonight / Sentimental Street / Goodbye / Forever All Over Again / Slap Like Being Born / When You Close Your Eyes / New York Time / Don't Tell Me You Love Me / Sister Christian / (You Can Still) Rock In America
SEVEN, Sony (1998)
Sign Of The Times / Jane's Interlude / Panic In Jane / Don't Ask Me Why / Kong / Mother Mayhem / Soul Survivor / Sea Of Love / Peace Sign / When I Call On You / Revelation

BRAD GILLIS:
ALLIGATOR, Spitfire (2000)
Alligator / Eyes (Your Eyes Are The Window To Your Soul) / Monche La Roughe / Chain Gang / Leap Of Faith / Swami / Circle Of Light / Survive / Heart Shaped Wings / Tanbark Tyrant

KELLY KEAGY:
TIME PASSES, (2001)

The Ozzy Sidemen Discographies

JOE HOLMES

LIZZY BORDEN:
VISUAL LIES, Roadrunner RR 9592 (1987)
Me Against The World / Shock / Outcast / Den Of Thieves / Visual Lies / Eyes Of A Stranger / Lord Of The Flies / Voyeur (I'm Watching You) / Visions
DAVID LEE ROTH:
YOUR FILTHY LITTLE MOUTH, Warner Bros. 9362454391-2 (1994) **28 UK, 78 USA**
She's My Machine / Everybody's Got The Monkey / Big Train / Experience / A Little Luck / Cheatin' Heart Café / Hey, You Never Know / No Big 'Ting / Yo Breathin' It / Your Filthy Little Mouth / Land's Edge / Night Life / Sunburn / You're Breathin It (Urban NYCMix)

MIKE INEZ

ALICE IN CHAINS:
DIRT, Columbia 472330-2 (1992) **11 SWEDEN, 42 UK, 6 USA**
Tem Bones / Dam That River / Rain When I Die / Down In A Hole / Sick Man / Rooster / Junkhead / Dirt / God Smack / Hate To Feel / Angry Chair / Would
JAR OF FLIES, Columbia 475713-2 (1994) **4 UK, 1 USA**
Rotten Apple / Nutshell / I Stay Away / No Excuses / Whale And Wasp / Don't Follow / Swing On This / Brother / Got Me Wrong / Right Turn / I Am I Inside / Love Story
ALICE IN CHAINS, Columbia (1995) **37 UK, 1 USA**
Grind / Brush Away / Sludge Factory / Heaven Beside You / Head Creeps / Again / Shame In You / God AM / So Close / Nothin' Song / Frogs / Good Night
MTV UNPLUGGED, Columbia 484300-2 (1996) **20 UK, 3 USA**
Nutshell / Brother / No Excuses / Sludge Factory / Down In A Hole / Angry Chair / Rooster / Got Me Wrong / Heaven Beside You / Would? / Frogs / Over Now / Killer Is Me

LEE KERSLAKE

GODS:
GENESIS, Columbia SCX 6286 (1968)
Towards The Skies / Candles Getting Shorter / You're My Life / Looking Glass / Misleading Colours / Radio Show / Plastic Horizon / Farthing Man / I Never Knew / Time And Eternity
TO SAMUEL A SON, Columbia SCX 6372 (1970)
To Samuel A Son / Eight O 'Clock In The Morning / He's Growing / Sticking Wings On Flies / Lady, Lady / Penny Dear / Long Time, Sad Time, Bad Time / Five To Three / Autumn / Yes I Cry / Groozy / Momma I Need / Candlelight / Lovely Anita

Ozzy Osbourne

TOE FAT:
TOE FAT, Parlophone PCS 7097 (1970)
That's My Love For You / Bad Side Of The Moon / Nobody / The Wherefores And The Whys / But I'm Wrong / Just Like Me / Just Like All The Rest / I Can't Believe / Working Nights / You Tried To Take It All

URIAH HEEP:
LOOK AT YOURSELF, Island ILPS 9169 (1971) **15 AUSTRALIA, 39 UK**
I Wanna Be Free / Look At Yourself / July Morning / Tears In My Eyes / Shadows Of Grief / What Should Be Done / Love Machine
DEMONS AND WIZARDS, Bronze ILPS 9193 (1972) **14 AUSTRALIA, 20 UK, 23 USA**
The Wizard / Traveller In Time / Easy Livin' / All My Life / Poetic Justice / Circle Of Hands / Rainbow Demon / Paradise / The Spell
MAGICIAN'S BIRTHDAY, Bronze ILPS 9213 (1972) **10 AUSTRALIA, 28 UK, 31 USA**
The Magician's Birthday / Sunrise / Spiderwoman / Blind Eye / Echoes In The Dark / Rain / Sweet Lorraine / Tales
LIVE 1973, Island ISLD 1 (1973) **17 AUSTRALIA, 23 UK, 37 USA**
Sunrise / Sweet Lorraine / Easy Livin' / July Morning / Tears In My Eyes / Gypsy / Circle Of Hands / Look At Yourself / The Magician's Birthday / Love Machine / Rock 'n' Roll Medley: Roll Over Beethoven – Blue Suede Shoes – Mean Woman Blues – Hound Dog – At The Hop – Whole Lotta Shakin' Goin' On
SWEET FREEDOM, Island ILPS 9245 (1973) **33 AUSTRALIA, 18 UK, 33 USA**
Sweet Freedom / Dreamin' / Stealin' / One Day / Seven Stars / I Had The Time / Circus / Pilgrim
WONDERWORLD, Bronze ILPS 9280 (1974) **26 AUSTRALIA, 23 UK, 38 USA**
Wonderland / Suicidal Man / The Shadows And The Winds / The Easy Road / So Tired / Something Or Nothing / I Won't Mind / We Got We / Dreams
URIAH HEEP DOWNUNDA, Bronze 25002 (1974) **36 AUSTRALIA**
(Australian release)
RETURN TO FANTASY, Bronze ILPS 9335 (1975) **22 AUSTRALIA, 7 UK**
Return To Fantasy / Shady Lady / Devil's Daughter / Your Turn To Remember / Beautiful Dream / Prima Donna / Why Did You Go / Showdown / A Year Or A Day
HIGH AND MIGHTY, Island ILPS 9384 (1976) **66 AUSTRALIA, 21 SWEDEN, 55 UK**
One Way Or Another / Weep In Silence / Confession / Woman Of The World / Misty Eyes / Midnight / Footprints In The Snow / Can't Keep A Good Band Down / Can't Stop Singing / Make A Little Love
FIREFLY, Bronze 28 791 XOT (1977) **35 SWEDEN**
Firefly / The Hanging Tree / Been Away Too Long / Who Needs Me / Rollin' On / Wize Man / Do You Know / Sympathy
INNOCENT VICTIM, Bronze 25543 XOT (1977) **44 AUSTRALIA**

The Ozzy Sidemen Discographies

Keep On Ridin' / Flyin' High / Roller / Free 'n' Easy / Choice / Illusion / Free Me / Cheat n' Lie / The Dance
FALLEN ANGEL, Bronze 26449 XOT (1978)
Fallen Angel / Woman Of The Night / Falling In Love / Save It / One More Night / Last Farewell / Put You Lovin' On Me / I'm Alive / Whad' Ya Say / Love Or Nothing
ABOMINOG, Bronze BRON 538 (1982) **34 UK**
Too Scared To Run / Chasing Shadows / On The Rebound / Think It Over / Hot Night In A Cold Town / That's The Way It Is / Running All Night (With The Lion) / Hot Persuasion / Prisoner / See Your Soul
HEAD FIRST, Bronze BRON 545 (1983) **46 UK**
The Other Side Of Midnight / Lonely Nights / Sweet Talk / Love Is Blind / Rool – Overture / Red Lights / Rollin' The Rock / Staring Through The Heart / Weekend Warriors
EQUATOR, Portrait PRT 261414 (1985) **79 UK**
rockerama / Bad Blood / Angel / Lost One Love / Holding On / Party Time / Poor Little Rich Girl / Skool's Burning / Heartache City / Night Of The Wolf
LIVE IN MOSCOW, Legacy (1988)
Bird Of Prey / Stealin' / Too Scared To Run / Corrina / Mister Majestic / The Wizard / July Morning / Easy Livin' / That's The Way It Is / Pacific Highway
RAGING SILENCE, Legacy (1989)
Hold Your Head Up / Blood Red Roses / Voice On My TV / Rich Kid / Cry Freedom / Bad Man / More Fool You / When The War Is Over / Lifeline / Rough Justice
STILL 'EAVY, STILL PROUD, Legacy LLP133 (1990)
Gypsy / Lady In Black / July Morning / Easy Livin' / The Easy Road / Free Me / The Other Side Of Midnight / Mr. Majestic / Rich Kid / Blood Red Roses
DIFFERENT WORLD, Legacy (1991)
Blood On Stone / Which Way Will The Wind Blow / All God's Children / All For One / Different World / Step By Step / Seven Days / First Touch / One On One / Cross That Line
SEA OF LIGHT, SPV SPV085-76952-P (1995)
Against The Odds / Sweet Sugar / Time Of Revelation / Mistress Of All Time / Universal Wheels / Fear Of Falling / Spirit Of Freedom / Logical Progression / Love In Silence / Words In The Distance / Fires Of Hell / Dream On
SPELLBINDER LIVE, CBH SPV 085-76992-2 (1996)
Devil's Daughter / Stealin' / Bad Bad Man / Rainbow Demon / Words In A Distance / The Wizard / Circle Of Hands / Gypsy / Look At Yourself / Lady In Black / Easy Livin' / Sail The Rivers (Studio Version)
SONIC ORIGAMI, Eagle rock EAGCD043 (1998)
Between Two Worlds / I Hear Voices / Perfect Little Heart / Heartless Lands / Only The Young / In The Moment / Question / Change / Shelter From The Rain / Everything In Life / Across The Miles / Feels Like / The Golden Palace

Ozzy Osbourne
JAKE E. LEE

BADLANDS:
BADLANDS, Atlantic 781 966-2 (1989) **35 SWEDEN, 39 UK**
High Wire / Dreams In The Dark / Jade's Song / Winter Call / Dancing On The Edge / Streets Cry Freedom / Hard Driver / Rumblin' Train / Devil's Stomp / Seasons / Ball And Chain
VOODOO HIGHWAY, Atlantic 7567-82251-2 (1991) **74 UK**
The Last Time / Show Me The Way / Shine On / Whiskey Dust / Joe's Blues / Soul Stealer / 3 Day Funk / Silver Horses / Love Don't Mean A Thing / Voodoo Highway / Fire And Rain / Heaven's Train / In A Dream

JAKE E. LEE:
A FINE PINK MIST, Pony Canyon PCCY 01008 (1996)
Exithouse / Demon A Go Go / Soulfinger / The Rapture / I Magnify / The Velvet Fire / Atomic Holiday / Galaxy Of Tears / Luna Gitana / Bludfuk

BADLANDS:
DUSK, Pony Canyon PCCY-1334 (2000)
Healer / Sun Red Sun / Tribal Moon / The River / Walking Attitude / The Fire Lasts Forever / Dog / Fat Cat / Lord Knows / Ride The Jack

GUEST SESSIONS:
ANN LEWIS, Meiki (1988)
ANN LEWIS, Rude (1990)
ANN LEWIS, K rock (1992)
ANN LEWIS, rockadelic (1993)
RAID, Atushi Yokoseki Project (1993)
AIR PAVILION, Sarrph Cogh (1994)
ROB ROCK, Age Of Creation (2000)

ROY MAYORGA

THORN:
BITTER POTION, (1995)
SHE RISES LIKE THE SUN, (1995)

CAUSE FOR ALARM:
BIRTH AFTER BIRTH, (1997)

CRISIS:
HOLLOWING, (1997)

SOULFLY:
SOULFLY, Roadrunner (1998)

The Ozzy Sidemen Discographies

RANDY RHOADS

QUIET RIOT:
QUIET RIOT, Columbia (1978)
It's Not So Funny / Mama's Little Angels / Tin Soldier / Ravers / Back To The Coast / Glad All Over / Get Your Kicks / Look In Any Window / Just How You Want It / Riot Reunion / Fit To Be Tied / Demolition Derby
QUIET RIOT II, Columbia 25AP 1192 (1979)
Slick Black Cadillac / You Drive Me Crazy / Afterglow (Of Your Love) / Eye For An Eye / Trouble / Killer Girls / Face To Face / Inside You / We've Got The Magic

RUDY SARZO

As well as his appearance on numerous recordings as bassist Sarzo would also act as producer for Spanish language rock acts such as Logos for their 'Generacion Mutante' album of 1996 and Fuego Adentro's 1997 effort 'Somos Libres'.

QUIET RIOT:
QUIET RIOT II, Columbia 25AP 1192 (1979)
Slick Black Cadillac / You Drive Me Crazy / Afterglow (Of Your Love) / Eye For An Eye / Trouble / Killer Girls / Face To Face / Inside You / We've Got The Magic
METAL HEALTH, Epic 25322 (1983) **1 USA**
Metal Health (Bang Your Head) / Cum On Feel The Noise / Don't Wanna Let You Go / Slick Black Cadillac / Love's A Bitch / Breathless / Run For Cover / Battle Axe / Let's Get Crazy / Thunderbird
CONDITION CRITICAL, Epic EPC 26075 (1984) **71 UK, 15 USA**
Sign Of The Times / Mama Weer All Crazee Now / Party All Night / Stomp Your Hands, Clap Your Feet / Winner Takes All / Condition Critical / Scream And Shout

M.A.R.S.:
PROJECT:DRIVER, Roadrunner (1987)
Nations On Fire / Writings On The Wall / Stand Up And Fight / Nostradamus / Unknown Survivor / Fantasy / Slave To My Touch / I Can See It In Your Eyes / You And I

WHITESNAKE:
SLIP OF THE TONGUE, EMI EMD 1013 (1989) **11 SWEDEN, 10 UK, 10 USA**
Slip Of The Tongue / Cheap 'n' Nasty / Fool For Your Lovin' / Now You're Gone / Kitten's Got Claws / Wings Of The Storm / The Deeper The Love / Judgement Day / Slow Poke Music / Sailing Ships

SAM KINISON:
HAVE YOU SEEN ME LATELY?, (1990)

LEADER OF THE BANNED, (199-)

MANIC EDEN:
MANIC EDEN, CNR Music (1994)
Can You Feel It / Gimme A Shot / Fire In My Soul / Do Angels Die? / Pushing Me / Dark Side Of Grey / Keep It Coming / When The Hammer Comes Down / Ride The Storm / Can't Hold It

QUIET RIOT:
ALIVE AND WELL, Axe Killer 3049322 (1999)
Don't Know What I Want / Angry / Alive And Well / Ritual / Slam Dunk (Way To Go) / Too Much Information / Against The Wall / Overworked And Underpaid / Mama Weer All Crazee Now 1999 / Sign O The Times 1999 / Don't Want To Let You Go 1999 / Wild And The Young 1999 / Cum On Feel The Noize 1999 / Highway To Hell / Metal Health 1999
GUILTY PLEASURES, Bodyguard 7 (2001)
Vicious Circle / Feel The Pain / Rock The House / Shadow Of Love / I Can't Make You Love Me / Feed The Machine / Guilty Pleasures / Blast From The Past / Let Me Be The One / Street Fighter / Fly Too High

JOHN SINCLAIR

HEAVY METAL KIDS:
KITSCH, RAK SRAK 523 (1977)
Overture / Chelsea Kids / From Heaven To Hell And Back Again / Cry For Me / She's No Angel / Jackie The Lad / Docking In / Squalliday Inn
CHELSEA KIDS, Razor METALP 117 (1987)
Overture / Chelsea Kids / From Heaven To Hell And Back Again / Cry For Me / She's No Angel / Jackie The Lad / Docking In / Squaliday Inn / Delirious
LIVE AND LOUD, Link Records (1989)

LION:
RUNNING ALL NIGHT, A&M AMLH 64755 (1980)
Summer Ghosts / Cold Sheets (Winters In New York) / Running All Night (With The Lion) / Get Here Woman / Helpless / How Does It Feel / Sweet Fire / Diana

URIAH HEEP:
ABOMINOG, Bronze BRON 538 (1982) **34 UK**
Too Scared To Run / Chasing Shadows / On The Rebound / Think It Over / Hot Night In A Cold Town / That's The Way It Is / Running All Night (With The Lion) / Hot Persuasion / Prisoner / See Your Soul

ALEX SKOLNICK

TESTAMENT:
THE LEGACY, Megaforce Atlantic 781 741-1 (1987)

The Ozzy Sidemen Discographies

Over The Wall / Haunting / Burnt Offerings / Raging Waters / Curse Of The Legions Of Death / First Strike Is Deadly / Do Or Die / Alone In The Dark / Apocalyptic City
LIVE AT EINDHOVEN, Megaforce Atlantic 780 226-1 (1987)
Over The Wall / Burnt Offerings / Do Or Die / Apocalyptic City / Reign Of Terror
THE NEW ORDER, Megaforce Atlantic 781 849-2 (1988) **49 SWEDEN, 81 UK**
Eerie Inhabitants / New Order / Trial By Fire / Into The Pit / Hypnosis / Disciples Of The Watch / Preacher / Day Of Reckoning / Musical Death (A Dirge)
PRACTICE WHAT YOU PREACH, Megaforce Atlantic WX 297CD (1989) **40 UK, 77 USA**
Practice What You Preach / Perilous Nation / Envy Time / Time Is Coming / Blessed In Contempt / Greenhouse Effect / Sins Of Omission / Ballad (A Song Of Hope) / Nightmare (Coming Back To You) / Confusion Fusion
SOULS OF BLACK, Megaforce Atlantic 7567821432 (1990) **35 UK, 73 USA**
Beginning Of The End / Face In The Sky / Falling Fast / Souls Of Black / Abscence Of Light / Love To Hate / Malpractice / One Man's Fate / Legacy / Seven Days In May
THE RITUAL, East West 756782392-2 (1992) **48 UK, 55 USA**
Sermon / As The Seasons Grey / Ritual / Deadline / So Many Lies / Let Go Of My World / Agony / Troubled Dreams / Signs Of Chaos / Electric Crown / Return To Serenity

SAVATAGE:
HANDFUL OF RAIN, Bulletproof CDVEST 32 (1994)
Taunting Cobras / Handful Of Rain / Chance / Stare Into The Sun / Castles Burning / Visions / Watching You Fall / Nothing's Going On / Symmetry / Alone You Breathe (Criss's Song)

ATTENTION DEFICIT:
ATTENTION DEFICIT, Magna Carta (1998)

PHIL SOUSSAN

WILDLIFE:
WILDLIFE, Swansong (1983)
Somewhere In The Night / Just A Friend / Surrender / Charity / One Last Chance / Haven't You Heard The News / Midnight Stranger / Rock 'n' Roll Dreams / Downtown Heartbreak

BEGGARS & THIEVES:
BEGGARS & THIEVES, East West 7567-82113-2 (1990)
No More Broken Dreams / Billy Knows Better / Waitin' For The Man / Your Love Is In Vain / Isn't It Easy / Let's Get Lost / Heaven And Hell / Love

Ozzy Osbourne
Junkie / Kill Me / Love's A Bitch / Beggars And Thieves

VINCE NEIL:
EXPOSED, Warner Bros. 936245260-2 (1993) **44 UK, 13 USA**
Look In Her Eyes / Sister Of Pain / Can't Have Your Cake / Edge / Can't Change Me / Fine, Fine Wine / Living Is A Luxury / You're Invited But Your Friend Can't Come / Gettin' Hard / Forever

Although Phil does not perform on the album 'Exposed' includes five tracks co-written by the bassist.

STEVE LUKATHER:
LUKE, Miramar 23098 (1997)
The Real Truth / Broken Machine / Tears Of My Own Shame / Love The Things You Hate / Hate Everything About U / Reservations To Live (The Way It Is) / Don't Hang Me On / Always Be There For Me / Open Your Heart / Bag O' Tales / Bluebird / Pump (Live)

DANA STRUM

VINNIE VINCENT INVASION:
VINNIE VINCENT INVASION, Chrysalis CHR 1529 (1986)
Boys Are Gonna Rock / Shoot You Full Of Love / No Substitute / Animal / Twisted / Do You Wanna Make Love / Back On The Streets / I Wanna Be Your Victim / Baby O / Invasion
ALL SYSTEMS GO, Chrysalis CHR 1626 (1988)
Let Freedom Rock / Naughty Naughty / Ecstasy / That Time Of Year / Breakout / Burn / Love Kills / Dirty Rhythm / Deeper And Deeper / Heavy Pettin' / Ashes To Ashes

SLAUGHTER:
STICK IT TO YA, Chrysalis CCD 1702 (1990) **18 USA**
Eye To Eye / Burnin' Bridges / Up All Night / Spend My Life / Thinking Of June / She Wants More / Fly To The Angels / Mad About You / That's Not Enough / You Are The One / Give Me Your Heart / Desperately / Loaded Gun / Fly To The Angels (Acoustic) / Wingin' It
STICK IT TO YA LIVE, Chrysalis 21816 (1990)
Burnin' Bridges / Eye To Eye / Fly To The Angels / Up All Night / Loaded Gun
THE WILD LIFE, Chrysalis CCD 1911 (1992) **50 SWEDEN, 64 UK, 8 USA**
Reach For The Sky / Out For Love / The Wild Life / Days Gone By / Dance For Me Baby / Times They Change / Move To The Music / Real Love / Shake This Place / Streets Of Broken Hearts / Hold On/ Do Ya Know / Old Man / Days Gone By (Acoustic)
FEAR NO EVIL, SPV Steamhammer 085-76002 (1995)
Live Like There's No Tomorrow / Get Used To It / Searchin' / It'll Be Alright

The Ozzy Sidemen Discographies

/ Let The Good Times roll / Breakdown 'n' Cry / Hard Times / Divine Order / Yesterday's Gone / Prelude / Outta My Head / Unknown Destination
REVOLUTION, CMC International 06076-86214-2 (1997)
American Pie / Heaven It Cries / Tongue 'n' Groove / Can We Find A Way / Stuck On You / Hard To Say Goodbye / Revolution / Guck / Heat Of The Moment / Rocky Mountain Way / You're My Everything / I'm Gone / Ad Majorem Dei Gloriam
ETERNAL LIVE, SPV 085-18162 CD (1998)
Rock The World / Get Used To It / Shout It Out / Mad About You / Spend My Life / Fly To The Angels / Real Love / Dance For Me / Searchin' / Wildlife / Move To The Music / Up All Night
BACK TO REALITY, SPV 085-21432 CD (1999)
Killin' Time / All Fired Up / Take Me Away / Dangerous / Trailer Park Boogie / Love Is Forever / Bad Groove / On My Own / Silence Of Ba / Headin For A Dream / Nothin Left To Lose

BRIAN TICHY

CHINA RAIN:
BED OF NAILS, Dig It (1992)
You're Only Lonely Today / Bang On The Wall / Psychedelic Sex Reaction / Last Forever / Light Of My Love / Bed Of Nails / Before It's Too Late / I Loved You Lied / Valerine / Love Calls

SASS JORDAN:
RATS, (1993)

PRIDE AND GLORY:
PRIDE AND GLORY, Geffen GED 24703 (1994)
Losin' Your Mind / Horse Called War / Shine On / Lovin' Woman / Harvester Of Pain / The Chosen One / Sweet Jesus / Troubled Wine / Machine Gun Man / Cry Me A River / Toe'n' The Line / Found A Friend / Fadin' Away / Hate Your Guts

NICKLEBAG:
12 HITS AND A BUMP, Iguana 574-2 (1996)
Love Song (All Up In The World) / Hit It And Quit It / I Will / Indanee / Turning The Other Way / Too Many Mountains (Big Daddy mix) / Sweet Thang / Don't Know Why I Love You / Grow / Repitition / Soul Search (Mother mix) / Win / Hots On For Nowhere (Bump Track) / Soul Search (Bonus Bump) / Nicklebag mix)

VINNIE MOORE:
OUT OF NOWHERE, Music For Nations CD MFN 194 (1996)

Ozzy Osbourne

BERNIE TORMÉ

GILLAN:
GLORY ROAD, Virgin V 2171 (1980) **3 UK, 183 USA**
Unchain Your Brain / Are You Sure / Time And Again / No Easy Way / Sleeping On The Job / On The Rocks / If You Believe Me / Running, White Face, City Boy / Nervous
GLORY ROAD – FOR GILLAN FANS ONLY, Virgin (1980) (Limited Edition Double Album set)
Unchain Your Brain / Are You Sure / Time And Again / No Easy Way / Sleeping On The Job / On The Rocks / If You Believe Me / Running, White Face, City Boy / Nervous / Higher And Higher / Your Mother Was Right / Red Watch / Abbey Of Thelema / Trying To Get To You / Come Tomorrow / Dragon's Tongue / Post Fade Brain Damage / Egg-Timer (Vice Versa) / The Harry Lime Theme
FUTURE SHOCK, Virgin VK 2196 (1981) **45 SWEDEN, 2 UK**
Future Shock / Night Ride Out Of Phoenix / New Orleans / The Ballad Of Lucitania Express / No Laughing In Heaven / Sacré Bleu / Bite The Bullet / If I Sing Softly / Don't Want The Truth / For Your Dreams
ONE FOR THE ROAD, Virgin (1981) (Japanese release)
One For The Road / Lucille / Bad News / Mutually Assured Destruction / The Maelstrom / Take A Hold Of Yourself

ATOMIC ROOSTER:
HEADLINE NEWS, Towerbell TOWLP 4 (1983)
Hold Your Fire / Headline News / Taking A Chance / Metal Minds / Land Of Freedom / Machine / Dance Of Death / Carnival / Time / Future Shock / Watch Out – Reaching Out

BERNIE TORMÉ:
TURN OUT THE LIGHTS, Kamaflage KAMLP 2 (1982) **50 UK**
Turn Out The Lights / Painter Man / Lies / America / Getting There / Chelsea Girls / Oh No! / No Reply / Possession
ELECTRIC GYPSIES, Zebra ZEB 1 (1983)
Wild West / 20th Century / Lightning Strikes / Too Young / Call Of The Wild / D.I.S.E. / Presences / I Can't Control Myself / Go-Go
LIVE, Zebra MZEB 3 (1984)
Presences / Wild West / Turn Out The Lights / Lightning Strikes / Getting There / Too Young / No Easy Way
BACK TO BABYLON, Zebra ZEB 6 (1985)
All Around The World / Star / Eyes Of The World / Burning Bridges / Hardcore / Here I Go / Family At War / Frontline / Arabia / Mystery Train.
ALL AROUND THE WORLD, Zebra (1985)
BACK WITH THE BOYS, Rawpower RAW LP 010 (1986)
Come Tomorrow / My Baby Loves A Vampire / No Easy Way / Try And Stop Me / Don't Give Up Your Day Job / Turn Out The Lights / Wild West / What's Next? / Lies / Night Lights / All Day And All Of The Night / Back With The Boys

The Ozzy Sidemen Discographies

OFFICIAL BOOTLEG, Onsala ONS 3 (1987)
Frontline / Turn Out The Lights / Hardcore / Star / Burning Bridges / T.V.O.D. / My Baby Loves A Vampire / Love, Guns And Money
DIE PRETTY, DIE YOUNG, Heavy Metal HMRLP 94 (1987)
Let It Rock / The Real Thing / Ready / Sex Action / The Ways Of The East / Killer / Memphis Louise / Crimes Of Passion / Ghost Train / All Around The World
ARE WE THERE YET, Heavy Metal HMR 168 (1991)
Teenage Kicks / Come The Revolution / Let It Rock / All Around The World / Mystery Train / Search And Destroy / Shoorah Shoorah / Wild West / Star / Turn Out The Lights (Live) / Lies / Chelsea Girls
DEMOLITION BALL, Bleeding Hearts BLEED 2 (1994)
Fallen Angel / Black Sheep / Action / Ball And Chain / Slipaway / Long Time Coming / Spinnin' Your Wheels / Don't Understand / Industry / Draw The Line / U.S. Maid / Let It Go / Walk It / Man 'O Means
WILD IRISH, Retrowrek RETRK 103 (1997)
Rat / Ghost Walking / Follow The Leader / Bad Blood / Howling At The Moon / River / Walk Don't Run / Lonesome Train / One More Heartache / Yesterday And Nowhere
PUNK OR WHAT?, Retrowrek 104 (1998)
WHITE TRASH GUITAR, Retrowrek RETRK 105 (1999)
Chasing Rainbows / Credibility Joe / All I Want / Boy Who Ran Away / My Obsession / Shoot The DJ / Lone Wolf Blues / Healer / Dark Horizon / Pearls / Credibility Joe / Easy Action / Sea Of Pain / Purple Haze (Live)

SILVER:
SILVER, AOR Heaven (2000)
Silver / Pretender / Sister Love / Marianna / Christine / She Was Mine / Walk The Stage / Sergei's Revenge / Brother Kill Brother / The Writer / Far Behind / No More Tears / Silverous

GUEST SESSIONS:
RENE BERG, The Leather, The Loneliness And Your Dark Eyes (1991)

ROB TRUJILLO

SUICIDAL TENDENCIES:
LIGHTS, CAMERA... REVOLUTION, Epic 4665692 (1990) **59 UK**
You Can't Bring Me Down / Lost Again / Alone/ Lovely / Give It Revolution / Get Whacked / Send Me Your Money / Emotion No. 13 / Disco's Out, Murder's In / Go 'n' Breakdown
SUICIDAL TENDENCIES, Virgin OVED 384 (1991)
Suicide's An Alternative / You'll Be Sorry / Two Sided Politics / I Shot The Devil / Subliminal / Won't Fall In Love Today / Institutionalised / Memories Of Tomorrow / Possessed / I Saw Your Mommy... / Fascist Pig / I Want More / Suicidal Failure / Possessed To Skate / Human Guinea Pig / Two Wrongs Don't Make A Right (But It Makes Me Feel Better)

Ozzy Osbourne

THE ART OF REBELLION, Epic 4718852 (1992) **52 USA**
Can't Stop / Accept My Sacrifice / Nobody Hears / Tap Into The Power / Monopoly On Sorrow / We Call This Mutha Revenge / I Wasn't Meant To Feel This / Asleep At The Wheel / Gotta Kill Captain Stupid / I'll Hate You Better / Which Way To Be Free / It's Going Down / Where's The Truth
STILL CYCO AFTER ALL THESE YEARS, Epic 473749-2 (1993)
Suicide's An Alternative / Two Sided Politics / Subliminal / I Shot The Devil / Won't Fall In Love / Institutionalised / War Inside My Head / Don't Give Me Your Nothin' / Memories Of Tomorrow / Possessed / I Saw Your Mommy... / Fascist Pig / Little Each Day / I Want More / Suicidal Failure
SUICIDAL FOR LIFE, Epic 476885-2 (1994) **82 USA**
Invocation / Don't Give A Fuck / No Fuckn' Problem / Suicyco Muthafucka / Fucked Up Just Right / No Bullshit / What Else Could I Do / What You Need's A Friend / I Wouldn't Mind / Depression And Anguish / Evil / Love v Loneliness / Benediction

INFECTIOUS GROOVES:
THE PLAGUE THAT MAKES YOUR BOOTY MOVE (IT'S THE INFECTIOUS GROOVES), Epic 4687292 (1991)
Punk It Up / Therapy / I Look Funny / Stop Funkn' With My Head / I'm Gonna Be My King / Closed Session / Infectious Grooves / Infectious Blues / Monster Skank / Back To The People / Turn Your Head / You Lie.. And Yo Breath Stank / Do The Sinister / Mandatory Love Song / Infecto Groovalistic / Thanx But No Thanx
SARSIPPIUS ARK, Epic 473591-2 (1993)
Intro / Turtle Wax (Funkaholics Anonymous) / No Cover / 2 Drink Minimum / Immigrant Song / Caca De Kick / Don't Stop Spread The Jam / Three Headed Mind Pollution / Slo-Motion Slam / Legend In His Own Mind (Ladies Love 'Sip) / Infectious Grooves / These Freaks Are Here To Party / Man Behind The Man / Fame / Savor Da Flavor / No Budget / Dust Off The 8 Track / Infectious Grooves (2) / You Pick Me Up (Just Throw Me Down) "Therapy" / Do The Sinister / Big Big Butt By Infectiphibian / Spreck
GROOVE FAMILY CYCO, Epic 475929-2 (1994)
Violent And Funky / Boom Boom Boom / Frustrated Again / Rules Go Out The Window / Groove Family Cyco / Die Like A Pig / Do What I Tell Ya / Cousin Randy / Why / Made It
MAS BORRACHO, XIIIBis (2000)
Citizen Of The Nation / Just A Little Bit / Lock It In The Pocket (And Throw Away The…) / Good For Nothing / Borracho / Good Times Are Out To Get You / Wouldn't You Like To Know / Going, Going, Gone / 21st Century Surf Odyssey / Please Excuse The Funk / Fill You Up / What Goes Up / Leave Me Alone

The Ozzy Sidemen Discographies
PETE WAY

UFO:
UFO, Beacon BEAS 12 (1970)
Unidentified Flying Object / Boogie / C'mon Everybody / Shake It About / Come Away Melinda / Timothy / Follow You Home / Treacle People / Who Do You Love / Evil
UFO 2 - FLYING ONE HOUR SPACE ROCK, Beacon BEAS 19 (1972)
Silver Bird / Star Storm / Prince Kajuku / Coming Of Prince Kajuku / Flying
UFO LIVE, Gem (1974)
C'mon Everybody / Who Do You Love / Loving Cup / Prince Kajuku / Coming Of Prince Kajuku / Boogie For George / Follow You Home
PHENOMENON, Chrysalis 1059 (1974)
Too Young To Know / Crystal Light / Doctor, Doctor / Space Child / rock Bottom / Oh My / Time On My Hands / Built For Comfort / Lipstick Traces / Queen Of The Deep
FORCE IT, Chrysalis CHR 1074 (1975) **71 USA**
Let It Roll / Shoot Shoot / High Flyer / Love Lost Love / Out In The Street / Mother Mary / Too Much Of Nothing / Dance Your Life Away / This Kid's / Between The Walls
NO HEAVY PETTING, Chrysalis 1103(1976) **38 SWEDEN**
Natural Thing / I'm A Loser / Can You Roll Her / Belladonna / Reasons Love / Highway Lady / On With The Action / A Fool In Love /Martian Landscape
LIGHTS OUT, Chrysalis CHR 1127 (1977) **31 SWEDEN, 54 UK, 23 USA**
Too Hot To Handle / Just Another Suicide / Try Me / Lights Out / Gettin' Ready / Alone Again Or / Electric Phase / Love To Love
OBSESSION, Chrysalis CDL 1182 (1978) **31 SWEDEN, 26 UK, 41 USA**
Only You Can Rock Me / Pack It Up And Go / Arbory Hill / Ain't No Baby / Looking Out For No. 1 / Hot 'n' Ready / Cherry / You Don't Fool Me / Looking Out For No. 1 (Reprise) / One More For The Rodeo / Born To Lose
STRANGERS IN THE NIGHT, Chrysalis CJT 5 (1979) **8 UK, 42 USA**
Natural Thing / Out In The Street / Only You Can rock Me / Doctor, Doctor / Mother Mary / This Kid's / Love To Love / Lights Out / Rock Bottom / Too Hot To Handle / I'm A Loser / Let It Roll / Shoot Shoot
NO PLACE TO RUN, Chrysalis CDL 1239 (1980) **44 SWEDEN, 11 UK, 51 USA**
Alpha Centauri / Lettin' Go / Mystery Train / This Fire Burns Tonight / Gone In The Night / Young Blood / No Place To Run / Take It Or Leave It / Money, Money / Any Day
WILD WILLING AND THE INNOCENT, Chrysalis CHR 1307 (1981) **27 SWEDEN, 19 UK, 77 USA.**
Chains Chains / Long Gone / The Wild, The Willing And The Innocent / It's Killing Me / Makin' Moves / Lonely Heart / Couldn't Get It Right / Profession Of Violence
MECHANIX, Chrysalis CHR 1360 (1982) **38 SWEDEN, 8 UK, 82 USA**
The Writer / Somethin' Else / Back Into My Life / You'll Get Love / Doing It All For You / We Belong To The Night / Let It Rain / Terri / Feel It / Dreaming

Ozzy Osbourne

WAYSTED:
VICES, Chrysalis CHR 1438 (1983) **78 UK**
Love Loaded / Women In Chains / Sleazy / Night Of The Wolf / Toy With The Passion / Right From The Start / Hot Love / All Belongs To You / Somebody To Love
WAYSTED, Music For Nations MFN 31 (1984) **73 UK**
Won't Get Out Alive / The Price You Pay / Rock Steady / Hurts So Good / Cinderella Boys
THE GOOD, THE BAD, THE WAYSTED, Music For Nations MFN 43(1985)
Hang 'Em High / Hi Ho My Baby / Heaven Tonight / Manuel / Dead On Your Legs / Rolling Out The Dice / Land That's Lost The Love / Crazy 'Bout The Stuff / Around And Around
COMPLETELY WAYSTED, Rawpower RAWLP 019 (1986)
Women In Chains / Hang 'Em High / Won't Get Out Alive / Sleazy / Hot Love / Dead On Your Legs / Hurt So Good / Somebody To Love / Around And Around / Rock Steady / Love Loaded / Hi Ho My Baby / Toy With The Passion
SAVE YOUR PRAYERS, Parlophone 24 0638 1 (1986)
Walls Fall Down / How The West Was Won / Out Of Control / Heroes Die Young / Hell Comes Home / Heaven Tonight / Wild Night / Singing To The Night / Black 'n' Blue / So Long

UFO:
HIGH STAKES AND DANGEROUS MEN, Essential ESSCD 178 (1992)
Borderline / Primed For Time / She's The One / Ain't Life Sweet / Don't Want To Lose You / Burnin' Fire / Running Up The Highway / Back Door Man / One Of Those Nights / Revolution / Love Deadly Love / Let The Good Times Roll
LIGHTS OUT IN TOKYO (LIVE), JVC Victor VICP 5204 (1993)
Running Up The Highway / Borderline / Too Hot To Handle / She's The One / Cherry / Back Door Man / One Of Those Nights / Love To Love / Only You Can rock Me / Lights Out / Doctor, Doctor / Rock Bottom / Shoot Shoot / C'mon Everybody
WALK ON WATER, Zero Corporation XRCN 1237 (1995) (Japanese release)
A Self Made Man / Venus / Pushed To The Limit / Stopped By A Bullet (Of Love) / Darker Days / Running On Empty / Knock, Knock / Dreaming Of Summer / Doctor Doctor '95 / Lights Out '95 / Message For Japan

MOGG/WAY:
EDGE OF THE WORLD, Roadrunner RR 8804-2 (1997)
Change Brings A Change / All Out Of Luck / Gravy Train / Fortune Town / Highwire / Saving Me From Myself / Mother Mary / House Of Pain / It's A Game / History Of Flames / Spell On You / Totalled
CHOCOLATE BOX, Shrapnel (1999)
Muddy's Gold / Jerusalem / Too Close To The Sun / King Of The City / Living And Dying / This Is The Life / Death In The Family / Whip That Groove /

The Ozzy Sidemen Discographies

Last Man In Space / Sparkling Wine

UFO:
WEREWOLVES OF LONDON-LIVE, Zoom Club ZCRCD20 (1999)
Natural Thing / Mother Mary / A Self Made Man / Electric Phase / This Kids / Out In The Street / One More For The Rodeo / Venus / Pushed To The Limit / Love To Love / Too Hot To Handle / Only You Can Rock Me / Lights Out / Doctor Doctor / Rock Bottom
COVENANT, SPV (2000) 53 GERMANY
Love Is Forever / Unravelled / Miss The Lights / Midnight Train / Fool's Gold / The Middle Of Madness / Smell The Money / Rise Again / Serenade / Cowboy Joe / The World And His Dog / Mother Mary (Live) / This Kids (Live) / Let It Roll (Live) / Out In The Street (Live) / Venus (Live) / Pushed To The Limit (Live) / Love To Love (Live)

PETE WAY:
AMPHETIMINE, Zoom Club (2000)
That's Tuff / Hangin' Out / Fooled Again / American Kid (What A Shame) / Hole / Hole 2 / Crazy Again / Hard To Hold

ZAKK WYLDE

PRIDE 'N' GLORY:
PRIDE AND GLORY, Geffen GED 24703 (1994)
Losin' Your Mind / Horse Called War / Shine On / Lovin' Woman / Harvester Of Pain / The Chosen One / Sweet Jesus / Troubled Wine / Machine Gun Man / Cry Me A River / Toe'n' The Line / Found A Friend / Fadin' Away / Hate Your Guts

ZAKK WYLDE:
BOOK OF SHADOWS, Geffen 24964 (1996)
Between Heaven And Hell / Sold My Soul / Road Back Home / Way Beyond Empty / Throwin' It All Away / What You're Loonin' For / Dead As Yesterday / Too Numb To Cry / The Things You Do / 1,000,000 Miles Away / I Thank You Child

BLACK LABEL SOCIETY:
SONIC BREW, Spitfire 5004-2 (1998)
Bored To Tears / The Rose Petalled Garden / Hey You (Batch Of Lies) / Born To Lose / Peddlers Of Death / Mother Mary / Beneath The Tree / Low Down / T.A.Z. / Lost My Better Half / Black Pearl / World Of Trouble / Spoke In The Wheel / The Beginning… The Last
STRONGER THAN DEATH, Spitfire (2000)
All For You / Phoney Smiles, Fake Hellos / 13 Years Of Grief / Rust / Super Terrorizer / Counterfeit God / Ain't Life Grand / Just Killing Time / Stronger Than Death / Love Reign Down
ALCOHOL FUELED BREWTALITY – LIVE BLS, Spitfire SPITCD112

Ozzy Osbourne

(2001)
Lowdown / 13 Years Of Grief / Stronger Than Death / All For You / Superterrorizer / Phoney Smiles & Fake Hellos / Lost My Better Half / Bored To Tears / A.N.D.R.O.T.A.Z. / Born To Booze / World Of Trouble / No More Tears / The Beginning...The Last / Heart Of Gold / Snowblind / Like A Bird / Blood In The Wall / The Beginning...The Last
1919 ETERNAL, Spitfire (2002)

<u>GUEST SESSIONS:</u>
BRITNY FOX, Bite Down Hard (1990)
C.P.R., C.P.R. (1993)

Other Albums Which Include Sessions From Ozzy Osbourne Band Members:

<u>CAGE:</u>
CAGE, Nexus International KICP 542 (1997)
Walk On Water / My Shell / Mind's Eye / Train Song / Here And Gone / Soul To Soul / Save Me / Lie / Ticket

The CAGE album features contributions from three Ozzy players – drummers Carmine Appice and Randy Castillo with bassist Phil Soussan.

<u>VARIOUS ARTISTS:</u>
HUMANARY STEW : A TRIBUTE TO ALICE COOPER, Eagle EAG0062 (1998)
Under My Wheels / *School's Out* / No More Mr. Nice Guy / Welcome To My Nightmare / *Cold Ethyl* / Black Widow / Go To Hell / *Billion Dollar Babies* / *Only Women Bleed* / *Eighteen* / *Elected*

This tribute album, one of many crafted by Kiss guitarist Bob Kulick, would witness the involvement of some of the most highly rated players. Nestling in amongst the likes of The Who's Roger Daltrey, Slash of GunsN'Roses and members of Def Leppard would be a veritable army of Ozzy campaigners. Mike Inez is featured on the Roger Daltrey fronted 'No More Mr. Nice Guy', both Phil Soussan and Randy Castillo lent support to 'Welcome To My Nightmare', ironically fronted by Ronnie James Dio. Tommy Aldridge provided the backbone for 'Black Widow' in alliance with Iron Maiden members Bruce Dickinson and Adrian Smith whilst Zakk Wylde and Rudy Sarzo provided an interesting combination on 'Go To Hell' led by Twisted Sister's Dee Snider.

Ozzy Osbourne – Kith & Kin

Selected Ozzy Related Acts From The
www.rockdetector.com
Files

DON AIREY (UK)
A highly esteemed veteran of the genre, keyboard player Don Airey's CV reads like a Who's Who of rock starting with COZY POWELL'S HAMMER then BABE RUTH and includes performances with OZZY OSBOURNE, RAINBOW, WHITESNAKE, COLOSSEUM II, GARY MOORE, ULI JON ROTH and JETHRO TULL.

Airey first came to prominence in the rock world (previously he had his own act touring globally on cruise liners!) with COZY POWELL'S HAMMER in 1974 before joining the esoteric rock outfit COLOSSEUM II recording the *Strange New Flesh*, *Electric Savage* and *Wardance* albums. The man also found time to collaborate with none other than ANDREW LLOYD WEBBER on his 'Variations' theme for television arts programme 'The South Bank Show'.

Next port of call was with the ex-THIN LIZZY guitarist GARY MOORE, one of his credits including the arrangement on a track titled 'Biscayne Blues' which was to evolve, with the addition of Phil Lynott's vocals, into the famous 'Parisienne Walkways'. Airey departed from a fragmenting COLOSSEUM II in 1978 briefly uniting with BLACK SABBATH for their 'Never Say Die' album prior to reuniting with Cozy Powell in RAINBOW. Airey also found time to aid STRIFE with their 'Back To Thunder' effort.

Airey's tenure in RAINBOW lasted for three years and two major albums *Down To Earth* and *Difficult To Cure*. During time out keyboard contributions were added to MICHAEL SCHENKER GROUP's debut and OZZY OSBOURNE's *Blizzard Of Ozz* album including the trademark organ intro to 'Mr Crowley'.

With RAINBOW in constant flux Airey jumped ship to form part of OZZY OSBOURNE's band appearing on *Bark At The Moon* and *Speak Of The Devil*. By 1985 Airey was back helping out GARY MOORE for his *Out In The Fields* record, PHENOMENA, Yugoslavians WILD STRAWBERRIES, German Metal band SINNER's *Comin' Out Fighting*, ZENO, HELIX's *Wild In The Street* and ALASKA's *The Pack* before laying down work on WHITESNAKE's masterful *1987* album. The same year had Airey conducting live duties in America with JETHRO TULL and recording with Italians CROSSBONES before finally going solo. The resulting *K2* album, released only in Japan and Germany, sees guest performances from guitarist Gary Moore and the late Cozy Powell.

Further work with GARY MOORE on his *Still Got The Blues* album ensured. Airey has latterly played with JAGGED EDGE, TIGERTAILZ, SLAVERAIDER, FASTWAY, UFO, GRAHAM BONNET, JOE SATRIANI, ULI JON ROTH, BRIAN MAY, COZY POWELL, ELECTRIC LIGHT ORCHESTRA, JUDAS PRIEST's *Painkiller* and even wrote the British Eurovision song contest winner for KATRINA & THE WAVES!

1998 had Airey as part of THE CAGE, a band founded together with erst-

Ozzy Osbourne

while BLACK SABBATH vocalist TONY MARTIN and members of Italian Metal act CROSSBONES.

Airey toured Britain in 1999 as part of COLIN BLUNSTONE's band. 2001 had reports that Airey had formed part of a brand new 'supergroup' including his familiar sparring partner Neil Murray on bass, former YNGWIE MALMSTEEN band members vocalist MARK BOALS and drummer Anders Johansson alongside Rolf Munkes and Lance King.

Not content with that union Airey would also figure in the all star SILVER project fronted by former MICHAEL SCHENKER GROUP vocalist Gary Barden and including BERNIE TORMÉ, DEMON DRIVE's Michael Voss and H-BLOCKZ drummer Marco Minnemann.

Airey would join his ex-RAINBOW colleague vocalist GRAHAM BONNET for a British club tour to close out 2001. He would add to his career CV of major acts by joining no less than DEEP PURPLE in March of 2002 for dates in Russia.

Albums:
K2, 121 Records (1989)

ALICE IN CHAINS (Seattle, WA, USA)
Line-up: Layne Staley (vocals), Jerry Cantrell (guitar), Mike Inez (bass), Sean Kinney (drums)

ALICE IN CHAINS formed in 1986 originally with a Glam image, but would find huge commercial success as the very epitome of Grunge. The band had previously gone under the name of DIAMOND LIE.

Vocalist Layne Staley was just ridding himself of a Glam act he was fronting when he teamed up with guitarist Jerry Cantrell and erstwhile GYPSY ROSE bassist Mike Starr. Staley, known then as Candy Staley, had for three years fronted SLEZE, an outfit comprising of guitarist Nicky, bassist Johnny Bacolas and drummer Bam Bamm. Another one time SLEZE member, bassist Jimmy Sheppard would later go on to Metal band SANCTUARY. Drummer Sean Kinney had previously played with his grandfather's band THE CROSSCUTS. An early ALICE IN CHAINS / SLEZE member, bassist Johnny 'Yanni Bacolas', would later found SECOND COMING.

Following a handful of gigs ALICE IN CHAINS soon signed with major label Columbia. Initial product was the June 1990 'We Die Young' EP, now a much sought after rarity.

The original title of the band's first album was *Gash*, but the record company objected. They chose *Facelift* as an alternative due to the fact that many of the songs ALICE IN CHAINS had written prior to recording had been scrapped in the studio and succeeded by songs that differed drastically in style to those originally planned for the album.

Their debut hit the American music scene at the height of Grunge and ALICE IN CHAINS, morose yet engaging songs captivated the rock audience. The band gained valuable further exposure with an appearance as a bar band performing 'Would?' in the Cameron Crowe movie *Singles*, which also featured PEARL JAM's Eddie Vedder. Touring found the band as support to

Selected Ozzy-Related Acts From The Rockdetector Files

MEGADETH on their European dates and an appearance on the 'Clash Of The Titans' touring package with MEGADETH, SLAYER and ANTHRAX. Supporting VAN HALEN Cantrell missed a support gig on December 1st, the guitarist was out on a hunting expedition and thought November had 31 days! The band followed *Facelift* quickly with the mini album *Sap* after which bassist Mike Starr quit. He would go on to form MY SISTER'S MACHINE then SUN RED SUN.

1992's *Dirt*, with new four-stringer ex-SURE FIRE and OZZY OSBOURNE man Mike Inez, gave the band a top ten album. Incidentally, SLAYER's Tom Araya features on the *Dirt* album lending a blood-curdling scream to the untitled track.

The band went out on tour in America with Inez's previous employer, Staley, who had fractured his ankle, appearing onstage in a wheelchair! Tour T shirts depicted an x-ray of the singers damaged limb.

Staley put in a vocal duet on the BOB DYLAN tune 'Ring Them Bells' with Ann Wilson on fellow Seattle act HEART's 1993 album *The Road Home*. ALICE IN CHAINS themselves went out on the road as part of the 'Lollapalooza' tour.

The band contributed two tracks ('What The Hell Have I' and 'A Little Bitter') to the soundtrack of the *Last Action Hero* movie starring Arnold Schwarzanegger. As 1993 ended both *Dirt* and *Last Action Hero* albums went platinum.

Staley put together an act THE GACY BUNCH (after the mass murderer John Wayne Gacy) changing this band title later to MAD SEASON. This project was billed by the media as a Grunge 'supergroup', including as it did SCREAMING TREES Barrett Martin and PEARL JAM's Mike McCready. The MAD SEASON album *Above* fared well and hit platinum status.

Meantime Staley's priority act scored their second American number 1 with the eponymous 1995 album. An 'MTV Unplugged' session followed, with guitarist Scott Olsen sitting in on the proceedings, putting ALICE IN CHAINS back into the American top 5 once more.

ALICE IN CHAINS put in four gigs opening for the 1996 KISS reunion tour before the band retiring into the shadows.

JERRY CANTRELL had a solo cut included on the soundtrack album for the Jim Carey movie *The Cable Guy*, a portent of what was to follow.

The band were out of the limelight for such a lengthy period wild rumours began to circulate about the fate of individual members. These speculations went as far as claiming that Staley had contracted gangrene due to his drug problem and that the singer was having surgery to remove fingers or even an arm.

Inez briefly rejoined the OZZY OSBOURNE band.

Cantrell was to further pursue a solo route with the release of a full-blown album *Boggy Depot* in April 1998. Although all the members of ALICE IN CHAINS contributed, rumours still abounded as to the state of Staley's health. Cantrell took drummer Kinney out on the road with him to support *Boggy Depot* in a touring band that also, rather surprisingly, included ex-QUEENSRYCHE guitarist Chris De Garmo.

The 1999 box set *Music Bank* included the first new ALICE IN CHAINS

Ozzy Osbourne

material plus demos and unreleased material.

Late 2000 found Inez and Kinney demoing material with Chris De Garmo in a new act titled SPYS 4 DARWIN. By 2001 demand for the still inactive ALICE IN CHAINS was still at such a high that the *Live* album was issued to satisfy demand. March of 2002 found Mike Inez adding to his growing list of high profile band credits by joining Seattle AOR superstars HEART.

Albums:
FACELIFT, CBS 467201-4 (1990)
SAP, Columbia 74182 (1992) (USA release)
DIRT, Columbia 472330-2 (1992)
JAR OF FLIES, Columbia 475713-2 (1994)
ALICE IN CHAINS, Columbia (1995)
MTV UNPLUGGED, Columbia 484300-2 (1996)
MUSIC BANK, Columbia (1999)
BEST OF THE BOX, Columbia (1999) (Promotion release)

BADLANDS (USA)
Line-Up: Ray Gillen (vocals), Jake E. Lee (guitar), Greg Caisson (bass), Eric Singer (drums)

BADLANDS was the vehicle for former OZZY OSBOURNE guitarist extraordinaire JAKE E. LEE to exorcise some Blues demons. BADLANDS were to release a brace of finely crafted rock albums of the old school but fell apart before any tangible success.

The band line-up comprised of Lee, former BLACK SABBATH men vocalist RAY GILLEN and drummer Eric Singer together with ex-GHOST RIDE, SURGICAL STEEL and STEELER bassist Greg Chaisson. Immediately before BADLANDS Chaisson had been a founder member of BRITTON. The bassist had encountered Lee earlier when trying out for a position with the guitarist's former employer OZZY OSBOURNE.

Whilst Eric Singer had also played with LITA FORD and GARY MOORE previously, Gillen had recently been working with ex-THIN LIZZY and WHITESNAKE guitarist JOHN SYKES's BLUE MURDER project that had, at one time, also been fronted by ex KING KOBRA singer MARK FREE.

Whilst Free had quickly established that the project was not for him, Gillen stayed slightly longer but was ousted from the band due to record company pressure. He became involved with BADLANDS after Lee had told Eric Singer that he was on the look out for a vocalist. Singer initially played drums with the fledgling group as a favour to Gillen, but as the project became more substantial the drummer signed up on a full-time basis.

Taking their cue from '70s Blues Rock outfits, the quartet recorded debut product with SAVATAGE producer Paul O' Neill and engaged David Thoener at the mixing stage. The self-titled debut was released through *Hit Parader* editor Andy Secher's Atlantic affiliated Titanium label in May 1989.

By 1990 Singer had opted out to join the ALICE COOPER band before forming a more permanent liaison with KISS. His position in BADLANDS was taken by former RACER X vocalist Jeff Martin.

Selected Ozzy-Related Acts From The Rockdetector Files

British shows in mid-1992 had Lee announcing that Gillen was out of the band and that black female vocalist Debbie Holiday had already usurped his position. However, such was the outcry that the band was forced to reinstate their original frontman.

Once back in Los Angeles Lee drafted in vocalist John West. This version of BADLANDS lasted about six months before West opted out. The singer joined the MICHAEL LEE FIRKINS BAND, worked with COZY POWELL then created ARTENSION.

Martin became the drummer for PAUL GILBERT's live band then teamed up with Progressive Metal band BLACK SYMPHONY. Martin rejoined RACER X for their 'Technical Difficulties'. By 2000 Martin found himself behind the drum kit for UFO's European tour.

GREG CHAISSON would later play in covers band THE RELICS. The man has also issued a 1995 solo Christian rock album *It's About Time* which features his erstwhile BADLANDS colleague Eric Singer on drums.

Albums:
BADLANDS, Atlantic 781 966-2 (1989)
VOODOO HIGHWAY, Atlantic 7567-82251-2 (1991)
DUSK, (2000)

BLACK LABEL SOCIETY (USA)
Line-Up: Zakk Wylde (vocals / guitar), Nick Catanese (guitar), S.O.B. (bass), Philth Ondich (drums)

Exceptionally heavy and uncompromising trio founded by ex OZZY OSBOURNE and ALLMAN BROTHERS guitarist ZAKK WYLDE following his more Southern flavoured PRIDE & GLORY. Wylde also spent time rehearsing with GUNS N' ROSES and songs written during this period were used for the debut BLACK LABEL SOCIETY album.

Wylde made it into celluloid in 2000 appearing in the movie *Metal God* as guitarist for actor Mark Wahlberg's fictitious band STEEL DRAGON. This movie would be eventually released in August 2001 with a new title of *Rock Star*.

BLACK LABEL SOCIETY toured America in 2000 with CROWBAR and SIXTY WATT SHAMEN. The initial dates were marred though when Ondich fell ill necessitating CROWBAR's drummer Craig Nunemacher stepping into the breach for many shows.

2001 brought renewed fortunes for Wylde as it emerged that the guitarist was back in the Ozzy camp recording for a projected album. BLACK LABEL SOCIETY meanwhile formed part of the summer 'Ozzfest' touring festival promoting the live-cum-acoustic album *Alcohol Fuelled Brewtality*. By June bassist S.O.B. had parted ways with the act and Mike Inez, an erstwhile OZZY OSBOURNE band colleague, stepped into the breach.

The band returned in 2002 touting a new studio album *1919 Eternal* promoting this with yet more 'Ozzfest' shows, this time on a European leg.

Ozzy Osbourne

Albums:
SONIC BREW, Spitfire 5004-2 (1998)
STRONGER THAN DEATH, Spitfire (2000)
ALCOHOL FUELLED BREWTALITY, Spitfire SPITCD112 (2001)
1919 ETERNAL, Spitfire SPITCD176 (2002)

BLACK OAK ARKANSAS (USA)
Line-Up: Jim Dandy (vocals), Ricky Reynolds (guitar), Stan Knight (guitar), Harvey Jett (guitar), Pat Daugherty (bass), Tommy Aldridge (drums)

Born and raised in the small town of Black Oak, Arkansas (or neighbouring hamlets), school friends Jim 'Dandy' Mangrum and Ricky Reynolds formed their first band whilst in High School and September 1965 witnessed the group's first live show at Reynolds Park Community Centre in Pasragould, Arkansas.

1969, after having been finally chased out of town thanks to a reputation for hell raising and ripping off the neighbourhood in order to pawn their ill-gotten gains for new band equipment the boys wound up in New Orleans.

Relocated, the group (originally known as THE KNOWBODY ELSE) were signed to Hip Records and issued a self-titled album (re-issued by the Stax label in 1974 as *The Early Times*) before attracting the interest of the Atlantic label after a show in Los Angeles.

By the time they released their major label debut in 1971 the group had changed their name to BLACK OAK ARKANSAS in honour of their roots. The initial BLACK OAK ARKANSAS roster included vocalist Mangrum, guitarist Reynolds, guitarists Stan Knight and Harvey Jett, bassist Pat Daugherty and drummer Wayne Evans. However, Evans was replaced by Nashville-born Tommy Aldridge during 1972 and he took his place on tour that summer during which the live set *Raunch And Roll – Live* was captured. Some American sources have suggested that Aldridge had previously recorded with a band signed to Capitol called DAVID AND THE GIANTS who also included keyboard player Gregg Giuffria. Giuffria would go on to enjoy a fair amount of success with the Pomp Rock outfits ANGEL, GIUFFRIA and HOUSE OF LORDS in the '70s and '80s. Aldridge was to spend some time in the latter group in the early '90s although he has gone on record to claim to one of the authors of this publication that he had never played with Giuffria before joining HOUSE OF LORDS. Whatever, Aldridge would certainly make his name bashing the tubs for BLACK OAK ARKANSAS.

Officially the band debuted with self-titled effort in 1971 produced by IRON BUTTERFLY men MIKE PINERA and Lee Dorman. The album struck an immediate chord with the American Rock public; especially the renewed attitude the band gave the GUY MITCHELL hit 'Singin' The Blues'. The band kept up a hectic schedule of recording and touring throughout the '70s. Highlights included a British tour opening for BLACK SABBATH, although the good ol' BBC mysteriously banned the *High On The Hog* album's 'Jim Dandy To The Rescue'!

A further line-up change occurred after the *Street Party* album, ex-BLOODROCK guitarist Jimmy Henderson replacing Harvey Jett.

Selected Ozzy-Related Acts From The Rockdetector Files

Henderson had recently worked with Mangrum discovery RUBY STARR, a singer now managed by BLACK OAK ARKANSAS mentor Butch Stone. She had been discovered by the singer working in a bar in Evansville, Indiana and had been tapped by Mangrum to appear on the aforementioned *Jim Mangrum To The Rescue* before signing to Capitol as a solo artist.

The band toured Europe in 1974 with support acts STACKRIDGE and SASSAFRAS.

In 1975 BLACK OAK ARKANSAS left Atlantic for pastures new at MCA Records, *Ain't Life Grand* being their parting shot on the former label. The first album of the MCA contract, *X Rated*, arrived in the stores later in the year. Atlantic offered the *Live Mutha* album the following year whilst a second MCA record, *Balls Of Fire* followed.

During 1976 BLACK OAK ARKANSAS were augmented with the full-time talents of Ruby Starr. Having released three albums in the interim (*Ruby Starr*, *Grey Ghost* and *Scene Stealer*, the latter two of which find Tommy Aldridge guesting), Starr made her live debut at no less a gig than at the huge California Jam event.

Unfortunately, 1976 also marked the departure of Tommy Aldridge. The drummer had seemingly wanted out of the band for some two years but was unable to quit due to the nature of his contract. As Aldridge went off to work with PAT TRAVERS, BLACK OAK ARKANSAS recruited Joel Williams from CABOOSE, TARGET and RUBY STARR's GREY GHOST in his place and begin to pursue slightly different musical avenues with the addition of the all-girl backing group HOT BUTTERED SOUL live.

However, by 1977 Mangrum remained the sole original member as Reynolds, Daugherty and Knight all followed Aldridge out of the door to be replaced by Greg Reding, Andy Tanas and ex-HOT DOGS guitarist Jack Holder respectively, all three appearing on *Race With The Devil*.

This was the first album in a new deal with the Atlanta, Georgia, based Capricorn Records. A second album with the label, *I'd Rather Be Sailing* appeared later the same year before BLACK OAK ARKANSAS went into exile, mainly due to a heart attack suffered by Mangrum in 1980!

Guitarist Jack Holder turned up in the Butch Stone managed hard rock outfit COBRA in 1983 with whom he recorded the *First Strike* album on Epic. Holder later worked with the AOR/Pop Rock outfit DRAMA and EDDIE DEGARMO.

Andy Tanas would be drafted into another of Butch Stone's 80s interests, Swiss Metal band KROKUS, for a short term of employment in 1984.

JIM DANDY would be reunited with Ricky Reynolds for Dandy's own *Ready As Hell* album. The BLACK OAK ARKANSAS moniker was unable to be used at the time due to a number of legal wrangles. The duo stuck together for the full bore BLACK OAK ARKANSAS release 'The Black Attack Is Back' in the '80s.

There was a rumour circulating at the time of IAN GILLAN's enrolment into BLACK SABBATH that Jim Mangrum's name had been bandied around in connection with the vacancy prior to the ex-DEEP PURPLE vocalist landing the job.

In the latter half of 1991 Mangrum was involved in a bad car accident in which he sustained three broken vertebrae and wasn't expected to be able to walk again. However, the singer made a miraculous recovery and was performing again by the spring of 1992. During 1996 BLACK OAK ARKANSAS toured with FOGHAT, MOUNTAIN, IRON BUTTERFLY and HEAD EAST. The group were still active (albeit on the bar circuit) the following year with a line-up comprising Jim Dandy, Rick Reynolds, Pat Daugherty, guitarist Rocky Athas and drummer Johnnie Bolin. The latter is the brother of late DEEP PURPLE guitarist TOMMY BOLIN and had previously recorded with DVC, amongst others, back in 1981.

Thenew incarnation of BLACK OAK ARKANSAS have a studio album in the can and were last heard of shopping for a new deal.

Incidentally, Harvey Jett turned up in 1996 in a Christian outfit titled BAND OF GOLD.

In 1998 the group were the subject of one of the latest in a string of popular live album releases culled from the 'King Biscuit Flower Hour' concert series vaults.

Of all the BLACK OAK ARKANSAS members, Tommy Aldridge has enjoyed perhaps the most illustrious career. After leaving the band, the drummer worked with PAT TRAVERS, OZZY OSBOURNE, MARS PROJECT DRIVER, HOUSE OF LORDS, WHITESNAKE, YNGWIE MALMSTEEN and MANIC EDEN. 2000 found the drummer as a member of ELEMENTS OF FRICTION and by 2001 Aldridge was ensconced in Motor City Madman TED NUGENT's live band.

Albums:
BLACK OAK ARKANSAS, Atco 354 (1971)
KEEP THE FAITH, Atco 381 (1972)
IF AN ANGEL CAME TO SEE YOU, WOULD YOU MAKE HER FEEL AT HOME?, Atco 7008 (1972)
RAUNCH N' ROLL– LIVE, Atco 7019 (1973)
HIGH ON THE HOG, Atco 7035 (1973)
STREET PARTY, Atco 101 (1974)
AIN'T LIFE GRAND, Atco 111 (1975)
X-RATED, MCA MCF 2734 (1975)
LIVE! MUTHA, Atco 128 (1976)
BALLS OF FIRE, MCA MCF 2762 (1976)
10 YEAR OVERNIGHT SUCCESS, MCA MCF 2784 (1976)
RACE WITH THE DEVIL, Capricorn 2429 156 (1977)
THE BEST OF BLACK OAK ARKANSAS, Atco (1977)
I'D RATHER BE SAILING, Capricorn CP 0207 (1978)
THE BLACK ATTACK IS BACK, Heavy Metal HM USA 63 (1986)
HOT & NASTY: THE BEST OF BLACK OAK ARKANSAS, Rhino 2 71146 (1992)
KING BISCUIT FLOWER HOUR LIVE, King Biscuit (1998)
THE WILD BUNCH, Deadline 705 (1999)
LIVE, EMI 24496 (2000)

Selected Ozzy-Related Acts From The Rockdetector Files

BLACK SABBATH (UK)
Line-Up: Ozzy Osbourne (vocals), Tony Iommi (guitar), Geezer Butler (bass), Bill Ward (drums)

Cited by many to be THE original Heavy Metal band, BLACK SABBATH have had a massive influence on the genre and have sold countless millions of albums. BLACK SABBATH, steered into their chosen doom/occult leanings by bassist and songwriter Geezer Butler, impose an enormous legacy upon the Heavy Metal scene. Guitarist Tony Iommi has laid down many of the classic all time riffs and is a versatile Blues inspired musician revered as a guitar hero despite having lost some fingertips in a 1966 machine accident, which nearly put paid to his chosen career.

Until 1978 the band was fronted by the irrepressible Ozzy Osbourne. Now renowned as one of the true legends of Metal from his BLACK SABBATH years and his subsequent, massively successful solo career, Osbourne's trademark vocal style and outrageous on and off stage behaviour have gained the Brummie true rock idol status.

Created in 1967 in the heart of industrial Birmingham, a skinhead then known as Ozzy Zig, Tony Iommi, Terry 'Geezer' Butler and Bill Ward first united, albeit briefly, under the name POLKA TULK BLUES BAND. Osbourne's first attempts at singing came just after leaving school when, together with guitarist Jimmy Phillips, he founded the short-lived act THE PROSPECTORS. Previously Iommi and Ward had been part of THE REST, a band fronted by ex-METHOD FIVE vocalist Chris Smith. The group later changed its name to MYTHOLOGY.

Osbourne and Butler, the latter a rhythm guitarist at this point, were members of RARE BREED, an act that lasted a mere two gigs. Previous to this Osbourne had stints with local bands THE BLACK PANTHERS and APPROACH as well as having served a short term in the forbidding Winson Green prison for burglary. It was during his incarceration at Her Majesty's pleasure that the singer gave himself his now famous 'Ozzy' and smiley face tattoos by rubbing floor cleaning paste into his skin.

The quartet joined forces when MYTHOLOGY lost both singer and drummer. With the recruitment of Osbourne and Ward, MYTHOLOGY changed its title to MUSIC MACHINE adding saxophonist Alan Clark and Jimmy Phillips on slide guitar. Before long MUSIC MACHINE became the POLKA TULK BLUES BAND and trimmed down to a quartet, with Butler adopting a new role as bass player by taking two strings off his lead guitar. Phillips meanwhile would go onto become a keyboard player performing with PURPLE ONION, FROG and MAGIC ROUNDABOUT.

Within a short space of time the revised band had altered their moniker to the shortened POLKA TULK before another name change was enforced, the foursome becoming EARTH.

Signing up to a management deal with Jim Simpson (who later was to manage fellow brummies JUDAS PRIEST) the band started the grind of playing the Rock and Blues clubs. Their first taste of Europe came when Simpson booked a tour of Germany. The shows included a date at Hamburg's infamous Star Club (the once famous haunt of THE BEATLES), before getting the band in a four-track studio to record their first demo. This recording, featuring the tracks 'Song For Jim' and 'The Rebel' in 1969, enabled the band to gain a deal with the then 'Progressive Rock' experimental label Vertigo Records, an arm of Fontana Records. BLACK SABBATH had already put in an appearance in the capital with a batch of gigs at the legendary Marquee Club in March of 1969.

Upon signing they were to discover that another act called EARTH had just released a single in Germany, thus necessitating a name change. According to legend it was a Dennis Wheatley novel that inspired Butler to come up with BLACK SABBATH. Despite the deal, BLACK SABBATH were financially in difficult times and it was at this point that Iommi actually left to join JETHRO TULL for all of two weeks, to replace the departed Mick Abrahams.

Although Iommi's stay in JETHRO TULL was brief he did appear with the band at the legendary ROLLING STONES *Rock 'n' Roll Circus* film session. However, he was soon back in the fold and BLACK SABBATH recorded their first Rodger Bain produced album for a miserly £600 on a four-track machine. (Interesting to note as an aside that the engineer for the first two albums was none other than 'Colonel' Tom Allom, himself later to find fame as a producer for JUDAS PRIEST).

The band's first product as BLACK SABBATH sunk without trace. A single, 'Wicked Woman (Don't Play Your Evil Games With Me)', a cover of THE CROWS track, had seen a release in January 1970. However, in February, the album *Black Sabbath* emerged upon an unsuspecting world, laden with many what are now widely regarded as all-time classics; such as 'Black Sabbath', 'The Wizard' and 'N.I.B.' The latter was allegedly at the time thought to be 'Nativity In Black' but is actually a strange reference to the shape of Butler's beard! The album's almost Neanderthal bludgeoning heaviness and thick industrial riffing took rock fans by storm. Quite simply the band had delivered a unique brand of hard rock on the unsuspecting masses. The debut reached Number 8 in the British charts with virtually no assistance from radio airplay.

Live dates to promote the album saw the band opening up proceedings in Cardiff. The British tour would include such salubrious venues as the East Ham Dukes Head, Salisbury's Alexis Disco and the Croydon Greyhound. The band would venture into Germany, appearing at festivals alongside RORY GALLAGHER, DEEP PURPLE, FREE, STATUS QUO and BLACK WIDOW. The band also played later British shows including a support to PINK FLOYD. The group returned to Germany in August.

Shortly after wrapping up recording for their second album in June of 1970, provisionally titled *War Pigs*, again with Rodger Bain, in August 1970 BLACK SABBATH played the 10th Plumpton Jazz and Blues festival alongside HUMBLE PIE and YES. Prior to the album release the record company changed the album title to *Paranoid*. The record company objected to *War Pigs* due to the prevailing Vietnam War and also as there was a feeling 'Paranoid' could be a possible hit. The 'War Pigs' title itself had been changed, the original composition entitled 'Walpurgis'.

The single 'Paranoid' reached Number 4, (which still remains BLACK

Selected Ozzy-Related Acts From The Rockdetector Files

SABBATH's biggest hit to date), with the album reaching the dizzy heights of Number 1! The album, with the now more renowned classics such as 'Hand Of Doom', 'Fairies Wear Boots' and 'Iron Man', had BLACK SABBATH exploring a much more varied field of interests than its predecessor's predilection for the occult.

In America the second album reached Number 12 and settled in for a long chart stay, eventually clocking up a 65week residency. The band's first American shows also occurred, with support slots to MOUNTAIN prior to a headline tour.

There would be virtually no respite for the quartet as live promotion for the sophomore outing saw the band back on the road in the UK during September starting off in Wales yet again – this time at the Swansea Brangwyn Hall. Three shows in Switzerland were undertaken before a short burst of live activity in the Low Countries and by October BLACK SABBATH were putting in inaugural gigs in Scandinavia. The close of the month witnessed another first as a Philadelphia appearance signalled the start of a long trail of roadwork in the United States. BLACK SABBATH's first American trip would also see a run of three San Francisco Fillmore West gigs opening up for ARTHUR LEE'S LOVE and the JAMES GANG.

August 1971 saw the release of the last Rodger Bain produced BLACK SABBATH album *Master Of Reality*. The record peaked at Number 5 in the British charts, but provided the band with a strong 'out of the box' seller in America, being certified gold before its release.

The band backed up this success Stateside by a lengthy bout of touring, which by this time was beginning to take it's toll both mentally and physically on the individual members. *Volume 4* (originally to be titled *Snowblind*) gave the band another top ten British album and featured the classic ballad 'Changes', featuring YES keyboard player RICK WAKEMAN, alongside the more brutal 'Snowblind'.

Completists may wish to know that TONY IOMMI also recorded a session for FREEDOM, later SNAFU vocalist BOBBY HARRISON's solo album 'The Funkist'. FREEDOM were also part of Patrick Meehan's management stable and the band opened for BLACK SABBATH on numerous occasions. Titled *The Funkist* the album saw a release in America on the Capitol label in 1973.

The band returned to America to work on *Volume 4*'s follow up but found for the first time their flow of ideas had ebbed. Relocating to rehearse in the suitably spooky setting of a Welsh castle dungeon Iommi came up with the classic riff for the track 'Sabbath Bloody Sabbath' and the creative juices started to flow once more. In late 1973 BLACK SABBATH released the renowned *Sabbath Bloody Sabbath* album to worldwide critical acclaim.

For live work, keyboard player Gerry Woodruffe was added and BLACK SABBATH put in one of their most important American appearances at the California Jam festival in 1974 alongside EMERSON LAKE & PALMER and DEEP PURPLE, playing to an audience of over quarter of a million people.

However, touring excesses and managerial nightmares had taken the band to breaking point, with TONY IOMMI and OZZY OSBOURNE reportedly becoming ever more confrontational. By now the band had shifted their busi-

Ozzy Osbourne

ness affairs to the notorious Don Arden. 1975's *Sabotage* kept the flame alive and the band put in another enormous American tour supported by KISS. The *Sabotage* album included a rarity for the band as initial copies included an unaccredited track 'Blow The Jug'. This was actually BILL WARD singing the NITTY GRITTY DIRT BAND track captured unawares by a studio engineer. Later pressings do not include this moment.

The compilation *We Sold Our Souls For Rock 'n' Roll* charted well too, but many thought the 1976 experimental effort *Technical Ecstasy* to be way below par. The album did include a first for the band though as Ward took lead vocals for the first time ever on the track 'It's Alright'. American dates saw the band on the road supported by the unlikely duo of REO SPEEDWAGON and THE RAMONES.

In November 1977 Osbourne announced he was bowing out from the band. Ozzy set about creating a fresh band with NECROMANDUS guitarist Barry Dunnery but due to the chaotic circumstances prevailing at the time this project floundered. Another stab at building a solo band found Ozzy in league with former DIRTY TRICKS personnel guitarist John Frazer-Binnie, bass player Terry Horbury and drummer Andy Bierne but just as this group readied themselves for rehearsals in London Osbourne promptly rejoined BLACK SABBATH.

In the interim BLACK SABBATH had endeavoured to fill the void with ex-IDLE RACE, FLEETWOOD MAC and SAVOY BROWN vocalist David Walker. Recordings were made with Walker for the next album, but the liaison was short-lived and, scrapping the previous songs, Osbourne was enticed back for one last album *Never Say Die*, a record featuring HIGHWAY's John Elstar on harmonica. The only track to surface from the Walker era was a version of 'Junior's Eyes' on the bootleg *Archangel Rides Again*. Walker later rejoined SAVOY BROWN.

Touring Britain in 1978, BLACK SABBATH appeared tired and uninspired; a state of affairs sharply put into focus by having the youthful VAN HALEN as guests stealing the honours from the headliners throughout the tour. Upon the tour's completion OZZY OSBOURNE quit for the last time, eventually resurfacing as a solo artist under the initial band handle of BLIZZARD OF OZZ for an immensely successful post BLACK SABBATH career.

The past reared its head with the release of a live album *Live At Last*. Hardly the greatest sound quality and issued with no involvement from the band, the album at least gave fan's an 'official' live recording of the Osbourne fronted line-up. Such was BLACK SABBATH's standing that despite misgivings *Live At Last* charted high.

In 1980, BLACK SABBATH announced that former ELF and RAINBOW vocalist Ronnie James Dio had joined the fold. Butler also departed and for a while was supplanted by WORLD OF OZ/QUARTZ man Geoff Nichols. As Nichols shifted over to the keyboard role (a role he has occupied ever since, sometimes as bona fide band member or, more often than not, as hired hand), ex-RAINBOW bassist Craig Gruber took the role. Apparently at this juncture the band was merely to be titled SABBATH. By the time of recording for their comeback album Butler had returned along with the full band name.

Management and legal hassles surrounded the band as the pressure was on

Selected Ozzy-Related Acts From The Rockdetector Files

for a farewell tour with Ozzy, but despite the adversities BLACK SABBATH came up trumps with a massively successful album entitled *Heaven And Hell*. According to some reports many of Gruber's bass lines were left intact for the finished record but the American did not want his name to appear anywhere on the finished package.

Produced by Martin Birch, this record spawned many classics, including 'Children Of The Sea', the title track and even a hit single in 'Neon Nights', which saw BLACK SABBATH once more on the TV show *Top Of The Pops*. Dio, a vocalist of quite awesome talents, certainly lent the epic touch of majesty Iommi needed as a foil for his increasingly monolithic riffing and fittingly *Heaven And Hell* soon racked up over a million sales in America.

BLACK SABBATH put on a monstrous tour of America with BLUE OYSTER CULT billed the 'Black n' Blue' tour. Support came from MOLLY HATCHET and RIOT. However, shortly after the album was recorded, Ward was unceremoniously replaced mid-tour, as the years on the road finally took their toll on his health and sense of purpose with the band. Members of MOLLY HATCHET were later to claim that such was the magnitude of ill-luck BLACK SABBATH were dragging around with them that at one open air show a solitary cloud deluged rain onto BLACK SABBATH on stage leaving the audience completely dry!

BLACK SABBATH drafted in ex-AXIS, BRUZER and DERRINGER drummer Vinnie Appice, who, incidentally, was asked to join OZZY OSBOURNE's new band at the same time but had declined.

Maintaining their momentum BLACK SABBATH swiftly turned out another spectacular album in *Mob Rules* which, if anything, saw BLACK SABBATH getting even heavier. Strangely the album artwork, by artist Greg Hildebrandt, sparked rumours that amidst the rubble strewn about in the foreground of the painting was the barely disguised legend 'Kill Ozzy'!

The band would make their mark on the British singles charts once again with the title track as Dio had proven that *Heaven And Hell* was no one-off and delivered yet another quality clutch of songs. In America the album fell short of the platinum sales mark but still bolstered the band's reputation.

The subsequent tour, kicking off with a show in Hawaii to 20,000 people, witnessed BLACK SABBATH solidifying their return to the fore. Sadly, prior to the release of a proposed double live album *Live Evil*, Dio left amidst a cloud of insults and accusations.

Bizarrely, BLACK SABBATH accused Dio of sneaking in the studio after the rest of the band had gone, to push up the vocal levels on *Live Evil*. To cap it all Osbourne had issued a double live album *Speak Of The Devil* chock full of BLACK SABBATH classics as performed by his band stealing the band's fire for *Live Evil*. The press were only too eager to fan the flames and keep the verbal feud alive, which naturally succeeded in dragging the once glorious name of BLACK SABBATH down into the mud. BLACK SABBATH would, directly due to Tony Iommi's stoicism, never lay down arms but were about to enter turbulent times.

Vinnie Appice was given the push along with Dio and the drummer joined the singer in forming DIO during 1983. The debut DIO album was widely regarded as a remarkable Metal album (with sales to match) and a big point-

Ozzy Osbourne

er to the direction BLACK SABBATH would have gone had Dio stayed the course.

The band's next move took the rock world by total surprise as it was announced that BLACK SABBATH's new singer was none other than former DEEP PURPLE man Ian Gillan alongside a reinstated BILL WARD. Many GILLAN fans felt betrayed, as Gillan had, only weeks before, quit a British tour purporting to be severely affected with a throat infection that would put him out of action for months. GILLAN band members also leaked the news that an abortive attempt at putting DEEP PURPLE back together again had prompted the singer's move. When this proposed union faltered Gillan got the welcome call from BLACK SABBATH.

Bill Ward was also reinstated for recording having been pulled from his latest venture MAX HAVOC.

The ensuing album *Born Again*, featuring an incredibly garish sleeve designed by *Kerrang!* art director Krusher Joule, was slated by critics, and the combination of Gillan and BLACK SABBATH certainly jarred with many fans. Regardless, an equal number praised this strange alliance. The record still achieved a high British chart placing and good international sales. (Someone in GUNS N' ROSES certainly had been listening. Spot the widely recognised identical riff!)

Shortly after recording *Born Again* Ward was forced to quit due to recurring health problems – reforging ties with MAX HAVOC on the production front – and was quickly replaced by ELECTRIC LIGHT ORCHESTRA drummer Bev Bevan. Headlining the Reading festival that year BLACK SABBATH rubbed salt in the wounds by dragging out DEEP PURPLE's 'Smoke On The Water' as an encore.

Incidentally, the notorious Stonehenge stageset scene in spoof Rockumentary 'This Is Spinal Tap' was strongly rumoured to have been based on actual events surrounding the BLACK SABBATH stage set for the *Born Again* tour, with the finished 'stones' being too big to fit into venues!

Controversy continued to follow the latest incarnation of the band wherever they roamed. At a gig in Zwolle, Holland, one insulted fan even threw a wheelchair on stage in protest at the sullying of the BLACK SABBATH legend. An American tour, with LITA FORD as opener, proved less than successful and this line-up soon fell apart, harried by the press from all quarters. In 1984 BLACK SABBATH was in turmoil. Without a vocalist the band were in consultation with producer Spencer Proffer regarding possibly working together on an album. Proffer was a hot ticket having worked on the recent QUIET RIOT number one album *Metal Health*. The producer suggested BLACK SABBATH hook up with former STEELER vocalist Ron Keel. The young American passed the audition and cut a series of demos. However, relations between Proffer and BLACK SABBATH were curtailed and Keel was also put out of the frame. This was not before news stories of his tenure with the band were leaked though. Keel went on to major label success with his own eponymous band KEEL as BLACK SABBATH began the hunt once more for a singer.

Finally the band announced that Ward had rejoined and unveiled new vocalist, an American, David Donato, whose past credits listed various small

Selected Ozzy-Related Acts From The Rockdetector Files

time Californian club bands, such as HERO, HEADSHAKER and VIRGIN. The tape that secured Donato the job was recorded with ex DEEP PURPLE bassist GLENN HUGHES and KISS guitarist Mark Norton in a band titled DALI. But within weeks Donato was out of the picture, later to emerge as frontman to ex-KISS guitarist Mark Norton's act WHITE TIGER.

July 13th 1985 Live Aid event provided the catalyst for an impromptu reunion of the original BLACK SABBATH, but negotiations for a more permanent venture proved fruitless and Geezer Butler returned to Britain to set up a more AOR orientated act that performed a handful of club shows.

The line-up for the GEEZER BUTLER BAND included guitarist Pedro Howse, vocalist Richie Callison and drummer John Mee. A later line up had ex-BIRD OF PREY vocalist Kyle Michaels fronting the band, later of MASI. It was for the initial auditions for what was originally planned as Iommi's solo album *Seventh Star* that the American TV evangelist Jeff Fenholt actually rehearsed with the band for a short period.

Fenholt claims to have been a 'member' of the band between January and May 1985 and demos recorded with Iommi have been posted on the web. Former ARMAGEDDON vocalist Fenholt now often puts in appearances on evangelical TV shows during which claims are made that he was a member of the band. Immediately after his BLACK SABBATH liaison Fenholt fronted JOSHUA for one album then DRIVER for a brief period. Strangely Fenholt apparently became involved with the widow of famed surrealist artist Salvador Dali, recording in her studio. Fenholt's parents were later to sue their own son for $12,000,000 in damages after he claimed they had beaten him as a child.

With BLACK SABBATH effectively falling apart, TONY IOMMI (who had been dating former RUNAWAYS guitarist LITA FORD) got back to business by recording a solo album entitled *Seventh Star*. The album was originally to have featured three vocalists in Ronnie James Dio, JUDAS PRIEST's Rob Halford and ex-DEEP PURPLE and TRAPEZE star GLENN HUGHES. As it turned out, Hughes cut all the songs.

Persuaded by management and record company, this album was eventually to see the light of day under the rather unwieldy title of *Black Sabbath Featuring Tony Iommi* and paradoxically was also to be one of the band's brightest moments musically.

The album gave Iommi more freedom to explore the bluesier side of his nature and, combined with an awesome vocal display from Hughes, *Seventh Star*, produced by Jeff Glixman, is without doubt a classic album.

Iommi formed a new band around this album with Hughes, drummer Eric Singer, ex-AMERICADE and WHITE LION bassist Dave 'The Beast' Spitz and long-time keyboard player Geoff Nichols.

The American tour started out in Cleveland on March 21st with support acts W.A.S.P. and ANTHRAX, but Hughes still suffered from unreliability and alleged drug-related problems. The singer claimed to have been punched the day before the debut gig by a member of BLACK SABBATH's crew and that blood was choking his throat, thus affecting his performance. Whatever the real cause the rest of the band were concerned enough to rehearse a stand-by singer in RAY GILLEN.

Ozzy Osbourne

Upon discovering Gillen sound checking with the band Hughes quit following a Connecticut show on March 29th, leaving Gillen to pick up the pieces. The following European tour, with support act ZENO, played to half-empty houses despite the excellence of the new material and superior style of Gillen's vocals. It seemed the fans had simply had enough of constant line-up changes.

BLACK SABBATH retired to the studio, aided by producer Jeff Glixman. Unfortunately, Glixman upped and left midway through recording. His place was taken by Vic Coppersmith who lasted little longer. Further turmoil followed as Gillen did not stick around long enough to finish recording the next album *Eternal Idol*, opting instead to join former OZZY OSBOURNE guitarist JAKE E. LEE's new Blues Rock act BADLANDS. Gillen would die tragically young in 1994. His legacy with BLACK SABBATH remains with a set of highly sought-after bootleg recordings of the original album sessions. Singer also quit during recording to join GARY MOORE (and later KISS). Former RAINBOW and OZZY OSBOURNE bassist Bob Daisley was enlisted to help the band out of a tight spot as producer Chris Tsangarides finally finished the album.

Regrouping yet again, Iommi pulled in Birmingham's TONY MARTIN, previously with THE ALLIANCE and TOBRUK, to fill the vacant vocal spot. *Eternal Idol* showcased Martin's vocal abilities, unfortunately tainted by a remarkable resemblance to Dio. Despite the undoubted quality of the songs displayed on the album, indeed *Eternal Idol* is often hailed as an overlooked classic, these could do little to stem the tide and it fared badly in the charts. Touring was erratic and a massive *faux pas* by the band resulting from gigs at South Africa's Sun City venue, forced the band's management to issue a formal apology upon their return. BLACK SABBATH then took to the road in Europe, with ex-VIRGINIA WOLF bassist Jo Burt in the ranks.

1988 BLACK SABBATH put in a surprise low-key appearance at a local night club, the Oldbury Top Spot, performing for charity. A lucky handful of fans witnessed one of the strangest ever BLACK SABBATH line-ups for this one-off gig comprised of Iommi, Martin, drummer Bev Bevan and keyboardist Geoff Nichols handling bass duties.

An amusing BLACK SABBATH-related story emerged in April '88 when *Kerrang!* magazine ran an 'exclusive' story related to plans for top Welsh crooner Tom Jones to join the band, the combination revealing their intention to record a concept album and undertake a tour based upon the dual subjects of bullfighting and Welsh mining. The story was, of course, a well-conceived April Fool's Day hoax enjoyed by both Iommi and Tom Jones!

By this time not only had the fans stomached enough but Vertigo dropped the band shortly after *Eternal Idol*'s release. Undaunted, BLACK SABBATH signed to Miles Copeland's IRS label and set about rebuilding their career with a clutch of strong album releases, kicking off with *The Headless Cross*. A new album naturally witnessed a further line-up shuffle, with Iommi and Martin drafting in ex-RAINBOW, WHITESNAKE and MICHAEL SCHENKER GROUP drummer COZY POWELL and little known bassist Lawrence Cottle. The latter had made his mark previously on GARY MOORE's *After The War* album and with sessions for ERIC CLAPTON.

Selected Ozzy-Related Acts From The Rockdetector Files

For live work Cottle was supplanted by former WHITESNAKE and VOW WOW bassist Neil Murray. Still, *Headless Cross* proved a welcome return to form and saw strong sales across Europe. The album sold particularly well in Europe and Scandinavia, rebuilding a great degree of BLACK SABBATH's lost credibility. BLACK SABBATH toured Russia with Brit female Rockers GIRLSCHOOL, Europe with AXXIS as guests before American dates supported by METAL CHURCH and KINGDOM COME.

Another superb album *Tyr*, loosely based on Norse mythology – Tyr being the Viking War God – found BLACK SABBATH solidifying their return. Shows in Europe were opened by CIRCUS OF POWER.

In late 1991 the band suffered a serious setback when Powell was badly injured. The drummer's horse, Pip, suffered a heart attack and fell on Powell, fracturing his hip.

BLACK SABBATH continuously kept negotiating with OZZY OSBOURNE for his return, but in 1992, following many false starts, Iommi and Butler opted finally for the next best thing by teaming up once more with Dio.

Geezer Butler had jammed with DIO in America on the 'Lock Up The Wolves' tour performing 'Neon Nights', after which the proposal to join forces once more was mooted. The idea was a necessary step for both parties as DIO had suffered from less than capacity attendances on their American tour and BLACK SABBATH were in limbo following Ozzy's opt-out of reunion plans. With Dio rejoining, TONY MARTIN pursued a solo project, releasing a 1992 album for Vertigo in Germany. He would also contribute lead vocals to two MISHA CALVIN albums.

Powell's position was taken by Vinnie Appice. The resulting album was the Mack produced *Dehumanizer*, which, despite being a heavyweight offering, failed to capture previous Dio-era glories, mainly due to a clutch of mediocre songs.

BLACK SABBATH toured Europe followed by a stint in America where Ozzy was nailing the lid on his live work by performing his last two shows at Costa Mesa. The Oz invited BLACK SABBATH to play on the same bill then reunite for a few songs one last time following his performance. The idea was anathema to Dio, who promptly announced he was quitting once more. This was not before another ugly war of words had ensued, including a fax to journalists from the Ozzy management camp detailing the paltry attendance figures DIO the band had mustered last time they played the Costa Mesa venue. Remarkably BLACK SABBATH did play at the Ozzy shows with JUDAS PRIEST vocalist Rob Halford fronting the band, the singer having learnt the entire set in two days!

During all this activity ex-members Cozy Powell and Neil Murray refounded one of Cozy's old acts COZY POWELL's HAMMER with guitarist MARIO PARGA and singer Peter Oliver. This line-up only lasted one gig before the recruitment of another BLACK SABBATH face TONY MARTIN. The band toured Europe billed as TONY MARTIN & FRIENDS. Powell and Murray would stick together to form SAINTS AND SINNERS.

1994 saw another excellent, if overlooked, album *Cross Purposes* surfacing. Although initially planned as an Iommi/Butler project album, akin to

Ozzy Osbourne

Iommi's *Seventh Star*, record company pressure saw its release under the BLACK SABBATH banner.

SABBATH toured America once again, with vocalist Tony Martin and new drummer Bobby Rondinelli (ex-RAINBOW) this time, in an all British Metal package with MOTÖRHEAD, prior to a well-received European jaunt with '70s BLACK SABBATH idolising support act CATHEDRAL and Americans GODSPEED. Still, in August 1994, Rondinelli quit prior to dates in South America and his place on the drum stool was once more in the hands of original member BILL WARD.

The BLACK SABBATH 'tribute' album *Nativity In Black* was launched at the Los Angeles Foundations Forum. Essentially a selection of up-and-coming, mainly American acts such as BIOHAZARD, WHITE ZOMBIE and TYPE O NEGATIVE paying homage to their heroes, the album nonetheless featured some interesting combinations; such as OZZY OSBOURNE and THERAPY?'s rendition of 'Iron Man' and MEGADETH performing 'Paranoid' . Also included was a track by the BULLRING BRUMMIES, a studio outfit consisting of JUDAS PRIEST/FIGHT vocalist Rob Halford, Geezer Butler, FIGHT guitarist Brian Tilse and THE OBSESSED guitarist Wino.

With one more original BLACK SABBATH member back in the line-up another one departed. Geezer Butler quit in September 1995, going on to work on a solo album under the band handle of G//Z/R. By the following month it was announced that the group had reinstated the *Headless Cross/Tyr* era rhythm section of Neil Murray and COZY POWELL, alongside TONY IOMMI and TONY MARTIN.

Unfortunately, the resulting album, *Forbidden*, did not match the class of its predecessors, sounding rushed and lacking overall sound quality. The somewhat pedestrian production was handled by BODY COUNT guitarist Ernie C. and the album featured vocalist ICE T. guesting on the lead cut 'Illusion Of Power'.

Still, BLACK SABBATH once more set out on tour in America, co-headlining with MOTÖRHEAD for a second time. Prior to the end of these dates Powell was forced to leave to deal with personal problems and in came Bobby Rondinelli yet again to complete the schedule.

In mid-1996 it appeared that TONY IOMMI was once more working with Rob Halford for an album project, although the former JUDAS PRIEST vocalist still had commitments to his new Industrial project TWO. These sessions were subsequently put on ice and Iommi began recording solo material with his old ally GLENN HUGHES and former TRAPEZE and JUDAS PRIEST drummer Dave Holland for a projected solo album.

Before this project was finalised however, and from out of the blue, BLACK SABBATH with its classic line-up relented to fan pressure and reunited.

OZZY OSBOURNE had put together a touring extravaganza in America, modestly titled 'Ozz-fest'. The bill included his own band together with PANTERA, COAL CHAMBER and POWERMAN 5000 to which the classic BLACK SABBATH were due to headline. Osbourne, Iommi and Butler forged the reunion, but Ward felt unable to commit himself citing health rea-

Selected Ozzy-Related Acts From The Rockdetector Files

sons, both physical and mental.

BLACK SABBATH undertook the tour, which established itself as one of the biggest draws on the American touring circuit that year, aided by OZZY OSBOURNE & FAITH NO MORE drummer Mike Bordin.

Whilst the American dates were under full steam Butler put out his second, and highly commendable, solo affair with his band now dubbed GEEZER, in the form of *Black Science*. Enterprising bootleggers had also got hold of the Iommi/Hughes/Holland studio recordings and cheekily issued them as *Eighth Star*. Meantime, ex-drummer Bobby Rondinelli would be announced as joining BLUE OYSTER CULT in February 1997.

The BLACK SABBATH legend was kept alive by the release of Ozzy's compilation album, *The Ozzman Cometh*. Alongside more familiar solo Ozzy outings the CD also boasted four early unreleased BLACK SABBATH tracks with demo versions of 'Fairies Wear Boots', 'Behind The Wall Of Sleep', 'War Pigs' and 'Black Sabbath'.

The band, fronted by Ozzy, announced two shows at the Birmingham NEC in early December '97, bringing FEAR FACTORY as support. Both shows sold out with a live album issued in 1998 titled *Reunion*. However, on May 19th Ward, who had been suffering chest pains for some time, suffered what was later discovered to be a mild heart attack. With Ward's health still a subject of concern Vinny Appice was pulled from the ranks of DIO in 1998 to occupy the drum stool. Ward took most of the summer out recuperating until, after checks to see if he could to resume his rightful position, the drummer did attend the BLACK SABBATH headlined 'Ozzfest' at Milton Keynes in June where to everyone's amusement Osbourne welcomed him on stage then pulled Ward's trousers down in front of 60,000 bemused onlookers.

SABBATH put in their last ever live gigs dubbed 'The Last Supper' at Birmingham's NEC in late December 1999 with Ward back behind the kit. Appice created his own act HUNGER FARM.

2000 found Iommi busy on his solo album with numerous high profile guests including Ozzy and PANTERA's Phil Anselmo. The guitarist did take time out to perform with impromptu club act BELCH, a band that featured his ex-SABBATH friend Bev Bevan and comedian Jasper Carrott on vocals. Osbourne himself was hard at work on a further solo album. TONY IOMMI, after three decades, finally got around to issuing his first solo album proper *Iommi*. Both Osbourne and Ward were included on the track 'Who's Fooling Who'. Ward meantime was still endeavouring to complete his third solo album provisionally titled *Beyond Aston*. A projected reissue of his first album *Ward One – Along The Way* was shelved when two songs that featured Ozzy on lead vocals created business complications.

BLACK SABBATH did reunite for a summer 2000 show although after the event they probably wished they hadn't. A surprise performance after an OZZY OSBOURNE gig at the Anaheim 'Weenie Roast' festival ended in debacle when a revolving stage snagged the band's gear resulting in a long embarrassing silence and lengthy delays.

Undaunted BLACK SABBATH would rise yet again during 2001 demonstrating renewed vigour as the main attraction at the California ESPN Action, Sports & Music Awards ceremony on April 7th.

Ozzy Osbourne

This showing would provide a taster for another full-blown 'Ozzfest' global touring festival. Backing up the steadfast Brummies were contemporary acts such as SLIPKNOT, TOOL, PAPA ROACH, AMEN, SOULFLY, DISTURBED and BLACK LABEL SOCIETY. MARILYN MANSON would also figure but only for the American dates. Even Geezer Butler's son got involved with his act APARTMENT 26. Also announced was that Ozzy's plans for a solo album would be put on hold whilst recording of a brand new BLACK SABBATH album was undertaken.

A warm-up show just prior to the UK Ozzfest was held at the Birmingham Academy on May 22nd with the band donating all proceeds from the gig to the homeless persons charity St. Basil's. Another display of nostalgia came in October with the long overdue officially sanctioned release of archive live material. Divine Recordings, the label established by Sharon Osbourne, would announce the release live tapes culled from the 'Sabotage' world tour entitled suitably *Live in '75*. However, just after a track listing and release had been set the album was cancelled.

May of 2001 also witnessed a treat for fans when ex-BLACK SABBATH men Tony Martin and Neil Murray joined RONDINELLI, the band spearheaded by another Sabbath veteran Bobby Rondinelli. Martin would also find time to front BAILEY'S COMET for a British club tour and promote the *Cage 2* album, his second in union with Italian guitarist Dario Mollo.

Quite surreally, an Estonian outfit RONDELLUS made quite an impact upon the BLACK SABBATH faithful in March of 2002. The group of classically trained medieval folk artists re-interpreted an entire album of Sabs classics sung in operatic style, played on original medieval instruments with lyrics translated into Latin!

Albums:
BLACK SABBATH, Vertigo VO 6 (1970)
PARANOID, Vertigo 6360 011 (1970)
MASTER OF REALITY, Vertigo 6360 050 (1971)
VOLUME 4, Vertigo 6360 071 (1972)
SABBATH BLOODY SABBATH, Vertigo WWA 005 (1973)
SABOTAGE, NEMS 9119 001 (1975)
WE SOLD OUR SOULS FOR ROCK 'N' ROLL, NEMS 6641 335 (1976)
TECHNICAL ECSTASY, Vertigo 9102 750 (1976)
ATTENTION VOL. 1, Fontana 6438 057 (1975)
ATTENTION VOL. II, WWA WWA 101 (1975)
THE ORIGINAL, NEMS (1976)
GREATEST HITS, NEMS NEL 6009 (1977)
NEVER SAY DIE, Vertigo 9102 751 (1978)
ROCK LEGENDS, Vertigo 6321 120 (1978) (Australian release)
STARGOLD, NEMS 0084.501 (197-)
LIVE AT LAST, NEMS BS001 (1980)
HEAVEN AND HELL, Vertigo 9102 752 (1980)
ROCK HEAVIES, Vertigo (1980)
MOB RULES, Mercury 6V02119 (1981)
LIVE EVIL, Vertigo SAB 10 (1983)

Selected Ozzy-Related Acts From The Rockdetector Files

BORN AGAIN, Vertigo VERL 8 (1983)
BEST OF BLACK SABBATH, NEMS (1983) (Picture Disc)
30 ANOS DE MUSICA ROCK, Vertigo 8222971 (1985) (Mexican release)
HAND OF DOOM, Victoria JS90164 (1984) (Spanish box set release)
THE BLACK SABBATH COLLECTION, Castle CCSLP 109 (1985)
SEVENTH STAR, Vertigo VERH 29 (1986)
THE ETERNAL IDOL, Vertigo VERH 51 (1987)
BLACKEST SABBATH, Vertigo (1989)
BLACKEST SABBATH, Vertigo 838 818-2 (1989) (UK version)
HEADLESS CROSS, IRS EIRSA 1002 (1990)
BACKTRACKIN', Knight (1990)
BACKTRACKIN', Masterpiece TRK CD 103 (1990) (UK Version)
THE BLACK SABBATH COLLECTION VOLUME II, Castle CCS CD 199 (1990)
TYR, IRS EIRSA 1038(1991)
THE OZZY OSBOURNE YEARS, Essential ESB CD 12 (1991)
THE OZZY OSBOURNE YEARS, Essential ESB 142 (1991) (Vinyl Version)
THE MASTERS OF HEAVY METAL, Castle CHC 7022 (1991)
THE BLACK SABBATH STORY, Castle CHC 7028 (1991)
DEHUMANIZER, IRS EIRS CD 1064 (1992)
CROSS PURPOSES, IRS (1994)
IRON MAN, Spectrum 550720-2 (1994)
CROSS PURPOSES LIVE, PMI 7243 491314 3 9 (1995)
FORBIDDEN, IRS 7243 8 30620 2 7 (1995)
1970-1983 BETWEEN HEAVEN AND HELL, Rawpower RAWCD 104 (1995)
THE SABBATH STONES, IRS 7243 8 37532 2 2 (1996)
UNDER WHEELS OF CONFUSION, Essential ESF CD 419 (1996)
REUNION-LIVE, Epic 491954-9 (1998)
THE BEST OF BLACK SABBATH, Rawpower RAW DD145 (2000)
BESTSELLER, Barracuda (2000) (Russian release)
ROCK CHAMPIONS, EMI (2001)

DESPERADO (USA / UK)
Line-Up: Dee Snider (vocals), Bernie Tormé (guitar), Mark Russell (bass), Clive Burr (drums)

One of Heavy Metal's enduring 'might-have-beens'. The all star DESPERADO, convened during 1989 by the larger-than-life former TWISTED SISTER vocalist DEE SNIDER, ex-GILLAN and OZZY OSBOURNE guitarist BERNIE TORMÉ, bass player Mark Russell and IRON MAIDEN drummer Clive Burr, managed just one gig (in Birmingham, UK) and an unreleased album.

Elektra, just weeks before the album launch, mysteriously scotched the entire project. BERNIE TORMÉ resumed his solo career. Snider and Russell stuck together to found WIDOWMAKER, with Snider's TWISTED SISTER colleague Joe Franco on drums and latter day SAVATAGE (amongst many

Ozzy Osbourne

others) guitarist Al Pitrelli, taking DESPERADO songs with them. Further DESPERADO material would see the light of day on Snider's solo album *Never Let The Bastards Grind You Down*.

The DESPERADO album leaked out in 1996 on the Destroyer label, most likely a semi-official issue via one of the band members.

Albums:
BLOODIED BUT UNBOWED, Destroyer (1996)

DIRTY TRICKS (UK)
Line-Up: Kenny Stewart (vocals), John Frazer Binnie (guitar), Terry Horbury (bass), Andy Bierne (drums)

Meat 'n' potatoes hard rockers DIRTY TRICKS formed in 1974 and delivered three unpretentious Hard Rock albums for the Polydor label. The band debuted live at London's Marquee Club as openers to DUX DELUXE during January of 1975. DIRTY TRICKS debuted with an eponymous Rodger Bain produced set promoted by support tours in the UK to both ARGENT and BUDGIE.

In June of 1975 Australian drummer John Lee, a former member of DINGOES, BLACKFEATHER and ARIEL, joined the fold. Lee would quit following the third album *Hit And Run* and was superseded by Andy Bierne. Tony Visconti would be on hand to produce the band's second effort. Touring for this release would witness British support dates to the STREETWALKERS and gigs across America as guests to CHEAP TRICK, BLUE OYSTER CULT and BOB SEGAR. The group bowed out in 1977 with *Hit And Run*, another Visconti produced affair.

After the group had finally called it quits the Binnie/Horbury/Bierne triumvirate put in some rehearsals with OZZY OSBOURNE, then having just decamped from BLACK SABBATH. This proposed band folded as Osbourne duly rejoined BLACK SABBATH.

Bassist Terry Horbury would then join VARDIS in 1983, guitarist John Frazer Binnie wound up joining the high profile ROGUE MALE in the early '80s. Bierne eventually turned up in PRAYING MANTIS, SCORCHED EARTH and GRAND PRIX. Stewart meantime hooked up with erstwhile SIDEWINDER and STALLION guitarist STUART SMITH to found FRENCH KISS, a band unit completed by drummer Kelvin 'Yatta' Yates. Stewart and Smith later relocated to America forging INFORMER.

DIRTY TRICKS members Binnie, Horbury and Stewart evolved into tribute band STAIRWAY TO ZEPPELIN during the '90s fronted by one 'Robert Planet' a.k.a Kenny Stewart.

Albums:
DIRTY TRICKS, Polydor 2383 351 (1975)
NIGHTMAN, Polydor 2383 398 (1976)
HIT AND RUN, Polydor 2383 446 (1977)

Selected Ozzy-Related Acts From The Rockdetector Files
FAITH NO MORE (USA)
Line-Up: Mike Patton (vocals), Jim Martin (guitar), Bill Gould (bass), Roddy Bottum (keyboards), Mike Bordin (drums)

San Franciscans FAITH NO MORE, founded in 1980, have undoubtedly pushed the boundaries of rock in all directions with a diverse set of influences creating a new musical genre as they went. Thrash, funk, pop and hardcore are all on display but all with more than enough guitar to keep rock fans happy.

Guitarist 'Big Sick' Jim Martin had journeyed through the Californian music scene making an appearance in as many bands with widely differing musical styles. Along with drummer Mike Bordin, the guitarist had first stepped into the limelight with E.Z.Y. STREET, an act that also included in its ranks future METALLICA bassist Cliff Burton. E.Z.Y. STREET pursued the commonly-trod path of ROLLING STONES and LED ZEPPELIN covers, the line-up being finalized by vocalist Kevin Costa and rhythm guitarist Dan Magalhaeo.

This first incarnation folded when Burton quit for TRAUMA and Bordin followed suit teaming up with SHARP YOUNG MEN. The latter, wherein Bordin received his nickname 'Puffy' due to his outrageous afro hairstyle, also boasted soon-to-be FAITH NO MORE man, bassist Bill Gould.
Gould had previously been a member of THE ANIMATED, an act which featured then keyboard player Chuck Moseley.

Martin busied himself with numerous side projects appearing in many 'Battle of the Bands' contests including the three guitar crossover army of VICIOUS HATRED, a blues act with a horn section PIGS OF DEATH and AGENTS OF MISFORTUNE, yet again teaming up with Cliff Burton.

Meanwhile E.Z.Y. STREET continued evolving into RECLUSE before a very nebulous version of FAITH NO MORE kicked into gear during 1985 as SHARP YOUNG MEN recruited guitarist Mark Bowen and keyboard player Roddy Bottum alongside Bordin and Gould.

In an early line-up Courtney Love, later to be propelled to world stardom as undisputed leader of HOLE and, more significantly, the widow of NIRVANA's Kurt Cobain, featured, but she was swiftly fired. Her stay lasted four gigs.

Bowen, it was clear was not working out and so, upon Cliff Burton's recommendation Jim Martin was hired as was Chuck Moseley, leaving his then band HAIRCUTS THAT KILL.

FAITH NO MORE's self-financed debut and subsequent club tour provoked world-wide interest enough for a deal to be signed with ex-QUIET RIOT manager Warren Enter and from there to Warner Bros. subsidiary Slash Records. The resulting album *Introduce Yourself*, produced by the LOS LOBOS duo of Steve Berlin and Matt Wallace, more than justified Warner Bros. faith in the band and the accompanying single *We Care A Lot* quickly became a huge club and MTV hit. The band toured America as support to RED HOT CHILI PEPPERS in late 1987. Despite healthy sales and praiseworthy press, the band, in a foretaste of what was to come, reportedly tore itself apart resulting in the departure of Moseley, first to BAD BRAINS (leaving before recording anything) before forming his own act CEMENT.

Ozzy Osbourne

Chuck Moseley's place was taken by MR. BUNGLE's Mike Patton and the even more adventurous third album *The Real Thing* broke FAITH NO MORE out of the underground and into global chart success with a string of hit singles and well-received live shows. This progression could not hide the fact that internal disputes were constantly wracking the band as various members publicly voiced their dislike for one another. Nevertheless FAITH NO MORE toured relentlessly.

Post world tour Patton returned to his pre-FAITH NO MORE act MR. BUNGLE to record a humorous, if somewhat sick, album as well as finding time to guest for John Zorn's NAKED CITY before the band re-assembled to record the 1992 *Angel Dust* album.

The record gave the band another hit, solidifying their reputation. All of *Angel Dust's* spin-off single releases charted in Britain and provided fans with some interesting asides such as a cover of and DEAD KENNEDY's 'Let's Lynch The Landlord' as B-sides to 'A Small Victory'. A re-released format of the same A-side later in the year saw the track remixed by KILLING JOKE guitarist Youth.

1993 gave FAITH NO MORE their biggest British hit as their cover of the COMMODORES smooth ballad 'I'm Easy' peaked at Number 3. The same year a collaboration with BOO YA TRIBE also put the band back in the charts with 'Another Body Murdered' from the soundtrack to the movie *Judgement Day*.

The band themselves maintained a high live profile guesting as part of the METALLICA/GUNS N' ROSES stadium extravaganza in America and putting in an appearance at the British Phoenix Festival.

By December 1993 the all-too-obvious disagreements within the band saw the ousting of Martin (who had been more than vocal in his lack of affection for *Angel Dust*) and recruitment of MR. BUNGLE guitarist Trey Spruance.

Whilst recording a new album it was learned that Bottum would not be taking part, the musician involved in a personal battle against drug addiction. The band's touring schedule lasted a matter of months, with Spruance soon being ejected in favour of former guitar tech Dean Menta, following the release of *King For A Day*. Amidst rumours of an impending split, FAITH NO MORE were put on ice as the individual members pursued solo ventures.

Patton got to work with MR. BUNGLE once again, while Bottum created IMPERIAL TEEN releasing the *Seasick* album on London Records. Bordin leapt back into the limelight as drummer for OZZY OSBOURNE and the BLACK SABBATH reformation whilst Gould busied himself with production including a stint in Moscow with Russian Punks NIAVE.

FAITH NO MORE were to return in 1997 with the modestly titled *Album Of The Year* with new guitarist John Hudson, previously with SYSTEMS COLLAPSE. Although not a huge seller the record did provoke much laudatory and well deserved praise and the band accomplished a well-attended American theatre tour.

Ex-guitarist JIM MARTIN also returned to the fray with his debut solo offering, *Milk And Blood*, which featured a re-working of FAITH NO MORE's 'Surprise! You're Dead'.

FAITH NO MORE finally announced their collapse on April 20th 1998.

Selected Ozzy-Related Acts From The Rockdetector Files

The band had been confirmed as support to AEROSMITH on their European tour but frictions within the band proved too tortuous to endure.

Bordin continued his duties with OZZY OSBOURNE. Gould involved himself in production for acts such as Finland's CMX and German supergroup RAMMSTEIN.

Patton founded a fresh act titled FANTOMAS with noted ex-SLAYER/GRIP INC. drummer Dave Lombardo, ex-MELVINS guitarist Buzz Osbourne and MR. BUNGLE bassist Trevor Dunn. The group was later reported to be using the handle DIABOLIK. Bottum forged on with a second IMPERIAL TEEN album. Gould, in collusion with FEAR FACTORY's Dino Cazeres and Raymond Herrera, founded his own record label Kool Arrow during 2000. All three of course (albeit anonymously) also operate the notorious 'Mexican' Death Metal band BRUJERIA.

Albums:
FAITH NO MORE, Mordan (1985)
INTRODUCE YOURSELF, Slash (1987)
THE REAL THING, Slash 828 217 1 (1989)
LIVE AT THE BRIXTON ACADEMY, Slash (1991)
ANGEL DUST, Slash (1992)
KING FOR A DAY – FOOL FOR A LIFETIME, Slash (1995)
ALBUM OF THE YEAR, Slash 828 901-2 (1997)

LITA FORD (USA)

Ex-RUNAWAYS guitarist Lita Ford (real name Rosanna) struck a huge blow for female rock with a string of accomplished heavy chart albums in addition to combining stunning looks with virtuoso guitar playing.

London-born to British parents, Lita's family emigrated to America when the would-be star was a mere toddler. Getting her first guitar at the age of 11, she attended her first concert (BLACK SABBATH at Long Beach Arena) at 13. Gaining employment at a local hospital a year later, having lied about her age, she saved up $400 to buy a Gibson SG and promptly learnt the BLACK SABBATH and DEEP PURPLE back catalogues.

Lita wound up in the RUNAWAYS at 16 after substituting for the bass player in a friend's band. Kim Fowley, looking for promising female musicians in order to piece together his dream of a jailbait, all-girl Rock band, originally asked her to audition as a bassist. However, after discovering she actually played guitar was promptly blown away by her prowess and offered her the gig, only for Ford to quit after three days due to Fowley's obnoxious treatment.

Having tried to find a suitable replacement Ford was back in the band following a plea from the other members of the band asking her to return to the fold, by which time the group was holed up in Cherokee Studios in Los Angeles recording demos.

Post-RUNAWAYS, Lita intended forming a new band with the band's drummer, Sandy West, but unable to find suitable musicians the pair split. Lita worked as a beautician before picking up the guitar once more and took vocal

Ozzy Osbourne

lessons in order to train her voice for the role of a front woman. Her first post-RUNAWAYS performance came as guest guitarist on the Punk act THE STEPMOTHERS 1981 album on the RUNAWAYS cover 'American Nights'.

Signed by Mercury Records (ironically the same label that had eagerly been sold THE RUNAWAYS by the band's guru Kim Fowley), Ford hooked up with Canadian guitarist NEIL MERRYWEATHER (who produced the debut album *Out For Blood*) and drummer Dusty Watson. Both were soon replaced for slightly younger, leaner models once Ford began to tour in earnest, her live band soon comprising of ex-KNACK and MASTERS OF THE AIRWAVES bassist Randy Rand and former MOTELS drummer Randy Castillo. The latter had, just prior to hooking up with Ford been a member of guitarist MITCH PERRY's band CODE BLUE. With this line-up Ford, opened for RAINBOW and BLACK SABBATH during late 1983.

The original artwork used on the American release of *Out For Blood* (depicting a scantily clad Ford tearing apart a blood filled guitar) was considered to be too strong an image for the British end of PolyGram and thus the record was released in an extremely toned-down sleeve. The clothing was just as skimpy, but the guitar now held by Ms Ford remained intact without a drop of the red stuff to be found!

Out For Blood's follow-up, *Dancin' On The Edge* was released in 1984 and produced by Lance Quinn. Whilst Castillo played on the record, Rand had departed (joining STONE FURY then AUTOGRAPH). The bass parts were thus recorded by Hugh McDonald, a man who would replace Alec John Such in BON JOVI some ten years later.

The album also featured a couple of co-writing credits for one Jeff Lieb, who also appeared playing synthesisers and singing back-ups on the title track. Under his stage name of JEFF PARIS Mr. Lieb would create his own cult following a few years later!

For the tour Castillo was replaced by Eric Singer (later of KISS). Castillo promptly joined STONE FURY to hook up with Rand once more and would of course later journey through OZZY OSBOURNE's band and MÖTLEY CRÜE.

Lita actually recorded a third album for PolyGram, entitled *The Bride Wore Black*. The cover was to have featured Ford dressed in a specially made black wedding dress, but the album was never released and, as a result, Lita parted company with the label. She still owns the dress!

1988's Mike Chapman-produced relaunch album *Lita* was backed by an impressive arsenal of big-time managers and name session musicians. Lita was now benefiting from business guidance from Sharon Osbourne, wife of OZZY OSBOURNE, and the album featured no less than PAT BENATAR drummer Myron Grombacher as well as noted keyboard player David Ezrin. Ford had also drafted guitarist STEVE FISTER. Fister had applied to audition for OZZY OSBOURNE but was manoeuvred into Ford's camp.

The album also boasted guest appearances from ex-boyfriend MÖTLEY CRÜE bassist Nikki Sixx (who co-wrote 'Falling In And Out Of Love') and OZZY OSBOURNE himself aided a duet 'Close My Eyes Forever' which gave Lita a huge American hit single. A further album track 'Can't Catch Me' was co-written with MOTÖRHEAD's infamous LEMMY.

Selected Ozzy-Related Acts From The Rockdetector Files

Ford would hit the headlines once again, although this time for the wrong reasons, when her marriage to W.A.S.P. guitarist Chris Holmes quickly floundered. Fister decamped to join STEPPENWOLF later working with DEREK ST. HOLMES and PAT TRAVERS.

The 1991 released *Dangerous Curves* record, produced by Tom Werman, featured Matt Bissonette (A=440 / DAVID LEE ROTH) on bass, Grombacher on drums and a cameo guitar part for HEART guitarist Howard Leese.

1993 also found Lita playing herself in the American TV comedy show 'Herman's Head'

In 1994 Malibu Comics, using their Rock-It imprint, released an official LITA FORD comic book, intended to be the first in an on-going series. Certainly, the plot indicated that future editions were only a formality, a scantily-clad Lita battling with the evil forces of a thinly disguised Tipper Gore led P.M.R.C., with DEEP PURPLE's RITCHIE BLACKMORE making a mysterious cameo appearance.

Signing to the German label Zyx Records, more noted for their Techno product, Lita returned with a heavily Grunge-influenced affair simply titled *Black*, featuring fiancé Jim Gillette, ex-FASTWAY and KATMANDU vocalist Dave King and the legendary JEFF SCOTT SOTO all on backing vocals.

Lita actually married the former TUFF and NITRO front man Jim Gillette in 1995 and the pair began working on a totally new band project tentatively titled RUMBLE TRIBE.

Her other plans included the release of a second comic book and complimentary CD-ROM plus the endorsement of Gibson's new Nighthawk line of guitars.

A number of plans were, only naturally, put on hold as Lita and Jim celebrated the birth of their first child, James, in May 1997 and they were still planning to release some form of product at a later date despite rumours of a RUNAWAYS reunion that Lita was certainly very keen on.

Interestingly, to highlight Ford's popularity as a solo artist, she was still winning awards in America in 1998 despite not having released a record for three years. She beat off the current crop of female recording artists to win *Metal Edge* magazine's readers poll as 'Best Female Performer'!

During 2001 Ford, kept in the public eye by the release of an archive live album, would be resident in Florida having given birth to her second child.

Albums:
OUT FOR BLOOD, Mercury MERL 26 (1983)
DANCIN' ON THE EDGE, Vertigo VER 13 (1984)
LITA, RCA 6397-1-R (1988)
STILETTO, RCA 52090 (1990)
DANGEROUS CURVES, RCA 90592 (1991)
BEST OF LITA FORD, RCA 7863 66047-2 (1992)
BLACK, Zyx 20330-2 (1995)
LIVE GREATEST HITS, Deadline (2000)

Ozzy Osbourne

G//Z/R (UK)
Line-Up: Burton C. Bell (vocals), Pedro Howse (guitar), Geezer Butler (bass), Deen Castronovo (drums)

The first project, outside of BLACK SABBATH, of bassist Geezer Butler to find a release was the 1995 G//Z/R band. Butler had ventured out of the BLACK SABBATH confines previously in the '80s with various acts.

GEEZER BUTLER BAND of 1985 included guitarist Pedro Howse, vocalist Richie Callison and drummer John Mee. Former PERSIAN RISK vocalist Carl Sentance (later of GHOST and KROKUS) also operated with Butler briefly. A later line-up had ex-BIRD OF PREY vocalist Kyle Michaels fronting the band, later of MASI.

Sallying back and forth between BLACK SABBATH in the '80s and '90s Butler, a member of OZZY OSBOURNE's band at the time forged an extremely heavy proposition in 1995.

Joining in were FEAR FACTORY vocalist Burton C. Bell. G//Z/R also comprised Bell's fellow American Deen Castronovo (formerly with such diverse acts as WILD DOGS, BAD ENGLISH and HARDLINE) who was also part of OZZY OSBOURNE's rhythm section at the time of the album's release.

For the second album, *Black Science*, Bell had opted out due to commitments with FEAR FACTORY.

Albums:
PLASTIC PLANET, Rawpower RAWCD 105 (1995)

GEEZER (UK)
Line-Up: Clark Brown (vocals), Pedro Howse (guitar), Geezer Butler (bass), Deen Castronovo (drums)

Essentially BLACK SABBATH bassist Geezer Butler's G//Z/R solo project with a revised name, GEEZER debuted in 1997 with the *Black Science* record showcasing the vocal talents of new singer Clark Brown who replaced the unavailable FEAR FACTORY frontman Burton C. Bell.

The most amazing aspect of the *Black Science* record was that the songs were influenced by subjects far removed from the usual Heavy Metal cliched subject matter. A careful listen to the lyrics will pick up references to a multitude of passions close to Butler's heart, including Sci-Fi TV series *Captain Scarlet*, *Secret Service*, *Dr Who* and *Fireball XL5* plus Aston Villa Football Club!

Drummer Deen Castronovo, Butler's rhythm partner in the OZZY OSBOURNE band and previously with WILD DOGS and HARDLINE, would completely change musical direction back to mellower material as he landed the most prestigious of AOR drummer's positions in JOURNEY.

Brown contributes guest vocals to ex-TESTAMENT, DEATH, CANCER and OBITUARY guitarist JAMES MURPHY's 1999 *Feeding The Machine* album.

By 2000 Brown was fronting LD/50, a band including bassist Oddie

Selected Ozzy-Related Acts From The Rockdetector Files

McLaughlin, drummer Jeremy Colson and ex-FORBIDDEN and TESTAMENT guitarist Glen Alvelais. In late 2001 it was announced Brown had joined American crew BEKWENHEIMER.

Albums:
BLACK SCIENCE, Eagle EAGCD001 (1997)

ROBIN GEORGE (UK)

Guitarist / vocalist / songwriter Robin George was previously with QUARTZ, the BYRON BAND and MAGNUM before opting for a solo career and George's first solo project was LIFE with keyboard player Mark Stanway (who later went on to join MAGNUM) and ex-TRAPEZE bassist Pete Wright and drummer Dave Holland. LIFE released one single in 1980, 'Too Late'/'Castles', on the Media label.

Before launching his own project George worked as a producer working on such records as DIAMOND HEAD's *Sweet And Innocent* and releases from both QUARTZ and WITCHFINDER GENERAL.

The man's much hyped debut solo single was the 'History' 12" issued in September 1983 by Arista featuring George on vocals and guitar with old LIFE colleagues Dave Holland, by then a member of JUDAS PRIEST, on drums and the then MAGNUM keyboard player Mark Stanway.

The record was simultaneously released on 7" format under a different title and was to have also been the first guitar-shaped picture disc but was pipped to the post by DEF LEPPARD's 'Photograph'. Nevertheless, it gained George massive press attention as a guitar hero in the making and songsmith (TED NUGENT later covered 'Go Down Fighting'), including the front cover of *Kerrang!* (a feat unheard of for an unknown artist at the time), prompting Bronze Records to sign him up for the following year

George's long awaited album *Dangerous Music* eventually surfaced in 1985 and had been recorded with a long cast list of notables including Holland, bassists PHIL LYNOTT of THIN LIZZY and ace session man Pino Palidino together with the ever-faithful Mark Stanway on keyboards.

In early 1985 George assembled a touring band comprising ex-WILDLIFE bassist Phil Soussan, former MAGNUM drummer Kex Gorin and ALLIANCE keyboardist Eddie George. The latter was soon to depart for MAGNUM, although his stay in that particular outfit was extremely brief to say the least! Eddie George was not only succeeded in Robin George's band by Mark Stanway but the latter also replaced him in MAGNUM as well, Mark opting to rejoin the group after a period spent away from the ranks. In addition, George added second guitarist Huw Lucas (ex-KOREA and TROUBLE) to the band now known as DANGEROUS MUSIC after the album title.

Following a series of low-key British club gigs the band supported ULI JON ROTH across Europe in February. However, Stanway was taken ill midway through the tour and his place was temporarily filled by Alan Nelson.

In June 1985 bassist Phil Soussan chose to take up a high profile offer from the OZZY OSBOURNE band and was replaced by former RENAISSANCE man Jon Camp.

Ozzy Osbourne

Robin George was to have been a member of the reformed THIN LIZZY together with PHIL LYNOTT and drummer Brian Downey, but sadly this project was curtailed by Lynott's tragic death and with 1986 underway George was performing selected club dates with former ASIA vocalist JOHN WETTON.

The demise of his solo career prompted George to hook up with former DIAMOND HEAD mainman and vocalist Sean Harris to form NOTORIOUS. As it turned out they had chosen an apt name and a catalogue of misfortune and large investments of both time and money led to an ill-fated album release which was deleted within weeks of i's American release, mainly due to a change in record company personnel.

In 1992 George produced the *Powergame* album for Brummie Metal outfit MARSHALL LAW and worked on production for GLENN HUGHES, but was back in action playing the British club circuit in 1993 billed as Robin George's WORLD. This band featured vocalist/bassist JOHN WETTON together with EMERSON LAKE & PALMER drummer Carl Palmer and journeyman ex-RAINBOW keyboard player DON AIREY.

George would also assist ex-LED ZEPPELIN vocalist ROBERT PLANT with demos for his *Now And Zen* album. Proving his prowess once more George also was auditioned for the vacant spot left in DEF LEPPARD following Steve Clark's death. George made it into the last two candidates position. Although Vivian Campbell secured the job DEF LEPPARD gave George a guitar as a token of their respect.

Opting to later resurrect LIFE (initially with ex-MARSHALL LAW drummer Lee Morris, before, after six months, Morris left to join PARADISE LOST) George recorded an album using the handle for release in 1995. Musicians comprised vocalist Nick Tart, bassist Chris Cliff and ex-HOOTERS and SHADES OF GREY drummer Bill Rudolph. The band played a set of originals and covers at the Now And Then Records 'Gods '96' event at Maximes in Wigan prior to the independent label releasing an album's worth of material entitled Cocoon almost a year later.

Not content to sit back and rest on any laurels, Robin George actually has another solo album awaiting a deal and further material recorded with LIFE in the can.

Albums:
DANGEROUS MUSIC, Bronze BRON554 (1985)

HEAVY METAL KIDS (UK)
Line-Up: Gary Holton (vocals), Cosmo (guitar), Barry Paul (guitar), Rob Thomas (bass), John Sinclair (keyboards), Keith Boyce (drums)

Never as inspiring as their grand moniker suggested, the HEAVY METAL KIDS nonetheless possessed the ability to create rough 'n' ready rock 'n' roll. The band built themselves quite a fanbase, especially in the London area, and issued a series of commendable, if sometimes overlooked, albums. It is known that a pre-JUDAS PRIEST vocalist ROB HALFORD auditioned for the band in their early days.

Selected Ozzy-Related Acts From The Rockdetector Files

Featuring ex-BLUE MAX keyboardist DANNY PEYRONEL, the HEAVY METAL KIDS' first two albums were recorded with Peyronel and guitarist Cosmo, although Danny joined UFO in 1975 for their *No Heavy Petting* album.

The band actually split following the second album *Anvil Chorus*, but reformed with keyboard player John Sinclair and guitarist Barry Paul, although with the band's eventual demise Sinclair formed LION before joining SAVOY BROWN and then URIAH HEEP. Sinclair, besides gaining performing credits on the classic spoof movie *Spinal Tap*, would also become long-term live keyboard player for OZZY OSBOURNE, a position he enjoys to this day.

Post UFO Peyronel then journeyed back to his birthplace of Argentina to join RIFF before relocating to Spain and joining BANZAI. Whilst in Spain Peyronel created a short-lived 'supergroup' consisting of CREAM drummer GINGER BAKER, ex-MOODY BLUES and WINGS guitarist Denny Laine and ex-FAMILY and BLIND FAITH bassist Ric Grech. The project fell apart and Peyronel founded acclaimed Spanish-based rockers TARZEN.

TARZEN originally comprised Peyronel, his erstwhile BANZAI colleague Salvador Dominquez on guitar, ex-GRAND PRIX bassist Ralph Hood and Danny's brother Michel on drums. Before long Dominiquez was ousted in favour of ex-STAMPEDE, GRAND SLAM and L.A. SECRETS guitarist Lawrence Archer in 1986. Peyronel would also enjoy acclaim as a hit songwriter penning MEAT LOAF's 'Midnight At The Lost And Found' as well as songs for sultry Soul diva SADE.

Drummer Keith Boyce would find his talents employed by Blues Rock veterans SAVOY BROWN.

Chirpy frontman Gary Holton embarked on a solo career which saw a brief tenure in seminal Punk act THE DAMNED in late 1978 and a European released album. Holton also hit the British charts in 1984 with his version of 'Catch A Falling Star', The singer had found fame as a TV actor alongside Jimmy Nail, playing the (King birding), Cockney bricklayer Wayne in the ITV series *Auf Wiedersehn Pet*. Sadly, at the height of his acting career, Holton died in tragic circumstances in 1985 during filming of the second series.

The HEAVY METAL KIDS were resurrected in 2002 for an album entitled *A Hundred Skeletons*. DANNY PEYRONEL, who also issued a solo record *Make The Monkey Dance* the same year, would handle lead vocals and keyboards alongside Ronnie Thomas on bass and Keith Boyce on drums. Joining this trio would be Italian guitarist Marco Guarnerio.

Albums:
HEAVY METAL KIDS, Atlantic K 50047 (1974)
ANVIL CHORUS, Atlantic K 50143 (1975)
KITSCH, RAK SRAK 523 (1977)
CHELSEA KIDS, Razor METALP 117 (1987)
LIVE AND LOUD, Link (1989)

Ozzy Osbourne

KING KOBRA (USA)
Line-Up: Mark Free (vocals), David Michael Phillips (guitar), Mick Sweda (guitar), Johnny Rod (bass), Carmine Appice (drums)

A band that in their heyday sported a typical Los Angeles Glam look (all members having bleached hair except odd man out Carmine Appice who opted for red and black) KING KOBRA's recorded output showed a remarkable maturity and depth in both the musicianship and songwriting departments.

Formed by veteran rock drummer CARMINE APPICE, who had become a legend in his own lifetime thanks to his involvement with VANILLA FUDGE and ROD STEWART. Appice holds the dubious honour of co-writing Stewart's global smash 'Do Ya Think I'm Sexy'!

The original intention was to put a touring line-up of D.N.A. (the 'Supergroup' project he was engaged in with RICK DERRINGER) for dates in Japan. Appice was introduced to vocalist MARK FREE by guitar player Ronnie Mancuso (who was working with Appice on the VANILLA FUDGE re-union album *Mystery*). Mancuso had played with Free in the short-lived Los Angeles club band MODERN DESIGN and suggested that Free was perfect for the position.

The D.N.A. tour didn't occur, however, with Appice taking up an offer to tour Europe and America with OZZY OSBOURNE. Upon the drummer's abrupt mid-tour ousting from Ozzy's band he contacted Free again. Although originally intending to use the singer on a solo album (Appice's first effort, a self-titled release, had been issued through WEA in 1982), the pair eventually pieced together KING KOBRA in early 1984. The pair recruited ex-STORMTROOPER guitarist Mick Swedasky (aka. Mick Sweda) to team him up with fellow axeman David Michael Phillips aka David Henzerling. The latter, an ex-member of THE SCHOOLBOYS had previously had short, non-recording spells with ICON and KEEL. The role of bassist came down to two candidates in the auditions – Johnny Rod and Gary Moon. It would be Rod, a native of St. Louis, who completed the quintet whilst Moon went on to NIGHTRANGER.

All these musicians had been found through advertisements placed in 'Musicians wanted' ads specifically requesting top class, blonde players to join the peroxide Free and thus contrast Appice's black and red mane.

Hooking up with ex-Aucoin employee Alan Miller, who took on the role of manager, the band gained a two album recording deal with Capitol Records. KING KOBRA began working with producer Spencer Proffer (who had produced the VANILLA FUDGE reunion album *Mystery*) with the resulting debut album, *Ready To Strike*, appearing in early 1985 and the band immediately hitting the road in America.

The second album, *Thrill Of A Lifetime*, mystified many fans impressed by the debut. In fact the album failed to gain a British release, FM Revolver picking up on the album for British release.

The album included, 'Iron Eagle (Never Say Die)' the group's contribution to the movie *Iron Eagle*, the video for which depicted the band getting their long locks shorn for 'Military Service', leaving fans aghast at the very

Selected Ozzy-Related Acts From The Rockdetector Files

thought of a hard rock band at the time having anything but lonine manes!

MARK FREE quit before the recording of the band's third album, frustrated by the lack of a deal as their contract was not being renewed by Capitol. Free baled out favouring a different musical direction and would follow other horizons, both musically and sexually – he was eventually to undergo surgery to become a woman.

At this point, the band went through an extremely rocky period, hit by several line-up changes in an attempt to get a third album together. Bassist Rod had also quit to join W.A.S.P. (although he did contribute to the new record before leaving) whilst Sweda teamed up with Marq Torien and Loni Black to put together the BULLETBOYS.

Torien had originally replaced MARK FREE in the frontman's role and Loni Black (aka Lonnie Vincent) taking Johnny Rod's place on bass, but the liaison was brief. One or two of the tracks the Torien led incarnation of KING KOBRA recorded as demos, 'Kissin' Kitty' for example, would wind up on the first BULLETBOYS album a couple of years later.

Originally due to become one of the first signings to KISS' GENE SIMMONS label, the uncertainties regarding Simmons' distribution plans at that time led to Appice forming his own Rocker Records label for KING KOBRA's parting shot, having been influenced by his pal Ann Boleyn's New Renaissance outfit. For Europe Appice was keen to follow Boleyn's HELLION into signing a licensing deal with Music For Nations.

A third KING KOBRA album, simply titled *III*, was recorded with the new line up of Appice, Phillips, ex-BUSTER BROWN and MONTROSE vocalist Johnny Edwards, guitarist Jeff Northrup and bassist Larry Hart. This trio had been discovered by Appice playing in Sacramento under the handle of NORTHRUP and the album consisted of Appice/Phillips compositions married to a few numbers from the NORTHRUP files. The album marked a return by the band to the heavyweight form of the *Ready To Strike* debut and found ex-KISS drummer PETER CRISS on backing vocals. The track 'Meanstreets Machine' was originally found on the 1980 'Singin', Shoutin' EP by the pre-ICON outfit THE SCHOOLBOYS. Also featured is the GENE SIMMONS penned 'Legends Never Die' and 'It's My Life', originally recorded by PLASMATICS vocalist WENDY O' WILLIAMS on her first solo album.

As KING KOBRA's flame died the members went their separate ways. During 1988 Appice busied himself by producing demos for SIBLING RIVALRY and NRG and working putting together the BLUE MURDER line-up with JOHN SYKES in Vancouver. This act briefly roped MARK FREE into early rehearsals until the singer decided things weren't working out and returned to Los Angeles. He was to record with Appice once more in the studio band BLACK ROSES, put together for the soundtrack of the horror flick of the same name. Mick Sweda was also involved, as was Italian guitarist Alex Masi and QUIET RIOT, GIUFFRIA and HOUSE OF LORDS bassist Chuck Wright. KING KOBRA also contributed 'Take It Off' for good measure, with ex-KING KOBRA six-stringer David Michael Phillips also supplying a track of his own.

Phillips had by now formed GERONIMO with vocalist Thomas Adam Kelly and recorded demos with W.A.S.P. bassist Johnny Rod and QUIET

Ozzy Osbourne

RIOT drummer Frankie Banali. The guitarist would also contribute to LIZZY BORDEN's 1989 album Master Of Disguise.

Edwards was the surprise replacement for LOU GRAMM in FOREIGNER's *Unusual Heat* album. Edwards also recorded a single album in harness with ex-KINGDOM COME guitarist Danny Stag and former COBRA and KROKUS drummer Jeff Klaven in the band ROYAL JELLY. The singer would reunite with erstwhile KING KOBRA colleagues Larry Hart and guitarist Jeff Northrup, after the six-stringer's term with SHORTINO and RAIL, on an album credited to J.K. NORTHRUP.

Appice reassembled KING KOBRA in late 2000 for a new album. The new record, which most fans agreed was a completely different animal to its predecessor, also included guest contributions from POISON and SAMANTHA 7 guitarist C.C. DeVille alongside EARL SLICK. The KING KOBRA line-up for the resulting album, 'Hollywood Trash' released in 2001, saw Appice joined by Mick Sweda, erstwhile MICHAEL SCHENKER GROUP vocalist Kelly Keeling and ex-LITA FORD guitarist STEVE FISTER. With recording complete, the drummer would then embark on an August VANILLA FUDGE reformation tour of America.

Albums:
READY TO STRIKE, Capitol 12386-1 (1985)
THRILL OF A LIFETIME, Capitol 12473-1 (1986)
KING KOBRA III, Rocker NRR26 (1988)
HOLLYWOOD TRASH, CRCL-4564 (2001)

LION (UK)
Line-Up: Gary Farr (vocals), Robin Le Mesurier (guitar), Steve Webb (guitar), Steve Humphrey (bass), John Sinclair (keyboards), Eric Dillon (drums)

A Los Angeles-based outfit of ex-pats, LION included guitarist Robin Le Mesurier, the wayward son of *Dad's Army* actor John Le Mesurier. Robin later toured as part of ROD STEWART's backing band.

Keyboard player John Sinclair, previously with the HEAVY METAL KIDS, has been a long standing member of the OZZY OSBOURNE band. Drummer Eric Dillon boasts stints with FAT MATTRESS, HEMLOCK and SAVOY BROWN.

GARY FARR had issued a 1969 solo album and previous to that had his own act GARY FARR & THE T. BONES which included KEITH EMERSON in the ranks.

Albums:
RUNNING ALL NIGHT, A&M AMLH 64755 (1980)

LIZZY BORDEN (USA)
Line-Up: Lizzy Borden (vocals), Joe Holmes (guitar), Michael Davis (bass), Joey Scott-Harges (drums)

Theatric Heavy Metal band suitably named after an infamous murderess and

Selected Ozzy-Related Acts From The Rockdetector Files

fronted by the almost afro-topped 'Lizzy Borden'.

For the 'Terror Rising' EP which includes a cover of the JEFFERSON AIRPLANE psychedelia classic 'White Rabbit', BITCH's Betsy makes an appearance on the track 'Don't Touch Me There' and ARMORED SAINT's Joey Vera guests on 'Catch Your Death' and 'Terror Rising'.

Added new guitarist Joe Holmes (ex-TERRIF) for the Max Norman-produced *Visual Lies* album.

The ambitious double live album, *Murderess Metal Roadshow* released in 1986, would include a rendition of the WINGS epic 'Live And Let Die'.

LIZZY BORDEN's debut British appearance came in 1987 with a headline slot at London's Marquee Club prior to a Reading Festival appearance on a bill headlined by ALICE COOPER.

Guitarist Gene Allen quit to found a project with ex-METAL CHURCH vocalist David Wayne in 1988. He would much later assume the mantle 'KaBong', contributing to the PHOENIX DOWN project of ex-ALICE COOPER guitarist KANE ROBERTS.

By 1989 LIZZY BORDEN was essentially a solo vehicle for the man himself, who had split the group and assembled a new bunch of musicians to assist in the recording of the *Master Of Disguise* album, a semi-conceptual affair mixed by Terry Brown

Joining Lizzy on the record came drummer Joey Scott-Harges (actually Lizzy's brother), original bassist Mike Davis, ARMORED SAINT bassist Joey Vera and more permanent four-stringer Bryan Perry, ex-KING KOBRA guitarist David Michael Phillips, New York axeman Ronnie Jude and co-producer Eliott Soloman on keyboards.

Former band member Joe Holmes put TERRIF back together with a new line-up that didn't include ex-ANGEL vocalist Frank Dimino, as had the original incarnation. The 1990 version included vocalist Dana Freebarin, drummer Tim Cosma and Holmes, LIZZY BORDEN bass-playing buddy Mike Davis. The band failed to last the course and Holmes later found high profile work with DAVID LEE ROTH and OZZY OSBOURNE.

Without a deal now the band soldiered on throughout 1992 on the American club circuit with new member Swedish bassist Martin Anderson.

LIZZY BORDEN returned in 1999 performing a well-received set at the 'Bang Your Head' festival in southern Germany on a major bill headlined by W.A.S.P., MOTÖRHEAD, DIO and DEEP PURPLE. The band put on a back-to-theatrics full blood 'n' gore spectacle. It was not all good news for the band though. Lizzy himself was arrested at the airport on the way back to America and asked to explain why he was in possession of a blood soaked axe!

Ex-bassist Michael Davis was found on the Los Angeles club circuit in 2000 as a member of BRANOM, an act including erstwhile HERICANE ALICE, BANGALORE CHOIR and BAD MOON RISING drummer Jackie Ramos, former BOY ELROY guitarist Brian Davis and ex-CLOUD NINE vocalist Tim Branom.

Japanese versions of LIZZY BORDEN's 2001 comeback album *Deal With The Devil*, which included a raucous take on ALICE COOPER's 'Generation Landslide', came with a bonus track 'We'll Burn The Sky'. LIZZY BORDEN was comprised of Borden, guitarist Alex Nelson, bass play-

Ozzy Osbourne

er Marten Andersson (of LEGACY, JONAS HANSSON BAND and TAKARA) and long term drummer Joey Scott for this recording. Guest sessions would be on hand from ARMORED SAINT's Joey Vera and erstwhile LIZZY BORDEN man Michael Davis on bass.

This new unit would tour America during April of 2001 as guests to YNGWIE MALMSTEEN. Despite being out on a welcome high profile bout of touring, not everything ran smoothly and the band would find itself back in the media when at a gig in Charlotte, North Carolina, the band's guitar tech Ulrik Zander was shot three times attempting to foil a robbery. Fortunately Zander recovered and the tour went on.

Albums:
LOVE YOU TO PIECES, Roadrunner RR 9771 (1985)
MURDERESS METAL ROADSHOW-LIVE, Roadrunner RR 9702 (1986)
MENACE TO SOCIETY, Roadrunner RR 9664 (1986)
TERROR RISING, Roadrunner RR 9621 (1987)
VISUAL LIES, Roadrunner RR 9592 (1987)
MASTER OF DISGUISE, Roadrunner RR 9454-2 (1989)
BEST OF LIZZY BORDEN, Metal Blade ZORRO 72 (1994)
DEAL WITH THE DEVIL, Metal Blade (2000)

M-80 (USA)
Line-Up: Niki Buzz (vocals / guitar), Don Costa (bass), Sam Mann (drums)

M-80 were created by ex-VENDETTA guitarist Niki Buzz (real name Darrell Young) and bassist Don Costa, the latter being known as the man thrown out of OZZY OSBOURNE's band for being too outrageous.

Costa's stay in M-80 was short lived (as was Mann's). In 1984 Buzz recorded with ex-BODINE bassist Jeronimo Bos and drummer Gerard Haitsma in Holland on a record tentatively titled *Don't Feed The Animal*. He also put together the Dutch-based NIKI BUZZ BAND with Arco Boomer (bass) and Robbie Fiffer (drums), playing Dingwalls in London during October.

By 1985 and the recording of *The Maniac's Revenge* album, Buzz recruited ex-SAMSON bassist Chris Aylmer and drummer Ian Roberts.

Buzz would create the heavy Rap project THE ALARM before touring and playing with CURTIS KNIGHT. Latter bands included MIDNIGHT GYPSIES and LONE WOLF.

Albums:
M-80, Roadrunner (1984)
MANIAC'S REVENGE, Roadrunner RR 9801 (1985)

MANIC EDEN (HOLLAND / USA)
Line-Up: Ron Young (vocals), Adrian Vandenberg (guitar), Rudy Sarzo (bass), Tommy Aldridge (drums)

A bluesy hard rock outfit put together by Adrian Vandenberg, Rudy Sarzo and

Selected Ozzy-Related Acts From The Rockdetector Files

Tommy Aldridge following the break up of the multi-platinum WHITESNAKE. The trio's output, even prior to their high profile WHITESNAKE stint was notable with the Sarzo/Aldridge rhythm axis having made its name with OZZY OSBOURNE. Sarzo had come to the fore with QUIET RIOT whilst Aldridge's pedigree included work with BLACK OAK ARKANSAS, PAT TRAVERS and GARY MOORE. Dutchman Adrian Vandenberg had made his mark with his own act VANDENBERG.

The instrumental triumvirate had originally begun working with former HOUSE OF LORDS vocalist JAMES CHRISTIAN and had already begun writing together after negotiating a Japanese record deal before Christian quit. The singer was reportedly unhappy at the direction the group was going in, feeling that it was merely WHITESNAKE with himself on vocals in place of DAVID COVERDALE. Eventually, the trio settled on ex-LITTLE CAESAR vocalist Ron Young to replace the departed frontman.

Although the band intended to tour Europe, following the release of the album on the continent by the French label CNR Music, the only live appearances undertaken were a series of acoustic sets in record stores owned by the FNAC chain in France. Adrian Vandenberg quit soon afterwards to resume his writing partnership with DAVID COVERDALE for a final WHITESNAKE album, eventually released in 1997.

Young founded DIRT.

Albums:
MANIC EDEN, Now & Then (1994)

M.A.R.S. (USA)
Line-Up: Rob Rock (vocals), Tony MacAlpine (guitar), Rudy Sarzo (bass), Tommy Aldridge (drums)

The much touted and even more individually talented M.A.R.S. supergroup assembled by Shrapnel boss Mike Varney was quick to splinter after an indifferent response to their sole release. M.A.R.S. had originally been created as a band project by the ex-OZZY OSBOURNE rhythm team of bassist Rudy Sarzo (who had just left QUIET RIOT) and drummer Tommy Aldridge. Managed at the time by Ronnie James Dio's wife Wendy's Niji stable, the pair initially worked with ex-YNGWIE MALMSTEEN vocalist JEFF SCOTT SOTO and former STEELER guitarist Kirk James.

By September '85 James had been succeeded by ex-ROUGH CUTT guitarist Craig Goldy, who had quit GIUFFRIA to team up with Sarzo and Aldridge in what was now DRIVER and they were looking for a new singer after Soto's defection back to YNGWIE MALMSTEEN.

By the following year Goldy had been tempted away by DIO and had been replaced by Mike Varney discovery TONY MACALPINE, one of the vaunted new guitar heroes being guided by the Shrapnel boss.

Meantime, ROB ROCK had been added on vocals and this quartet recorded an album (produced by Mike Varney) before Rock began a career as a foil for burgeoning guitar merchants as he teamed up with JOSHUA, then Chris Impelliterri in IMPELLITERRI and German guitar god AXEL RUDI PELL.

Ozzy Osbourne

MacAlpine, meantime, resumed his solo career after the group had tried out the enigmatically-titled Zeus on vocals (previously with MAYDAY) from New York in order to attempt to succeed Rock.

By the time the album (after many a delay) had been issued through Shrapnel in America and Roadrunner in Europe under the M.A.R.S. banner (complications over the DRIVER name caused the switch) Sarzo and Aldridge adopted the new band name of NRG. The duo recorded further demos with the aforementioned Zeus, keyboardist Phil Lupo and new guitarist Lanny Cordolla (ironically, like Craig Goldy, also previously with GIUFFRIA).

NRG reportedly scored a deal with Elektra but the project was abandoned when Sarzo chose to rejoin QUIET RIOT in May 1987 in addition to signing up with WHITESNAKE where he linked up with Aldridge once more. The pair would form MANIC EDEN once DAVID COVERDALE had put WHITESNAKE on ice. Lanny Cordolla, meantime, rejoined former bandmate Greg Giuffria in HOUSE OF LORDS.

It's worth noting that the DRIVER name was resurrected by Rock during 1989 when he put a band together using the name alongside ex-JOSHUA bandmates Emil Lech Brando and Greg Shultz plus guitarist Roy Z and drummer Reynold 'Butch' Carlson. Roy Z later formed hip Los Angeles outfit TRIBE OF GYPSIES.

Albums:
PROJECT:DRIVER, Roadrunner (1987)

MOGG/WAY (UK)
Line-Up: Phil Mogg (vocals), Jeff Kollman (guitar), Pete Way (bass), Aynsley Dunbar (drums)

Essentially founded as a vehicle for UFO linchpins vocalist Phil Mogg and bassist PETE WAY to pursue music following the collapse (due to guitarist Michael Schenker handing in the towel) of UFO's massively successful 1995 American tour, unable to use the name UFO due to contractual reasons Mogg and Way opted to use their surnames and stride forward. Mogg had remained since the late '60s as the central linchpin of UFO. Way, another UFO founder member, had remained steadfast too until 1982 when he opted out, journeying through FASTWAY, OZZY OSBOURNE's band and the anarchic WAYSTED. The two reunited in a revitalised UFO during the late '80s.

The duo were offered the services of young American guitarist GEORGE BELLAS for the album. Bellas was to issue a solo album *Turn Of The Millenium* the same year the MOGG/WAY debut emerged.

The group was rounded out by drummer Aynsley Dunbar, whose reputation harks back to bands such as JETHRO TULL, RETALIATION, OZZY OSBOURNE, JEFFERSON STARSHIP and the formative years of JOURNEY. The resulting album featured a re-working of UFO's 'Mother Mary'. Having kissed and made up with Michael Schenker UFO would reform once more in late 1997 with Simon Wright on drums and undertake exhaustive touring throughout Europe well into early 1998.

Selected Ozzy-Related Acts From The Rockdetector Files

MOGG/WAY reunited again for a second album *Chocolate Box*, this time with new guitarist Jeff Kollmann of EDWINDARE and THE TRUTH. Joining Mogg and Way were UFO cohorts Paul Raymond and Simon Wright. Additional guitar and keyboards came from Luis Moldonado.

UFO with Schenker reunited in 1999 (with Aynsley Dunbar on drums) but Mogg also found time to busy himself on a projected solo album in cahoots with Kollmann. Meantime Way issued his first purely solo album *Amphetamine*.

By the time UFO's 2000 touring line up was announced it emerged that Dunbar was out but MOGG/WAY man Moldonado was in.

Phil Mogg also spent time in 2000 working on a projected solo album with Kollman, provisionally billed as STONETOWNE. JEFF KOLLMAN also cut tracks for ex-ARTENSION and BADLANDS vocalist JOHN WEST's solo album *Permanent Marks* and issued his own solo album 'Shedding Skin' in 2000.

PETE WAY also released his debut solo record *Amphetamine* the same year. Former guitarist George Bellas re-emerged as part of the RING OF FIRE project band in 2001.

Albums:
EDGE OF THE WORLD, Roadrunner RR 8804-2 (1997)
CHOCOLATE BOX, Shrapnel (1999)

GARY MOORE (IRELAND)

Widely recognised by rock fans for his time spent in the ranks of THIN LIZZY, Gary Moore has continued to pursue a prolific solo career that has often elevated the man into the British charts. Moore's most enduring solo hit, of course, was 1979's brooding instrumental 'Parisienne Walkways'. Throughout the '80s GARY MOORE elevated his career with a series of finely crafted hard rock albums. His output would then become more Celtic orientated and would then switch direction totally to a purist blues vein achieving a second round of success for the guitarist.

The teenage guitarist's entry into the music world came with SKID ROW before going solo followed his off-and-on relationship with THIN LIZZY.

In 1979 Moore would rehearse with erstwhile BLACK SABBATH vocalist and fellow Jet Records artist OZZY OSBOURNE but this proposed project came to naught. During 1980 Moore rehearsed with ex-DEEP PURPLE vocalist GLENN HUGHES and drummer Mark Nauseef for what was to become G-FORCE. However, Hughes departed and bassist Willie Dee (actually ex-CAPTAIN BEYOND frontman Willy Daffern) and vocalist Tony Newton brought the band up to strength.

G-FORCE would be short-lived. So, after a stint with the GREG LAKE BAND – including an American tour – Moore set about constructing a new band, leading to the recording of the *Corridors Of Power* album, a record that would seriously push his name to the fore.

For *Corridors Of Power*, which featured a cover of FREE's 'Wishing Well', Moore at first enrolled MICHAEL SCHENKER GROUP vocalist Gary

Barden. Although Barden demoed the material, Moore opted to take the lead vocal mantle himself for the actual album and assembled a line-up of WHITESNAKE bassist Neil Murray and ex-DEEP PURPLE and WHITESNAKE drummer Ian Paice together with keyboard player Tommy Eyre of the GREG LAKE BAND. At the time of recording the WHITESNAKE duo of Murray and Paice were both uncertain about their future within that group. Murray would leave Moore in late 1983 and was replaced by ex-RAINBOW and NINJA bassist Craig Gruber. Paice left in mid-1984 to join the reformed DEEP PURPLE and his place was temporarily filled by Bobby Chouinard, on loan from American artist BILLY SQUEIR's band.

In the interim, and upon completion of the album, ex-TED NUGENT vocalist Charlie Huhn was drafted in for live work although he would leave at the end of 1982, along with Tommy Eyre. The pair were replaced by ex-URIAH HEEP and LONE STAR vocalist JOHN SLOMAN and keyboard player Don Airey respectively. With this new line-up Moore toured America supporting RUSH.

For the 1985 album *Run For Cover* Moore assembled a more awesome list of contributing musicians and no less than four producers. The men at the production helm included Andy Johns, Peter Collins, Mike Stone and Beau Hill. Musicians included THIN LIZZY's PHIL LYNOTT, GLENN HUGHES and ex-RAINBOW and OZZY OSBOURNE man Bob Daisley on bass. Lynott, Moore himself and Hughes on vocals, three different drummers in Paul Thompson, Charlie Morgan and ex-BLACK ROSE and CHANNEL man Gary Ferguson and keyboards courtesy of UFO man Neil Carter, DON AIREY, previously with RAINBOW, and Andy Richards.

The liaison with GLENN HUGHES was meant to result in the structuring of a permanent band, but the man's well known problems with substance abuse proved the undoing of this effort. Amidst bizarre accusations of overeating, an addiction to Mars Bars and other erratic behaviour, Hughes quit and flew home to Los Angeles. Whatever, the GARY MOORE band would appear at the prestigious Castle Donington 'Monsters Of Rock' festival that year on an awesome bill that included AC/DC, VAN HALEN, OZZY OSBOURNE, ACCEPT, Y&T and MÖTLEY CRÜE.

In early 1985 Moore reunited with PHIL LYNOTT to record the single 'Out In The Fields', recorded with drummer Charlie Morgan and keyboard player Andy Richards. The success of the single provided the pair with a welcome return to the singles charts.

Later on in 1985 Moore once again performed a lengthy series of shows in Britain with his touring band, which now consisted of Neil Carter and a rejoining Gary Ferguson. 1986 saw Moore touring his band heavily again – including a special guest appearance at MARILLION's 'Garden Party' festival at Milton Keynes – before hooking up with QUEEN for a series of massive European shows and a headliner in Finland. Later that year the guitarist also found time to contribute to ex-BLODWYN PIG man Jack Lancaster's solo album 'Deep Green'.

Whilst 1987's *Wild Frontier* offered a Gaelic flavour to the Moore sound, 1989's *After The War* followed a similar path. The latter record stayed heavy, but did find Gary ditching some of the more Celtic influences.

Selected Ozzy-Related Acts From The Rockdetector Files

During this period the band line-up remained stable with Moore's songwriting partner Neil Carter on keyboards, drummer COZY POWELL and bassist Bob Daisley. The album featured Gary's tribute to the now deceased PHIL LYNOTT in the song 'Blood Of Emeralds' as well as a scathing attack on the band KINGDOM COME in 'Led Clones'. This latter track featured a guest vocal appearance by old acquaintance OZZY OSBOURNE.

As a new decade beckoned so did a fresh musical outlook for Moore. The guitarist abandoned his hard rock leanings and launched into headlong into the blues. His 1990 album *Still Got The Blues* opened up a whole new audience in America as well as other parts of the globe. In Sweden, for example, the album even topped the national charts.

Moore would form BBM with ex-CREAM veterans, frontman JACK BRUCE and drummer GINGER BAKER in 1993 for an album and well-received tour. By 1995 Moore was once more solo, slotting in a tribute concert for former FLEETWOOD MAC guitarist PETER GREEN in London during May and returned in 1997 with an altogether different new record entitled *Dark Days In Paradise*.

In 2000 Swedish Metal band THRYFING covered 'Over The Hills And Far Away' for their *Urkraft* album.

2001 proved a busy year for Moore. He put in appearances on JOHN MAYALL'S BLUESBREAKERS *Along For The Ride* and JIM CAPALDI's *Living On The Outside* albums. The guitarist, alongside ERIC CLAPTON, also united with his former BBM colleague JACK BRUCE on his new solo album on a re-recorded version of the CREAM classic 'Sunshine Of Your Love'. Numerous re-issues and box sets commemorating Gary's career also surfaced.

Touring throughout the year commenced with British dates, a May 27th appearance at the 'Bishopstock' festival alongside PETER GREEN and TAJ MAHAL and then on June 16th the famous Irish Fleadh event with NEIL YOUNG and VAN MORRISON.

In the Autumn of 2001 Moore formed a confederation once more with JACK BRUCE and, along with drummer Gary Husband, committed two JOHN LEE HOOKER songs 'I'm In The Mood' and 'It Serves Me Right To Suffer' to a tribute album.

Albums:
GRINDING STONE, CBS 65527 (1973)
BACK ON THE STREETS, MCA (1978)
CORRIDORS OF POWER, Virgin V 2245 (1982)
ROCKIN' EVERY NIGHT – LIVE IN JAPAN, Virgin ZIDCD1 (1983)
LIVE, Jet (1983)
VICTIMS OF THE FUTURE, Ten 205 914 (1984)
DIRTY FINGERS, Jet (1984)
WE WANT MOORE (LIVE), Ten (1984)
MORE & GUITAR CRAZY, MCA (1984)
RUN FOR COVER, Ten DIXP 16 (1985)
ANTHOLOGY, Rawpower RAWLP023 (1986)
WHITE KNUCKLES, Castle CLC 5069 (1986)

Ozzy Osbourne

EMERALD AISLES, Virgin (1986)
WILD FRONTIER, Ten DIXG 56 (1987)
LIVE AT THE MARQUEE, Castle CLC 5070 (1987)
PARISIENNE WALKWAYS, MCA (1987
A PORTRAIT OF GARY MOORE, Castle CHC 7082 (1987)
PARISIENNE WALKWAYS, Castle CBC 8022 (1988)
AFTER THE WAR, Virgin (1989)
NUCLEAR ATTACK, Teldec (1989)
MILESTONES, Castle Communications (1989)
STILL GOT THE BLUES, Virgin (1990)
THE COLLECTION, Castle CCSCD273 (1991)
AFTER HOURS,Virgin CDV 2684 (1992)
BLUES ALIVE, Virgin CDVX 2716 (1993)
BALLADS AND BLUES 1982-1994, Virgin CDV 2768 (1994)
BLUES FOR GREENY, Virgin CDV2784 (1995)
DARK DAYS IN PARADISE, Virgin CDV 2826 (1997)
OUT IN THE FIELDS: THE VERY BEST OF, Virgin (1998)
A DIFFERENT BEAT, Rawpower PAW 142 (1999)

MOTHER'S ARMY (AUSTRALIA / USA)
Line-Up: Joe Lynn Turner (vocals), Jeff Watson (guitar), Bob Daisley (bass), Carmine Appice (drums)

An outfit of illustrious pedigree fronted by ex-FANDANGO, RAINBOW, YNGWIE MALMSTEEN, DEEP PURPLE singer JOE LYNN TURNER.

MOTHER'S ARMY, over a series of three commendable melodic hard rock albums, made a significant impact in Japan. Joining Turner were characters of no less distinction with erstwhile VANILLA FUDGE, CACTUS, OZZY OSBOURNE, KING KOBRA drummer CARMINE APPICE, NIGHT-RANGER guitarist JEFF WATSON and Australian Bob Daisley, a veteran of OZZY OSBOURNE, RAINBOW, URIAH HEEP, BLACK SABBATH and YNGWIE MALMSTEEN.

Both Daisley and Appice had figured on Watson's 1991 solo album *Lone Ranger*.

Daisley was also to be found having contributed to the STREAM album *Nothing Is Sacred*, released around the same period. STREAM was a project put together by German guitarist Peter Scheithauer.

The second MOTHER'S ARMY album found Appice supplanted by ex-JOURNEY, JEFFERSON STARSHIP, JETHRO TULL, MOGG/WAY drummer Aynsley Dunbar.

Daisley deputised for DIO on their late 1998 Scandinavian dates as rumours flew regarding a possible RAINBOW reunion featuring Ronnie James Dio, RITCHIE BLACKMORE and Daisley. This project never got off the ground.

Albums:
MOTHER'S ARMY, FEMS (1993)
PLANET EARTH, USG 1018-2 (1998)

Selected Ozzy-Related Acts From The Rockdetector Files
FIRE ON THE MOON, USG 1027-2 (1998)

MÖTLEY CRÜE (USA)
Line-Up: Vince Neil (vocals), Mick Mars (guitar), Nikki Sixx (bass), Randy Castillo (drums)

The notorious bad boys of American Rock. MÖTLEY CRÜE, surviving many personal traumas, took the sleazier elements of American Rock 'n' Roll and made it their very own throughout the '80s. The band led the Los Angeles Glam movement and always maintained their lead in album and concert ticket sales.

17-year old Seattle native Frank Ferrano quit a dim past filled with fledgling outfits like SLEAZE and FORCED ENTRY. The bassist headed to Los Angeles via a stint working on his grandparents, farm in Idaho.

Once in Hollywood, Ferrano found work in a music store and then a liquor store by day and played in the clubs by night. In fact, Ferrano, alias Nikki Sixx, had just left LA club band LONDON when he met Greek-born drumming wildman Tommy Lee Bass, nicknamed 'T-Bone' because he was so skinny. The drummer had been playing in SUITE 19 and, just prior to his enlistment, with SAPPHIRE alongside future ARMORED SAINT bassist Joey Vera. The latter actually attended Lee's first meeting with Sixx although their relationship would sour when a car which Lee was driving was involved in an accident injuring Vera. There are rumours that the insurance pay-out for this crash paid for ARMORED SAINT's debut demo.

Lee and Sixx decided to team up by forming the extremely short-lived CHRISTMAS before searching for a guitarist and front man.

The duo noticed an ad in classifieds mag *The Recycler* placed by guitarist Bob Deal, a minister's son originally from Terre Haute, Indiana, who, claiming to be sick of playing in a never-ending succession of useless cover bands, advertised himself as a: 'loud, rude, aggressive guitarist'. Sixx and Lee (having dropped his real surname) were extremely interested.

Deal, finding he had much in common with this enticing rhythm team signed up for the cause, changing his name to the more exotic Mick Mars in the process.

A search for a second guitarist led them to infamous Hollywood club The Starwood to check out the rhythm guitarist of ROCK CANDY, James Alverson, but the trio come away impressed with the band's singer, Vince Neil Wharton.

This caused a bit of a dilemma for this fledgling new band as Sixx had already offered the vocalist's position to a singer identified only as O' Dean. But Vince Neil (as he became) got the job and Mars came up with the name MÖTLEY CRÜE and, a month later, the group made their live debut at The Starwood opening for Y&T.

In desperate need of a manager, Sixx having handled all business affairs since MÖTLEY CRÜE's inception, Mick Mars brings Alan Coffman into the fold. The brother-in-law of one of the guitarist's friends, Coffman's wealth was attributed to a career in the construction industry, a remarkably common pursuit of men seeking to finance Rock bands in the '80s, strangely enough!

Ozzy Osbourne

With Coffman's money MÖTLEY CRÜE were able to record a single, 'Stick To Your Guns', in June 1981 in a limited edition pressing of 1,000 copies, which were promptly given away to fans at the band's subsequent gigs. Today an original copy of the single (it has been bootlegged), which was backed with 'Toast Of The Town', can command in the region of £100 from collectors.

Increasing their following with shows both in and outside of LA, the band threw caution to the wind and entered a recording studio once more in December 1981 to lay down tracks for a full blown album, taking three days and costing in the region of $7,000 to complete.

The first pressing of *Too Fast For Love* was in a limited run of 900 copies and can be distinguished from the second pressing by way of its white band logo instead of the red of the second. The second pressing finds the singer's shag-do considerably toned down!

The *Too Fast For Love* album proved to be a sell out and rumours abounded in 1982 of an impending British tour opening for, of all people, WISHBONE ASH!! The rumours prove, naturally, to be unfounded. Instead of heading over to Britain, MÖTLEY CRÜE wound up on a rather embarrassing headlining stint in Canada, playing discos and gay bars and suffering the indignation of having their stage props and items of stage clothing confiscated by Canadian customs, who considered the items to be offensive weaponry. With the buzz growing on the band by the day, Elektra Records' Tom Zutuat stepped in to sign the band. The label immediately issued *Too Fast For Love* for major consumption, albeit with a re-mix from producer Roy Thomas Baker and less the track 'Stick To Your Guns' in order to improve the overall sound quality.

At the close of 1982 MÖTLEY CRÜE headlined the Santa Monica Civic Theatre and attracted new management in the form of the New York-based Doc McGhee and Doug Thaler. Things begun to take off in a big way from here on. Early 1983 is spent opening for KISS on the 'Creatures Of The Night' tour. In May MÖTLEY CRÜE appeared on the bill of the huge US Festival's Metal Day alongside QUIET RIOT, OZZY OSBOURNE, JUDAS PRIEST, TRIUMPH, the SCORPIONS and VAN HALEN, playing to crowds of some 350,000 people.

November MÖTLEY CRÜE's long-awaited second album, *Shout At The Devil* is unleashed, produced by Tom Werman and featuring soon-to-be-classic Metal anthems in 'Looks That Kill', 'Bastard' (reportedly written in honour of former manager Coffman!) and the title track itself.

1984 found MÖTLEY CRÜE out on the road with OZZY OSBOURNE and earning themselves a reputation for being one of the wildest bands on the road. In August the band finally hit Britain as the opening act on a particularly strong 'Monsters Of Rock' bill at Donington headlined by AC/DC and VAN HALEN. The CRÜE stayed in Europe at the invitation of IRON MAIDEN to open up for the Brits on the continental leg of their 'Powerslave' tour before returning to Britain in November with a headline show at the Dominion Theatre in London.

On his return to Los Angeles Neil tragically became involved in a far more damaging incident when his car was involved in a serious accident. His pas-

Selected Ozzy-Related Acts From The Rockdetector Files

senger, Nicholas 'Razzle' Dingley – the British-born drummer with HANOI ROCKS – was killed and the two occupants of the other car were badly injured.

Neil was subsequently charged with vehicular manslaughter. A lengthy prison sentence was expected, but, extremely surprisingly, the singer was given a mere 30-day jail term, 200 hours community service and ordered to pay a $2.6 million dollar compensation package to Razzle's relatives and the driver and passenger of the other vehicle.

During downtime Tommy Lee forged a union with ex-RUNAWAYS members CHERIE CURRIE and bassist Vickie Blue for a projected project band but this act never got beyond rehearsals.

MÖTLEY CRÜE's new album, once again with Tom Werman at the helm, was unveiled in 1985. Entitled *Theatre Of Pain*, a more studied affair in places, it featured a rousing cover of BROWNSVILLE STATION's 'Smokin' In The Boys Room', virtually making the song their own, and allowed the band to begin headlining in America, supported by Japanese Metal band LOUDNESS.

The Arena tour unveiled Tommy Lee's fairground ride drum solo on an outrageously innovative revolving drum-kit.

By January 1986 the quartet were back on European soil again, including playing nine dates in Britain with their heroes CHEAP TRICK opening.

On May 10th Tommy Lee married *Dynasty* and *T.J. Hooker* actress Heather Locklear back home in California, having first met her backstage at an REO SPEEDWAGON show, of all places. Sixx was Lee's best man.

A month later Vince Neil finally found the time to serve his sentence and spends a mere 20 days in the Gardena City slammer. In fact, Neil only served 18 days, as he was given time off for good behaviour.

A new MÖTLEY CRÜE opus, *Girls Girls, Girls*, was issued during May 1987 and found the band in a far heavier mood than *Theatre Of Pain*. The tour was bigger than ever (including the introduction of backing singers Emi Canyn and Donna McDaniel as the NASTY HABITS), initially hitting the road with the resurrected WHITESNAKE in the opening slot.

The tour was massively successful, with GUNS N' ROSES also opening a little later on, before MÖTLEY CRÜE played their first dates in Japan. Scheduled European shows in early 1988 were cancelled at the last minute, with the management citing exhaustion as the cause. However, the original press line claimed the band feared the weight of the snow on the venue roofs meant that they wouldn't be able to take the band's lighting rig for fear of damaging the buildings. However, rumours abounded that the real reasons for pulling the dates lay with the band's excessive lifestyle with some reports even speculating as to the death of Nikki Sixx.

The truth, when revealed, had seen Sixx come dangerously close to meeting his maker. Upon arrival back from touring Japan and a vacation in Hong Kong, the bassist overdosed on heroin and was found in his hotel room at the Hollywood Plaza by a couple of members of GUNS N' ROSES, blue in the face. Sixx was pronounced dead at the scene by paramedics but, after having been given a shot of adrenaline to the heart, regained his life signs. It's estimated that Nikki was actually dead for two minutes.

Ozzy Osbourne

The curse of drugs was further rammed home when manager Doc McGhee was arrested in January 1988 for his part in smuggling 40,000lbs of Colombian marijuana into the United States in 1982. He promptly received a five-year suspended prison sentence, a $15,000 fine and was ordered to set up the 'Make A Difference' anti-drugs foundation.

1988 also found Sixx embroiled in a rather bizarre lawsuit in which one Matthew Trippe claimed to have been enlisted by McGhee Entertainment to replace the real Nikki Sixx following a car crash in 1983. Trippe claimed to have toured, written and recorded as Nikki Sixx. His lawsuit against the band centred upon unpaid royalties following his alleged sacking from the band in 1985 in order to bring the original back following Trippe's arrest in Florida for his incarceration for an involvement in an armed robbery.

The story generated massive press exposure, especially in Europe, but the whole thing was put to bed when Trippe dropped his case in December 1993 and disappeared back into obscurity after attempting an extra run for his money with the formation of a short-lived outfit called SIXX PACK.

Doc McGhee saw fit to organise two shows in Moscow during August 1989 as part of his anti-drugs campaign, putting the MÖTLEY CRÜE on a bill that also featured BON JOVI, the SCORPIONS, OZZY OSBOURNE, SKID ROW, CINDERELLA and Russian groups GORKY PARK, BRIGADA S and NUANCE. By the time the whole thing was over a row had erupted between MÖTLEY CRÜE and McGhee centring on his alleged favouritism of management stablemates BON JOVI. The fracas led to Tommy Lee punching Doc in the face and a split in the McGhee Entertainment empire. The band signed with McGhee's erstwhile business partner Doug Thaler instead and went back to work on their new record, produced by former PAYOLA man Bob Rock in Vancouver's Little Mountain Studios.

The album, titled 'Dr. Feelgood', promoted MÖTLEY CRÜE to global superstardom, going multi-platinum status with apparent ease (it hit the number one spot in the States), firing off numerous hit singles and prompting a mammoth almost universally sold-out world tour. The album boasted an enviable array of studio guests, giving an indicator as to the fact that MÖTLEY CRÜE had definitely arrived in the big league. Guesting were AEROSMITH's Steven Tyler, CHEAP TRICK's Robin Zander and Rick Nielsen, BRYAN ADAMS, SKID ROW and NIGHTRANGER's Jack Blades.

MÖTLEY CRÜE appeared on two compilation albums during the latter part of the year, the *Make A Difference* release with a cover of Tommy Bolin's 'Teaser' and the *The Adventures Of Ford Fairlane* movie soundtrack with 'Rock 'n' Roll Junkie'. Vince Neil played a small cameo role in the movie, playing a singer who passes away whilst on stage...

With all this activity one studio session from 1989 did get lost. The band teamed up with rappers 2 LIVE CREW founding a project titled CRÜE TO CREW and laid down the song of the same name intended for the soundtrack to the movie *Hanging With The Hombres*. The tapes were left to gather dust until their appearance in 1997 on a 2 LIVE CREW compilation album.

In 1990 Mick Mars married Emi Canyn, one half of the voluptuous NASTI HABITS duo, whilst Nikki Sixx tied the knot with model Brandi Brandt.

Selected Ozzy-Related Acts From The Rockdetector Files

A decade after forming in Los Angeles MÖTLEY CRÜE celebrated their ten year anniversary with the release of the compilation, greatest hits style album aptly titled *A Decade Of Decadence*. The album came complete with two new tracks – 'Primal Scream' (released as the first single from the album) and a cover of the SEX PISTOLS 'Anarchy In The UK'.

Before it hit the stores the band once more played at Donington (as coincidence would have it, the 'Monsters Of Rock' event was again headlined by AC/DC). Three days before the show the quartet performed a 'secret' club gig billed as the FOURSKINS at the Marquee Club in London. The gig, played in sweltering heat, was a sell out and a riot.

In January 1992 Elektra re-issued 'Home Sweet Home' as a single, albeit in the remixed form it appeared in on the *Decade...* album. The band set to work on a brand new studio album, working towards the Punkier approach touched upon with 'Primal Scream', one tentative track boasting the title of 'I'm A Victim Of A Psycho Bitch', but the band's plans began to look rather loaded against Vince Neil. Soon enough the blond frontman was out of the group.

Neil soon set about work on a solo career creating THE VINCE NEIL BAND, initially in league with high profile players ex-BILLY IDOL guitarist STEVE STEVENS and former OZZY OSBOURNE bassist Phil Soussan. The ex-frontman's debut proved promising and charted high but reviews and general reception for the follow-up were not exactly complimentary. To further enhance the gloom the singer suffered the devastation of the death of his daughter Skylar.

MÖTLEY CRÜE meanwhile had found their new frontman. John Corabi had previously been headhunted by SKID ROW pre-Sebastian Bach as well as being tapped to front BRITNY FOX after the departure of Dean Davidson. Philadelphia native Corabi had resisted both offers to move back East in order to pursue his musical career in Los Angeles, opting to join RACER X at a time when they were going through a transitional period when they evolved into THE SCREAM.

Corabi had recorded one album with the band, *Let It Scream*, in 1991 on the Hollywood label and that had led to a tour with the BULLETBOYS and a one-off show in London.

Although MÖTLEY CRÜE had shown some interest in KIK TRACEE vocalist Stephen Shareaux and had actually jammed with the band, Corabi was the man they wanted.

However, despite a high initial chart placing for the 'Mötley Crüe' album fans, interest soon waned in both Corabi and the new toned down image of the band. Corabi was soon ousted (the man later created UNION with ex-KISS guitarist Bruce Kulick) and to nobody's surprise Neil was back in the fold.

Sixx announced plans for a solo album release in early 1997 that had been recorded at his home studio in collaboration with BOXING GHANDIS vocalist/guitarist David Darling, but the record had not been released by the close of the year.

Geared up for a massive promotion campaign to promote the comeback reunion album *Generation Swine*, they were convinced of its chances. MÖTLEY CRÜE had to this juncture sold in excess of 35 million albums and, despite the relative disappointment of the Corabi-fronted effort, industry hopes were high for a return to traditional rock 'n' roll values. There was even a new, non-alcoholic beer tied in with the marketing campaign 'Motley Brue'.

The band themselves boosted expectations with their debut appearance at the Livestock festival where a crowd of over 25,000 turned up to witness the event. Further dates upfront of the album were more low-key including a somewhat strange pairing as MÖTLEY CRÜE opened for TYPE O NEGATIVE for which, typically, the British 'Rock' press found the need to stick the boot in, berating the band for being 'shit'.

The album itself, stifling the critics by crashing into the Billboard chart at number 4, which included an industrial rework of 'Shout At The Devil', proved to be a diverse collection of material with Neil singing much lower in range than usual. Both Sixx and Lee also offered lead vocals on one song each, Lee choosing to perform the track 'Brandon', a song dedicated to his son by third wife *Baywatch* actress Pamela Anderson.

Instead of hosting the usual array of listening parties for the media, MÖTLEY CRÜE chose to perform the album in its entirety on a ten-date nationwide American promotion tour up front of *Generation Swine's* June 24th Stateside release. MÖTLEY CRÜE fans could actually attend these shows either through winning radio contests or buying a limited number of tickets put on sale, monies from ticket sales going to the Skylar Neil Foundation set up by Vince in memory of his daughter to aid the care and research for children with cancer. The group participated in Question & Answer sessions following their performances.

Seemingly unconcerned with the then politically correct notions of the media, the MÖTLEY CRÜE tour proceeded to delve into decadence almost straight away. Both Sixx and Lee were arrested in Phoenix for allegedly inciting a riot. Neil was accused of assaulting a member of the audience whilst the whole band were put on a charge for somehow letting a hardcore porn video be aired to their waiting fans at one gig at the Pittsburgh Civic Arena!

The first single in Britain, 'Afraid', was released with 'Rave' mix and 'Swine' mix versions married to a cover of IGGY POP and DAVID BOWIE's 'Lust For Life' and Tommy Lee's 'Welcome To Planet Boom'. The latter track was originally on the *Quartenary* Japanese released album of 'solo' recordings and also featured in Pamela Anderson Lee's *Barb Wire* movie.

Now in full swing with UNION, Corabi filed a claim against his former bandmates that the band owed him a substantial amount of money.

1998 began on a sour note for Tommy Lee, the drummer not only being served with divorce papers by wife Pamela but also facing a jail term for assaulting the actress. Indeed, Lee was initially sentenced to six months after breaking a probation order incurred on him for an assault on a photographer some months previously.

Lee's prison term came at a time when MÖTLEY CRÜE announced that they had parted company from Elektra and had plans to go it alone on their own Mötley label (distributed by BMG). As the band's immediate future looked a bit uncertain Neil spent the downtime continuing his association with motor sport working as a celebrity crew man with the FedEx Champ Car series racing outfit Team Green, who Neil's Canadian buddy Paul Tracy and

Selected Ozzy-Related Acts From The Rockdetector Files

Scot Dario Franchitti drove for during 1998.

Neil himself was also involved in a sex tape scandal when a video involving the singer and two girls (one of whom was Janine Lindenmulder) appeared although, unlike the Tommy Lee and Pamela Anderson tape, Neil was reported to be unconcerned about its availability.

On the eve of the release of MÖTLEY CRÜE's debut live album *Entertainment Or Death* in a shock move Lee quit the band after an altercation with Neil. The drummer soon got to work on his Nu-Metal project band METHODS OF MAYHEM. During May of 1999 the band pulled in ex-OZZY OSBOURNE drummer Randy Castillo and got back to touring. Castillo's investiture proved to be a completion of a circle, Tommy Lee having first proposed him for the position in Ozzy's band. August arena dates saw German veterans the SCORPIONS as openers.

Nikki Sixx was expected to continue working on his 58 solo project while MÖTLEY CRÜE remained inactive. The bassist also launched his own label Americoma in 2000, first offering being the debut by LAIDLOW produced by Sixx himself.

Summer 2000 had MÖTLEY CRÜE back on the road headlining the 'Maximum Rock' tour to promote new album *New Tattoo* alongside MEGADETH and ANTHRAX. Interestingly one of the band's new backing singers is MEAT LOAF's daughter Pearl! Things did not run all smoothly though as Castillo ruptured a stomach ulcer while playing with his side act AZUL just prior to the tour, necessitating HOLE's Samantha Maloney occupying the drumstool for the first batch of dates, much to Courtney Love's amusement!

During the Autumn MÖTLEY CRÜE were due to tour Australia with strong support from THE SCREAMING JETS but these dates were pulled. Castillo was still out of action, the public now aware that the drummer was undergoing treatment for cancer.

As 2000 drew to a close it emerged that in a surprise move Tommy Lee had joined OZZY OSBOURNE's band. However, whatever the validity of this claim, the union was hotly denied and Lee was certainly absent from the next public Ozzy band line-up. Two tribute albums emerged the same year titled *Kickstart My Heart* and *Shout At The Remix*. In 2001, upfront of the band's autobiography, miniature die-cast MÖTLEY CRÜE racing cars arrived in the toy stores.

Another new product arrival for 2001 was a live DVD filmed in Salt Lake City on July 5th, 2000 on the 'Maximum Rock' tour and the 'New Tattoo' tour. As well as the live tracks on video, backstage footage and the promotional clip for 'Hell On High Heels' the DVD also included a recently found track 'Nobody Knows What It's Like To Be Lonely', actually the first song ever recorded by the band.

The same year would reveal the band's contribution to the American record industry in terms of sheer album sales. At this juncture *Dr. Feelgood* was leading the pack in the rankings of American album sales at six million and counting with *Shout At The Devil*, *Theatre Of Pain* and *Girls, Girls, Girls* all boasting four million apiece.

As 2002 broke ex-drummer Samantha Maloney revealed her new outfit,

Ozzy Osbourne

THE CHELSEA, an all-girl act completed by former SMASHING PUMPKINS and HOLE bassist Melissa Auf Der Maur on guitar and A PERFECT CIRCLE's Paz Lenchantin on bass. Meantime Nikki Sixx was set to guest on erstwhile MARVELOUS 3 main man BUTCH WALKER's debut solo record and drummer Randy Castillo forged a fresh band project in alliance with OZZY OSBOURNE and ALICE IN CHAINS bassist Mike Inez.

Sadly Randy Castillo lost his battle against cancer in late March of 2002.

Albums:
TOO FAST FOR LOVE, Leathur (1982)
TOO FAST FOR LOVE, Elektra K 52425 (1982)
SHOUT AT THE DEVIL, Elektra 960 289-1 (1983)
THEATRE OF PAIN, Elektra EKT 8 (1985)
GIRLS, GIRLS, GIRLS, Elektra EKT 39 (1987)
RAW TRACKS, Elektra P-6261 (1988) (Japanese release)
DR. FEELGOOD, Elektra EKT 59 (1989)
DECADE OF DECADENCE, Elektra 7559 61204-2 (1991)
MÖTLEY CRÜE, Elektra 7559 61534-2 (1994)
QUARTERNARY, Elektra (1994) (Japanese Release)
GENERATION SWINE, Elektra 7559-61901-2 (1997)
SUPERSONIC AND DEMONIC RELICS, Motley (1999)
ENTERTAINMENT OR DEATH, Spitfire 553.0058.23 (1999)
NEW TATTOO, Spitfire (2000)

VINCE NEIL (USA)
Line-Up: Vince Neil (vocals), Steve Stevens (guitar), Phil Soussan (bass), Vikki Foxx (drums)

Fired by MÖTLEY CRÜE in February 1992 Vince Neil almost immediately received a request from the Walt Disney company to create a song for their *Encino Man* production, a comedy starring Pauly Shore and re-titled *California Man* for European consumption. Collaborating with TOMMY SHAW and Jack Blades from DAMN YANKEES the trio came up with 'You're Invited (But Your Friend Can't Come).'

Putting together his post-MÖTLEY CRÜE solo outfit, Neil finally settled on ex-ENUFF Z' NUFF drummer Vikki Foxx and former OZZY OSBOURNE, BILLY IDOL and BEGGARS AND THIEVES bassist Phil Soussan. After having talked with the likes of RATT's WARREN DE MARTINI and WHITESNAKE's Adrian Vandenberg, amongst others, erstwhile BILLY IDOL, ATOMIC PLAYBOYS and JERUSALEM SLIM guitarist Steve Stevens landed the job.

The resulting album charted high in America, undoubtedly due to the singer's profile and track record whilst fronting MÖTLEY CRÜE.

During 1992 Neil continued his involvement in the Indy Lights racing series, a step down from the fully fledged CART championship, as a driver and sponsor. In his first race in Long Beach Neil retired due to crashing on the third lap after trying to avoid a spinning car.

Stevens was long gone by the time of the second album and in his stead

Selected Ozzy-Related Acts From The Rockdetector Files

came ex-WILDSIDE man Brent Woods. Ex-NEW HAVEN bassist Robbie Crane was also drafted. *Carved In Stone* was held back from release for many months due to Neil's daughter Skylar losing her battle against cancer shortly after recording had finished.

Touring resulted in Crane and Neil ending up in a fist fight. Needless to say the bass player lost his position, with SLAUGHTER's Dana Strum a temporary replacement.

Neil somewhat predictably, despite those bitter words in the world's media upon his departure, returned to MÖTLEY CRÜE for their 1997 *Generation Swine* album. The blond frontman's appearance made a noticeable difference for the positive in MÖTLEY CRÜE's album sales.

Crane worked with the former RATT / ARCADE vocalist Stephan Pearcy on his VERTEX project prior to joining RATT for their 1997 reformation tour of America. Foxx had joined BULLETBOYS by 2000.

Neil, now sporting somewhat of a Hawaiian beach bum image, assembled a fresh band for a headlining summer 2001 national jaunt dubbed the 'Voices Of Metal' tour backed up by STEPHEN PEARCY'S RATT, SLAUGHTER and BRITNY FOX. Alongside Neil and the loyal Brent Woods, band members included the UNION rhythm section of bassist Jamie Hunting and drummer Brent Fitz.

Mid-way through the dates, Hunting exited in acrimonious circumstances and was swiftly replaced by Neil's erstwhile colleague Phil Soussan. With the tour wrapped up, Soussan only having covered for three gigs, Hunting and Neil settled their differences in time for a September appearance in Buenos Aires, Argentina.

Albums:
EXPOSED, Warner Bros. 936245260-2 (1993)
CARVED IN STONE, WEA 9362 45877-2 (1995)

NIGHTRANGER (USA)
Line-Up: Jack Blades (vocals / bass), Brad Gillis (guitar), Jeff Watson (guitar), Alan Fitzgerald (keyboards), Kelly Keagy (Vocals / drums)

With roots entrenched in the eclectic Jazz and Funk Rock combo RUBICON, NIGHTRANGER's name would become synonymous with well-crafted melodic hard rock.

Bassist Jack Blades and guitarist BRAD GILLIS had both been part of the RUBICON experience, recording two albums with the group before turning into the harder-edged STEREO, by which time drummer KELLY KEAGY had signed up.

As STEREO became RANGER, Brad Gillis was invited to tour with OZZY OSBOURNE in the wake of Randy Rhoads' tragic death. Gillis stuck with OZZY OSBOURNE for nearly a year and appears on the live *Speak Of The Devil* album.

With Blades and Keagy joining forces with former MONTROSE and GAMMA keyboardist Alan Fitzgerald in the interim, upon Gillis' return from Europe with Ozzy the quartet drafted in Sacramento-based guitarist JEFF

Ozzy Osbourne

WATSON.
Watson had made quite a name for himself already. Starting out on his musical path as a singing waiter, the guitarist founded his first act JUNE BLITZ which later evolved into the JEFF WATSON BAND fronted by vocalist Jim Vigir. With this act Watson scored heavy radio success with songs produced by none other than RONNIE MONTROSE.

As the JEFF WATSON BAND's popularity grew, the act found themselves supporting the likes of HEART, TED NUGENT and SAMMY HAGAR and also enrolled a fresh vocalist in ERIC MARTIN, later to find massive commercial success with MR. BIG.

Watson though was enticed away to the fledgling NIGHTRANGER by Alan Fitzgerald who had aided the group on the production front.

The band, initially known as RANGER, signed to the MCA-affiliated Boardwalk label founded by ex-Casablanca Records boss Neil Bogart. The NIGHTRANGER moniker was adopted after the discovery of a Country & Western group had already claimed the RANGER name. The band earned themselves a reputation on the live circuit and, ably assisted by veteran Bay Area-based promoter Bill Graham, the band scored valuable exposure opening for the likes of JUDAS PRIEST, DOOBIE BROTHERS and SANTANA. The band made an immediate impact with one of the most riff-laden AOR albums of the decade in the debut *Dawn Patrol* release. Touring as support to the likes of SAMMY HAGAR, NIGHTRANGER began to establish themselves as one of America's most promising hard rock acts, one made for the arenas and the enormo-domes of the world.

However, despite their undeniable quality as a Hard Rock band, NIGHTRANGER struggled throughout their career to break away from the huge success of more featherweight hit singles as 'Sister Christian' and 'Goodbye'. The Boardwalk label, owned by Neil Bogart, was soon swallowed up by the corporate giant MCA Records after his death and NIGHTRANGER found themselves under increasing pressure to produce hit singles. Nevertheless NIGHTRANGER built up a solid legacy of touring, pushing sales to their peak with 1985's *Seven Wishes* album which reached the Billboard top ten. The album included the track 'Interstate Love Affair', originally a contribution to the *Teachers* movie soundtrack.

1987's *Big Life* found NIGHTRANGER switching producers, enlisting Kevin Elson to the cause in place of Pat Glasser who they had worked with on their previous three albums.

Big Life was a tad more experimental than previous efforts, the band not adverse to using drum machines and various effects on the album which featured backing vocals from former 707 and future THE STORM vocalist Kevin Chalfant.

As an aside, the video for 'The Secret Of My Success' – a track from the album – featured MÖTLEY CRÜE's VINCE NEIL and Tommy Lee on saxophones and pop satirist WEIRD AL YANKOVIC on trumpet.

After a gruelling tour trek in America supporting the *Big Life* album, Alan Fitzgerald was to depart (reportedly tired of the road) and the Keith Olsen-produced *Man In Motion* album saw keyboards supplied by sessioneers Alan Pasqua and John Purdell. Following recording, the band pulled in a permanent

Selected Ozzy-Related Acts From The Rockdetector Files

keyboard player, Jesse Bradman (ex-KILLERWATT, EDDIE MONEY and ALDO NOVA).

NIGHTRANGER officially broke apart in April 1989. MCA promptly issued a *Greatest Hits* album as Blades went forward to retain a high profile as part of DAMN YANKEES, a unit that outstripped NIGHTRANGER in commercial popularity built by the bassist and wildman guitarist TED NUGENT, ex-STYX guitarist TOMMY SHAW and drummer Michael Cartellone.

Brad Gillis was to team up with a budding solo artist called MIKE REEVES and songwriter Todd Meagher. Gillis co-wrote with Meagher on material for the project, which was produced at Gillis' Gilrock Studios. MISTRESS, BILLY SATELLITE and .38 SPECIAL guitarist Danny Chauncey was also involved.

Alameda, California, native Reeves had met Gillis when the guitarist had happened upon him playing a high school gig and was invited by Gillis to join his side project, THE ALAMEDA ALLSTARS, which is where Mike first met Chauncey.

The MIKE REEVES BAND also comprised ex-RICK DERRINGER bassist Tommy Sprayberry, keyboard player Brian Craig and drummer Ronny Sieff.

Jeff Watson, meantime, put a group together with bassist David Sikes (ALDONOVA / GIUFFRIA / BOSTON), drummer Billy Carmassi (ALDO NOVA) and adding Jesse Bradman on vocals, although Bradman also created a new act with former WILD HORSES / DIO bassist Jimmy Bain.

NIGHTRANGER were resurrected in late 1991 for live dates.

Watson released the ironically titled solo album *Lone Ranger* on Roadrunner Records in 1992. Assisting him with this venture were such luminaries as Gillis, VAN HALEN frontman SAMMY HAGAR, ex-OZZY OSBOURNE bassist Bob Daisley, veteran ex-VANILLA FUDGE / CACTUS drummer CARMINE APPICE, JOURNEY drummer Steve Smith and noted jazz-rock guitarist ALLAN HOLDSWORTH.

By 1993 Daisley and Appice had helped Watson co-found his MOTHERS ARMY side project. Fronted by ex-FANDANGO, RAINBOW and DEEP PURPLE vocalist JOE LYNN TURNER, this outfit has released three commendable albums to date.

The 1996 NIGHTRANGER album *Feeding Off The Mojo*, saw the band as a trio of Gillis, Keagy and bassist Gary Moon. Songs included a cover of PETER FRAMPTON's 'Do You Feel Like I Do' and THE BEATLES 'Tomorrow Never Knows'. The band also collaborated with JEFF PARIS for the track 'Last Chance'.

The following year bore witness to a reunion of the original band and the release of an album, *Neverland*, to celebrate the event. The resurrected group toured America in support of the album, playing a combination of headlining shows and playing on bills with the likes of REO SPEEDWAGON, TED NUGENT and JOE WALSH.

The reunion of the original group had first occurred during the summer of 1996, Blades hooking up with his former colleagues for a tour of Japan that led to a bidding war with interested Japanese labels. A deal was signed and

Ozzy Osbourne

Ron Nevison engaged to produce what would become *Neverland*. Following the album's release NIGHTRANGER put in successful headline shows in America.

Rumours suggested that a third DAMN YANKEES album was also on the cards. However, the new NIGHTRANGER album was the first to emerge. Titled *Seven* and released in Japan during the Spring of 1998 it found the group back on form.

NIGHTRANGER put in an arena tour of America in the summer of 1999 as part of the 'Rock Never Stops' extravaganza including TED NUGENT, SLAUGHTER and QUIET RIOT.

Gillis issued a further solo album *Alligator* in 2000 as NIGHTRANGER spent the summer touring America once again.

KELLY KEAGY put in a guest vocal on SURVIVOR guitarist JIM PETERIK's *World Stage* album the same year. Peterik returned the favour by guesting on Keagy's 2001 solo album *Time Passes*. Other familiar faces included Gillis, Blades and Moon.

Albums:
DAWN PATROL, Boardwalk EPC 25301 (1982) 38 USA
MIDNIGHT MADNESS, MCA (1983) 15 USA
SEVEN WISHES, MCA MCF 3278 (1985) 10 USA
BIG LIFE, MCA DMCF 3362 (1987) 28 USA
MAN IN MOTION, MCA 6238 (1988) 81 USA
GREATEST HITS, MCA DMCG 6055 (1989)
LIVE IN JAPAN, MCA MCAD-10024 (1990)
FEEDING OFF THE MOJO, Semaphore 50 528-422 (1996)
NEVERLAND, Sony (1997)
ROCK MASTERPIECE COLLECTION, MCA Victor (1997) (Japanese release)
ROCK IN JAPAN '97, Zero Corporation (1997) (Japanese release)
SEVEN, Sony (1998)

PRIDE AND GLORY (USA)
Line-Up: Zakk Wylde (vocals / guitar), James Lomenzo (bass), James Tichy (drums)

A distinctly Southern-flavoured power trio put together by guitarist ZAKK WYLDE following his exit from the OZZY OSBOURNE band. Immediately post-Ozzy, the guitarist had toured America with a band including ex-RONDINELLI, WHITE LION and ACE FREHLEY bassist James LoMenzo, erstwhile WHITE LION and ACE FREHLEY drummer Greg D'Angelo and keyboard player Kevin Jones. These dates culminated in supports to LYNYRD SKYNYRD. Wylde also toured live as part of the legendary ALLMAN BROTHERS replacing Dickey Betts.

The PRIDE AND GLORY band was a distinctly '70s retro affair even featuring Zakk on banjo.

Lomenzo and Tichy remained together to tour with GUNS N' ROSES guitarist Slash in SLASH'S SNAKEPIT during 1995.

Selected Ozzy-Related Acts From The Rockdetector Files

Brian Tichy was touring with FOREIGNER during 1998 as he also put his own band B.A.L.L. together in Los Angeles taking up the role of a vocalist/ guitarist. By 2000 he had joined the OZZY OSBOURNE band and in late 2001 was touting a new band project MIRROR DOWN.

Wylde returned to the scene with the raucous BLACK LABEL SOCIETY. LoMenzo would be found in the HULA MONSTERS and KILLER WHALES.

Albums:
PRIDE AND GLORY, Geffen GED 24703 (1994)

QUIET RIOT (USA)
Line-Up: Kevin DuBrow (vocals), Randy Rhoads (guitar), Rudy Sarzo (bass), Frankie Banali (drums)

The original incarnation of QUIET RIOT was pieced together in 1975 by the ex-VIOLET FOX duo of guitarist Randy Rhoads and bassist Kelli Garni together with frontman Kevin DuBrow. They were cheekily dubbed a 'quiet riot' by a visiting STATUS QUO guitarist Rick Parfitt and the name stuck. The band was rounded out by drummer Drew Forsyth. Rhoads, who split a previous act VIOLET FOX which featured Rhoads brother Doug on drums, had pulled in DuBrow after an audition at the guitarist's house. Funnily enough this first attempt of DuBrow's to front the new band was rejected but his eventual persistence paid off as he was finally asked to join.

CBS Records in Japan picked up on the group and released two albums, *Quiet Riot* (1978) and *Quiet Riot II* (1979) – the latter of which featured new bassist Rudy Sarzo. Kelli Garni would re-emerge in 1985 playing with Randy Rhoads' brother Kelle's band EMERALD.

The band split when Randy Rhoads, upon the recommendation of future SLAUGHTER bassist Dana Strum, hooked up with OZZY OSBOURNE having become frustrated in his efforts to get an American record deal for QUIET RIOT. Sarzo was to follow him, after a brief stint replacing Felix Robinson in ANGEL during 1981, into the former BLACK SABBATH vocalist's band once touring commenced, replacing Bob Daisley.

Whilst Rhoads and Sarzo were enjoying the success of a rejuvenated OZZY OSBOURNE, DuBrow stayed in Los Angeles, forming the modestly titled DUBROW with former SATYR guitarist Bob Stefan. Bass guitar was supplied by erstwhile SNOW bassist Tony Cavazo. This band later included former SWEET 19 and DOKKEN guitarist Greg Leon. Original QUIET RIOT drummer Drew Forsyth would turn up in 1989 in HIGHLANDER with guitarist Craig Collins Turner.

In fact DUBROW became QUIET RIOT following the tragic death of Rhoads in an air crash whilst on tour with OZZY OSBOURNE in 1982.

DuBrow had already hooked up with ex-SNOW guitarist Carlos Cavazo (Tony's brother, replacing Leon who was later to form GREG LEON'S INVASION and enjoy a brief stint in ROUGH CUTT and MARSHALL LAW) and retained the services of Wright.

Chuck Wright actually plays bass on two tracks on the resurrected QUIET

Ozzy Osbourne

RIOT's 'debut' album *Metal Health*. Although Carlos' brother and ex-SNOW member Tony recorded tracks for the record, Kevin DuBrow claims his work was re-recorded once Rudy Sarzo had rejoined the group after leaving OZZY in the wake of the Rhoads tragedy.

Rudy Sarzo had always been trying to get his friend, drummer Frankie Banali, into the band in the Randy Rhoads period, having played with him for 12 years in the bar circuits of Florida, New York and Illinois. Banali, eking out a living playing sessions as well as being a member of STEPPENWOLF guitarist Michael Monarch's band STEEL MONARCH, was obviously an ideal choice to replace the long departed Drew Forsyth once the decision was taken to re-name DUBROW as QUIET RIOT. As a direct result of working on the *Metal Health* album Frankie, who had just finished working with HUGHES/THRALL was tapped by producer Spencer Proffer to play drums on Australian legend BILLY THORPE's *East Of Eden's Gate* album. Pat Regan played all keyboards on *Metal Health*.

The album surpassed everyone's expectations, hitting the resurgence of Heavy Metal at its peak. The band's SLADE cover 'Cum On Feel The Noise' reached the American top 5 whilst the album itself made it all the way to Number 1. QUIET RIOT visited Britain in March 1984 playing dates supported by Mancunian Glamsters ROX.

Despite the denials by DuBrow that QUIET RIOT would not be recording another SLADE cover 'Mama Weer All Crazee Now' was laid down for the *Condition Critical* album. The band even ended up releasing it as a single, although it could only manage to peak at Number 51 in the American charts as it was in hot competition with a version of the same song by Irish band MAMA'S BOYS who got their effort to Number 54.

QUIET RIOT fragmented under a barrage of criticism. Sarzo teamed up with his erstwhile OZZY OSBOURNE colleague Tommy Aldridge to form the backbone behind what would become a project band DRIVER with vocalist BOB ROCK and guitarist TONY MACALPINE.

The pair had originally worked together as SARZO/ALDRIDGE and recruited ex-YNGWIE MALMSTEEN vocalist JEFF SCOTT SOTO and former STEELER guitarist Kirk James to the band managed by Ronnie James Dio's wife Wendy's management company Niji. Ex-QUIET RIOT bassist Chuck Wright was persuaded to rejoin the band, the man having left the ranks of GIUFFRIA. The third album braved the media storm and still managed a worthy chart placing in America.

QUIET RIOT toured Japan in 1986 with WANG CHUNG and LIFE BY NIGHT man JEFF NAIDEAU on keyboards.

Early 1987 brought with it the rumour that Kevin DuBrow had parted company with the band, a tale later confirmed as fact at the end of March as the singer bowed out, citing personal differences with the other members of the group as the reason for the split.

After producing demos by Florida outfit JULLIET, DuBrow planned on forming a new band and recording a solo album with ex-RAINBOW drummer COZY POWELL and ex-WHITESNAKE and THIN LIZZY guitarist JOHN SYKES, although such plans came to naught.

Ex-ROUGH CUTT vocalist PAUL SHORTINO was announced as

Selected Ozzy-Related Acts From The Rockdetector Files

DuBrow's replacement in April 1987 and the band began work on a new album for Pasha.

Rather bizarrely, in June the same year Rudy Sarzo was reported to have quit the NRG project that DRIVER/M.A.R.S. had evolved into after the departure of ROB ROCK and TONY MACALPINE. Sarzo rejoined QUIET RIOT after Chuck Wright had gone back to GIUFFRIA in order to record what would become the debut HOUSE OF LORDS album.

However, Sarzo had also linked up with Tommy Aldridge again to form the rhythmic backbone in the latest WHITESNAKE line-up in addition to recording the new QUIET RIOT album. This period of serious moonlighting would lead to Sarzo having to relinquish his position in QUIET RIOT by the end of the Summer to concentrate fully on his role in WHITESNAKE. He was replaced in QUIET RIOT by Sean McNabb.

Session player Jimmy Johnson played bass on two songs on the resulting *Quiet Riot* album. All keyboard parts come courtesy of Jimmy Waldo, veteran of NEW ENGLAND, ALCATRAZZ and BLACKTHORNE.

Due to poor sales, the group splintered in 1989 with Shortino and McNabb sticking together to form BADD BOYZ and later reforming ROUGH CUTT. The bassist would later figure in GREAT WHITE.

Frankie Banali temped with W.A.S.P. and FASTER PUSSYCAT whilst Carlos Cavazo was keeping a rather low profile. Banali would reunite with DuBrow on the projected debut album for Tampa's JULLIET with the singer acting as producer and Banali as session drummer. However, although a full album was recorded, these tapes were shelved and JULLIET's record arrived revamped by SURVIVOR's Frankie Sullivan.

In January 1990 it was revealed that Kevin DuBrow had pieced together a new group under the name of LITTLE WOMEN with guitarist Sean Manning, bassist Kenny Hillery and drummer Pat Ashby. DuBrow and Cavazo reunited in 1991 with a band titled THE HEAT. As it turned out QUIET RIOT was to re-emerge in 1993 with the low key *Terrified* album. Joining DuBrow for this outing were Cavazo, Banali and Hillery. Wright made an appearance on backing vocals and some tracks featured the drumming of RAINBOW, BLUE OYSTER CULT and BLACK SABBATH man Bobby Rondinelli.

Another effort *Down To The Bone* surfaced the following year with Wright back in the bass position. The bassist would later depart to work with HONEY on a tour of Korea then with ANTONIO NADIR.

Back on the road with QUIET RIOT DuBrow suffered a personal setback when it was claimed that he threw an audience member from the stage into the crowd breaking the leg of Susan Hawkins. A judgement went against the singer who was ordered to pay $105,000 in damages.

The 'classic' line-up of DuBrow, Cavazo, Sarzo and Banali reunited in May 1997 at the F Musicfest in Los Angeles. After a number of shows in Canada the band made another comeback appearance in Las Vegas on May 30 with a show at The Joint (situated in the Hard Rock Hotel) in conjunction with the KOMP 92.3 radio station (the station DuBrow had been DJ-ing for). The gig was recorded for a possible live album. The group also recorded a version of 'Highway To Hell' for an AC/DC tribute album. This track would quite surreally be remixed for inclusion on the record by '80s British Shock Popsters

Ozzy Osbourne

SIGUE SIGUE SPUTNIK.
Unfortunately for Cavazo, the same year the guitarist's home was broken into, the robbers giving Cavazo a severe beating in the process.

Back in business QUIET RIOT guested for UFO on their European dates. QUIET RIOT also later toured Germany during 1999 promoting their comeback album *Alive And Well* and America as part of 'The Rock Never Stops' touring bill that also included TED NUGENT, SLAUGHTER and NIGHTRANGER.

DuBrow's past came back to haunt him when the vocalist was arrested and jailed overnight for failing to pay the 1994 ruling for breaking a fan's leg. The singer pleaded poverty. Meantime, in more positive news, Cavazo produced the debut album from SWIRL during 1999.

QUIET RIOT proved their staying power in 2000. To highlight the band's pulling power they performed two gigs in 24 hours by playing a show in Korea then hopping on a plane back to America for another show. They also put in three American shows within a day, playing in front of 19,000 people in 24 hours.

QUIET RIOT were back in the limelight in mid 2001 being announced as special guests on POISON's mammoth 'Glam Slam Metal Jam' American arena tour alongside WARRANT and ENUFF Z' NUFF. The band also issued a new album *Guilty Pleasures*, which received generally commendable reviews, on Bodyguard Records.

Banali would also figure on another current album, having laid down drums on W.A.S.P.'s 'Unholy Terror' opus. Sarzo meantime formed part of ex-SHOUT vocalist KEN TAMPLIN's new project band CRUSADE. DuBrow would put in a further tribute album appearance, fronting up a version of 'Welcome To The Jungle' on an April 2002 Deadline Records GUNS N' ROSES collection.

Albums:
QUIET RIOT, Columbia (1978)
QUIET RIOT II, Columbia 25AP 1192 (1979)
METAL HEALTH, Epic 25322 (1983)
CONDITION CRITICAL, Epic 26075 (1984)
QUIET RIOT III, Epic EPC 26945 (1986)
TERRIFIED, Moonstone 28096 3102-2 (1993)
THE RANDY RHOADS YEARS, Rhino 812271445-2 (1993)
DOWN TO THE BONE, Kamikaze (1994)
ALIVE AND WELL, Axe Killer 3049322 (1999)
GUILTY PLEASURES, Bodyguard (2001)

RAINBOW (UK)
Line-Up: Ronnie James Dio (vocals), Ritchie Blackmore (guitar), Bob Daisley (bass), David Stone (keyboards), Cozy Powell (drums)

Perceived by many as the vehicle used by ex-DEEP PURPLE guitarist RITCHIE BLACKMORE to enhance his own solo standing, RAINBOW nevertheless produced some exceptional hard rock albums throughout its tumul-

Selected Ozzy-Related Acts From The Rockdetector Files

tuous career. With an ever-fluid line up Blackmore remained the linchpin throughout it all and established RAINBOW as one of the major rock bands of its time.

Always a volatile relationship, Blackmore and DEEP PURPLE had almost parted ways in 1972. The guitarist set up a band project titled BABY FACE projected to include THIN LIZZY bassist PHIL LYNOTT, ex-FREE vocalist PAUL RODGERS and DEEP PURPLE drummer Ian Paice. BABY FACE never got beyond a few jam sessions and both Lynott and Blackmore persevered with their own bands.

Blackmore finally split from DEEP PURPLE seemingly in disgust at the new funkier direction of the *Stormbringer* album and the rest of the band's refusal to record the QUATERMASS track 'Black Sheep Of The Family'. Previously the guitarist had worked with one of DEEP PURPLE's support bands ELF, whose first album had been produced by ROGER GLOVER and Ian Paice, and with this band he cut his first solo album *Richie Blackmore's Rainbow* in 1975.

With the album making an impression on the American charts, Blackmore was sure post-DEEP PURPLE success was attainable. The line-up for RAINBOW Mk 1 was virtually ELF plus Blackmore obviously without redundant guitarist Steve Edwards. Featuring vocalist Ronnie James Dio, bassist Craig Gruber, Mickey Lee Soule on keyboards and drummer Gary Driscoll.

The inaugural RAINBOW did not survive long as Blackmore dispensed with those he did not deem up to par. Gruber had left by July 1975 (later to form the short lived NINJA) and Driscoll and Lee Soule the following September. A replacement drummer was found in COZY POWELL from STRANGE BREW (which also had among its ranks ex-HUMBLE PIE guitarist Dave Clemson) whilst keyboards were handled by Tony Carey (ex-BLESSINGS) and bass by Scotsman Jimmy Bain (ex-HARLOT / STREET-NOISE).

RAINBOW debuted in late 1975 playing the West Coast of America with a very troublesome rainbow stage prop that unfortunately interfered with the band's PA sound.

RAINBOW went into the studio in early 1976 to record the second album before heading out on more American dates running from May until August before finally hitting Europe. The European tour coincided with the release of what many regard as the finest RAINBOW recording, *Rainbow Rising* featuring the classic 'Stargazer'. The British tour completely sold out and RAINBOW rounded off the year with their first Japanese dates.

Quick to capitalize on this initial success the rather lukewarm live album *Rainbow On Stage* was released. The line-up was soon in disarray as after a world tour Bain was unceremoniously fired (he went on to form the ill-fated WILD HORSES) whilst Carey was also given his marching orders only to be reprieved for six months.

Bain's place was filled by ex-URIAH HEEP, TEMPEST and COLOSSEUM bassist Mark Clarke but after 1977 recording sessions in France, Blackmore scrapped both the tapes and gave the boot to Clarke and finally Carey. The recordings were resumed with former WIDOWMAKER bassist Bob Daisley. The position of keyboard player was auditioned by ex-CURVED

Ozzy Osbourne

AIR and ROXY MUSIC man Eddie Jobson, Mark Stein of VANILLA FUDGE and PROCUL HARUM's Matthew Fisher. However, it was a relative unknown, former SYMPHONIC SLAM man David Stone, who eventually stepped in.

Before the release of the third album RAINBOW once more performed another sell-out UK tour and completed the world tour in Japan during February 1978. *Long Live Rock n' Roll* presented a much cleaner sound and heralded the beginning of RAINBOW's concentrated assault on the American market. Ditching the infamous rainbow prop the band spent many months slogging across the States. Following the tour Stone and Daisley were asked to leave (the bassist soon hooking up with URIAH HEEP) and rumours abounded that Dio was next on the list.

In January 1979 Dio finally announced he was quitting to join BLACK SABBATH. With the virtual disintegration of the band Blackmore was forced to re-think and opted to invite his former DEEP PURPLE colleague bassist Roger Glover to join the band and produce the next album. Keyboard player DON AIREY was recruited from COZY POWELL'S HAMMER but Blackmore's next potential enlistee proved more elusive. Former DEEP PURPLE Mk 2 frontman IAN GILLAN was asked to join but declined, instead offering Blackmore a job in his band! Blackmore did perform one show with GILLAN's band at the Marquee in December 1979 but this was as far as any liaison between the two legends went. STRIFE bassist Gordon Rowley was also asked by Blackmore to join RAINBOW. He lasted one day before forming NIGHTWING.

Blackmore requested the services of TRAPEZE vocalist Pete Goalby who flew from England to the guitarist's home in Connecticut to rehearse. Goalby was offered the job and RAINBOW set about recording the *Down To Earth* album. However, severe personality clashes developed and recording was halted as Glover was delegated to perform the unpleasant task of informing Goalby he was no longer welcome in Blackmore's eyes. Goalby's stay in RAINBOW lasted just six weeks and the vocalist soon was offered another prime position as frontman for URIAH HEEP.

RAINBOW began auditioning singers and finally settled on ex-MARBLES vocalist GRAHAM BONNET. Recording commenced once more and the next album *Down To Earth* shed many of the earlier Dio-esque fantasy lyrics and gave RAINBOW a number of charting singles.

The band went on the road in America once more, this time supporting BLUE OYSTER CULT before headlining. In February 1980 the band toured Britain backed up by the hit single 'All Night Long'. Blackmore's reputation for moods was further enhanced when he refused to encore at Wembley Arena resulting in a near riot.

In May the band toured Japan and yet again were blighted by rumours of various members being sacked. The rumours crystallized into fact when Powell played his last gig with RAINBOW at their headlining appearance at the first 'Monsters Of Rock' festival at Castle Donington on August 16th, 1980, alongside acts such as JUDAS PRIEST, SCORPIONS and SAXON. His replacement American Bobby Rondinelli (ex-SAMANTHA) was already waiting in the wings having just declined an offer to join KISS.

Selected Ozzy-Related Acts From The Rockdetector Files

Bonnet was to pack his bags (and beach shirts) toward the end of 1980. The singer would pursue an erratic path through MICHAEL SCHENKER GROUP then ALCATRAZZ.

By the time 1981's *Difficult To Cure* album, recorded in Sweden, was on the streets RAINBOW had another American member. New Jersey born JOE LYNN TURNER had previous experience cutting four albums with RCA act FANDANGO. Bonnet's official parting shot was the inclusion of two live RAINBOW tracks on the 'Monsters Of Rock' album of the event but in actual fact the former singer had laid down vocals for the next album, subsequently re-recorded by Turner. RAINBOW once more got to grips with America, touring on a bill with the PAT TRAVERS BAND beginning in March before touring Britain then Japan. During the Japanese dates Airey announced he was leaving and was quickly replaced by ex-MORNING THUNDER and BOSTON man David Rosenthal who debuted on *Straight Between The Eyes*. Despite success in Europe and Japan RAINBOW were still finding the going tough in America.

Bent Out Of Shape was a much harder-edged affair than the previous two albums and featured new drummer Chuck Burgi (ex-BRAND X and BALANCE) in place of Rondinelli (later to form RONDINELLI and join SUN RED SUN). The band was effectively put on hold while Blackmore negotiated with Ian Gillan to reform the Mk 2 DEEP PURPLE line-up.

Turner signed to Elektra to pursue an ill-fated solo career before teaming up with YNGWIE MALMSTEEN for a stormy working relationship that still managed to deliver the Swedish axe guru's best selling album to date, *Odyssey* before coming full circle, reuniting with Blackmore in DEEP PURPLE for the *Slaves And Masters* opus. Latterly Turner has fronted MOTHER'S ARMY with another former RAINBOW man bassist Bob Daisley. Rondinelli worked with QUIET RIOT and BLACK SABBATH. Rosenthal joined Dutch band HAMMERHEAD.

Live In Germany is a set featuring the Dio/Blackmore/Powell/Bain/Carey line up from 1976.

Bizarrely, Blackmore was linked to the reformation of WHITESNAKE in 1994 whilst still a member of DEEP PURPLE but rumours of a RAINBOW reformation continued unabated. Blackmore finally walked out on DEEP PURPLE prior to some Japanese dates. In late 1994 Blackmore was rehearsing as a solo artist in Connecticut with ex-LA PAZ, PRAYING MANTIS and MIDNIGHT BLUE vocalist Doogie White. The singer had first come to Blackmore's attention when the ambitious Scotsman had dropped off a tape with DEEP PURPLE's tour manager at Blackmore's last London gig with his old troupe.

Also involved in these formative steps was VIRGIN STEELE/ RONDINELLI bassist Rob DeMartino. This inevitably culminated in a RAINBOW reformation with the addition of ex-ALICE COOPER/BLUE OYSTER CULT bassist Greg Smith, keyboard player Paul Morris and drummer John O'Reilly. Before long O'Reilly had jumped to BLUE OYSTER CULT and ex-RAINBOW drummer Chuck Burgi, who had been replaced by O'Reilly in BLUE OYSTER CULT, joined the fold. Eventually Burgi returned to BLUE OYSTER CULT and O'Reilly was back in position for

Ozzy Osbourne

RAINBOW. This bizarre scenario of swapping drummers between the two acts did not end there as Burgi's place in BLUE OYSTER CULT was taken shortly after by Bobby Rondinelli – ex-RAINBOW!

1994 also saw the release of an album with strong RAINBOW connections. The band RED DAWN featured ex keyboard player David Rosenthal, drummer Chuck Burgi and bassist Greg Smith.

RAINBOW completed a highly successful tour of Europe during the winter of 1995, marred only by the apathetic rejection of the British media. RAINBOW was duly put on ice once again.

White released an album of pre-RAINBOW material titled *Eros Of Love And Destruction* with his side project CHAIN in 1996. Featured musicians included FM keyboard player Jem Davis and VAN DAMME guitarist Ashley John Limer.

During the latter half of 1997 White reunited with Smith another ex-RAINBOW/BLUE OYSTER CULT man drummer Jon Miceli to forge an untitled act completed by GUN/BRUCE DICKINSON guitarist Alex Dickson. However, Dickson landed the plum job of guitarist for ROBBIE WILLIAMS. By 1999 White was to be found fronting XFM, a covers band led by erstwhile FM guitarist Andy Barnett.

O'Reilly formed WESTWORLD with TNT frontman Tony Harnell issuing a debut album in 1999. The same year a confederation of name German rockers billed as CATCH THE RAINBOW formed a project uniquely dedicated to covering RAINBOW songs. The 1999 album, conceived in the main by HELLOWEEN drummer Uli Kusch, would see vocal contributions from BRAINSTORM's Henne Basse, HELLOWEEN's ANDI DERIS and PRIMAL FEAR's Ralph Scheepers.

Guitars would be laid on by GAMMA RAY's Henjo Richter, the HELLOWEEN pairing of ROLAND GRAPOW and Michael Weikath. Bass came courtesy of erstwhile GAMMA RAY man Uwe Wessel, GRAVE DIGGER's Jens Becker and HELLOWEEN's Marcus Grosskopf with keyboards supplied by ROUGH SILK man Ferdy Doernberg, HELLOWEEN's Jørn Ellerbrøck and ZED YAGO's Markus Glossner.

The resulting album *A Tribute To Rainbow* achieved high sales in mainland Europe.

Despite the success of the last RAINBOW album, Blackmore's next move was to issue a folk-rock album under the title Blackmore's Night in collaboration with his girlfriend Candice Night.

Rumours abounded towards the close of the year that Blackmore had approached both Ronnie James Dio and Bob Daisley to recreate a classic RAINBOW line up. Dio would not deny the stories and indeed Daisley joined DIO for their Scandinavian tour.

White created CORNERSTONE in 2000 in alliance with ROYAL HUNT bassist Steen Morgensen and the album *Arrival*. The singer has also assembled his own ICE project band and holds the dubious honour of being known to millions as the voice on the 'Action Man' toy TV advert! By September 2001 White was ensconced in Swedish guitar maestro YNGWIE MALMSTEEN's live band.

More recently Blackmore has stated that a RAINBOW reformation cannot

Selected Ozzy-Related Acts From The Rockdetector Files

be ruled out.

Albums:
RITCHIE BLACKMORE'S RAINBOW, Oyster OYA 2001 (1975)
RAINBOW RISING, Polydor 2490 137 (1976)
ON STAGE, Polydor 2657 016 (1977)
LONG LIVE ROCK 'N' ROLL, Polydor POLD 5002 (1978)
DOWN TO EARTH, Polydor POLD 5023 (1979)
DIFFICULT TO CURE, Polydor POLD 5036 (1981)
STRAIGHT BETWEEN THE EYES, Polydor POLD 5056 (1982)
BENT OUT OF SHAPE, Polydor POLD 5116 (1983)
FINYL VINYL, Polydor PODV 8 (1986)
LIVE IN GERMANY, Connoisseur DP VSOP CD 155 (1990)
STRANGER IN US ALL, RCA 7432 1303372 (1995)

SILVER (UK / GERMANY)
Line-Up: Gary Barden (vocals), Bernie Tormé (guitar), Michael Voss (bass), Don Airey (keyboards), Marco Minnemann (drums)

SILVER boast a quite awesome pedigree of established rock talent. The band, convened in 2001, witnessed a welcome return to action by former MICHAEL SCHENKER GROUP vocalist Gary Barden. Joining the singer would be former GILLAN and OZZY OSBOURNE guitarist BERNIE TORMÉ, H-BLOCKX drummer Marco Minnemann and MAD MAX, CASANOVA and DEMON DRIVE bassist Michael Voss. Keyboards were in the hands of a true veteran – DON AIREY of RAINBOW, OZZY OSBOURNE and WHITESNAKE fame.

The resulting eponymous album took many by surprise being infused with a strong Gothic streak. None too surprising perhaps, bearing in mind that SISTERS OF MERCY man Andreas Bruhn had a hand in co-writing much of the material. Included was a remake of 'Walk The Stage', originally sang by Barden on the 1983 MICHAEL SCHENKER GROUP album *Built To Destroy*.

Albums:
SILVER, AOR Heaven (2001)

SLAUGHTER (USA)
Line-Up: Mark Slaughter (vocals), Tim Kelly (guitar), Dana Strum (bass), Blas Elias (drums)

Formed, phoenix-like, from the ashes of VINNIE VINCENT INVASION by vocalist Mark Slaughter and bassist Dana Strum in 1989. Strum had also been involved in the late '70s act BADAXE and with the short-lived but influential MODERN DESIGN as well as carving his name into the rock history books by hooking OZZY OSBOURNE up with the legendary late guitar hero Randy Rhoads. Guitarist Tim Kelly had very briefly been a member of Heavy Metal band ODIN.

Ozzy Osbourne

SLAUGHTER immediately hit the big time in 1990 with the release of their debut album *Stick It To Ya* and the smash hit single 'Up All Night'. This debut was followed by the even more successful 'Fly To The Angels', both reaping the benefits of heavy exposure on MTV in the United States where the group was to tour with KISS. Indeed, SLAUGHTER would go on to score no fewer than eight MTV Number 1 videos and *Stick It To Ya* would eventually gain double platinum status. Incidentally, the model on the debut album cover was briefly married to RATT guitarist Robbin Crosby.

The band had convened in Los Angeles whilst Slaughter and Strum were producing demos for the North Carolina outfit WHITE HEAT (who became FIREHOUSE once signed to Epic Records). The duo met guitarist Tim Kelly, a veteran of a number of local bands in Philadelphia at Cherokee Studios. Houston resident Blas Elias, previously a member of BLACK SHEEP, was then added after auditioning for the position.

Due to the band's success on the road Chrysalis opted to release a live mini album, appropriately titled *Stick It To Ya Live* and containing five tracks.

SLAUGHTER toured America during 1992 opening for OZZY OSBOURNE in support of *The Wild Life* album. Strum's services were later hastily employed in the VINCE NEIL band when an inter-band fist fight saw the rapid mid-tour exit of previous incumbent Robbie Crane.

As the Grunge explosion decimated the 'hair band' genre SLAUGHTER wisely stuck to their guns, continuing to knock out bona fide hard rock albums that sustained them through the lean years. The group would also display their stoicism on the road, maintaining constant annual touring year on year.

1997 album *Revolution* saw the band seemingly drifting into a '60s era Psychedelia direction. *Revolution* was recorded at their own De La Casa Studios in Las Vegas and the CD version features an enhanced multi-media portion featuring video footage, photos, bios, demo recordings and live material compiled by Elias and Strum. The first single choice from *Revolution* was intended to be the opening track 'American Pie'.

Sadly, Tim Kelly was killed in a car accident on February 5, 1998. Kelly, who was driving from Baghdad, Arizona to Kingman, was involved in a collision with an on-coming semi-articulated truck that had jack-knifed in front of him. Kelly was taken to hospital but died from head injuries sustained in the accident. Kelly had played his last shows with SLAUGHTER at Detroit's Harpo's club on November 14 and 15, 1997.

SLAUGHTER were expected to continue, although reports suggested that Tim Kelly would not be permanently replaced. As it transpired Jeff Blando eventually fulfilled the position.

The band put in a series of shows toward the end of 1998 as part of 'The Rock Never Stops' American tour alongside FIREHOUSE, WARRANT and QUIET RIOT.

Blando filled in as live guitarist for the 2000 tour by the reformed SAIGON KICK. The band were back out on the road in the summer of 2001 forming part of the 46 date 'Voices Of Metal' tour alongside VINCE NEIL, VIXEN and STEPHEN PEARCY'S RATT.

Blas Elias would grace the big screen in the fall of 2001 playing the drummer of fictitious band BLOOD POLLUTION in the Mark Wahlberg movie

Selected Ozzy-Related Acts From The Rockdetector Files

Rock Star. SLAUGHTER's tenacity and fan support could be evidenced when, during 2001, the band received more MTV airings than in the previous five years.

Albums:
STICK IT TO YA, Chrysalis CCD 1702 (1990)
STICK IT TO YA LIVE, Chrysalis 21816 (1990)
THE WILD LIFE, Chrysalis CCD 1911 (1992)
FEAR NO EVIL, SPV Steamhammer 085-76002 (1995)
REVOLUTION, CMC International 06076-86214-2 (1997)
ETERNAL LIVE, SPV 085-18162 CD (1998)
BACK TO REALITY, SPV 085-21432 CD (1999)

STONE FURY (USA)
Line-Up: Lenny Wolf (vocals), Bruce Gowdy (guitar), Randy Rand (bass), Randy Castillo (drums)

The product of manager/mentor Marty Wolff's fevered imagination, STONE FURY was pieced together in Los Angeles during 1983.

German-born frontman Lenny Wolf had been playing in a group called FUNHOUSE in Hamburg and was introduced to Marty Wolff (no relation) by his then guitarist. Wolf and FUNHOUSE recorded some demos and Marty took them to Elektra in Los Angeles with a view to getting a deal, but things didn't work out and Lenny wound up quitting FUNHOUSE in order to go to Los Angeles.

Marty Wolff introduced Lenny to guitarist Bruce Gowdy upon the German's arrival in Los Angeles and this pairing recorded 'Life Is Too Lonely' and 'Tease' as demo tracks.

Having returned to Germany, Lenny Wolf was amazed to find something of a bidding war had erupted between a number of major labels looking to sign this new 'group' on the strength of the two tracks. MCA Records won the day, the then untitled project signing to the label on 4th May 1983.

With the record pretty well written, Gowdy introduced drummer Jody Cortez into the line-up. He would be followed by bassist Rick Wilson.

The STONE FURY debut album, *Burns Like A Star*, was released in 1984 and the group shot a video in London for the track 'Break Down The Walls' a few weeks before it hit the racks. The debut sold well but just failed to break into the American charts.

Jody Cortez quit late in 1984, ex-LITA FORD drummer Randy Castillo promptly replacing Cortez for touring purposes. Castillo's LITA FORD colleague Randy Rand filled the bass slot as Wilson opted out as STONE FURY opened up for AEROSMITH. Castillo would, post-STONE FURY, go on to higher profile work enjoying a lengthy term with OZZY OSBOURNE and in 1999 joining MÖTLEY CRÜE. He would sadly pass away on March 26th 2002 succumbing to a lengthy battle with cancer.

Let Them Talk album saw STONE FURY essentially trimmed to the duo of Wolf and Gowdy and teamed with producer Richard Landis. Sessioners included bassist Dean Cortez, keyboards from Alan Pasqua and drums by

Vinnie Colaitua. Strangely, the record was a disappointment, veering off into more pop rock territory as the duo went all experimental, eschewing the ZEPPELIN-esque traits of *Burns Like A Star*. Such a drastic change in direction led, needless to say, to STONE FURY's demise.

As Lenny Wolf went off to resurrect the earlier STONE FURY sound with the trés ZEPPELIN influenced KINGDOM COME, Bruce Gowdy put the Progressive influenced WORLD TRADE together with LODGIC and YES man Billy Sherwood before forming UNRULY CHILD with ex-KING KOBRA and SIGNAL vocalist MARK FREE.

Meantime, Jody Cortez had played drums in a session capacity on CINDERELLA's *Night Songs* debut in 1986.

To cash in on the success of KINGDOM COME, MCA released the compilation album *The Best Of Stone Fury* in June 1988 which turned out to be a reasonable representation of both albums, nonetheless, with five tracks taken from each.

Jody Cortez had a busy 1997 appearing on albums by TAMARA CHAMPLIN, PHIL CHRISTIAN and BIG MOUTH.

Albums:
BURNS LIKE A STAR, MCA 5522-1 (1984)
LET THEM TALK, MCA 5788 (1986)
THE BEST OF STONE FURY, MCA 42208 (1988)

SUICIDAL TENDENCIES (USA)
Line-Up: Mike Muir (vocals), Rocky George (guitar), Mike Clark (guitar), Rob Trujillo (bass), R.J. Herrera (drums)

SUICIDAL TENDENCIES, created in 1982 by vocalist Mike Muir, are one of the few hardcore acts to break out onto the world circuit. Muir and his cohorts often appeared in photographs in the distinctive Los Angeles gang culture dress style of eyes hidden behind bandannas and check shirts held by the neck button. Later this image would develop through the skateboard culture fuelled by songs such as 'Possessed To Skate'.

Amongst the underground hardcore circles the self-titled debut was recognised as a classic but as the band grew more conventional rock sensibilities would come to the fore.

The band signed to major label Virgin in 1986 as MTV support for the video to 'Institutionalised' raised the band's profile considerably, pulling them clear of their indie hardcore roots and breaking the charts on both sides of the Atlantic. *Join The Army* saw the departure of Estes and Smith as the band debuted guitarist Rocky George and drummer R.J. Herrera.

Bassist Louiche Mayorga joined his erstwhile bandmates Estes and Smith to form UNCLE SLAM, debuting the new act with the *Say Uncle* album on Caroline Records during 1988.

The Mark Dodson produced *How Will I Laugh...* saw the band being enlarged with the addition of ex-NO MERCY rhythm guitarist Mike Clark and bassist Bob Heathcote.

SUICIDAL TENDENCIES were seemingly in ascendancy into the big

Selected Ozzy-Related Acts From The Rockdetector Files

league. Their controversial name made them ripe targets for the moral majority. California's police department, fearing Muir's crew was merely a front for a Los Angeles gang, even went so far as to ban the band performing in their hometown. The notorious moral campaigner Tipper Gore-led pressure group P.M.R.C. kept up a campaign against the band claiming that a number of teenage suicides were directly attributable to the band.

SUICIDAL TENDENCIES brought in bassist Rob Trujillo for *Lights, Camera... Revolution*. The album track 'Send Me Your Money', a forthright attack on American television evangelists proved a huge hit with the fans and quickly became a staple of live shows. Both Muir and Trujillo captured more than their fair share of the limelight at this juncture, creating side project act INFECTIOUS GROOVES together with erstwhile JANE'S ADDICTION drummer Stephan Perkins. This side project band would go on to release two well-received albums and test the duo's stamina as INFECTIOUS GROOVES often opened the show for SUICIDAL TENDENCIES.

Perhaps wishing to amend previous mistakes, the band's next album *Still Cyco After All These Years* was actually a complete re-recording of their debut.

For the *Art Of Rebellion* album, what was to be SUICIDAL TENDENCIES's highest selling record reaching Number 52 in the Billboard charts, noted producer Peter Collins was utilized. The band once more announced a new recruit in VANDALS drummer Josh Freece who incidentally took over the drum stool in INFECTIOUS GROOVES too.

Suicidal For Life had SUICIDAL TENDENCIES recording without a permanent drummer. Freese joined the limbo-bound GUNS N' ROSES then PEARL JAM and A PERFECT CIRCLE. WHITE LION and Y&T man Jimmy DeGrasso deputised for the album sessions before he joined up full time with MEGADETH.

SUICIDAL TENDENCIES folded after this release. Rocky George created SAMSARA with CRO MAGS members Harley Flanagan and Parris Mayhew. Trujillo found himself enjoying a lengthy term with the OZZY OSBOURNE band, having had an interim stint with PALE DEMON.

SLAYER covered 'Memories Of Tomorrow' for inclusion on their *Undisputed Attitude* covers album. However, the track only made it onto the Japanese pressing.

The band returned in 1999 signed to Germany's Nuclear Blast label. In mid-2001 Brooks Wackerman returned to the ranks back from his touring stint filling in with A PERFECT CIRCLE. Drummer Josh Freese would also re-enlist.

By early 2002 Rocky George had re-emerged touting a fresh act HARLEY'S WAR in union with ex-CRO MAGS frontman Harley Flanagan and former WARZONE guitarist Jay Vento.

Albums:
FIRST ALBUM, Frontier FLP1011 (1987)
JOIN THE ARMY, Virgin V2424 (1987) **81 UK, 100 USA**
HOW WILL I LAUGH TOMORROW WHEN I CAN'T EVEN SMILE TODAY, Virgin CDV 2551 (1988)

Ozzy Osbourne

CONTROLLED BY HATRED – FEEL LIKE SHIT... DEJA VU, Epic 4653992 (1989)
LIGHTS, CAMERA... REVOLUTION, Epic 4665692 (1990) **59 UK**
SUICIDAL TENDENCIES, Virgin OVED 384 (1991)
THE ART OF REBELLION, Epic 4718852 (1992) **52 USA**
STILL CYCO AFTER ALL THESE YEARS, Epic 473749-2 (1993)
SUICIDAL FOR LIFE, Epic 476885-2 (1994) **82 USA**
PRIME CUTS, Epic 484123-2 (1997)
FREEDUMB, Nuclear Blast (1999)
FREE YOUR SOUL... SAVE YOUR MIND, Nuclear Blast NB 528-2 (2000) **92 GERMANY**

TERRIF (USA)
Line-Up: Dana Freebarin (vocals), Joe Holmes (guitar), Mike Davis (bass), Tom Cosmo (drums)

Act assembled by ex-ANGEL vocalist Frank Dimino in the mid-'80s after his first post-ANGEL act THE RUFFIANS had disintegrated.

Moving to Portland, Oregon, Dimino put a new group, TERRIF together, featuring guitarist Joe Holmes, bassist Emil Lech Brando and drummer Tom Cosmo. Demos were recorded before Dimino, frustrated at the lack of progress, moved back to Los Angeles. Dimino and his former ANGEL colleagues Punky Meadows and Barry Brandt, united again in late 1985 in an attempt to resurrect ANGEL.

Lech promptly joined SOUND BARRIER before stints with JOSHUA for their *Speed Of Light* record and by 1989 DRIVER. Holmes meanwhile joined LIZZY BORDEN for their 1987 album *Visual Lies* before quitting that band to recreate TERRIF. This second version of the band comprised Holmes, Cosmo, ex-LIZZY BORDEN bassist Mike Davis and vocalist Dana Freebarin.

TERRIF folded for good when Holmes landed the job as six-stringer for DAVID LEE ROTH. The guitarist scaled even greater heights when he was inducted into the ranks of the OZZY OSBOURNE band in 1995.

By 2000 Davis was a member of BRANOM, a Los Angeles act comprising of former CLOUD NINE vocalist Tim Branom, ex-BOY ELROY guitarist Brian Davis and erstwhile HERICANE ALICE, BANGALORE CHOIR and BAD MOON RISING drummer Jackie Ramos.

BERNIE TORMÉ (UK)

Irishman Bernie Tormé is a talented guitarist with great character and renowned for some particularly wild axework and theatrics. Such showmanship brought him close to 'guitar hero' status whilst in GILLAN.

Tormé first made his name as guitarist with Irish bands WORMWOOD and URGE, prior to relocating to London forming SCRAPYARD in 1976. A hard rock trio of Tormé, bassist Bernie Hagley (also playing with VANITY FAIR at the time) and drummer Roger Hunt, SCRAPYARD gigged solidly throughout the London area.

Selected Ozzy-Related Acts From The Rockdetector Files

Hagley was to depart and the band were swiftly brought back up to strength with the addition of former ZZEBRA bassist John McCoy. However, this union lasted only a matter of months with Tormé striking out on his own as THE BERNIE TORMÉ BAND. McCoy meanwhile soldiered on with Paul Samson on guitar as SCRAPYARD became McCOY.

Playing hard rock but with a Punk image – Tormé having cut off his long hair to keep in vogue – the band managed to release two singles and contribute tracks to the Punk compilation album *Live At The Vortex*. THE BERNIE TORMÉ BAND, still a trio format with the guitarist augmented by bassist Phil Spalding and drummer Mark Harrison, put in some British supports to GILLAN, the headline act now featuring McCoy on bass.

An album was recorded for Jet Records but remains unreleased. Disillusioned, Tormé took up his old colleague John McCoy's offer to hook up with GILLAN. Spalding joined Punktress TOYAH then MIKE OLDFIELD, ORIGINAL MIRRORS and the platinum supergroup GTR led by guitarists STEVE HOWE and STEVE HACKETT.

Harrison went on to THE NIPPLE ERECTORS and DIRTY STRANGERS.

After his split from GILLAN in 1981, Tormé joined the warhorse rock act ATOMIC ROOSTER, appearing on their *Headline News* album and undertaking two tours of Germany and Italy.

But fate was to stall progress in trying to assemble another solo band when Tormé was asked to fill in for Randy Rhoads in OZZY OSBOURNE's band following the American guitarist's tragic death. Torme's stint on OZZY OSBOURNE's American tour lasted but two weeks, with the pressure being too much for the Irishman. Returning to London with OZZY OSBOURNE's blessing, Tormé, who had before he left suggested his own replacement to OZZY OSBOURNE in ex-RUBICON man Brad Gillis, set back to work on his own band ELECTRIC GYPSIES.

The fresh line-up featured two erstwhile GENERATION X men, second guitarist Bob 'Derwood' Andrews and drummer Mark Laff together with former BETHNAL bassist Everton Williams.

The *Turn Out The Lights* album featured SAXON drummer Nigel Glockler, bassist Phil Spalding and Bernie's ex-GILLAN partner Colin Towns on keyboards. For live work ELECTRIC GYPSIES consisted of Tormé handling both vocals and guitar, Williams on bass and drummer Frank Noon, the latter being on temporary loan from STAMPEDE.

During downtime in 1982 Tormé's name surfaced on his ex-GILLAN cohort keyboard player Colin Towns solo LP *Making Faces*, which – although recorded whilst Tormé was in GILLAN – only saw a later Japanese release.

The *Live* album (released during 1984) featured original IRON MAIDEN member Ron 'Rebel' Matthews on drums. (Matthews was much later to resurface in 1999 as part of ATOMIC ROOSTER).

A later British tour saw the addition of bassist Chris Heilmann (later to turn up in US act SHARK ISLAND) and ex-FRAMED drummer Ian Whitewood with vocalist Kef.

In 1984 ex-GIRL vocalist PHIL LEWIS joined the band on a supposed temporary basis following vocalist Kef's sudden departure, before joining on

Ozzy Osbourne

a full time basis. Two albums (using the TORMÉ handle rather than ELECTRIC GYPSIES) and successive British touring put the band in the press, but momentum seemed to be waning. Lewis relocated to Los Angeles to join American act L.A. GUNS.

The ELECTRIC GYPSIES soldiered on, now with ex-LONDON COWBOYS vocalist Steve Dior, but a further line-up blow came when Whitewood quit to join SHAM 69, his place being taken by erstwhile BEKI BONDAGE drummer Ben Bennett.

Tormé formed the short-lived RUSSIAN HIPPIES in 1988 with Bennett, vocalist Gary Owens and ex-BOMBSHELLS bassist Marc Russell. However, progress was minimal so Tormé and Russell travelled to America at the request of former TWISTED SISTER vocalist DEE SNIDER to join the vocalist's DESPERADOS outfit. Owens later joined SAMSON.

The DESPERADOS project of Tormé, Snider, Russell and ex IRON MAIDEN drummer Clive Burr initially scored a huge deal with Atlantic Records. However, after more than two years the band had switched to Elektra and, having laid down an album, discovered the label had no intention of releasing it.

Thus far the DESPERADOS album has only surfaced in bootleg form and although Dee Snider offered Tormé a position in another new act he was putting together – WIDOWMAKER – the Irishman opted to return to London. Upon his return Tormé put in a guest guitar appearance on former HANOI ROCKS guitarist RENE BERG's *The Leather, The Loneliness And Your Dark Eyes* album in 1991. Another project band was titled MUTANT with Blacken and Magpie of MOURNBLADE.

The year 1994 saw another solo release, *Demolition Ball*, with the guitarist joined in the studio by Gary Owens once more with a rhythm section of bassist John Pearce and drummer Chris Jones.

Early 1997 found the guitarist involved in Mick Underwood's reformation of the cult act QUATERMASS. Although Tormé wrote material for the album, *Long Road*, he was to opt out before recording of the album.

The guitarist's own solo album of that year, *Wild Irish*, recorded with Pearce and Jones, came out limited to merely 500 numbered copies.

Maintaining this renewed momentum, a further studio album was issued in 1999, one track including lead vocal from Dee Snider. In 2001 Tormé figured on a UFO tribute album entitled *Only UFO Can Rock Me*.

Bernie returned to the band format for SILVER. Convened in 2001, SILVER witnessed a welcome return to action by former MICHAEL SCHENKER GROUP vocalist Gary Barden. Joining Tormé and Barden for the eponymous album would be H-BLOCKX drummer Marco Minnemann and MAD MAX, CASANOVA and DEMON DRIVE bassist Michael Voss. Keyboards were in the hands of a true veteran – DON AIREY of RAINBOW, OZZY OSBOURNE and WHITESNAKE fame.

Albums:
TURN OUT THE LIGHTS, Kamaflage KAMLP 2 (1982) 50 UK
ELECTRIC GYPSIES, Zebra ZEB 1 (1983)
LIVE, Zebra MZEB 3 (1984)

Selected Ozzy-Related Acts From The Rockdetector Files
BACK TO BABYLON, Zebra ZEB 6 (1985)
ALL AROUND THE WORLD, Zebra (1985)
BACK WITH THE BOYS, Rawpower RAW LP 010 (1986)
OFFICIAL BOOTLEG, Onsala ONS 3 (1987)
DIE PRETTY, DIE YOUNG, Heavy Metal HMRLP 94 (1987)
ARE WE THERE YET, Heavy Metal HMR 168 (1991)
DEMOLITION BALL, Bleeding Hearts BLEED 2 (1994)
WILD IRISH, Retrowrek RETRK 103 (1997)
PUNK OR WHAT?, Retrowrek 104 (1998)
WHITE TRASH GUITAR, Retrowrek RETRK 105 (1999)

UFO (UK)
Line-Up: Phil Mogg (vocals), Michael Schenker (guitar), Pete Way (bass), Paul Raymond (keyboards), Andy Parker (drums)

A hugely influential hard rock band noted for the soulful talents of vocalist PHIL MOGG and superb songwriting abilities based around the triumvirate of Mogg, bassist PETE WAY and wayward guitarist Michael Schenker. UFO have successfully married strong melodies with some legendary riffs in a combination that has achieved world-wide success. The band's progress has only been marred by the various members' admitted excess of drugs and alcohol, which has resulted in the band's career being rather turbulent at times.

UFO was formed initially as THE BOYFRIENDS as a trio of Way, guitarist Mick Bolton and drummer Tic Torrazo. The group would journey its way through other guises (such as HOCUS POCUS, THE GOOD, THE BAD THE UGLY and ACID) before adding drummer Colin Turner to replace Torrazo. Upon adding vocalist Phil Mogg the band changed titles to UFO and soon ditched Turner in favour of Andy Parker. UFO debuted with a live appearance at Fagin's Blues Workshop in late 1969.

The early teenage incarnation of UFO achieved success in Germany and Japan with their first three albums, including a Number 1 single with a take on EDDIE COCHRAN's 'C'mon Everybody'. In Germany both 'Boogie For George' and 'C'mon Everybody' fared well on the national singles charts. Still teenagers, UFO toured Japan to superstar status. Such was the influence of 'C'mon Everybody' the band were forced to play it live on a Japanese tour 23 years later!

Estimates put sales of the first three albums, including the *Live* opus, at over three million in Germany such was the band's popularity there. However, it was after signing to Chrysalis in 1974 that things really started to take off globally. The material prior to the *Phenomenon* album was experimental, spacey rock but things would begin to change following Mick Bolton's departure.

In January 1972 ex-SHAGRAT, BLODWYN PIG and LANCASTER guitarist Larry Wallis joined the fold, but his tenure was relatively short, and in November 1972 Wallis quit to join PINK FAIRIES and later MOTÖRHEAD. In 1973 ex-SKINNY CAT guitarist BERNIE MARSDEN had a brief stint before UFO teamed up with Michael Schenker in June 1973. UFO had been on tour in Germany with support act the SCORPIONS and 'borrowed' Schenker from the German group as Marsden found himself stuck in England.

Ozzy Osbourne

The loan turned out to be more permanent in spite of Marsden arriving the next day and fulfilling his obligations on the final leg of the tour. UFO were so impressed by Schenker that Marsden was shown the door once live dates had ended. Marsden subsequently joined ex-JETHRO TULL bassist Glen Cornick in WILD TURKEY before finding international recognition in WHITESNAKE.

UFO would then record demos, including the Marsden co-composition "Oh My", at Rockfield Studios in Monmouthshire. Producer for these sessions was pop artist DAVE EDMUNDS. He in turn would suggest his cousin, PAUL CHAPMAN as contender for the guitar position. These tapes included tracks which eventually wound up on the *Phenomenon* album and would secure the deal with major label Chrysalis Records.

The *Phenomenon* album, produced by TEN YEARS AFTER bassist Leo Lyons, boasted what were to become two all-time classic rock tracks, namely 'Rock Bottom' and 'Doctor Doctor'. For live work during this period UFO hired the aforementioned second guitarist PAUL CHAPMAN, previously with UNIVERSE and SKID ROW, to augment Schenker.

UFO began 1974 with a gig at the Belgian Linkebeek Festival during January before a lengthy run of British and European club and pub dates. The band would also put in several appearances at the BBC which would much later turn up on live albums. In October of 1974 UFO put in their inaugural American shows, gigging at the infamous Los Angeles Whiskey club and supporting STEPPENWOLF amongst others, also putting in a showing on Don Kirshner's weekly concert TV show. Although the *Phenomenon* album failed to crack the Billboard charts the influential *Rolling Stone* magazine predicted that UFO would become "a very big act in an extremely short time."

During late 1974 UFO would begin recording of their sophomore Chrysalis outing *Force It*, still undertaking the odd club gigs during breaks in recording. Now managed by Wilf Wright, who also handled ROBIN TROWER, the band's next record would have production handled by Leo Lyons once again and included his TEN YEARS AFTER colleague CHICK CHURCHILL on keyboards.

UFO humbly rounded off the year with a gig at the less than salubrious Nottingham Boat Club.

UFO's young German guitarist had made his mark as a serious guitar talent on the early Chrysalis releases. By January 1975 UFO trimmed back down to a single guitar band dispensing with Chapman's services, the Welshman creating IONA, a band that evolved into LONE STAR.

1975's *Force It* continued the upward trend for the band. The band's American tour included legendary live broadcasts from the Los Angeles Record Plant, tapes from which would become highly prized on the bootleg market. UFO's concentration on America would also saw a virtual non stop run of gigs through October up until late November when the tour was rounded off as support to EDGAR WINTER in New York.

1976's *No Heavy Petting*, again with Lyons at the helm, UFO had added ex-HEAVY METAL KIDS keyboardist DANNY PEYRONEL to embellish their sound. UFO toured Britain in April of that year with support bands NUTZ and DIRTY TRICKS before setting off in May for American dates,

Selected Ozzy-Related Acts From The Rockdetector Files

including opening the established 'Day On The Green' festival, and a burst of headlining club shows, one of which had the fledgling VAN HALEN as openers. Other shows had UFO paired with FLEEETWOOD MAC, FOGHAT, STYX and NAZARETH.

Peyronel broke away upon the American tour's completion in July 1976. Later in the year ex-CHICKENSHACK and SAVOY BROWN keyboard player Paul Raymond took Peyronel's position. Raymond had also been a member of THE SAVAGES and THE CIRCLES in the mid-'60s.

Peyronel later turned up in BLUE MAX, issuing one album in 1978, and Spanish acts BANZAI and TARZEN as well as the Argentinian-based RIFF. The ex-UFO man would also find acclaim as a hit songwriter penning MEAT LOAF's 'Midnight At The Lost And Found' as well as work for Soul diva SADE.

UFO debuted with Raymond playing three sold-out gigs at London's Marquee.

Although UFO had made steady progress to that point, their album's potential was hindered by lacklustre production. However, 1977's *Lights Out* saw the band utilising the services of Ron Nevison and sowing the first seeds of their American success.

Unfortunately, on the eve of their debut American tour supporting RUSH, Schenker performed what was to be the first of his notorious disappearing acts. Former guitarist PAUL CHAPMAN (now firmly ensconced in LONE STAR) was hastily drafted in on a temporary basis before the wayward Schenker was located in Europe and persuaded to finish the tour.

In spite of internal frictions UFO's persistence had paid off with American radio taking to 'Too Hot to Handle,' and the *Lights Out* album remaining on the Billboard charts for nearly half a year peaking at Number 23 and earning the band a well-deserved gold album.

American reaction to the band's polished hard rock sound meant that it was sensible to relocate. The band all moved to Los Angeles and began recording *Obsession*, once more produced by Ron Nevison, in February 1978.

They returned home for a successful British tour during the summer and a further run of American dates with BLUE OYSTER CULT and with co-headliners JUDAS PRIEST followed, but by October Schenker had quit for good returning to Germany for another brief liaison with the SCORPIONS.

Meantime Chapman had been for an audition with the SCORPIONS during the June of the same year but would instead step into the breach with UFO once more and make his mark with the band for a quick burst of American dates, then on their January 1979 British tour. The awesome live album *Strangers In The Night* (captured whilst UFO still featured Schenker superbly on form) was released to enormous acclaim, finally heralding UFO as a major band in their home country.

The album boasts probably more classic cuts than any other live effort, featuring as it does 'Doctor, Doctor', 'Lights Out', 'Rock Bottom', 'Only You Can Rock Me', 'Shoot, Shoot', 'Too Hot To Handle' and 'Love To Love'. The live version of 'Doctor, Doctor' cracked the British charts and witnessed UFO promoting its release with a *Top Of The Pops* TV appearance.

Following the British dates the band once more set off for the American touring circuit, where by now they were capable of selling out arenas in some areas. Dates also included more shows guesting for RUSH and a mid-slot billing at the California 'World Music' festival. UFO's status was now such that members appeared as celebrity guests on the *Hollywood Squares* TV quiz show. UFO really got to grips with America during the summer of 1979 with a lengthy touring leg initially with JUDAS PRIEST as openers, both British acts coincidentally promoting groundbreaking live albums. However, in Chicago roles were reversed and UFO became the opening act. UFO then added a further leg with AC/DC as their guests.

In August of 1979 the group cut their debut product with Chapman *No Place to Run*. Production was handled by the esteemed BEATLES producer George Martin at his studios on the Caribbean island of Montserrat. The sessions were just completed prior to the island being ravaged by Hurricane Camille.

The album was launched in America upfront of a European release. It fared well, reaching Number 59 on the Billboard charts and UFO closed the year with a taster tour of their homeland in December as a portent of things to come for a full blown British tour in 1980.

In America UFO were by now headlining sold out arenas. More live action followed in Britain supported by GIRL and UFO was announced as headliner at the Reading Festival. However, prior to the gig Raymond was ousted in favour of ex-WILD HORSES keyboardist and rhythm guitarist Neil Carter. UFO slotted in a further British tour to close the year supported by FIST. Raymond soon found employment with Michael Schenker in the German's impressive new outfit MICHAEL SCHENKER GROUP.

1981 saw another strong album *The Wild, The Willing And The Innocent*, produced by the band themselves. Amply displaying Mogg's almost film noir approach to lyric writing, the album was bolstered by diverse experimentation, such as a string section and the haunting 'Profession Of Violence'. Keyboards on the album were supplied by former LONE STAR and URIAH HEEP man JOHN SLOMAN.

Another mammoth world tour ensued, including dates alongside OZZY OSBOURNE in America, before heading for Switzerland to record *Mechanix*. Producer Gary Lyons was employed as UFO struggled to maintain a fresh approach to the hard rock sound.

Despite including barnstorming stage favourites, such as 'Let It Rain' and 'We Belong To The Night', PETE WAY reportedly found much of the material too limp and verbalized this opinion in many interviews. Indeed, after the American tour supporting OZZY OSBOURNE the bassist quit, quickly finding a new writing partner in ex-MOTÖRHEAD guitarist Eddie Clarke in a new act titled FASTWAY. However, this high profile union was nixed by Way's contractual obligations to Chrysalis Records and despite the ex-UFO man having written the bulk of the material on the debut FASTWAY record, his contribution remained unaccredited. The bassist also put in the hours producing records for COCKNEY REJECTS and TWISTED SISTER. The liaison was short-lived as Way jumped ship to another celebrated alliance, joining OZZY OSBOURNE's touring band, before forming WAYSTED.

UFO stuck to their guns, with Chapman filling in on bass for studio work

Selected Ozzy-Related Acts From The Rockdetector Files

on the next album. Although a strong record, *Making Contact's* headway was severely hindered by numerous setbacks. For the European leg of the tour bass duties were handled by then TALAS bassist BILLY SHEEHAN, but during a show in Athens, Greece, Mogg collapsed onstage causing a near riot with Sheehan being struck by an object thrown from the audience.

The band took some time off before their British tour, during which it was planned to record dates for a live album. By this time Sheehan had returned home (still nursing his wounds from Greece) and bass was supplied by erstwhile DAMNED and EDDIE AND THE HOTRODS member Paul Gray, of whom many commented on his resemblance to Way both in looks and stage moves. The live recordings were strangely only issued in the form of one side of a family tree-based tribute album entitled *Headstone*.

After the final tour Chapman, Carter and Parker recorded some demos with Chapman handling vocals with a view to securing a new deal. Considerations were made to approach CHEAP TRICK's Robin Zander for the lead vocalist spot but Carter opted to join GARY MOORE on tour in America.

PAUL CHAPMAN relocated to Florida and formed D.O.A. with Americans David Edwards on vocals, guitarist Robert Journey, drummer Paul Barron and bassist Steve Chikitus. A further act, GHOST, included ex-PERSIAN RISK vocalist Carl Sentance.

Chapman rejoined his old UFO sparring partner PETE WAY in WAYSTED later in the year after which it was alleged that Chapman also played live gigs in Florida under the title of UFO!

Following his short stint with UFO, Paul Gray formed a new act titled SING SING with ex-MEMBERS guitarist Nigel Bennett and former EDDIE & THE HOTRODS drumming colleague Steve Nichol. Gray also briefly joined Swedish Metal band HEAVY LOAD in 1987. The bassist would later work on the live circuit with ex MOTÖRHEAD guitarist 'Fast' Eddie Clark's act FASTWAY.

Andy Parker, meantime, moved to Los Angeles, joining SCARLETT. Later moves included reuniting with Way in WAYSTED then American acts DR. WISH and REXX AND JOHNSSON.

In 1984 Mogg travelled to America to recruit a guitarist for the revitalised UFO and for a time YNGWIE MALMSTEEN was strongly rumoured to have landed the job with DOKKEN's fret burner GEORGE LYNCH supposedly also in the running. However, Japanese/American ex-BOY WONDER and THUNDERWING guitarist Tommy McClendon gained the honours. Paul Raymond rejoined the ranks alongside bassist Gray and former DIAMOND HEAD drummer Robbie France.

UFO set out on a British tour supported by TOBRUK to debut the new material and revised line up before recording began. The resulting *Misdemeanour* album featured some very strong songs but was crippled by Nick Tauber's lightweight production. The rather thin guitar sound of McClendon, who by now was renamed somewhat bizarrely 'Atomik Tommy M' didn't help matters either.

As ex-MAGNUM drummer Jim Simpson replaced France (who later journeyed through WISHBONE ASH and SKUNK ANANSIE), UFO performed

Ozzy Osbourne

a strong headline set at the Poperinge festival in Belgium, before playing the DEEP PURPLE reunion Knebworth show that year. The band toured Britain with PALLAS and SHY as support in 1985, then somewhat oddly settled on opening for ACCEPT on a European jaunt. America followed (where the album had been totally remixed) with the group performing on a disastrous club tour, during which Raymond quit to be briefly replaced by David Jacobson, a previous colleague of McClendon's.

Following the somewhat lukewarm response to *Misdemeanour*, UFO effectively split, but not before recording a mini-album (*Ain't Misbehavin*) for the indie FM Revolver label. This release only served to show that Mogg was sorely missing his old songwriting partners, as the material was strictly second rate.

During the ensuing period of inactivity, Mogg passed on his experience by dabbling in management and looking after the affairs of THE QUIREBOYS, a band which included his nephew Nigel Mogg on bass, before performing one gig as UFO at the *Metal Hammer* magazine party in December 1987. The line up Mogg assembled for this show included guitarist Myke Gray (ex JAGGED EDGE) and Gray. McClendon had long since departed, although before returning to America had played guitar on Irish act WINTER'S REIGN's album *The Beginning*.

Simpson was briefly a member of U.S.I., toured with BONNIE TYLER before joining BUDGIE in 1988. He would later join Newcastle act the RED DOGS. Gray would rejoin EDDIE & THE HOT RODS and later reunite with the DAMNED. (By the turn of the millennium Gray and Simpson had reunited with former DAMNED man Alan Lee Shaw in a new act MISCHIEF.)

Way meantime, having dissolved WAYSTED, bought a property near Mogg in Birmingham, enabling the pair to start writing together again. The duo cut new tracks with a succession of guitarists, including Myke Gray (by then a member of SKIN), the STARFIGHTERS' Rik Sanford and Tony Glidewell. With Sanford much of the material for the band's next eventual album was laid down. SAVATAGE's Chris Caffrey was also the subject of discussion at one stage. Discussions, although unfruitful, were also in place with both Schenker and PAUL CHAPMAN as well.

It would take a number of years before Mogg and Way committed to a line-up of guitarist Laurence Archer, previously a member of STAMPEDE, GRAND SLAM and RHODE ISLAND RED, with ex-WILD HORSES and ULI JON ROTH drummer Clive Edwards.

This line up recorded the commendable *High Stakes And Dangerous Men* album, produced by Kit Woolven (also featuring keyboardist DON AIREY and backing vocals from ex-NIGHT singer Stevie Lange). The new record had been named after a Wild West novel Mogg was reading at the time but with a slight name change from the original and slightly derogatory *High Stakes And Desperate Men*!

From a series of sell-out Japanese shows the band culled the live *Lights Out In Tokyo* set. The rejuvenated UFO played Britain with the addition of ex-STRANGER and TOBRUK keyboard player Jem Davis. The group promptly completed two successful UK headline tours with the RED DOGS and WRAITH as opening acts. In typical fashion, European shows ended in

Selected Ozzy-Related Acts From The Rockdetector Files

Russia with Mogg, fortunately on the last date of the tour, falling offstage and breaking his leg!

The *High Stakes* album was purposely held back from an American release as the possibility of reuniting the classic 1978 line-up grew stronger. In some downtime, Way and Archer produced the WRAITH album *Danger Calling*.

Archer and Edwards joined MEDICINE HEAD when it became apparent that Mogg and Way were intent on reuniting the classic line-up.

After putting in work with the idea of teaming back up with PAUL CHAPMAN, it was finally announced in 1993 that the 1978 line-up had reformed for a very low-key tour of Germany. The alliance was pushed through so quickly that tour promoters were unaware of Schenker's involvement. The shows, with support act QUIET RIOT, were a huge success for UFO as they played the classic *Strangers In The Night* set plus some of Schenker's own *Thank You* record.

Testing the waters in America, UFO performed at a festival in San Antonio in April 1994 alongside MOTÖRHEAD, BLUE OYSTER CULT and YNGWIE MALMSTEEN. UFO signed to Zero Corporation Records in Japan for a phenomenal advance later the same year to record the superb *Walk On Water* album, which arrived towards the end of 1995.

In the interim, an album was released in 1994 titled *TNT*. Issued on Essential Records, the record comprises the *Lights Out In Tokyo* recordings plus previously officially unavailable live material that earlier appeared as the *Parker's Birthday* bootleg from Texas in 1979.

UFO began a high profile American tour with support acts TRIANGLE and LODE in late June 1995, including a headline slot at the Milwaukee Festival and runs of four sold-out nights in Chicago, Los Angeles and San Francisco. Parker by now had laid down his drumsticks for good and his position was taken by ex-TYTAN, AC/DC, DIO and RHINO BUCKET drummer Simon Wright. The tour continued on into November, with the band returning to many cities to play larger venues. Most venues sold out and UFO confounded the critics by proving so successful with no American record deal or financial back up.

Trouble struck later in the tour when Schenker disappeared mysteriously yet again (old habits die hard!), necessitating the cancellation of many shows. Rumours abounded concerning fistfights between Mogg and Schenker and another collapse into substance abuse from Way. The band duly folded once more, unable to continue the dates without Schenker, as contractual obligations stipulated the guitarist's appearance.

UFO reunited for rehearsals with ex-EUROPE guitarist JOHN NORUM. Although Wright contributed to John Norum's solo album *World's Away* this proposed UFO union was short-lived. Schenker had apparently a contract stating that the band could not be titled UFO without his involvement.

In the meantime, American fans had the pleasure of live gigs by UFO tribute band FAUCET that very often included a certain Mr. Way! An added acknowledgement of UFO's influence on the rock scene came in March 1996 when the IRON MAIDEN single 'Lord Of The Flies' featured a cover version of UFO's 'Doctor Doctor' on the B-side. British Metal band SAVAGE cov-

Ozzy Osbourne

ered 'Hot 'n' Ready' for the Japanese version of their 1996 album *Holy Wars*. During mid-1996 Mogg and Way, signing to MOTÖRHEAD's manager Todd Singerman, formed a studio project band with DIO drummer Vinnie Appice and guitarist Tracy G for a Heavy Metal project, but UFO once more resumed negotiations with both Schenker and Chapman. However, the illustrious *Parker's Birthday* bootleg re-appeared the same year albeit quietly sanctioned by the band apparently as a precursor to another stab at a reformation with PAUL CHAPMAN. Oddly the CD credited the last track as being 'Shoot, Shoot' although in fact the song is absent from the sound recording.

Amidst this hive of activity, Mogg and Way also busied themselves by recording an album together with American guitarist George Bellas and ex-JEFFERSON STARSHIP and JOURNEY drummer Aynsley Dunbar. The resulting album, *Edge Of The World*, which included backing vocals supplied by MR. BIG's ERIC MARTIN, emerged in 1997 under the band name of MOGG/WAY. The album cover and style of the act's logo left nothing to the imagination.

After the emergence of the MOGG/WAY album UFO settled their differences with Schenker. The errant guitarist had in the meantime issued a further solo album, *Written In The Sand*, and a live effort recorded in Japan entitled *The Michael Schenker Story Live*. The band also negotiated a long-overdue European release for the *Walk On Water* album.

The band put in a lengthy and well-attended tour of Europe (with DANGER DANGER opening on the Continent) which included a run of British gigs in early 1998 supported by DIRTY DEEDS before predictably Schenker jumped ship once more, in the middle of a Japanese tour.

Mogg and Way knuckled down with recording a new album, enlisting Raymond and Wright. PAUL RAYMOND also began work on a further solo album for which Mogg aided on lead vocals.

The errant German guitarist meanwhile, still professing future commitments to UFO, toured with MICHAEL SCHENKER GROUP as part of the 1998 G3 guitar tour alongside ULI JON ROTH and JOE SATRIANI and issued a further MICHAEL SCHENKER GROUP album *The Unforgiven*. Another guitarist from the UFO family also made a return to the limelight the same year. Since the close of the *Misdemeanour* dates Tommy McClendon had kept a surprisingly low profile but would re-emerge touting a fresh act SOULMOTOR, a union with TESLA bassist Brian Wheat. McClendon would also guest on the TOMMY TUTONE album *Rich Text Files* the same year.

UFO was far from a spent force in 1999, though, with negotiations still taking place between Mogg, Way and Schenker for a further album. Not content to remain idle, a further MOGG/WAY album was recorded with ex-EDWINDARE/THE TRUTH guitarist Jeff Kollmann (including contributions from Raymond and Wright) and Way was busying himself planning a further WAYSTED project. Raymond issued his third solo album *Man On A Mission* which included a drastic re-work of 'Lights Out' and Mogg on guest vocals. Rounding off the year a 'semi-official' live album *Werewolves Of London* crept out much to fans, pleasure, although this had not been sanctioned by Schenker.

A new millennium broke for the band with PETE WAY ensconced in

Selected Ozzy-Related Acts From The Rockdetector Files

Rockfield Studios in Wales cutting his first solo album. Schenker issued an instrumental record whilst still giving the green light for a full UFO reunion. Wright was out of the picture though having rejoined DIO.

Meantime it was announced that the year 2000 would also see the release of a UFO tribute album.

UFO settled their differences with Schenker and pulled in Aynsley Dunbar on drums again to cut a new UFO album *The Covenant*. Meantime Way issued his first purely solo effort *Amphetamine* as Mogg busied himself on his first solo album working with MOGG/WAY and COSMO SQUAD guitarist JEFF KOLLMAN and drummer Shane Galaas.

UFO were all set to tour Britain in 2000 with support from ULI JON ROTH. European dates were to have GLENN HUGHES and MOON DOC supporting. The band sported yet another new look with Mogg, Schenker and Way joined by rhythm guitarist/keyboard player Luis Moldonado from MOGG/WAY and former BADLANDS, BLACK SYMPHONY and RACER X drummer Jeff Martin.

Quite incredibly UFO disintegrated in full public gaze during the British dates. Schenker, much to fans' amazement vastly overweight, was reportedly headbutted by QUIREBOYS vocalist SPIKE at an after-show party in Newcastle.

These rumours appeared to be confirmed when at the Manchester show the German walked onstage sporting two black eyes and the word 'Spike' written on his forehead. What followed was a débacle with Schenker refusing to play lead solos, deliberately bashing into Mogg and even offering his guitar to the singer at one point. With the audience booing, the guitarist Schenker proclaimed "This audience sucks and so do I". With UFO leaving the stage Schenker promptly marched back on to taunt the audience further. Needless to say all further shows were cancelled.

With UFO seemingly rescued from the brink the band's name was kept in the public eye in early 2001 by the tribute album *Only UFO Can Rock Me*. Featured players were RAINBOW's Dougie White, MOTÖRHEAD's Phil Campbell, FASTWAY singer LEA HART, ex-OZZY OSBOURNE and GILLAN guitarist BERNIE TORMÉ, Bob Skeat of WISHBONE ASH, ex-GRIM REAPER vocalist Steve Grimmett and even former UFO keyboard player Jem Davis.

As Schenker wrapped up recording of his latest MICHAEL SCHENKER GROUP album, the wryly titled *Be Aware Of Scorpions*, it would emerge that he had joined forces with Way once more for a round of studio sessions billed as PLOT. This alliance would be debuted as the support act to Schenker's own American tour. Another outing of interest to hardcore UFO fans arrived in early 2002 as former keyboard player DANNY PEYRONEL debuted his solo career with the *Make The Monkey Dance* album. Included would be a re-interpretation of Peyronel's 'Highway Lady', originally found on the *No Heavy Petting* album. Phil Mogg meantime finally announced the title of his solo project to be STONETOWNE.

Further attention would be bestowed upon the band by the release on Smallstone Records of the compilation album *Sucking In The '70s*. This collection comprised of modern rock acts paying homage to '70s heroes and

Ozzy Osbourne
FIREBALL MINISTRY duly weighed in with a cover of 'Doctor, Doctor'. Meantime, all this peripheral activity masked the fact that UFO themselves, with the Mogg/Schenker/Way axis joined by drummer Aynsley Dunbar once again, were back in the recording studio laying down a new album reportedly titled *Sharks*.

Albums:
UFO, Beacon BEAS 12 (1970)
UFO 2 – FLYING ONE HOUR SPACE ROCK, Beacon BEAS 19 (1972)
BEST OF UFO, Teldec (1973)
THE BEGINNING VOL. 8 – UFO, Decca Beacon 6 21655 AF (1973)
UFO LIVE, Gem (1974)
PHENOMONEN, Chrysalis 1059 (1974)
FORCE IT, Chrysalis CHR 1074 (1975) **71 USA**
SPACE METAL, (1976)
NO HEAVY PETTING, Chrysalis 1103(1976) **38 SWEDEN**
LIGHTS OUT, Chrysalis CHR 1127 (1977)
OBSESSION, Chrysalis CDL 1182 (1978)
STRANGERS IN THE NIGHT, Chrysalis CJT 5 (1979)
PROFILE OF UFO, Teldec (1979)
THE BEST OF UFO, Decca (1979)
NO PLACE TO RUN, Chrysalis CDL 1239 (1980)
WILD WILLING AND THE INNOCENT, Chrysalis CHR 1307 (1981)
MECHANIX, Chrysalis CHR 1360 (1982)
MAKING CONTACT, Chrysalis CHR 1402 (1983)
HEADSTONE, Chrysalis CTY 1437 (1983)
MISDEMEANOUR, Chrysalis CHR 1518 (1985)
SPACE METAL, Teldec 628363 (1985)
COLLECTION, Castle Collectors CCSLP 101 (1985)
AIN'T MISBEHAVIN', FM Revolver WKFM XD107 (1988)
BBC RADIO 1 LIVE IN CONCERT, Windsong WINDCD016 (1991)
HIGH STAKES AND DANGEROUS MEN, Essential ESSCD 178 (1992)
LIGHTS OUT IN TOKYO (LIVE), JVC Victor VICP 5204 (1993)
TOO HOT TO HANDLE – THE BEST OF UFO, Music Club MCCD 153 (1994)
TNT (LIVE 1979 & 1992), Essential ESD 218 (1994)
WALK ON WATER, Zero Corporation XRCN 1237 (1995) (Japanese release)
DOCTOR, DOCTOR, Karussel 550 743-2 (1995)
BEST OF UFO, Munhwa MHRL 1204 (1995) (Korean release)
HEAVEN'S GATE LIVE, M&M M&MCD 1 (1995)
CHAMPIONS OF ROCK, Disky CR862552 (1996)
THE X FACTOR: OUT THERE... AND BACK, Snapper Music SMDCD122 (1997)
ON WITH THE ACTION – LIVE AT THE ROUNDHOUSE 1976, Zoom Club ZCRCD1 (1997)
BBC IN SESSION AND LIVE IN CONCERT, Windsong 72434 94403 21 (1999)

Selected Ozzy-Related Acts From The Rockdetector Files
LIVE IN LONDON, Brilliant BT 33037 (1999)
WEREWOLVES OF LONDON – LIVE, Zoom Club ZCRCD20 (1999)
THE COVENANT, SPV (2000)

URIAH HEEP (UK)
Line-Up: Pete Goalby (vocals), Mick Box (guitar), Bob Daisley (bass), John Sinclair (keyboards), Lee Kerslake (drums)

URIAH HEEP have remained a steadfast contributor to quality British hard rock. During their lengthy, a 25-year history the band has toured the world relentlessly and charted consistently, although are probably appreciated more outside of their homeland.

URIAH HEEP originated from London outfit THE STALKERS, which formed in 1965 as a beat combo. During 1967 the band featured guitarist Mick Box, bassist Ricky Hurd and drummer Roger Penlington. THE STALKERS lost their lead vocalist and Penlington offered the services of his cousin, David Byron (real surname Garrick) to fill the position.

Byron and Box, wishing to turn professional, later evolved THE STALKERS into SPICE during 1968. Following a few line up shuffles – which saw the rhythm section of bassist Barry Green and drummer Nigel Pegrum ousted (Pegrum turning up in Progressive Rockers GNIDROLOG for two albums) – SPICE finally settled on Box, Byron, organist Roy Sharland, ex-GODS bassist Paul Newton and drummer Alex Napier.

The band's affairs were handled by Gerry Bron at the time and he signed them to his Hit Records Productions company, resulting in the single 'What About The Music' in the same year on the United Artist label. Newton only appeared on the B-side of this single ('In Love') as he was recruited mid-session.

SPICE were regulars on the club circuit and in early 1969 secured a prestigious residency at London's Marquee Club. At this stage in the band's development many cover versions bolstered the live set, and both Box and Byron were earning a living wage by covering successful pop songs of the day for Avenue Records. SPICE also recorded demo tapes under another name, THE PLAY.

Undergoing an identity crisis, the band began recording their debut album as SPICE, but initial recordings were shelved and by the time the album was completed SPICE had evolved into a completely different creature.

With the addition of ex-TOE FAT and GODS guitarist KEN HENSLEY to take the place of Sharland (who had joined ARTHUR BROWN and founded FUZZY DUCK, releasing one album) the band adopted a new name. The handle URIAH HEEP came from the character in Charles Dickens *David Copperfield*.

URIAH HEEP came onto the scene in 1970 with the *Very 'Eavy, Very Umble* album. The imagery and band title were all the more apt, it being the hundredth anniversary of the death of Charles Dickens that year. The British version of the album featured a photograph of Byron sprayed with theatrical cobwebbing, but the American version featured a bizarre worm like dragon.

The first URIAH HEEP line-up proper comprised Box, Byron, Newton and Hensley together with former SPENCER DAVIS GROUP, PLASTIC PENNY and ELTON JOHN drummer Nigel Olsson.

The debut album contained as its opening track the seminal 'Gypsy', a standard the band wrote as their first ever song and still a mainstay of their live set to this day.

After the release of the first album Olsson quit to rejoin ELTON JOHN (and later to become a successful producer) and was superseded by ex-BAKERLOO drummer Keith Baker. A further drumstool change came after the *Salisbury* album, when Baker was replaced by ex-CRESSIDA man Ian Clarke. *Salisbury* also featured guest keyboards courtesy of Manfred Mann and a title track weighing in at nearly 17 minutes. Once again, the American version of the album came with a different sleeve to the European original which featured a tank driving over a flower.

Interestingly, the song *Lady In Black* gained the band massive single success in Germany many years after the album release, scoring the coveted Number 1 single position and staying there for a massive thirteen weeks, earning the band a Golden Lion award.

HEEP were now beginning to make waves on the international scene and in 1971 undertook what was to be the first of many American tours. For these dates URIAH HEEP supported STEPPENWOLF and THREE DOG NIGHT, throwing the band into the fire playing massive arenas.

The band's third album, *Look At Yourself*, saw yet more changes. Ian Clarke was out in favour of Hensley's ex-TOE FAT colleague Lee Kerslake and Newton lost his place in November 1971 to ex-COLLOSSEUM and TEMPEST bassist Mark Clarke. His stay was short-lived and Clarke, later to turn up in RAINBOW and MOUNTAIN, was quickly despatched in favour of New Zealander and ex-THE NEW NADIR, KEEF HARTLEY BAND and MILLER ANDERSON BAND man Gary Thain.

The new line up crafted the *Demons And Wizards* album, URIAH HEEP's first record to be recorded on 16-track. Graced with one of noted fantasy artist Roger Dean's evocative paintings, the album was another solid effort, highlighted by the inclusion of live favourites 'Easy Livin'' and 'The Wizard'. *Demons And Wizards* gave the band another chart hit to rival 'Lady In Black'. The single charting everywhere except Britain. Not resting on their laurels the band got out another album, *The Magician's Birthday* before the close of the year.

URIAH HEEP were by now a truly international success with the Australian charts in particular featuring numerous albums and singles simultaneously.

Their debut live record quickly sold more than a million copies. *Sweet Freedom*, where the band recorded for the first time in France, spawned another hit single in 'Stealin''.

As with 'Easy Livin'', the 'Stealin'' single charted everywhere with the exception of the band's home country. By now, URIAH HEEP were regularly at the top of the Australian and New Zealand charts. Indeed, the band were the subject of a special double album release, titled *Downunda*, made available solely in those territories.

URIAH HEEP's line up remained thankfully stable until the 1974 album

Selected Ozzy-Related Acts From The Rockdetector Files

Wonderland. Another mammoth world tour ensued following the album's release, including shows in Australia and New Zealand. Thain, desperately ill from drug dependency, was to have his position ably filled by ex-KING CRIMSON, ROXY MUSIC and FAMILY bassist JOHN WETTON. 1975 Thain had suffered a massive onstage electric shock in Dallas, Texas resulting in the cancellation of an American tour. Thain was finally to overdose on pills on December 8th, 1975, resulting in his death. The band doggedly soldiered on with a 45-da te tour of America before successful British dates.

1975 also saw URIAH HEEP's position solidified as a band of international major status, with the release of a *Best Of* album. There were also two solo efforts in DAVID BYRON's *Take No Prisoners* (which had contributions from both Box and Kerslake) and Hensley's second solo record, *Eager To Please*, which featured ex-URIAH HEEP bassist Mark Clarke.

Unfortunately, URIAH HEEP slowly fragmented with constantly shifting line-ups, but still managed to release a string of albums. *Return To Fantasy* proved a highlight, peaking at Number 7 in the British charts but the follow-up *High And Mighty* was a patchy affair that failed to sell. Nevertheless, the band geared up for roadwork once more on a British tour that saw WIDOWMAKER (featuring a future HEEP member, bassist Bob Daisley) as strong support.

By this point in the URIAH HEEP saga DAVID BYRON's increasing reliance on drink and drugs was creating frictions within the band and becoming increasingly noticeable onstage. At the close of their 1976 Spanish tour Byron was asked to leave. The singer hastily created his own band, ROUGH DIAMOND with ex-BAKERLOO, COLOSSEUM and HUMBLE PIE guitarist Clem Clempson, and Wetton departed soon after, eventually to find American stardom with ASIA.

During this time of flux ex-DEEP PURPLE vocalist DAVID COVERDALE actually rehearsed with URIAH HEEP, before he in turn asked Box and Kerslake to help kick-start his own WHITESNAKE project. Also involved at this juncture was former ACE KEFFORD STAND and BEDLAM bassist Denny Ball.

Finally the gaps were filled. Ex-LUCIFER'S FRIEND vocalist John Lawton and ex-DAVID BOWIE and WISHBONE ASH bassist Trevor Bolder joined as the band soldiered on, although the musical style took a radical detour into more pop orientated territory.

1977's *Firefly* album received critical praise and, with renewed vigour, URIAH HEEP commenced touring once more, opening with an American support slot to KISS. However, sales were lacking and *Firefly* was to remain outside the charts.

The ensuing *Innocent Victim* also made no headway in the British charts but put URIAH HEEP back on the map, being the band's best-selling album to date in Germany, where the single 'Free Me' also fared well.

1978's *Fallen Angel* combined radio friendly material, such as 'Come Back To Me' and 'All Or Nothing', alongside bona fide hard rockers. Although the band's tours continued to be well-attended *Fallen Angel* proved a poor seller. As the band once more ensconced themselves in the recording studio both Lawton and Kerslake quit.

More new recruits included ex-MANFRED MANN drummer Chris Slade,

Ozzy Osbourne

filling the gap left by Kerslake and former LONE STAR vocalist JOHN SLOMAN. The band actually auditioned Pete Goalby for the vocalist position but favoured Sloman, who was being billed at the time by many as the new Robert Plant.

Post-HEEP Kerslake had set about forging a fresh group in alliance with erstwhile MANFRED MANN bassist Colin Pattendon and then unknown future GO WEST vocalist Pete Cox. This venture was brought to an abrupt halt when the drummer was inducted into the new OZZY OSBOURNE band, Kerslake going on to grace the monumental *Blizzard Of Oz* and *Diary Of A Madman* records.

The frictions that had caused Kerslake's departure would unfortunately resurface. In the middle of recording *Conquest* in 1980 KEN HENSLEY left the band, apparently unable to reconcile himself with Sloman's vocal style. Hensley went on to release his third solo album, *Free Spirit*, on Bronze Records in 1981. He would also create a fresh act titled SHOTGUN which featured Denny Ball on bass, guitarist Derek Marshall, ex-KINKS keyboard player Ian Gibbons and SILVERHEAD drummer Pete Thompson. SHOTGUN put in one gig at London's Marquee (to which all of URIAH HEEP turned up!) before folding. Hensley then joined American Southern Rockers BLACKFOOT.

Hensley's position was taken in November 1980 by Canadian Greg Dechart, who had worked together with Sloman in the act PULSAR. With this configuration of personnel, URIAH HEEP cut the 'Think It Over' single and set out on a poorly attended British tour in November 1980.

Sloman, seeing the writing on the wall from both fans and critics, departed in early 1981 and was to hook up with GARY MOORE. Sloman was also involved in ex-TYGERS OF PAN TANG guitarist JOHN SYKES, project BADLANDS with WHITESNAKE bassist Neil Murray, although this project faltered as Sykes was drafted into THIN LIZZY.

Chris Slade joined GARY NUMAN and much later AC/DC. Dechart joined MIKE AND THE MECHANICS.

Box tried to reform the band with bassist Trevor Bolder, but the latter succumbed to an offer from WISHBONE ASH and set off for pastures new. Desperate not to let the name just fizzle out, Box even asked Byron to rejoin. The offer was declined.

Mick Box finally got URIAH HEEP back off the ground with the release of the Ashley Howe produced *Abominog* in 1982. The new URIAH HEEP boasted a line up of ex-TRAPEZE and RAINBOW vocalist Pete Goalby, ex-HEAVY METAL KIDS keyboardist John Sinclair, former RAINBOW and WIDOWMAKER bassist Bob Daisley and a returning Lee Kerslake. The drummer had just left the OZZY OSBOURNE band along with Daisley.

Box and company actually waited for Goalby to finish an American tour with TRAPEZE before recording and in the meantime had auditioned former ARGENT man John Verity in the interim. Verity would later have a brief liaison with MICHAEL SCHENKER GROUP and issue albums under his own steam as the JOHN VERITY BAND.

URIAH HEEP's first move with Goalby was a theatre tour of America with support coming from British act GRIM REAPER as *Abominog*

Selected Ozzy-Related Acts From The Rockdetector Files

rejuvenated the band's career, bringing in many new fans, and the album was a world-wide success. The single, 'That's The Way That It Is', even secured a placing in the American national charts, and the band put in a storming performance at the Castle Donington 'Monsters Of Rock' festival.

URIAH HEEP pulled out all the stops during 1983 promoting the *Head First* album, where the new line-up of Box, Goalby, Sinclair, Kerslake and former bassist Trevor Bolder (Daisley having drifted back once more to OZZY OSBOURNE) undertook a gruelling world tour. Starting in Europe then adding America (supporting DEF LEPPARD, JUDAS PRIEST, RUSH and ZZ TOP), Japan, India, Hong Kong, Malaysia, Singapore and back once more to America, URIAH HEEP pulled out all the stops.

URIAH HEEP also appeared at the Belgian Heavy Sound festival in the same year alongside GARY MOORE, GOLDEN EARRING, ANVIL and BARON ROJO. The band was now intent on making drastic changes to their organisation following the 'Head First' world tour, splitting from both management and long-time record company Bronze to sign with Portrait, an affiliate of CBS Records. The first fruits of this liaison being the excellent *Equator* album.

This renaissance period for the band came to a close when in 1985 Pete Goalby left, suffering from vocal problems which culminated in his voice collapsing during an Australian tour. He was at first replaced by American, ex-JOSHUA vocalist Steven Fontaine for a series of American club dates before URIAH HEEP drafted in former PRAYING MANTIS and GRAND PRIX vocalist Bernie Shaw. Following on from a chaotic period the advent of the Canadian vocalist would signal a period of much needed stability within the ranks. Fontaine meantime created RINGLEADER for a 1989 album.

The band, parting company with Sinclair who teamed up with OZZY OSBOURNE, also added another ex-GRAND PRIX member, keyboard player Phil Lanzon, who had recently been touring with the reformed SWEET and briefly had been involved with LIONHEART.

The band actually announced they were splitting in March 1986 but by 1987 were on tour in Russia, having secured a new deal with Legacy Records. These dates in Russia saw the band playing to a massive 185,000 people and gave URIAH HEEP the honour of being the first major rock act to play the Soviet Union. Topping off a busy year, URIAH HEEP headlined the Reading Festival for the second time in their career.

1991 again saw URIAH HEEP touring throughout both North and South America, before finishing the *Different World* album. Unwilling to wait for a producer of their choice, Bolder took over the production mantle. URIAH HEEP's 1995 European tour saw John Lawton fronting the band once more, putting his act LUCIFER'S FRIEND on hold briefly, to fill in for Shaw who had throat problems. Before the call Lawton had been concentrating his efforts on his own band GUNHILL.

With the latest album, *Sea Of Light*, selling well across Europe, the band extended their tour to take in the Czech Republic, Scandinavia and Brazil.

In 1996 the fourth, official URIAH HEEP live album arrived in *Spellbinder Live*. Like *Sea Of Light*, the album was released through CBH Records.

URIAH HEEP's 1998 album *Sonic Origami,* produced by Pip Williams of

Ozzy Osbourne

STATUS QUO fame, pushed the band toward AOR territory, even including a song written by SURVIVOR's Jim Peterik. British touring found the band supported by Liverpool's DEADLINE. Meantime top German Metal act GAMMA RAY covered 'Return To Fantasy' on their *Somewhere Out In Space* album. The band themselves rounded off 2000 with a December Christmas party held at the Mermaid Theatre in London. The event would be recorded for posterity and issued as the *Acoustically Driven* live album, part of a set also including its counterpart *Electronically Driven*. With renewed interest in the band these albums spawned two singles, reworked versions of the classics 'Come Away Melinda' and 'Lady In Black'.

The band was back on the live trail in 2001 undertaking a joint sell-out UK tour with fellow veterans NAZARETH prior to headline European dates with American guests SURVIVOR.

A long overdue tribute album *A Return To Fantasy* was issued in August 2001 on the German Century Media label. The record comprised of ANGEL DUST's take on 'Easy Livin'', American Metal act LIEGE LORD with 'Too Scared To Run', Swedes TAD MOROSE on 'Rainbow Demon', German axe hero AXEL RUDI PELL's rendition of 'July Morning', Christian rockers NARNIA's version of 'Sunrise', FREEBASE with 'Suicidal Man', Metal crusaders SACRED STEEL with 'Return To Fantasy' and German Metal vets BLIND GUARDIAN's 'The Wizard'. Kai Hansen's GAMMA RAY offered 'Look At Yourself', NIGHTINGALE delivered 'Stealin'', LANA LANE's 'Weep In Silence', ONWARD with 'Bird Of Prey' and the suitably titled EASY LIVIN's attempt at 'Circle Of Hands'. The same year the vast bulk of URIAH HEEP's catalogue would be re-issued *en masse*, with extensive liner notes and bonus rare and demo tracks, by the Sanctuary group.

In related activity many fans were surprised to witness ex-member KEN HENSLEY teaming up with another erstwhile URIAH HEEP singer John Lawton and bassist Paul Newton for a new band project SALISBURY. An album was rumoured to be on the cards but following a handful of European gigs SALISBURY folded.

A significant weekend would occur for URIAH HEEP fans in London during December of 2001 as the band celebrated the 21st anniversary of the *Magician's Birthday* album. Three days of Heep-related events included a performance by the JOHN LAWTON BAND at the Borderline Café on Thursday 6th, URIAH HEEP themselves with a guesting KEN HENSLEY at the Shepherds Bush Empire on Friday 7th and a joint KEN HENSLEY and JOHN WETTON gig at the Forum venue on Saturday 8th.

Albums:
VERY 'EAVY, VERY 'UMBLE, Vertigo 6360 006 (1970)
SALISBURY, Vertigo 6360 028 (1971)
LOOK AT YOURSELF, Island ILPS 9169 (1971)
MAGICIAN'S BIRTHDAY, Bronze ILPS 9213 (1972)
DEMONS AND WIZARDS, Island ILPS 9193 (1972)
SWEET FREEDOM, Island ILPS 9245 (1973)
LIVE 1973, Island ISLD1 (1973)
DOWNUNDA, Bronze 25002 (1974)

Selected Ozzy-Related Acts From The Rockdetector Files

WONDERLAND, Island ILPS 9280 (1974)
THE BEST OF – PART 1, Bronze 28784 XOT (1975)
RETURN TO FANTASY, Bronze ILPS 9335 (1975)
HIGH AND MIGHTY, Island ILPS 9384 (1976)
INNOCENT VICTIM, Bronze 25543 XOT (1977)
FIREFLY, Bronze 28791 XOT (1977)
FALLEN ANGEL, Bronze 26449 XOT (1978)
CONQUEST, Bronze BRON524 (1980)
ABOMINOG, Bronze BRON 538 (1982)
HEAD FIRST, Bronze BRON 545 (1983)
EQUATOR, Portrait PRT 261414 (1985)
LIVE IN EUROPE 1979, Rawpower RAWLP 080 (1987)
LIVE AT SHEPPERTON '74, Castle (1988)
LIVE IN MOSCOW, Legacy (1988)
RAGING SILENCE, Legacy (1989)
DIFFERENT WORLD, Legacy (1991)
RARITIES FROM THE BRONZE AGE, Sequel NEXCD 184 (1992)
THE LANSDOWNE TAPES, RPM 115 (1993)
SEA OF LIGHT, SPV 085-76952-P (1995)
SPELLBINDER – LIVE, CBH 085-76992-2 (1996)
LIVE ON THE KING BISCUIT FLOWER HOUR, BMG 707 10-88027-2 (1997)
SONIC ORIGAMI, Eagle Rock EAGCD043 (1998)
ACOUSTICALLY DRIVEN, Classic Rock Legends CRL0676 (2001)
ELECTRICALLY DRIVEN, Classic Rock Legends CRL0715 (2001)

WAYSTED (UK)
Line-Up: Fin (vocals), Paul Chapman (guitar), Pete Way (bass), Andy Parker (drums)

PETE WAY, one of the true great characters and noted songwriters of the British rock scene, split from UFO in 1982 following disillusionment with UFO's supposed more commercial direction on the *Mechanix* album. Way almost immediately formed FASTWAY with erstwhile MOTÖRHEAD guitarist Eddie Clarke but prior to any recording the bassist baled out to join OZZY OSBOURNE's touring band for British dates in 1982. Upon completion of OZZY OSBOURNE shows the errant bassist got together a new band project. The aptly named WAYSTED with new hot-shot guitarist Ronnie Kayfield (formerly with HEARTBREAKERS), former UFO colleague Paul Raymond on keyboards, Scottish ex-FLYING SQUAD vocalist Fin (real name Ian Muir) and ex-STAMPEDE, WILD HORSES and DEF LEPPARD drummer Frank Noon.
    WAYSTED soon scored a deal with Chrysalis. The debut album was produced by Mick Glossop who ironically earlier in the year had produced UFO's *Making Contact*.
    It proved Way's desire to rock harder than the UFO he had departed was as true as his word with an extremely heavy album, high on guitar content and

Ozzy Osbourne

all topped with Fin's gravel-edged raucous vocals.

Guitarist Barry Benadetta was added to the band's support slot to the MÖTLEY CRÜE / OZZY OSBOURNE tour package in America. Line-up problems ensued and by the end of the American tour both Benadetta and Kayfield were out.

Raymond was fired just prior to WAYSTED's support slot to DIO on his European tour of 1984. This tour was to result in much 'undisciplined' behaviour and excess, including the much documented scene when a blitzed Way carried on singing the UFO chestnut 'Too Hot To Handle' oblivious to the fact that the rest of the band had finished the set. By the end of the tour WAYSTED returned home trimmed down to the writing partnership of Way and Fin.

WAYSTED again shifted their line-up in the summer enrolling ex-ANGELIC UPSTARTS drummer Decca Wade and ex-JESS COX BAND guitarist Neil Shepard. In late 1984 WAYSTED underwent yet another line up shake-up with Way managing to entice his former UFO colleagues guitarist PAUL CHAPMAN and drummer Andy Parker to join the band. Chapman had previously been asked by Way to show Shepard how to play the UFO numbers but the union proved more permanent and following a handful of gigs Shepard exited.

In the hiatus between UFO and WAYSTED Chapman had formed a band in Florida entitled D.O.A. whilst Parker was playing with Los Angeles act SCARLET. Chapman's band comprised of vocalist David Edwards, guitarist Ronnie Damsani, bassist Steve Chikitus, keyboard player Jimmy Delella and drummer Paul Barron. Before long D.O.A. evolved into CIRCUS CIRCUS with the addition of former ALLIED FORCES singer Danny Vaughn.

The revised line up of WAYSTED with the enviable line up of three ex-UFO men opened for IRON MAIDEN on their UK tour after which Parker left. Former MOTÖRHEAD man Philthy Phil Taylor occupied the drum position for a few months but left to open a position for former HUMBLE PIE and FASTWAY drummer Jerry Shirley.

For recording of *The Good, The Bad, The Waysted* the band also drafted in keyboard player Jimmy DeLilla from Chapman's ex-outfit D.O.A. Fin finally left in late 1985.

Way regrouped once more with Chapman adding ex-WORLD WAR III drummer Johnny Dee and ex-D.O.A. and CIRCUS CIRCUS vocalist Danny Vaughn. This line-up, guided now by former UFO manager Wilf Wright, gained a deal with Capitol and released the excellent Simon Hanhart produced *Save Your Prayers* album.

The band set about promoting the album with dates in Europe guesting for STATUS QUO prior to supporting IRON MAIDEN in America during 1987. The band also put in a one-off show in Tel Aviv, Israel alongside MARILLION and ALVIN LEE. Chapman was replaced for August shows in America supporting HELIX with American guitarist Eric Gamens but with the end of the tour the band once more collapsed. Vaughn formed TYKETTO. Dee went on to join Philadelphia-based compatriots BRITNY FOX.

Both Dee and DiLella would join DORO's touring band of 1993.

In an effort to salvage the wreckage of WAYSTED and undeterred by the loss of their Capitol deal, Way recorded a batch of demos with Dee, guitarists

Selected Ozzy-Related Acts From The Rockdetector Files

Eric Gamens and Martin Chaisson (real name Martin Smith) together with QUIREBOYS vocalist SPIKE. The latter's act was managed by UFO frontman Phil Mogg, reuniting the two old friends once more.

WAYSTED faltered on with ex-TYGERS OF PAN TANG vocalist Jon Deverill and keyboard player Ged Ryland briefly flirting with the outfit prior to its demise. Gamens joined COLD SWEAT. Chaisson formed IF ONLY before turning up under the pseudonym 'Kettle' in APES, PIGS AND SPACEMEN.

Way inevitably reforged links with Mogg and reformed UFO in the early '90s initially with ex-GRAND SLAM, STAMPEDE and RHODE ISLAND RED guitarist Lawrence Archer and inevitably becoming part of the reunion of the classic UFO line up for the *Walk On Water* album.

The late '90s also saw Way and Mogg involved outside of UFO (often forced due to contractual reasons) with the MOGG/WAY project releasing two albums, *Edge Of The World* and *Chocolate Box*. By 1999 Way, although still committed to UFO, was contemplating a further WAYSTED project documenting his recent return from yet another episode of heroin addiction.

In the meantime fans were treated to the next best thing as the long-deleted *Save Your Prayers* album resurfaced. Demos for the original album were released with Chapman adding previously absent guitar solos. The *Wilderness Of Mirrors* album also added the previously unreleased 'Fortunate Son', a cover of the CREEDENCE CLEARWATER REVIVAL track. A further release of archive material, *Your Prayers Are Saved*, would include not only WAYSTED material but live UFO tracks and PAUL CHAPMAN's instrumental 'The Bells Of Berlin'.

Way issued his first pure solo album *Amphetamine* in 2000 as UFO launched their own *Covenant* opus.

Albums:
VICES, Chrysalis CHR 1438 (1983)
WAYSTED, Music For Nations MFN 31 (1984)
THE GOOD, THE BAD, THE WAYSTED, Music For Nations MFN 43 (1985)
SAVE YOUR PRAYERS, Parlophone 24 0638-1 (1986)
COMPLETELY WAYSTED, Rawpower RAWLP 019 (1986)
WILDERNESS OF MIRRORS, Zoom Club ZCRCD28 (1999)
YOU WON'T GET OUT ALIVE, Zoom Club (1999)
YOUR PRAYERS ARE SAVED, (2000)

WHITESNAKE (UK)
Line-Up: David Coverdale (vocals), Adrian Vandenberg (guitar), Vivian Campbell (guitar), Rudy Sarzo (bass), Tommy Aldridge (drums)

A veritable British rock institution fronted by the charismatic ex-DEEP PURPLE singer DAVID COVERDALE, a man blessed with a rich blues-soaked vocal and an unashamed macho stage presence. Although fraught with line-up changes, Coverdale's sheer single-mindedness and determination has seen the man turn WHITESNAKE into a multi-platinum selling act with global recognition.

Ozzy Osbourne

In 1977 Coverdale released the *Whitesnake* album into the teeth of the UK Punk rock explosion. It was a brave move as the album contained hard rocking R&B songs written whilst Coverdale was still in DEEP PURPLE. Coverdale was obviously still in two minds as to which direction to take during his immediate post-DEEP PURPLE days. The singer actually rehearsed with URIAH HEEP in 1976, cheekily trying to entice guitarist Mick Box into his new band.

Coverdale then collaborated with his old sparring partner, former JUICY LUCY, SNAFU and FRANKIE MILLER guitarist MICKY MOODY to assemble a line-up of session players for Coverdale's first solo album. The men involved were Simon Phillips on drums, ex-JUICY LUCY bassist Deslyle Harper and SNAFU pianist Tim Hinckley. Production was handled by DEEP PURPLE's bass player ROGER GLOVER.

The impact of the *Whitesnake* album inspired Coverdale to form a band around the project and next album, 1978's *Northwinds,* included Moody once more with more session players, former MAY BLITZ drummer Tony Newman, and the GREASE BAND's Alan Spenner on bass. Even DR. FEELGOOD's Lee Brilleaux contributed harp. Glover produced once more.

Founding WHITESNAKE as a band project Coverdale and Moody (bowing out from his day job with the FRANKIE MILLER band) pulled in all new cast. Included were former COLOSSEUM II, JUICY LUCY and NATIONAL HEALTH bassist Neil Murray, former UFO, BABE RUTH and COZY POWELL'S HAMMER guitarist BERNIE MARSDEN, ex-SNAFU and PALADIN keyboard player Pete Solley and ex-RUNNER drummer Dave Dowle. This line-up undertook a club tour, with Brian Johnston supplanting Solley, sponsoring many ecstatic reviews and the band's first official WHITESNAKE product, a four track EP titled 'Snakebite' sold in large numbers.

In Germany the record company created confusion by cobbling together the four 'Snakebite' EP tracks with four cuts from *Northwinds* to produce the *David Coverdale's Whitesnake* album.

WHITESNAKE quickly capitalized on this initial success by releasing *Trouble* in October of the same year which saw the reunion of Coverdale with his DEEP PURPLE colleague, keyboard player JON LORD.

In 1979 *Lovehunter* provided more fuel for the fire and also succeeded in enraging feminists with its Chris Achilleos-designed sleeve portraying a naked woman astride a huge snake. In America the artwork provoked such fury it even went out to some stores in a plain bag. WHITESNAKE toured the UK to even bigger crowds, this time supported by MARSEILLE.

By 1980 another ex-DEEP PURPLE veteran Ian Paice was on the WHITESNAKE drum stool which had many critics pondering whether Coverdale was attempting to re-create DEEP PURPLE. UK touring had GARY MOORE's new act G FORCE as openers.

The album *Ready 'n' Willing* broke new ground for the band when the single 'Fool For Your Loving' crashed into the charts. A song originally written for blues giant B.B. KING by Moody and Coverdale, it turned out so good they kept it for themselves.

Keeping the band on the boil, the previously only available in Japan live double album *Live... In The Heart Of The City* was also released later that

Selected Ozzy-Related Acts From The Rockdetector Files

year. WHITESNAKE toured in Europe opening for AC/DC and in America supporting JETHRO TULL.

1981 again saw WHITESNAKE with chart success with their album *Come An Get It*. The resultant tour of Britain climaxed in a five-night sold-out stint at London's Hammersmith Odeon. With the 1983 album *Slide It In* under their belts WHITESNAKE signed to Geffen Records in America. Further American dates followed as openers on a package headlined by JUDAS PRIEST.

The album was re-mixed for the American market and during this time Coverdale relocated to America. Moody quit to resurrect his YOUNG N'MOODY band only to be shortly followed by Hodgkinson. The bass position was filled by Neil Murray once more. Between WHITESNAKE terms Murray had been involved with INFORMER, a band involving ex-STALLION singer John Elstar, erstwhile STALLION and SIDEWINDER guitarist STUART SMITH and former STREETWALKERS and future IRON MAIDEN drummer Nicko McBrain.

With Murray back in the fold Moody's old position in WHITESNAKE was given to ex-TYGERS OF PAN TANG and THIN LIZZY guitarist JOHN SYKES complementing a much younger looking WHITESNAKE.

For WHITESNAKE's support stint in America to DIO, the ALASKA keyboardsman Richard Bailey was utilised on a temporary basis.

In 1985 guitarist Mel Galley and Murray departed to form the short-lived MGM project with MICKY MOODY. Galley and Murray would also both be involved in the PHENOMENA project album.

JOHN SYKES was also out of the picture and would forge ahead with his own BLUE MURDER project before embarking on a solo career.

WHITESNAKE now assembled what was thought to be by many a perfect video-presentable band as their record company geared Coverdale up for a massive push on the American market. Alongside Coverdale, WHITESNAKE now featured former OZZY OSBOURNE and BLACK OAK ARKANSAS drummer Tommy Aldridge, former SWEET SAVAGE and DIO guitarist Vivian Campbell, VANDENBERG guitarist Adrian Vandenberg and former QUIET RIOT and OZZY OSBOURNE bassist Rudy Sarzo. Not only were the level of talents assembled for the new look band extreme but so was the image. Honed for the video age, the band appeared to have spent as much time preparing their image and hair as their music.

The landmark *1987* album, which had keyboards courtesy of ex-RAINBOW man DON AIREY, gave WHITESNAKE the major success in America the band had striven for so long. In spite of the fresh look given to the band the album contained many songs co-written by Sykes and featured his guitar parts too as well as a re-recording of 1980's 'Fool For Your Loving'. A massive American tour capitalized on a clutch of American hit singles including the Number 1 ballad 'Here I Go Again'.

Coverdale married actress Tawny Kitaen in February 1989. Kitaen had already, by this point, played a large part in the rejuvenation of WHITESNAKE's fortunes, having been featured strongly as a central character in the band's last set of promotion videos.

1989's *Slip Of The Tongue*, although giving the band a top ten US album, saw the band struggling. Coverdale had added former ALCATRAZ and DAVID LEE ROTH guitarist STEVE VAI to the line-up and many purists felt Vai's quirky individualism sat ill at ease with the band's traditional hard blues. The follow up tour also struggled to sell out the same venues earlier dates had packed with ease.

WHITESNAKE was put on ice with Campbell forming SHADOWKING with FOREIGNER frontman LOU GRAMM before joining the multi-platinum arena act DEF LEPPARD.

Vandenberg, Sarzo and Aldridge created MANIC EDEN initially with HOUSE OF LORDS singer JAMES CHRISTIAN. The latter left, reportedly because he felt MANIC EDEN was merely a WHITESNAKE substitute and the band drafted in former LITTLE CAESAR vocalist Ron Young for a solitary album. Post MANIC EDEN Sarzo was to hook up once more with QUIET RIOT.

STEVE VAI resumed his solo activities.

In a shock move for fans of both camps, Coverdale hooked up with the ex-LED ZEPPELIN guitar legend JIMMY PAGE to create COVERDALE/PAGE. Page had gone on record at stating his displeasure at some of WHITESNAKE's later material such as 'Still Of The Night' bearing more than a little LED ZEPPELIN influence. The quality of the album silenced a few critics but American touring plans were scuppered and the band only performed live in Japan where the set included a mixture of WHITESNAKE and LED ZEPPELIN tunes among newer numbers.

In 1994 following the relatively moderate success of PAGE/COVERDALE Coverdale reformed WHITESNAKE based on the spur of a greatest hits compilation.

At first THUNDER guitarist Luke Morley was heavily rumoured to be in the band but this conjecture was soon squashed by THUNDER themselves. Another, more unlikely, name to be linked to the new line-up was none other than RITCHIE BLACKMORE!

As it turned out Adrian Vandenberg was quickly re-recruited from his MANIC EDEN project (with Rudy Sarzo, Tommy Aldridge and LITTLE CAESAR's Ron Young) alongside former RATT guitarist WARREN DI MARTINI. Sarzo came back in on bass with HEART's Denny Carmassi on drums and NELSON keyboard player Paul Mirkovich.

This line-up quickly undertook a highly successful European tour to back up the *Greatest Hits* album. However, European success for the *Greatest Hits* package was not matched in America where the album failed to chart. The band parted ways with their US label Geffen in the face of disappointing sales and the departure of A&R guru John Kalodner.

Rumours abounded in 1996 that Coverdale had rejoined DEEP PURPLE but these were scotched by confirmation that WHITESNAKE had entered the studio to work on a new album. Coverdale assembled a touring line-up consisting of guitarists Adrian Vandenberg and ex-MR. MISTER/EDDIE MONEY man Steve Farris, former THE FIRM and BLUE MURDER bassist TONY FRANKLIN and former MONTROSE, GAMMA and HEART drummer Denny Carmassi making his return to the ranks. Keyboards were handled by ex-DETROIT, STEPPENWOLF and DAVID LEE ROTH man Brett

Selected Ozzy-Related Acts From The Rockdetector Files

Tuggle.

The farewell world tour, dubbed 'The Last Hurrah!' took WHITESNAKE out on a high with the band returning to countries following scheduled dates due to ticket demand. When the dates finally came to a close in the Spring of 1998 Farris teamed up with GARY WRIGHT.

Although only comprised of Coverdale and Vandenberg, the acoustic Japanese release of 1998 *Starkers In Tokyo* was nevertheless issued under the WHITESNAKE tag.

1998 had ex-guitarists Moody and Marsden out on the road titled THE SNAKES even releasing an album in Japan. By 1999 had Moody, Marsden and Murray – now joined by ex-BAD COMPANY vocalist ROBERT HART and ex-RAINBOW man DON AIREY on keyboards, were treading the boards in an act titled COMPANY OF SNAKES.

Rumours abounded in early 2000 that Coverdale had been approached to front VAN HALEN, hotly denied by both parties. Coverdale emerged with a further solo album.

Albums:
WHITESNAKE, Purple TPS 3509 (1977)
NORTHWINDS, Purple TPS 3513 (1978)
TROUBLE, EMI INS 3022 (1978)
SNAKEBITE, Sunburst 1C 064-61290 (1978)
LOVEHUNTER, United Artists UAG 30624 (1979)
LIVE IN THE HEART OF THE CITY, United Artists SNAKE 1 (1980)
READY AND WILLING, United Artists UAG 30302 (1981)
COME AN' GET IT, Liberty LBG 30327 (1981)
THE BEST OF WHITESNAKE, Polydor (1981)
SAINTS 'N' SINNERS, Liberty LBG30354 (1982)
SLIDE IT IN, Liberty LBG 2400001 (1984)
1987, Liberty EMC 3528 (1987)
SLIP OF THE TONGUE, EMI EMD 1013 (1989)
GREATEST HITS, EMI 1065 (1994)
STARKERS IN TOKYO, Toshiba EMI TOCP 50314 (1997)
RESTLESS HEART, EMI 7243 856806 25 (1997)

WIDOWMAKER (UK)
Line-Up: Steve Ellis (vocals), Ariel Bender (guitar), Bob Daisley (bass), Paul Nichols (drums)

A late '70s supergroup fronted by erstwhile LOVE AFFAIR singer Steve Ellis. Guitarist Ariel Bender (real name Luther Grosvenor) is ex-MOTT THE HOOPLE and LOVE AFFAIR, bassist Bob Daisley is ex-CHICKEN SHACK and BROKEN GLASS while drummer Paul Nichols was previously with SKIP BIFFERTY and LINDISFARNE.

WIDOWMAKER debuted live opening for THE WHO in their football stadium gigs of 1975 before recording the eponymous first album.

Butler assumed vocal duties following Ellis's departure for the release of *Too Late To Cry*. Sometime HAWKWIND guitarist HUW LLOYD LANG-

Ozzy Osbourne

TON was added as second guitarist. WIDOWMAKER split in 1977 after achieving moderate success in America.

Daisley later turned up in many known metal bands such as URIAH HEEP, RAINBOW and as main songwriter and lyricist for most of OZZY OSBOURNE's albums.

Latterly Daisley has created MOTHER'S ARMY for a run of three albums in collaboration with NIGHTRANGER guitarist JEFF WATSON and fronted by ex-DEEP PURPLE and RAINBOW singer JOE LYNN TURNER.

Daisley recently toured with DIO. Guitarist LUTHER GROSVENOR issued a solo album.

Albums:
WIDOWMAKER, Jet 2310 432 (1976)
TOO LATE TO CRY, United Artists UAG 30038 (1977)

WILD DOGS (USA)
Line-Up: Matthew T. McCourt (vocals), Jeff Mark Horton (guitar), Danny Kurth (bass), Deen Castronovo (drums)

WILD DOGS achieved local notoriety in America's North West as a ferocious live act and would regularly appear at the Crossroads Centre in Bellevue, Washington (a suburb of Seattle) on bills that would usually also boast local heroes CULPRIT and OVERLORD. Interestingly, one of WILD DOGS' opening bands back in 1982 happened to be MYTH. This group would become QUEENSRYCHE.

WILD DOGS were fronted by vocalist Matthew McCourt, a man whose history spanned acts such as RUDE AWAKENING in 1978 with a pre-MALICE Mick Zane as well as THE VIOLATORS and THE RAVERS, both acts coincidentally featuring another future MALICE man guitarist Jay Reynolds. Just previous to WILD DOGS McCourt was singing for DMZ in 1981, reunited with Mick Zane, guitarist Jeff Horton and ranked alongside Pete Holmes – later of BLACK 'N' BLUE.

The group's first demo saw the band borrowing drummer Jaime St. James from fellow Portland outfit MOVIE STAR. St. James would become better known as a vocalist, fronting the group MOVIE STAR which subsequently transformed into BLACK 'N' BLUE. A permanent drummer would be found in Deen Castronovo just as WILD DOGS were signed by Mike Varney's Shrapnel label. However, McCourt would decamp to found EVIL GENIUS with a line-up of guitarists Kip Doran and Chris Jacobsen, bassist Ken Goldstein and drummer Ben Linton. EVIL GENIUS recorded an album although it would remain consigned to the vaults. McCourt's next move was to record a 1986 album with MAYHEM and later works with DR. MASTERMIND.

Managed by former JOURNEY and NIGHTRANGER lighting director Ken Mednick WILD DOGS, now comprising of Michael Furlong, Jeff Marks, Deen Castronovo and new bassist Rick Bartel recorded the *Reign Of Terror* album. MICHAEL FURLONG went on to record two highly commendable AOR type solo albums.

Selected Ozzy-Related Acts From The Rockdetector Files

Castronovo later came to prominence playing with BAD ENGLISH and HARDLINE. During downtime in HARDLINE's schedule Castronovo and McCourt resurrected WILD DOGS but the union was brief. The drummer resumed his ever-upward spiralling career with OZZY OSBOURNE and BLACK SABBATH bassist Geezer Butler's GEEZER venture. McCourt entered into various band ventures such as EASTSIDE STRANGLER with EVIL GENIUS guitarist Kip Doran and, for a fleeting spell, Deen Castronovo. By 1992 the singer was fronting up MEATHOOK in league with POISON IDEA's Kevin Sanders. McCourt auditioned for JUDAS PRIEST in 1993 but was unsuccessful.

It was not the end of the story though. Castronovo rekindled WILD DOGS once again in 1998. Although the drummer soon opted out of this latest reformation, to join the AOR megaband JOURNEY, McCourt would keep the flame alive. During August of 1999 WILD DOGS acted as support to a DOKKEN and GREAT WHITE double billing, guested for DIO in March of 2000 and BLUE OYSTER CULT the following year. An album of demos and outtakes, *Better Late Than Never*, also emerged. Confusingly for a short period the new look WILD DOGS operated as EVIL GENIUS before reverting back to WILD DOGS.

Besides WILD DOGS McCourt plays out the role of Rob Halford in JUDAS PRIEST covers band BRITISH STEEL.

Albums:
WILD DOGS, Shrapnel 1003 (1983)
MAN'S BEST FRIEND, Shrapnel 1012 (1984)
REIGN OF TERROR, Music For Nations MFN80 (1987)

WILDLIFE (UK)
Line-Up: Steve Overland (vocals), Chris Overland (guitar), Phil Soussan (bass), Mark Booty (keyboards), Jeff Rich (drums)

WILDLIFE's inaugural line-up comprised of brothers Chris and Steve Overland, bassist Nigel Widowson, keyboard player Mark Booty and drummer Richard Plumb. Widowson was supplanted by Bob Skeat whilst Plumb lost his spot to former HOTLINE drummer Pete Jupp, his previous act having also included 720 and BAD COMPANY guitarist Dave Colwell among their ranks.

Ex-BAD COMPANY drummer Simon Kirke replaced Jupp who joined SAMSON for the 1983 album. By early 1984 Kirke was out and replaced by Jeff Rich, formerly with JUDIE TZUKE. The last incarnation of WILDLIFE also saw the inclusion of former CUDDLY TOYS and REFLEX bassist Phil Soussan.

The Overland brothers and Jupp re-emerged with ILLEGAL TENDER, a short-lived outfit that included Soussan and Rich. ILLEGAL TENDER broke apart as Soussan joined ROBIN GEORGE then OZZY OSBOURNE. The four-stringer would also go on to work with BILLY IDOL, VINCE NEIL, his own band BEGGARS AND THIEVES and French star JOHNNY HALLI-

Ozzy Osbourne

DAY.
Rich found a more prominent haven in STATUS QUO. Undeterred the Overlands together with Jupp formed the popular AOR act FM, Booty surfaced with ex-STATUS QUO drummer John Coghlan's band PARTNERS IN CRIME. Skeat joined 3RD STONE, the TINA EGAN BAND and WISHBONE ASH. Kirke would of course rejoin BAD COMPANY.

Albums:
BURNING, Chrysalis (1980)
WILDLIFE, Swansong (1983)

ZAKK WYLDE (USA)

Not to be confused with the Canadian wrestler of the same stage name! Guitarist ZAKK WYLDE had shot to international prominence replacing JAKE E. LEE in the OZZY OSBOURNE band. When the mighty Ozz decided to temporarily retire from touring, Wylde formed a band to go out on the road in 1993 which included former RONDINELLI and WHITE LION bassist James LoMenzo, erstwhile ANTHRAX/WHITE LION/BLACKTHORNE drummer Greg D'Angelo and keyboard player Kevin Jones. The guitarist even got to support his heroes LYNYRD SKYNYRD the same year. Following his Southern-flavoured banjo totin' PRIDE & GLORY band and a short touring stint with the legendary ALLMAN BROTHERS, he issued his mellower solo album *Book Of Shadows*. Drums came courtesy of JOE WALSH and CROSBY, STILLS, NASH & YOUNG man Joe Vitale and bass from PRIDE & GLORY colleague Joe LoMenzo.

After briefly re-uniting with OZZY OSBOURNE and flirting with GUNS N' ROSES Wylde created the much rawer-edged BLACK LABEL SOCIETY for the debut *Sonic Brew* album.

The guitarist was signed up for his big screen debut forming part of the fictitious Metal band for the Mark Wahlberg movie *Metal God*. The guitarist, alongside 'band' members actor Mark Wahlberg, BONHAM drummer Jason Bonham and DOKKEN bassist Jeff Pilson, would grace the big screen in 2001 for the fictitious STEEL DRAGON for the movie renamed *Rock Star*. With a combination of musicians that strong, the lure to record STEEL DRAGON material for the movie was irresistible and the subsequent *Rock Star* soundtrack CD duly featured six STEEL DRAGON tracks with Wylde performing.

Wylde also is credited with a guest spot on BRITNY FOX's *Bite Down Hard* album and on C.P.R.'s 1993 eponymous album.
Wylde rejoined the OZZY OSBOURNE band in November 2000 featuring on the subsequent *Down To Earth* album. This move would not stall his ongoing BLACK LABEL SOCIETY career though.

On January 17th, 2002 the guitarist would land the honour of performing the US national anthem in front of a capacity crowd basketball game held in Los Angeles.

Albums:
BOOK OF SHADOWS, Geffen 24964 (1996)

Also available from

CHERRY RED BOOKS & ROCKDETECTOR

ROCKDETECTOR
A-Z of BLACK METAL

Garry Sharpe-Young

Over a decade Black Metal has spawned legions of bands making up a truly global rebellion. For the first time ever this ultimate authority documents detailed biographies, line-ups and full discographies with track listings of over 1,000 groups.
Including: CRADLE OF FILTH, DIMMU BORGIR, EMPEROR, MAYHEM, IMMORTAL, MARDUK, VENOM, WITCHFYNDE, BATHORY and MERCYFUL FATE.

Paper covers, 416 pages, £14.99 in UK

ROCKDETECTOR
A-Z of DEATH METAL

Garry Sharpe-Young

From the founding fathers such as NAPALM DEATH, CARCASS, DEATH, INCANTATION, IMPETIGO and MORBID ANGEL to the rise of Swedish Death Metal legends IN FLAMES, CARNAGE and AT THE GATES, the Death Metal of MARDUK, the Christian Death Metal of MORTIFICATION and the politically charged Noisecore of AGATHOCLES. All genres old and new are analyzed in depth with full career histories and detailed discographies.

Paper covers, 366 pages, £14.99 in UK

ROCKDETECTOR
A-Z of THRASH METAL

Garry Sharpe-Young

Without doubt Thrash Metal continues to make its mark in the biggest possible way. The 'big four' - METALLICA, MEGADEATH, ANTHRAX and SLAYER are all documented herre in the greatest possible detail with full, up to the minute histories, exclusive photographs and global discographies. Also covered are the legion of ground breaking Bay Area acts such as METAL CHURCH, TESTAMENT, EXODUS, DEATH ANGEL and HIRAX. The European Thrash explosion of KREATOR, RAGE, DESTRUCTION, SODOM, GRAVE DIGGER and HELLOWEEN, the PAGAN THRASH of SABBAT, the avant garde eccentricity of CELTIC FROST and the FUNK THRASH of MORDED- it's all here.
Includes 17 track Thrash Metal CD.
Paper covers, 302 pages and photographs throughout, £14.99 in UK

ROCKDETECTOR
A-Z of DOOM & GOTHIC METAL

Garry Sharpe-Young

From its beginning with instigators PENTAGRAM, ATOMIC ROOSTER and BLACK SABBATH including cult acts such as THE OBSESSED and TROUBLE to the new breed of MY DYING BRIDE, CATHEDRAL, PARADISE LOST, NOVEMBER's DOOM and CANDLEMASS, all bands in the Doom and Gothic genre are featured here.
Each and every band is included with an enormous wealth of historical detail and full global discography. From the full, weighty and unedited account of Black Sabbath's tortured history and spanning Stoner, Gothic and Darkwave, this book is the first to chronicle the underground world wide phenomena that is Doom.
Includes Doom & Gothic Metal CD.
Paper covers, 366 pages, £14.99 in UK

www.cherryred.co.uk

...from AC/DC to ZEPPELIN...

The renowned Danish photographer Jørgen Angel has taken more than
50 000 photos of rock stars
during his long career. Among those are AC/DC, Black Sabbath, Alice Cooper, Deep Purple, Nina Hagen, Jimi Hendrix, Ozzy Osbourne, Lou Reed, Sex Pistols, Thin Lizzy, The Who and Led Zeppelin. At Jørgen Angel Photography, Angel offers hand made prints of an exclusive selection of more than 1000 photos - a unique opportunity to obtain a high quality memorabilia item for you or as a gift.

JØRGEN ANGEL
Photography

Welcome at
www.angel.dk

Also available from CHERRY RED BOOKS

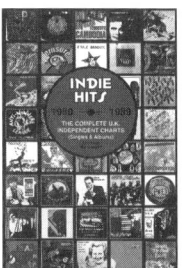

**Indie Hits
1980-1989**
The Complete UK
Independent Charts
(Singles & Albums)

Compiled by
Barry Lazell

Paper covers, 314 pages,
£14.99 in UK

**Songs In The
Key Of Z**
The Curious
Universe of
Outsider Music

Irwin Chusid

Paper covers, 311 pages,
fully illustrated,
£11.99 in UK

**Cor Baby, That's
Really Me!**
(New Millennium
Hardback Edition)

John Otway

Hardback, 192 pages and
16 pages of photographs,
£11.99 in UK

**The Legendary
Joe Meek**
The Telstar Man

John Repsch

Paper covers, 350 pages
plus photographs £14.99
in UK

All the Young Dudes
Mott the Hoople and
Ian Hunter
The Biography

Campbell Devine

Paper covers, 448 pages
and 16 pages of photo-
graphs, £14.99 in UK

Random Precision
Recording The Music
Of Syd Barrett
1965 – 1974

David Parker

Paper covers, 320 pages,
photographs through-
out, £14.99 in UK

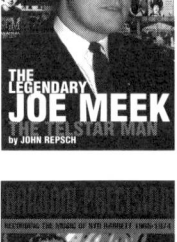

Embryo
A Pink Floyd
Chronology
1966 – 1971

Nick Hodges & Ian
Priston

Paper covers, 302 pages
and photographs
throughout, £14.99 in UK

Those Were The Days
An Unofficial History
Of The Beatles Apple
Organisation
1967-2002

Stefan Granados

Paper covers, 300 pages,
including photographs,
£14.99 in UK

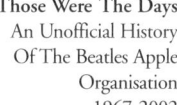

Johnny Thunders
In Cold Blood

Nina Antonia

Paper covers, 270 pages
and photographs
throughout,
£14.99 in UK

The Rolling Stones
Complete Recording
Sessions 1962-2002

Martin Elliott

Paper covers, 300 pages,
including photographs,
£14.99 in UK

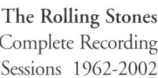

www.cherryred.co.uk

CHERRY RED BOOKS

We are always looking for interesting books to publish.
They can be either new manuscripts or re-issues of deleted books.
If you have any good ideas then please
get in touch with us.

CHERRY RED BOOKS LTD.
Unit 17, Elysium Gate West,
126-128 New King's Road
London SW6 4LZ

E-mail: iain@cherryred.co.uk
Web: www.cherryred.co.uk